MÉDECINS SANS FRONTIÈRES AND HUMANITARIAN SITUATIONS

This book explores the interaction between anthropology and humanitarianism, focussed on the organisation Médecins Sans Frontières (MSF).

The emphasis of the collection is on practising anthropology within humanitarian situations, reflecting on how anthropology contributes to the development of operational response. Each chapter presents an experience of working within a particular MSF project and highlights the real issues that anthropologists of humanitarian practice confront.

The volume will be of interest to scholars of anthropology, development studies and global health, as well as to NGO staff and health professionals.

Jean-François Véran is Associate Professor at the Federal University of Rio de Janeiro, Brazil. Between 2013 and 2019, he served as Anthropology Advisor in the Brazilian Medical Unit (BRAMU) of MSF Brazil.

Doris Burtscher has worked as a medical anthropologist with MSF since 2001. She is a medical anthropology referent in the MSF Vienna Evaluation Unit and lectures at the Medical University of Vienna, Austria.

Beverley Stringer is a social anthropologist and trained nurse based in London. With extensive field experience, she set up and leads the Social Science team for the Dutch operational section of MSF. She is a Visiting Fellow at the University of Sussex, UK.

MÉDECINS SANS FRONTIÈRES AND HUMANITARIAN SITUATIONS

An Anthropological Exploration

Edited by Jean-François Véran, Doris Burtscher
and Beverley Stringer

LONDON AND NEW YORK

First published 2020
by Routledge
2 Park Square, Milton Park, Abingdon, Oxon OX14 4RN

and by Routledge
52 Vanderbilt Avenue, New York, NY 10017

Routledge is an imprint of the Taylor & Francis Group, an informa business

© 2020 selection and editorial matter, Jean-François Véran, Doris Burtscher and Beverley Stringer; individual chapters, the contributors

The right of the editors to be identified as the authors of the editorial material, and of the authors for their individual chapters, has been asserted in accordance with sections 77 and 78 of the Copyright, Designs and Patents Act 1988.

All rights reserved. No part of this book may be reprinted or reproduced or utilised in any form or by any electronic, mechanical, or other means, now known or hereafter invented, including photocopying and recording, or in any information storage or retrieval system, without permission in writing from the publishers.

Trademark notice: Product or corporate names may be trademarks or registered trademarks, and are used only for identification and explanation without intent to infringe.

British Library Cataloguing-in-Publication Data
A catalogue record for this book is available from the British Library

Library of Congress Cataloging-in-Publication Data
Names: Véran, Jean-François, editor. | Médecins sans frontières (Association)
Title: Médecins Sans Frontières and humanitarian situations : an anthropological exploration / edited by Jean-François Véran, Doris Burtscher, and Beverley Stringer.
Description: Milton Park, Abingdon, Oxon ; New York, NY : Routledge, 2020. | Includes bibliographical references and index.
Identifiers: LCCN 2019058545 (print) | LCCN 2019058546 (ebook) | ISBN 9780367417956 (hardback) | ISBN 9780367419998 (paperback) | ISBN 9780367817244 (ebook)
Subjects: LCSH: Medical assistance. | Humanitarian assistance. | Medical anthropology.
Classification: LCC RA390.A2 M47 2020 (print) | LCC RA390.A2 (ebook) | DDC 362.17—dc23
LC record available at https://lccn.loc.gov/2019058545
LC ebook record available at https://lccn.loc.gov/2019058546

ISBN: 978-0-367-41795-6 (hbk)
ISBN: 978-0-367-41999-8 (pbk)
ISBN: 978-0-367-81724-4 (ebk)

Typeset in Bembo
by Apex CoVantage, LLC

Médecins Sans Frontières (MSF)/Doctors Without Borders is an international, independent, medical humanitarian organisation created in 1971 that delivers emergency aid to people affected by armed conflict, epidemics, health care exclusion and natural disasters. MSF offers assistance to people based only on need and regardless of race, religion, gender or political affiliation.

We would like to dedicate this book to people of all places, who for reasons beyond their control live disrupted, precarious lives. People who have lost loved ones and feel neglected and alone. People living in current crises affecting the world today – those moving away from danger, and those we hope find comfort and safety in the end.

CONTENTS

List of figures	*xi*
List of tables	*xii*
List of boxes	*xiii*
Acknowledgements	*xiv*
List of contributors	*xv*

Introduction: anthropology in humanitarian situations   1
Jean-François Véran, Beverley Stringer and Doris Burtscher

1   Changing contexts in humanitarianism: a challenge for
anthropology   27
Tammam Aloudat and James Smith

2   A medical operational perspective on anthropology in the
setting of MSF   39
William Hennequin and Kiran Jobanputra

3   Ethical considerations and anthropology: the MSF experience   61
*Beverley Stringer, Renée Teernstra, Darryl Stellmach and
Emilie Venables*

4   Emergency in practice: doing an ethnography of
malnutrition in South Sudan   77
Darryl Stellmach

x Contents

5 The paradox of safe birth: the interaction between anthropology and medical humanitarianism – the dilemma of an MSF medical strategy versus health-seeking behaviour of Pashtun women in Khost province, Afghanistan   93
Doris Burtscher

6 Whose culture needs to be questioned? access to HIV/AIDS treatment in Homa Bay, Kenya   114
Vanja Kovačič

7 Back to life – Ebola survivors in Liberia: from imaginary heroes to political agents   136
Umberto Pellecchia and Emilie Venables

8 Invisible dengue: epidemics and politics in Léogâne, Haiti   154
Jean-François Véran

9 Revealing causes beyond culture: an MSF surgical project through the lens of anthropology and health promotion   178
Paul Grohma and Ursula Wagner

10 "Yaya hankuri da mutani?" (How is your patience with the people?): a medical anthropological inquiry into treatment challenges in the Anka Local Government Area, Zamfara Heavy Metal Treatment Project, Nigeria   193
Annemieke Bont, Marit van Lenthe and Karla Bil

11 Dealing with the body social: an ethnography of dialogue in a health clinic, South Tehran, Iran   220
Mitra Asfari; Introduction by Mathilde Berthelot

12 Epilogue: the new missionaries – an anthropological reflection on humanitarian action in critical situations   242
Frédéric Vandenberghe and Jean-François Véran

Index   *252*

FIGURES

6.1	Patients' health-seeking pathways	120
6.2	Conceptual framework – interactions between the formal health sector and patients' barriers to HIV diagnosis and treatment	128
7.1	An example of harsh messages spread among the population	141
7.2	An MSF health promotion activity: celebrating the return of survivors at home	149

TABLES

I.1	Mapping of anthropology and social science in MSF	16
2.1	Overview of the three anthropological studies undertaken in the MSF Homa Bay project	57

BOXES

3.1	Example of gaining ethical approval: South Sudan	69
4.1	Statements, knowledge and assumptions	87
6.1	Wife inheritance	115
6.2	Traditional Luo diseases	124
7.1	Excerpts from MSF blog – Emilie Venables, December 2014	139
7.2	Distrust	143
7.3	Relativism	146
8.1	Send the disease: fieldwork narratives from Léogâne, 2012	164
8.2	An outreach at Beaussan (9 km from Léogâne)	170
10.1	Vignette: a description of a village where the intervention showed a successful outcome	202
10.2	Acknowledgement of the role of mining in the lead emergency and ready acceptance of the MSF intervention	203

ACKNOWLEDGEMENTS

We would like to thank Dr Ann Taylor for peer reviewing the ethics chapter and Michael Neuman and Frédéric Vandenberghe for their input and comments on the introduction. Much gratitude goes to Gordon Connell for copyediting the entire manuscript. We would like to acknowledge Sidney Wong, former Medical Director of MSF-Artsen zonder Grenzen in Amsterdam, for supporting the concept of the book. Special mention and credit go to Renée Teernstra for her tireless support to editors in shaping the manuscript.

Finally, this book could not have happened without the relentless willingness of the contributors to write, rewrite and exchange thoughts on how to make their chapters best fit in this book. Many thanks to Tammam, Mitra, Mathilde, Karla, Annemieke, Paul, William, Kiran, Vanja, Marit, Umberto, James, Darryl, Renée, Frédéric, Emilie and Ursula.

CONTRIBUTORS

Tammam Aloudat is a Syrian medical doctor with an MSc in Public Health in Developing Countries from the London School of Hygiene and Tropical Medicine (LSHTM). He has 18 years of medical humanitarian experience at both the project and headquarters levels with the International Federation of Red Cross and Red Crescent Societies (IFRC), Save the Children and Médecins Sans Frontières (MSF). He currently holds the position of Deputy Medical Director for MSF Switzerland, where his work incorporates the management of health projects, aspects of health in conflict, the development of health information systems, medical knowledge management, humanitarian medical ethics and the evolution of conflict and humanitarian response.

Mitra Asfari obtained her PhD in Anthropology at Paris 5 René Descartes University, France. She has mainly studied cultural and social life of a semi-itinerant group known as Gorbat in Iran (south of Tehran). She has collaborated with the MSF Clinic of South Tehran since 2015 as researcher and consultant. She conducts ethnographic research on the Gorbats' conceptions of body and illness, while trying to establish fruitful contact between the Gorbat population and MSF.

Mathilde Berthelot, MD, working with MSF since 2002. After several missions in the field in various countries, I have been working in Paris headquarter from 2008 as medical referent and later on operation manager for Afghanistan, Iran, Pakistan, Palestine, Georgia and Armenia. I have been in charge of the development of MSF projects in Iran between 2012 and 2019.

Karla Bil, RN, is a registered Intensive Care Unit nurse and currently holds a position as Health Advisor for Jordan, Southern Syria, Malaysia, Iraq and Nigeria at MSF-Artsen zonder Grenzen in Amsterdam, the Netherlands. In this position, she

xvi Contributors

is a member of the Public Health Department of the Dutch operational section of MSF, supporting the previously mentioned missions, and she started to support the programmes for lead poisoning in Nigeria in mid-2015. In this position, it is her responsibility to enforce the medical strategy for this programming.

Annemieke Bont is a medical anthropologist with a master's degree from the University of Amsterdam (UvA), the Netherlands. Between 2001 and 2015, she worked for MSF at both the project and headquarters levels. Since July 2015, she has been working as an independent researcher on hospital-based qualitative research projects in Berlin.

Doris Burtscher holds a PhD in Medical Anthropology and started her extensive research and fieldwork experience in 1992 in sub-Saharan Africa, the Middle East and Central Asia. Since 2001, she has worked as a medical anthropologist with MSF and has undertaken fieldwork within MSF and other NGOs in Mauritania, Kenya, Sierra Leone, Zimbabwe, Liberia, Niger, Eswatini, Lebanon, India, Chad, Iraq, Kyrgyzstan, Afghanistan, Uganda, Democratic Republic of Congo, Senegal and Albania. Doris currently works as a medical anthropology referent in the MSF Vienna Evaluation Unit, Austria, providing technical support to different projects and contexts in the MSF movement. Since 2005, she has been a lecturer at the Medical University of Vienna/Public Health department and gives lessons on medical anthropology and qualitative methodologies in different courses inside and outside MSF. Her main fields of interest include female sexual and reproductive health, HIV/AIDS, TB and MDR-TB, antibiotic use, misuse and resistance, malnutrition, mental health, health-seeking behaviour, SGBV and neglected disease.

Paul Grohma is a cultural anthropologist from Austria who has conducted field studies and evaluations for MSF projects since 2010. His research topics comprise health promotion, HIV/AIDS sensitisation and retention in care, community inclusion and communication, acceptance of treatment, antibiotics consumption and understanding, acceptance of electronic diagnostic devices (MSFeCARE) and influences of traditional health care and religious healing on the work of MSF. Since 2003, he has worked as electoral advisor and international observer for elections in Africa and the Middle East; also for MSF, his regional focus is Central Africa and the Great Lakes Region.

William Hennequin has been working with MSF for the past 16 years and is now a programme manager (based in Paris, France) following the Central African Republic (CAR), Chad, Libya and France. He conducted several fieldwork experiences, including as laboratory technologist, field coordinator and head of mission working in South Sudan, Uganda, Democratic Republic of Congo, Nigeria and Kenya.

Kiran Jobanputra trained in family practice and public health prior to joining MSF, where he has worked for the last 12 years. He is currently a deputy medical director based in London, UK, and leads a multi-disciplinary team of specialists working on the thematic areas of tuberculosis, malaria, NCDs, social sciences, epidemiology and public health intelligence. He has held several field roles, including field doctor, hospital director, project coordinator and medical coordinator, working in Somalia, Democratic Republic of Congo, Niger, Haiti, Swaziland, Kenya and China.

Vanja Kovačič is a medical anthropologist and focuses her work on more efficient delivery of aid and disease control programmes through engagement of all programme participants. Dr Kovačič studied biology at the University of Ljubljana, the control of disease vectors at London School of Hygiene and Tropical Medicine, medical anthropology at the University of Oxford and international health at Liverpool School of Tropical Medicine, UK. Her work as a researcher and field project coordinator was contributing towards disease control (leishmaniasis in Brazil, tsetse control in Uganda, Tanzania, Burkina Faso, Guinea-Conakry and Chad). She worked with MSF on HIV control programmes in Kenya and currently in Jordan and Iraq, where she conducted an anthropological research embedded in the MSF reconstructive surgery programme for the victims of war.

Umberto Pellecchia holds a PhD in Political Anthropology of African Societies from the University of Siena, Italy. After more than two years of fieldwork amongst the Sefwis of Ghana, West Africa, he taught Political Anthropology while diversifying his research subjects towards medical anthropology and migration. He worked for MSF as an anthropologist and project coordinator for seven years in South Sudan, Liberia, Malawi and Egypt. In 2017, he supported the MSF Luxembourg Operational Research Unit as Program Officer and Senior Researcher. He is currently collaborating with Greenpeace Belgium on environmental and social themes. He has published in international journals and is co-author of *La cura e il potere* (*The Cure and the Power*) and *Capitali migratori e forme del potere* (*Migration and Forms of Power*).

James Smith is a British medical doctor with an MA in Medical Anthropology from SOAS University of London and an MSc in Global Health and Development from University College London, UK. He maintains roles as an Honorary Research Fellow with the London School of Hygiene and Tropical Medicine's Health in Humanitarian Crises Centre (LSHTM HHCC), and as a physician of emergency medicine with the UK National Health Service (NHS). He has worked for MSF as a medical doctor in South Sudan, advocacy manager in Sierra Leone, researcher with the Unité de Recherche sur les Enjeux et Pratiques Humanitaires (UREPH), advisor to MSF Barcelona's Patient Safety and Dignity Initiative, and humanitarian affairs advisor. His current research interests broadly include humanitarian ethics; the intersect between migration, forced displacement and humanitarian response; aspects of global health governance; and state violence and its health and socio-political consequences.

Darryl Stellmach was a field worker with the Dutch operational section of MSF for ten years before he undertook graduate studies, earning master's and doctorate degrees in Anthropology from the University of Oxford, UK. His 2016 doctoral

xviii Contributors

thesis was a multi-sited ethnography of humanitarian emergency. His fieldwork followed MSF's response to the South Sudan conflict as it developed in real time. He continues to work at the crossroads of academia and the aid sector. He is currently Anthropology Implementer for the Manson Unit of MSF-UK, overseeing the integration of anthropologists into MSF's field operations and providing anthropological and other qualitative research to support emergency programmes and strategic decision making.

Beverley Stringer is a social anthropologist from SOAS, formally trained as a nurse practitioner, specialising in emergency paediatrics. She has many years of field experience working in health and anthropology in Somalia, Sudan, Palestine, Afghanistan, Uzbekistan, Tajikistan, Ethiopia, Democratic Republic of Congo, Zambia, Mexico and Colombia. Her research themes include community health systems, tuberculosis, HIV, reproductive health and Ebola. As well as carrying out research, she developed the Methodshop, a concept for a blended learning series focussing on mixed methods training and mentorship for epidemiologists, social scientists and clinical specialists. She has additional studies in public policy from King's College, London. Bev is a visiting fellow at Sussex University, UK.

Renée Teernstra holds a master's degree in Medical Anthropology and Sociology from the University of Amsterdam, the Netherlands, and currently works as the executive assistant of the medical director of MSF-Artsen zonder Grenzen in Amsterdam.

Frédéric Vandenberghe is Professor of Sociology at the Institute of Philosophy and Social Sciences of the Federal University of Rio de Janeiro in Brazil. He has published widely in the field of social theory. His most recent books are *What's Critical about Critical Realism? Essays in Reconstructive Social Theory* (Routledge, 2014); *Le réalisme critique. Une ontologie pour la sociologie* (with Margaret Archer) (Le Bord de l'eau, 2019); and *For a New Classic Sociology: A Debate (with Alain Caillé)* (Routledge, 2020).

Marit van Lenthe was born in 1970 in Dalfsen, the Netherlands. She spent the last two years of her secondary school at the international United World College of the Atlantic in Wales, UK, a school that promotes international understanding through education. After graduating as a medical doctor, she specialised to become a general practitioner and later as a tropical doctor. She completed a master's degree in International Health from Royal Tropical Institute, Amsterdam. She started working for MSF in 2003, in North Kivu, Congo, and joined headquarters in 2009 as a health advisor. As health advisor, she supervised programmes in Iraq, Ethiopia, Nigeria, Democratic Republic of Congo, Myanmar and Somalia. She does research on malaria for MSF. Marit is currently the president of MSF Holland.

Contributors **xix**

Emilie Venables has been working for MSF since 2012 in various roles, most recently as the Qualitative Research Focal Point within the Southern Africa Medical Unit (SAMU) and the Luxembourg Operational Research Unit (LuxOR). Her research interests include HIV/AIDS, sex work, Ebola and migration, as well as the role of anthropology in humanitarian aid. She has worked in a wide range of countries and contexts, including South Africa, Kenya, Liberia, Senegal, Democratic Republic of Congo, Italy, Lebanon, Malawi, Mozambique and Côte d'Ivoire. Emilie holds an MSc and a PhD in African Studies from the University of Edinburgh, UK, as well as a BA in Social Anthropology from the University of Cambridge and an MSc in Development Studies from SOAS University of London. Dr Venables is also an Honorary Research Associate with the Division of Social and Behavioural Sciences in the School of Public Health and Family Medicine, University of Cape Town, South Africa.

Jean-François Véran has a doctoral degree in Anthropology from the École des Hautes Études des Sciences Sociales (Paris, France) and is Associate Professor at the Federal University of Rio de Janeiro, Brazil. His work initially focussed on the construction of ethnicity in political mobilisation, particularly in Brazil in the context of access to land and the rights of ethnic minorities. He later sought to develop a theoretical reflection on the contributions of the French pragmatic sociology applied to the Brazilian context. Affiliated with the Movement of the MAUSS (Anti-utilitarian Movement in Social Sciences), he works alongside Alain Caillé and Frédéric Vandenberghe on the reception of the Convivialist Manifesto in Brazil and its applications in terms of public policy. He joined MSF in 2010 as a Health Promoter in Haiti, Guatemala and Honduras, and has been Anthropology Advisor in the Brazilian Medical Unit (BRAMU) of MSF Brazil since 2013. Using both qualitative (social cartography, ethnography) and quantitative (Population Assessment Tool) methodologies, he works in Latin America and Africa on anthropology in 'humanitarian situations', applied to migratory issues, the management of epidemic crises, sexual health, reproductive health and urban violence.

Ursula Wagner studied social and cultural anthropology and medical anthropology at the universities of Vienna, Utrecht and Amsterdam (Austria and the Netherlands). She has extensive work experience as a project manager in gender equality and diversity management, having worked on international projects in Ethiopia and Kosovo. She has conducted anthropological research on mental health care, reproductive health, medical ethics and female genital cutting in Austria, the Netherlands, Guatemala and Egypt. Her first mission with MSF was as flying health promotion activity manager in Chad; thereafter, she was in Egypt for an anthropological study. Currently she is working with IOM, the UN Migration Agency in the field of migration health, where she is supporting the development of public health projects and operational research, both in the humanitarian and development sectors.

INTRODUCTION

Anthropology in humanitarian situations

Jean-François Véran, Beverley Stringer and
Doris Burtscher

It usually begins with a deadlock signalled by a team of the international medical humanitarian organisation Médecins Sans Frontières (MSF) working in a humanitarian setting, a problem difficult to solve. For example: Kenya's prevalence and incidence of human immunodeficiency virus (HIV) in Homa Bay on the banks of Lake Victoria is four times higher than the national average; is it because local people practice sexual rites? Why would medical doctors in the region of Léogâne in Haiti refuse to recognise the existence of dengue and claim to be 'ideologically against' the disease? How does the traditional view of shame affect maternal health amongst the Pashtun in Afghanistan? Why would people with fractures in Chad seek an x-ray, but refuse hospital treatment; that is, accept the diagnosis, but not the cure? As anthropologists of MSF, all the contributors to this book have confronted several enigmas of this kind. They are the reasons we are usually involved in the first place. We do not try to solve the enigmas in the exact terms in which they are presented; our contribution is to help to unlock operational blockages. The first objective of this book is to show how, as anthropologists, we try to contribute to the success of a humanitarian medical response.

This intent to 'contribute' immediately locates us as first-degree believers in MSF's vision and mission. Like the medical doctors, we want to save lives and we respect the principles of impartiality, independence and neutrality that guide the organisation in its application of medical ethics, not transcendental, metaphysical, spiritual or philosophical aspirations of being anthropologists with a mission. In a much more pragmatic way, we are believers and we try to 'contribute' because, in our experience, anthropology actually works. We are sure that the concepts, analytical tools and methodologies of our discipline can indeed be helpful, when applied in a cooperative way, to an action intending to save lives and reduce suffering. We hope that the eight case-study chapters of this book will show this contribution of anthropology.

2 Jean-François Véran et al.

We practice 'applied anthropology'. Instead of advancing anthropology itself, we work with non-academic non-anthropologists to improve the provision of humanitarian aid. Our work is to pinpoint the comprehension gaps, unintended consequences or social blockages of a specific humanitarian project. As members of a team, we work to solve difficulties and help the project to reach the people that need help. We are not against the critical tradition of the discipline, but our critical thought is – at least at first – bound to the situations in which we were called to intervene. This is a restriction, but also a significant potential.

Doing 'applied anthropology' with the support of MSF's legitimacy, logistics and resources gives us privileged access to situations that would otherwise be impossible to reach. We are brought in to the centre of the world's most complex conflict zones, epidemics and natural disasters; contexts of emergency where social structures collapse, culture is challenged, resilience worn down. Applying anthropology in such peculiar circumstances produces a wealth of material we are pleased to share here. Also, we believe that by working at these extreme limits of humanity, where people struggle but refuse to die and be reduced to "bare lives" (Agamben, 1998), we can contribute to an anthropology of the 'humanitarian relationship' which we will locate in a postcolonial world. This is the second objective of this book.

We acknowledge that value-laden concepts, such as 'life', 'suffering' or 'humanitarian' can (and should) always be under the scrutiny of analytical deconstruction and perspectivism. Yet, our experience makes us pragmatic. To be workable, the humanitarian relationship has to be reduced to the lowest common denominator: survival. In a "critical event" (Das, 1996), an encounter occurs between, on the one hand, people who do not want to die (the people who need help and their families), and on the other hand, people (humanitarian workers) who do not want them to die, either, with all parties willing to act on that basis. It is our experience that this definition is fully and immediately operational.

The interface between critique and operational cooperation is the exact point where we situate our work. It also constitutes the core argumentation of the book. While we fully acknowledge the legitimacy and relevance of a vigilant anthropology of humanitarianism, this is not our main concern. Instead we locate at a face-to-face level where humanitarian action really happens. This book is about the practice of anthropology in humanitarian situations, and we hope that we can contribute to how this is understood.

As MSF anthropologists, we are involved in discussions carried out within three sub-fields of the discipline: the anthropology of humanitarian action, medical anthropology and applied anthropology. The first part of this introduction focuses on these discussions. The anthropology of humanitarian action, by raising a critical voice on the issues of power within the postcolonial agenda, can be read as call for responsibility in the way we do our fieldwork and in the need to confront the premises of the 'humanitarian order'. How do we, as insider anthropologists, stick to the MSF principles, while simultaneously submitting the conditions of the MSF charter to a critical examination? How do we hold together the reality of the principles and the principle of reality? Medical anthropology, for its part, constantly shows how the social aspects of an illness or an epidemic, the perceptions of health and pain, the diversity of therapeutic itineraries, etc., are by no means reducible to MSF's biomedical foundation. How, then, do we function as anthropologists within an organisation that relies on guidelines, techniques and protocols to perform medical responses to emergencies? What kind of dialogue can we have with our medical counterparts on the subtleties of the social construction of illness while large numbers of people are dying in an emergency setting? Finally, applied anthropology is by its nature oriented towards the solution of practical problems in a combination of methodology, engagement and advocacy. The issue here is that as an emergency medical organisation, MSF does not aim to bring lasting social changes to the places where it works. How does the anthropologist deal with the conflict of scale between the structural – and often complex – dimensions of their analysis and the actual context and time-limited constraints of their intervention? Under these circumstances, to what extend does 'applied anthropology' contribute to the solution of a problem or to its cyclical reproduction?

The second part of the introduction will locate anthropology within the history and the technical apparatus of MSF. It offers a description of the procedures and circumstances in which anthropologists are brought in during a humanitarian response. Frequently associated with or even assimilated to 'health promotion', 'community engagement' or 'outreach activities', the anthropologist rarely exists as 'just an anthropologist'. When they are eventually required to conduct an 'anthropological assessment', the specificity of their analysis is hard to defend in the face of two common reductions: to the generic methodological umbrella of 'qualitative studies', and to the misperception of their work as low-tech: anybody can 'talk to people', and the redundancy of their conclusion as 'everybody already knows that'. So, what is the aggregated value of the anthropologist, both within a specific project and at the same time when confronted with the necessity of reforming the humanitarian order?

Anthropology in humanitarian situations

Beshar and Stellmach (2017, p. 2) have asked a crucial question: "How have anthropologists engaged with institutions and action in the context of medical humanitarianism?" To answer it, they did extensive research and came up with a useful typology of three lines of thought that anthropologists have assumed: critique, translation and reform. "A critique of medical humanitarianism and its ties to colonialism and globalization. A translation of medical humanitarianism and its associated lexicon. A reform of medical humanitarianism from the inside out" (p. 3). Schematically, these strands refer to three analytical traditions of the discipline. Critique derives from Foucauldian genealogy that analyses the relationship between knowledge and power, translation from the cultural anthropology axiom that no culture is reducible to another and reform from historical engagement in the processes of change of social anthropology. As MSF insider anthropologists, we shall argue that our practice is located at the exact intersection of all three positions.

4 Jean-François Véran et al.

Our experience is that critique alone leads to a poor operational contribution, with immediate consequences in terms of legitimacy and permanence in practice. Translation, although sometimes necessary, may take unnecessary time and prove less efficient than finding a common idiosyncrasy and language. Reform is often needed and welcome, provided that it also focuses on concrete operational responses and does not limit itself to questioning the humanitarian order.

Critique: a constant – and tense – exercise

Deeply rooted within the critical tradition of anthropology, the anthropology of humanitarian action consists mainly in unearthing the power, symbolic violence and political stakes embedded within the humanitarian relationship. Just like Penelope, who destroyed at night the fabric woven during the day, critique always deconstructs the premises on which humanitarianism is based. To what does the concept of 'human' in humanitarianism refer? How is it constructed, imposed and operated?

As MSF anthropologists, we shall argue that critique is indeed our starting point. It is our point of departure, but not our standpoint. Our constant insertion in the practice of humanitarian action incites us to somehow criticise the critiques raised by some of our external counterparts.

Beyond compassion

In his influential critique of humanitarian reason, Fassin analyses the morality of humanitarianism. He argues that the growing impact of moral sentiments on politics has come at the expense of core values such as justice (Fassin, 2010). He denounces the fusion between the 'compassionate' and humanitarianism as an arbitrary regression of rights. He argues, for example, that the Geneva Convention of 1951 would have provided sufficient grounds to address the issue of migration in the European Union, but the migration 'crisis' emerged precisely because "moral sentiments" and even "emotional reflexes" were being invoked to justify asylum (p. 148). Fassin's critique is useful. It shows the necessity of a critical anthropology of emotions in the analysis of the humanitarian relationship. Within MSF, indeed, neither the legal bases of International Humanitarian Rights, nor the technical 'assessments' and 'guidelines', are stand-alone arguments for intervention. Moral arguments are always mobilised, as well.

MSF differentiates 'emergency assistance' – considered as self-obvious and justified – from the 'projects by choice' that result from a complex deliberation process. Regarding the latter, we have noted an increasing tendency to ground operational strategy – deciding where to start and when to close a project – on an ever-more-complex set of screenings and indicators. This technical development of operations is particularly salient during the project control cycle, when a 'project by choice' is submitted to the scrutiny of all sorts of advisors. The intention of this expertise is to block the mobilisation of controversial moral and emotional arguments that may be advanced by those who are close to a specific setting because of personal affinities, because they conducted the exploratory assessment or because they have had a long exposure to the context. Yet, we have also witnessed many (passionate) internal discussions opposing on the one hand, the compelling argument of relief of suffering, and on the other hand, the invocation of justice and balance against arbitrary decisions – why respond there if not here? These debates attest that the 'compassionate' is always there, like a ghost in the cupboard. Notwithstanding the complex set of technical tools, the ghost is still there, and this is why an anthropology of emotions is needed.

However, at both the headquarters and the operational level, Fassin's critique of a humanitarian reason governed by the 'compassionate' shows its limits when applied to concrete decision-making. Inverting Boltanski's analysis of "distant suffering" whereby the contemplation of the unfortunate's tragedy motivates the decision to financially support a humanitarian organisation (Boltanski, 2007), it is about showing how the "suffering in presence" that field anthropologists are exposed to, resituates the debate on the practical grounds imposed by crisis and emergency (p. xv).

As one cannot intervene in all theatres of suffering at the same time, 'compassion' is rarely useful for decision-making. Compassion cuts both ways: 'go' implies a symmetric 'no-go' that can tie up the organisation in never-ending moral dilemmas. MSF works in over 70 countries around the world, a reality that makes a "competition of victims" (Chaumont, 2017, p. 1) rather hard to organise, and this is why compassion tends to neutralise itself and leave space for the technical building of informed operational decisions.

This trickles down to the most practical operational levels. As insider anthropologists, we are constantly exposed to the emotional impact of a social or individual drama and to the moral dilemmas that appear in the everyday life of a project. But there again, as Fassin and Pandolfi put it, "the implementation of technical apparatuses allows one to suppress one's emotion while acting" (Fassin & Pandolfi, 2010, p. 245) eventually can be a challenge for those who are on their first assignment. Those who let compassion overtake a well-understood 'humanitarian reason' may at times face emotional burnout and be evacuated.

No, it's never just a medical intervention

We are perfectly aligned with Ticktin's critique that humanitarian projects have unintended consequences. For this reason, the position sometimes assumed by our medical counterparts that a humanitarian intervention is 'just a medical intervention' is wrong (Ticktin, 2014). The best intentions may provoke collateral damage and actually "does harm". As some of the chapters presented in this volume show clearly, a biomedical intervention is never *just* a biomedical intervention. As anthropologists, it is our job to show how an intervention always mobilises – both symbolically and at a very practical level – power relations, sometimes deeply rooted in colonial pasts and post-colonial presents. Indeed, we recall that in many settings, MSF is the first employer and has a significant economic impact. MSF can be a key public health actor and organiser. It is perceived as a moral entrepreneur while promoting sets of values that are not necessarily shared locally (neutrality, non-violence, impartiality and independence, for example). It affects local political and geopolitical perceptions, and it can also affect the balance of power, explicitly or in a subtle way (for example, by recruiting the son of the local authority). It activates post-colonial memories, thoughts and positioning, through the recurring tensions between international and local staff or through the perception of unequal treatment and access to care, as MSF was frequently accused of doing during the 2014/2015 Ebola epidemic in West Africa (Hofman & Au, 2017).

As anthropologists and through our work, we constantly draw attention to the fact that 'just biomedical interventions' may result in lasting behaviour change. Somehow, they always induce cultural change. This is the case, for example, when the linkage to care after a patient is found to be HIV positive implies lifetime enrolment onto antiretroviral treatment programmes. Responses to epidemics are frequently made with the backup of health promotion strategies aimed at changing hygiene habits. The very presence of MSF may challenge traditional healers' authority if there is no acknowledgement of their relevance. The projects focussing on sexual and reproductive health often induce conflicts within families that change the gender balance of power. Finally, the health-seeking behaviour of the people on which the success of a medical project depends is indeed about behaviour that may need to be adapted or changed through health promotion and 'community engagement' strategies.

Biomedical aid may have uncontrolled side effects that were not anticipated or desired by MSF. For example, as we cruelly experienced, the medicalisation of female medical cutting as a harm reduction strategy promoted by some MSF projects became an argument for the maintenance of the practice itself. Once it is medically compliant, a key argument against it loses it cogency (Shell-Duncan, 2001). Another frequent uncontrolled outcome of MSF's presence is when the organisation gets caught in local powers and interests, unwillingly and sometimes without even noticing; 84% of all MSF projects are run by national staff, compared to 16% international and headquarters staff, who may have an agenda that can't really be controlled by MSF (MSF, 2018b). For example, we have seen health promoters doing domiciliary visits with their portable radios tuned to their church or promoting another non-governmental organisation (NGO). Of course, international staff may also have parallel agendas.

Finally, as insider anthropologists, we fulfil the critical mission of our discipline by applying the formula of Michel Foucault: "People know what they do; frequently they know why they do what they do; but what they don't know is what what they do does" (Dreyfus & Rabinow, 1983, p. 187). We show that the biomedical-only argument for humanitarian responses is not sustainable, and we therefore warn that not knowing "what we do does" is not an option for MSF under the do-no-harm policy. In our understanding, the answer to this discussion is always to practice auto-ethnography by including the organisation itself in the scope of analysis. This methodological concern applies to all chapters of the book.

Engagement or objectivity? Beyond the debate

As previously argued, 'doing' applied anthropology means, in our case, joining a team effort to deliver medical assistance in humanitarian situations. The question of engagement may involve personal convictions, but in our programmes, it is brought down to the pragmatic 'here and now' of a specific project. It is not about defending a vision and a cause. We are experienced anthropologists, not the *intellectuels engagés* (engaged intellectuals) of Jean-Paul Sartre, who used his prestige politically to defend specific causes in the name of justice (Sartre, 1972). Neither are we the *spectateurs engagés* (committed observers) of Aron (1981), guardians of universal values beyond contemporary turmoil. We actually chose contemporary turmoil. We understand the argument that this commitment jeopardises from the very start the data we produce (Singer & Baer, 2011, p. 19), and that under these conditions, the fundamental principles of objectivity and independence of the discipline (Streber, 2017) can't always be respected.

If objectivity as an anthropologist means that one does not bring any external values into research, then, of course, we cannot pretend to adhere to Max Weber's principle of axiological neutrality (Weber, 2003). As we work for an organisation that promotes values that we also believe in, we are necessarily biased – and we are so by choice. However, does this axiological engagement make objectivity impossible in the conduct of our work? Does it condemn us to bad science, or even to anti-science? Symmetrically, we can ask whether we are militants, activists or missionaries. After all, aren't we committed to MSF's core ethical principles? One of these principles is neutrality. We do not take sides, at least not when we operate in a conflict zone. So, at the end of the day, where do we stand? Are we, perhaps, activists of neutrality?

Indeed, the dilemma that runs through the Scheper-Hughes versus d'Andrades discussion (D'Andrade & Scheper-Hughes, 1995) on objectivity versus militancy appears to us in somehow different terms. Scheper-Hughes dismisses "moral relativism" as "no longer appropriate in the world we live in" (p. 196). She affirms the necessity of grounding anthropological practice on strong ethics and assumes a militant posture against "the horrors of political violence". D'Andrade assumes the opposite position. For him, moral models and the objective model of science he defends are mutually incompatible. He sees in Scheper-Hughes' "primacy of the ethical" an attack against science. Her critique of oppression "doesn't do anything positive about bad conditions".

Trying to do something positive about bad conditions – saving lives and reducing suffering – is the *raison d'être* of MSF. We certainly agree with the argument that science does not exist in a social vacuum (Singer & Baer, 2011; O'Driscoll, 2009; Pool & Geissler, 2005). Our humanitarian anthropology starts from the conviction that it is the duty or moral responsibility of anthropologists to apply their knowledge and findings in order to reduce human suffering and improve the quality of human life (Streber, 2017, p. 32). So, whether or not we engage is not a dilemma for us. However, does our rejection of the dogma of Max Weber's "axiological neutrality" imply that we surrender 'science' to 'activism'?

8 Jean-François Véran et al.

The answer is in the way we frame our actions and the way we resolve an apparently contradictory injunction. 'Engage but do it in an objective way'. The biomedical professionals we work with understand and participate in the dilemmas of engagement ('Why here and not there?'). For them, once they are in front of patients, it is 'just' medical practice, with specific protocols, harsh working conditions, etc. They may be working with extreme medical challenges, but it is still medical practice with its 'cases', 'probabilistic diagnostics' and 'experimental protocols'. It is science in practice, certainly one d'Andrade would call 'objective'. Just as our medical colleagues do their job, we do ours. As we hope will be clear throughout the book, our commitment to MSF principles does not prevent us from applying the methodologies of the social sciences.

We acknowledge that in some cases, a research output sometimes takes on a life of its own. This is especially the case for any research used for advocacy purposes. In MSF there are processes in place to mitigate this, through communications departments and other checks, but despite that, uses and misuses can have serious unwanted consequences. Just to give an example: the published report *Forced to Flee Central America's Northern Triangle: A Neglected Humanitarian Crisis*,[1] partially based upon operational research conducted by Jean-François Véran, was quoted in 2019 by US President Donald Trump as an argument for building a border wall between Mexico and the USA in a complete manipulation of the report's content. This report showed the exceptional burden of violence during the migration route through Mexico and its impact on health and mental health and denounced a "neglected humanitarian crisis", but Donald Trump alleged that this burden would be supressed with the wall because nobody would try to cross the border any longer. More generally, the release of data may jeopardise the continuity of care to patients – and even the very presence of MSF. Like every other social scientist with fieldwork (Cefaï & Amiraux, 2002), we have to face the responsibility for any possible consequences of the publication of research for the study participants. In our case, the deliberation of what can and cannot be written is not only a meta-reflexive exercise with one's own sense of the 'do no harm' principle, but also a complex chain of external controls. The MSF anthropologist is not the owner of the data they produce; the organisation is. Every single chapter of this book passed various clearance gates.

Not everything is Foucauldable: the limits of critique

We can unlock the medical practice of MSF operations from a Foucauldian perspective. Following the path of Haraway, we can reveal the issues of power, sets of judgemental premises and sphere(s) of values that bias scientific research (Haraway, 1988). But how would that contribute to an emergency operation? 'Deconstruction', as we practice it, is not about shaking the epistemological premises of science, but about helping to remove operational blockages. Furthermore, working with medical practitioners, logisticians, etc., we cannot deconstruct scientific discourse at will. Cholera is caused by a vibrio, a type of bacteria that degrades the human

Introduction **9**

body's capacity to retain water. Symptomatology will be diarrhoea and vomiting, causing fast dehydration and death. Treatment is rehydration with all its subtleties and protocols. The anthropologist has nothing to say about that, and recognising this is a day-by-day lesson of humility. Not everything is Foucauldable.

If we were eternal whistle-blowers within an organisation committed to emergency responses in extreme situations, we would not last long. If it is true that anthropologists are often "more comfortable with the stance of critique than that of endorsement" (Bornstein & Redfield, 2011, p. 21), then it is about getting out of that comfort zone.

Are we cultural translators?

If, as Antoine de Saint-Exupéry puts it, "you become responsible, forever, for what you have tamed" (Saint-Exupéry, 1943, p. 60), then MSF anthropologists have a responsibility for how culture as a key concept of anthropology is handled within the organisation.

There are two ways of thinking we often encounter in our practice that are the opposite sides of the same cultural coin. One stems from the idea that local culture is a key factor to take into account for the success of a project. Ways then have to be found to remove 'cultural obstacles'. The other side is to raise ethical awareness of what should be the limits and impacts of a medical intervention. Following Homi Bhabha (2012), it is exactly at this interstice and liminality of the humanitarian situation that culture is located by humanitarian agents, and where the anthropologist is expected to intervene.

Uses and abuses of culture: a constant concern

Since 1971, MSF has worked in numerous countries. MSF – by the very nature of its social mission – is an organisation confronted by the challenges of cultural differences. In practice, this manifests itself with any nurse, paediatrician or emergency physician quickly understanding that although the biological body is universal, its social uses, its "techniques", as Marcel Mauss (1936, p. 5) put it, vary singularly from one place to another. However, in everyday medical practice, the 'cultural factor' doesn't translate into anything more than adjustments in the relationship with the patient – consented to as long as the integrity of treatment protocols is not at stake. It is about adapting the language, addressing the fears and body taboos, accepting the co-presence of biomedical and spiritual treatments, and being pedagogic rather than humiliating regarding hygiene issues.

These 'reasonable agreements' in the work routine correspond to a form of spontaneous cultural relativism, understood as the principle long established by Franz Boas (1982) that values and norms are relative to the context. Yet, the moral corollary that "cultural differences should not be judged by absolute standards" (Erickson & Murphy, 2003, p. 198) is not easy to practice in a biomedical environment where every protocol is presented as the best cure. The idea that there are 'cultural obstacles' to humanitarian action is often presented as a given fact in training, handbooks (Mac Ginty & Peterson, 2015) and context analysis. Not surprisingly, we often find international staff with an imagination populated by exotic representations of otherness, local staff sometimes deeply convinced that atavistic 'traditional' behaviour of uneducated people is the reason for MSF's difficulties, and local people believing that 'blaming it on culture' is what international organisations do. As will appear throughout the chapters of this book, the authors regularly came across conversations wherein culture was invoked as accountable for 'risky' practices ("amid cholera outbreaks they continue to embrace the bodies of the deceased") or inadequate health-seeking behaviour ("they believe that fever is an evil spirit so do not seek assistance").

In our anthropological assessments, we often find people who have learnt from other humanitarian workers to blame their own culture for their medical emergency. In Kenya, for example, an MSF report about HIV in Homa Bay County found that the Luo people blame their own sex rites for their exceptionally high rates of HIV. They had learnt from people working in health promotion (who sometimes portray themselves as – literally – culture removers) that HIV is about morals and 'good sexuality' against 'bad old practices'. One MSF worker said: "we try to remove that culture outside of them, we argue that in the whole world people don't obey the sex rites and don't have HIV for that" (Véran, 2017, p. 3). The MSF report found that the high levels of HIV in Homa Bay were partly a result of local resistance against unfounded criticism of local culture in the first place. This example shows how damaging, both ethically and in terms of humanitarian efficiency, it has been for humanitarian organisations to use culture to explain their failures.

Acculturation as contamination

Symmetrically, we also come across a 'post-relativist' reflection, especially at headquarters level, whereby professionals from both operations and medical departments worry about this stigma loaded onto cultural discourse. As a commitment to the ethical implications of the humanitarian relationship, they are convinced, as Taylor and Gutmann put it, that "recognition is not just a courtesy we owe people, but a vital human need" (Taylor & Gutmann, 1994, p. 26). Dealing appropriately with people's culture is crucial to recognition. At the same time, it is generally believed that an emergency aid programme should not affect local culture because this is not ethical and can be counter-productive.

Does the idea that culture must not be touched derive from the epidemiological concern of not contaminating local organisms and population? It relies anyway on the reification of culture as an ontological stock susceptible to corruption by contact. However, there is consensus within anthropology since Barth in 1969 that it is quite the contrary (Barth, 1969). It is understood that culture keeps remoulding itself by acculturation: this does not mean a-culturation (loss of culture) but ad-culturation (the production of cultures by reciprocal borrowings and adaptations) (Schwartz et al., 2010).

The 'leave the people alone with their culture' argument may quickly show its limits, because the culture in question is under the heavy stress of a crisis that is the reason for assistance in the first place. Indeed, MSF works in extremely vulnerable settings where the coping mechanisms provided by culture may not adequately function any longer. In a large African slum, for example, an unpublished MSF quantitative study found a 14% suicide attempt rate, and that 18% of the population suffered from severe mental health conditions. With the risk of being condescending, the cultural argument must be relativised when a local culture is shaken by a critical event. More than in any other context, the anthropologist in a humanitarian crisis must remember Fabian's warning about the abuse of the ethnographic present: they might observe the 'here and now' in a specific cultural configuration and erroneously conclude it is the way that culture 'is' in that location (Fabian, 1983). In times of crisis, the denial of absolute co-temporality between humanitarian agents and local people would be absurd. They too are 'here and now', and the culture they enact is put under just as much stress by the emergency situation as is the agents' own training and capacity.

The re-location of culture

How far can we go in the deconstruction of this cultural argument? The attempt by some experts to systematically 'de-culturalise' anthropological interventions does not necessarily result in a better understanding of what anthropology can provide in MSF. This is why the question "which anthropology do we talk about?" – raised in a special issue of the French journal *Humanitaire* with the title "Anthropologists and NGOs: a fruitful liaison?" (Atlani-Duault, 2007) – is fully endorsed in this book, and not an easy one to answer.

As a way to consider the question, we agree with Abu-Lughod, particularly in respect of the humanitarian relationship, on the need to be aware of how our anthropological discourse about culture may "enforce separations that inevitably carry a sense of hierarchy" (Abu-Lughod, 1991, p. 138). However, we wouldn't go as far as to suggest, as she does, that we should 'write without culture', even if the stigmatisation effect of such discourse, as we have mentioned, is a constant concern of ours. We need to write 'with culture' to understand better the operational difficulties of a specific project: if everything is not about culture, culture is still an analytical component we cannot simply bypass.

From our practical experience, we also don't agree with Hemmings that "anthropology [itself] has been handicapped by its cultural relativism and so-called literary turn" (Hemmings, 2005, p. 94), and that adherence to relativism and postmodernism, despite warnings, has reduced the credibility of anthropologists in health care (Kuznar, 1997; Lett, 1997; Rosenberg, 1995). As we previously argued, instead we have the opposite problem: we frequently relate to more cultural-relativist

12 Jean-François Véran et al.

biomedical colleagues than to other MSF anthropologists. In the end, because of operational pressures, we spend more time 'taking culture out' than bringing it in.

The added value of anthropology and the reform of the humanitarian order

From a sceptical perspective, the main argument is that the inputs of anthropology have already been integrated – or ought to be – within humanitarian work. As well as the methodological inputs of qualitative research already mentioned, local context, values and practices are widely seen to be key to MSF operations. MSF workers are required to be deeply involved with people in crisis, to show respect, empathy and precision with the aims of reducing suffering and making survival more likely. But these contributions are also seen as not being specific and technical enough. Anthropology quickly falls under the 'lesson learnt' and 'best practice' sections of MSF guidelines. Quite often, MSF anthropologists hear after their last report or presentation that the team of the project they had visited had already come to the same conclusions, implying that their assessment was not that necessary after all. This comes as a disappointment for the anthropologist but, in a more inclusive tone, others at headquarters acknowledge that anthropology has a lot to contribute, as long as it is limited to specific issues with strict terms of understanding on the definition of problems and the expected outcomes. There is no other position within the MSF apparatus that offers the same availability, methodologies, logistics and resources for the sole purpose of understanding an operational blockage. The lack of time for exclusive and dedicated listening and analysis is probably why the project came under difficulties in the first place.

This role of anthropologist is seen to be highly privileged by our medical colleagues, as we get to do 'outreach activities', 'talk to people', 'see their reality' and benefit from adapted security guidelines. This privileged position, however, is regularly challenged at the decisive moment a report is received and the operational recommendations are put under scrutiny. This is when most critics converge: reports are too often late, hard to read, insufficiently operational or not applicable. We did take these criticisms into account in the making of this book, by building chapters upon reports that have achieved a recognised impact.

Through this legitimisation process, we understood we had to be our own prescribers and proactively respond to a specific challenge. This was helped by being insider practitioners in MSF, where we were able to reproduce assessments with the use of participation methods with medical teams, as well as with communities, to bring results in real time, in line with expectations, with frequent as opposed to sporadic support. In that process we also learnt to be more MSF-compatible by imitating MSFs timeframes, jargon, acronyms and ways of working.

With the endorsement of anthropologists by headquarters, the momentum to recognise and apply the interdisciplinary value of the social sciences in public health programmes emerged, not least through varied practical applications between the different MSF sections, but also through a number of reflection workshops that

Introduction **13**

were organised between 2010 and 2018. They debated "what is anthropology good for?" and discussed how knowledge generated in humanitarian settings is used to make decisions. The idea for this book came out of such gatherings, where a more collective understanding of the growing momentum, challenges and value of anthropology was debated within the MSF movement. Through coming together as a group, the practice of anthropology has caught up with its present-day approval.

Finally, this real – but still fragile – approval corresponds to the very moment when postcolonial thinking trickled down within the MSF movement to become a systematic questioning of the way issues of power, symbolic violence, discrimination, fairness and equality of opportunity are addressed. In this context, a key dimension of our practice has been to downscale to practical dimensions the issues of power theoretically framed – since Foucault – within the nexus of knowledge and power, and that are embedded in the real-life humanitarian relationship. The recurrence of tensions between international and national staff, whether about practicalities such as wages or work routines, intermix with symbolic and always political issues plugged in to the colonial and postcolonial imagination and the phenomenological experience of discrimination. To say it in a prosaic way, a human resource issue, for example, in a project in the Democratic Republic of Congo involving a French or Belgian white male with the MSF white jacket is never just a human resource issue. This is also true for the complex web of conspiracy theories, accusations of poisoning or contamination, a hatred of 'white medicine' that ignores the spiritual forces at play, or a suspicion of hidden agendas such as allocated funds that never reach their targets. All these issues have resulted in an increased complexity of the agenda between the operational level and headquarters particularly concerning fairness of remuneration and, career planning for national staff (Shevchenko & Fox, 1995). As a result, mechanisms have been put in place to address any lack of diversity or inclusion and to report potential abuses of power or discrimination. There is a new code of conduct to be signed by all staff worldwide meant to avoid sexual and other exploitation (MSF, 2018a). MSF has clearly engaged with the postcolonial debate that Europe needs to be 'provincialised', which means that it should have no privileged position for any epistemological primacy and cultural leadership (Chakrabarty, 2008). *Provincializing Europe* is not merely an intellectual manifesto, but it is a concrete attempt to give better geostrategic non-European importance to what are still called 'branch offices' and 'partner sections'. The FAD sessions (Field Associative Debates) that MSF organises every year within every single one of its projects unpack an intense and emotional testimony of postmodern times. As anthropologists, we believe this is a meaningful moment where a new *episteme* is gaining its social standing and we are excited to join in.

This is why we have supported a transverse integration of power relation analysis and mitigation strategies, as a systematic component of all project definitions, terms of reference and operational research protocols as required criteria for MSF Ethical Review Board clearance. We have also supported a systematic 'reverse anthropology' analysis to be conducted in relevant projects. This consists of a targeted assessment of the way MSF and a project are perceived within the community's own

14 Jean-François Véran et al.

modes of analysis. This is nothing compared to a 'quick and dirty' satisfaction and notoriety survey.

We need to acknowledge our own awkwardness in the eyes of the people we are involved with. This is not *just* a matter of recognition, but the application of pure good sense following the precept of Strathern not to "lose out on intellectual resources" (Strathern, 2004, p. 1). In a more prosaic way, actually listening to people is the best way to 'think outside the box'. For that purpose, we have defined, and had approved by the MSF Ethical Review Board, a wide range of social science methodologies, from the quantitative Population Assessment Tool to participatory ateliers of social cartography. In the same vein, we have also been promoting a full co-definition of a project's objectives in a win–win perspective whereby the incorporation of local priorities strongly reinforces the chance of a project's acceptance. This implies that it is useful to be able at times to step out of MSF's core mission and to invest in activities that are not directly medical, such as community-building actions for local empowerment, the construction of a multi-functional meeting room near a health centre, or the restoration of a sports yard that can be used later to facilitate access for adolescents in sexual and reproductive health projects.

Synthesis

As a synthesis, we do agree with Stellmach that a tempered, well-understood practice of cultural relativism is not an option but a necessity for project success (Stellmach et al., 2017). When a humanitarian situation develops at the velocity of an emergency response, it is not only contact, but also coordination that is needed between very disparate groups of people.

This well-tempered practice is about giving equal analytic attention to all parties involved. Not choosing to give a preferential option to the patient's standpoint, rather than that of international doctors, community members or health care providers (Maretzki, 1985). This sense of responsibility to represent an as complete as possible emic perspective is our way to fight back against the stigmatisation, power issues and imputations that would inevitably come along with the location of an operational problem in the culture of the people involved. We do quite the contrary: we locate the culture of each party – including, of course, MSF itself – as a dialectic component of the humanitarian situation in which we work. The issues we are dealing with are never mere cultural atavisms and blockages; they are at least, as van Velsen puts it, "conflicting norms, discrepancies between people's beliefs and their professed acceptance of, or resistance to, certain norms usually imposed by external organizations on the one hand, and their actual behaviour on the other" (van Velsen, 2017, p. 142). This is why we do not explain 'cultures' independently from a situational analysis oriented towards the pragmatic resolution of an operational challenge. By 'situational analysis', we refer to the "anthropology of the concrete" inaugurated by Gluckman, van Velsen and the Manchester school (Kapferer, 2005, p. 85). It consists of observing behaviour in relation to a given situation, and not to the formal set of cultural norms alone. This obviously includes the way the humanitarian agents themselves really act in relation to their own values, rules and protocols. Humanitarian situations, probably more than any other, are characterised by their considerable "creative potential" (van Doorne, 1981, p. 503), realised and accelerated by the common objective of all parties to save lives, reduce suffering and do both urgently.

Anthropology at MSF: an inside-out position

Almost all the contributors to this book work first as international staff for MSF, and only secondarily as anthropologists. What this means in practice is that their experience of applying anthropology in MSF settings is from *within* the MSF apparatus or system itself; they have no issues about inside knowhow, nor are they excluded from the ways decision-making, governance and power operate within MSF. As previously clarified, the need for an anthropological perspective usually emerges within a project whereby the anthropologist becomes some sort of broker between what MSF intends to and what it can actually do. This type of MSF anthropologist cannot be found in a recent demarcation of types: accidental ethnographer, humanitarian practitioner or critical observer (Abramowitz & Panter-Brick, 2015). We choose to work in humanitarian settings, and the way we are practitioners includes critical observation, but also cooperation with the aid work. The anthropologists who are featured in this book have the advantage that they are sharing their experiences of anthropological practice from within MSF, while at the same time showcasing the value of their discipline.

The editors

The encounter of the three editors is itself an insight into this process. Medical practice led to anthropological questioning and – symmetrically – the academic study of anthropology eventually turned to a desire to apply it within humanitarian action. Beverley Stringer started with MSF as a nurse and was disillusioned with how she saw aid work in practice. After reading Harrell-Bond's *Imposing Aid* (1986), she realised that her concerns might be addressed by training in anthropology. Conversely, Jean-François Véran, an associate professor of the Federal University of Rio de Janeiro (Brazil), was disenchanted with the academic limitations of anthropology and went to Haiti in 2010 to work on the cholera outbreak as a health promoter and outreach activity coordinator. Finishing her PhD in medical anthropology, Doris Burtscher was uncomfortable that her thesis reached only a small academic audience in a library. Working with MSF helped her find a more meaningful way to practice medical anthropology. She started in 2001 as an anthropologist doing humanitarian work. This convergence of challenges that MSF ended up becoming is very recent. Many historians within MSF – and the three editors of this book – recall anthropologists being present on various assignments over the last 40 years or so, but accessible records show that only from the 1990s onwards (see Table I.1)

TABLE I.1 Mapping of anthropology and social science in MSF

While not exhaustive, the table presents an overview of work related to anthropology and the social sciences that we were able find in MSF digital files. A complete reconstruction of all physical archives within every branch of MSF proved difficult within the scope of the book. The table illustrates that outside of multiple studies for Ebola carried out in Liberia and Sierra Leone. South Sudan and Democratic Republic of Congo have higher numbers of requests for anthropological or social science inquiry where both locations also receive currently the highest investment in terms of patients treated and resources. Equally, people living in these places suffer a protracted experience of crisis, disruption and failure of the kind MSF is used to working. In general, social science has supported various MSF inquiries associated with its health priorities of the time, such as access to health care, HIV, tuberculosis, reproductive health, mental health and sexual violence in up to 40 missions in most continents of the world MSF is active.

Place	Topic	Year(s)
Afghanistan ×3	Antibiotic use; sexual and reproductive health; population perceptions of TB in Kandahar	2014; 2016; 2018–2019
Azerbaijan	Childhood immunisation and reproductive health	1999
Bangladesh Cox's Bazaar camp	Rohingya refugees	2019
Bangladesh Kamrangirchar and Hazaribagh	Health-seeking behaviour	2016
Cambodia ×2	Total malaria elimination; malaria health-seeking behaviour	2015; 2014
Central African Republic	Socio-political analysis	2015
Chad ×5	Malnutrition ×2; Darfur conflict and consequences; female genital mutilation, e-health; traditional medicine; surgery	2011; 2008; 2012; 2016; 2014
China	Public health needs	1997
Democratic Republic of Congo ×8	Health-seeking behaviour ×5; health care needs; health needs in a mining community; diabetes	2005, 2008, 2010, 2015, 2016; 2016; 2015; 2017
Djibouti	Health-seeking behaviour	2010
Eastern Europe	HIV	1998
Eswatini ×4	HIV×2; HIV/TB; TB	2011, 2016; 2013; 2008
Ethiopia	Sexual and reproductive health	2013
Guatemala	Sexual and reproductive health; sexual violence	2012; 2012
Guinea Bissau	Child health – socio-cultural constructions of child health; local perceptions on health	2015; 2015
Guinea Conakry	Community health	2014
Haiti	Cholera	2010
India ×3	Health-seeking behaviour ×2; socio-political analysis; malnutrition	2015, 2016; 2013; 2011

Place	Topic	Year(s)
Iran	Health-seeking behaviour	2015
Iraq	Sexual and reproductive health	2013
Italy	Migration	2015
Jordan	Reconstructive surgery refugees (Syria, Iraq, Yemen)	2019
Kenya ×5	Sexual and reproductive health ×3; sexual violence ×2; HIV and communication; differentiated models of HIV/NCD care	2010, 2010, 2010; 2013, 2013; 2003; 2015
Kyrgyzstan	TB	2014
Latin America	Situations of violence	2015
Lebanon	Mental health	2009
Liberia ×7	SGBV; Ebola ×5; health-seeking behaviour	2005; 2014, 2014, 2015, 2015, 2015; 2005
Malawi ×2	HIV from village perspective; sexual reproductive health: male inclusion and circumcision	2007; 2012
Mali	Health-seeking behaviour	2016
Mauritania	Health-seeking behaviour	2001
Mexico	Sexual violence	2016
Mozambique	HIV sex workers and PrEp	2015
Myanmar	Health-seeking behaviour ×2	2009, 2009
Niger ×3	Malnutrition ×3	2005, 2008, 2009
Nigeria ×2	Health-seeking behaviour; heavy metal treatment (lead poisoning)	2010; 2015
Pakistan	Health-seeking behaviour	2007
Russia	Homelessness	1992–2000
Siberia	Tuberculosis (TB)	1992–2000
Sierra Leone ×8	Health-seeking behaviour ×3; Ebola ×3; sexual and reproductive health; perception of health and illness	2004, 2013, 2015; 2016, 2018, 2018; 2016; 2004
Somalia ×2	Health-seeking behaviour; TB	2007; 2009
South Africa	HIV in Khayelitsha; sexual violence; oral HIV testing	2001
South Sudan ×10	Health-seeking behaviour ×4; socio-political analysis – culture and context ×2; HIV ×3; humanitarian emergency	2009, 2013, 2014, 2014; 2008, 2008; 1997, 2001, 2009; 2016
Tajikistan	Family health-seeking behaviour (TB); dealing with traumatic experiences	2012; 2000
Uganda ×2	Sexual and reproductive health; TB	2016; 2014
Ukraine	TB	2013
Uzbekistan ×4	TB ×3; health and illness behaviour	2014, 2016, 2016; 1998
Yemen	Risk exposure of medical personnel	2013
Zimbabwe	HIV – men taking risks in the context of HIV transmission	2004

18 Jean-François Véran et al.

did anthropology become a more regular resource for operations, prompted by the important work of Renee C. Fox (2014), on the HIV/AIDS epidemic in posta-partheid South Africa and the huge increase in homelessness and tuberculosis in post-socialist Russia.

Qualitative research: a back door

A more substantial presence and use of anthropology in MSF started with the expansion of qualitative techniques used in operational research, with the rise of the mixed-methods approach a prominent example. Anthropology and its relevance to humanitarian medical action was talked about in one-off workshops as early as 1996 (Riekje, 1996). For one of the MSF operational centres in Amsterdam, its entry point was clearly defined in the 2014–2019 strategic plan, to use appropriate qualitative methods to inform the choice, design and implementation of medical programmes. In the MSF operational research and medical support units, the last few years have seen an increase in the technical proficiency of mixed methods in research, with interdisciplinary cooperation and opportunities between epidemiologists, clinical specialists and social scientists more appreciated than before. Alongside this, the need for best practice models began to grow from guidelines on outreach work to com-munity engagement and health promotion – a mix of interventions and approaches that is akin to work often associated with anthropology. A focus on methods was a natural evolution for the demand for social science-type research with courses to support individuals and teams (such as the Structural Operational Research and Training course, SORT-IT; Methodshop: blended learning on mixed methods).[2]

Equally, toolkits for the implementation of qualitative methods came to be in high demand across the public health spectrum; for many years, such information had been collected without a systematic method of interpreting it. Collection of this type of narrative data became popular within humanitarian affairs, policy work, health promotion, assessments and evaluation. Emergency assessment tools, such as social cartography and the Population Assessment Tool, that include anthropologi-cal approaches and social science methods, are even more in demand. As well as a focussing on guidance and methods for fieldwork, the training of MSF volunteers began to include 'cross-cultural' course modules as part of the preparation for initial departure.

This growing integration comes with the tight connection to medical activi-ties that anthropologists have acquired within MSF. At the time this book was written in 2019, most of the permanent positions for anthropologists in MSF are based at headquarters, within the health departments and medical units as part of social science teams, or in some cases, at an evaluation unit and emergency desk. In the last ten years or so, health promotion workers, as a part of the public health programming in MSF, have included anthropologists as well as health promotion specialists and other paramedics. As a result, health promotion and anthropology are often seen by operations to be one and the same. More recently, 'community

Introduction **19**

engagement' has grown as a strategic component for operational planning, along with the increasing complication of humanitarian settings (see Chapter 3), and is thought to benefit from anthropology to support its approach. For the operational centre in Barcelona, humanitarian anthropology is integrated as an applied approach to solve practical problems as part of health promotion and community engagement. As with the accepted technical entry point for social sciences through qualitative research, anthropology – at least as a useful discipline to include for health promotion planning – is welcomed by MSF operations.

An ongoing challenge regarding this technical emphasis on the social sciences has been for anthropology to avoid being trapped and reduced to a qualitative component of research protocols. The risk of a methodological reduction of anthropology is increased by the growing use of protocols for MSF activities and for anthropological contributions to humanitarian work. The risk is that if MSF continues to represent its knowhow from within the technical apparatus of biomedical humanitarianism, the value of anthropology and the social sciences may be undermined. The eight case studies presented in this book show how anthropology has analytically contributed to the resolution of complex operational challenges, we clearly intend to resist 'technical reductionism' and aim to bring more attention to the strategically added value of the discipline.

Anthropologists embarked

To put this in context, the anthropologists in this book are part of the nearly 50,000 people working for MSF in 70 countries and over at least 90 projects. We are rare, but we are recruited in similar numbers to other 'advisors' in MSF – such as our fellow mental health advisors or infectious disease advisors.

MSF chooses anthropologists from a pool of people managed by the Human Resource Department. They must be matched by relevant experience and academic qualifications. Where possible, MSF works with a network of anthropologists corresponding to the tenet that both emic and etic perspectives are valued. This acknowledges that a locally employed anthropologist may still not be 'within' the social group being studied – as is the case with Chapter 11, which looks specifically at access to health for the Gorbat minority group in Iran. An anthropologist can work anything from four weeks to two years in an MSF project, with the option of returning to the location periodically to enhance the implementation of anthropological support. One of the key challenges has been to find a compromise between the longer timeframe of a traditional anthropological field study and the shorter-term needs for MSF emergency operations. Over time, we have understood spontaneously or were clearly notified that the permanent status of anthropology within the MSF movement depended on our capacity to aggregate value to other data production activities and to contribute in a direct way to MSF's core mission. Precisely, in a biomedical working environment, having as their colleagues the advisors for mental health, HIV, sexual and reproductive health, paediatrics, infectious

20   Jean-François Véran et al.

diseases, etc., all with very specific and clearly delimited job descriptions, the MSF anthropologist's aggregated value is an unknown quantity.

Chapter overview

Within the MSF movement and, more broadly, for those working in humanitarian situations this book is conceived as a facilitator for understanding the types of input anthropology can add to humanitarian action. Far from just cultural 'translation' or 'adaptation', the work of the applied anthropologist is presented in its full complexity and complementarity in the distinct moments of a project and the diverse contexts of its implementation. Particular attention was given to the operational recommendations that originated from the case studies and, eventually, their application and impact.

In accordance with the discussion on the uses and abuses of culture presented in this introduction, one piece of editorial guidance has been that chapters systematically 'locate' culture in their respective case studies. By doing this, we aim to clarify how the concept was invoked and mobilised by local people and MSF professionals, and finally retained – or not – in the final analysis of the situation by the anthropologist. We must admit that we had internal discussions around this issue, particularly regarding the chapter on discrimination at the point of access to health care faced by the Gorbat minority in Iran. In this chapter, culture is clearly presented as more of an explanatory factor than in the other chapters. We thought we would leave this discrepancy unaltered, as a way to restitute the unsettled debate within our group. The temporary answer is probably that the adding and taking away of culture is rather context related and that there is no one size fits all for cultural arguments.

Another piece of editorial guidance acknowledged that the chapters all have to navigate the interface between the 50-year-old tradition of modern medical anthropology and the emerging anthropology of humanitarianism. The discussion within each has been conducted with an operational and analytical double approach. We hope this will show how the professional discussions that arise from applying anthropology directly connect to more academic discussions on how to frame the humanitarian relationship within the critical anthropology of humanitarian action.

The editorial team gathered 11 papers, opening with Chapter 1: "Changing contexts in humanitarianism: a challenge for anthropology", which discusses changes in the humanitarian context related to the nature of conflict, the people being helped, the diseases being treated and how a more progressive humanitarian action could be achieved by integrating anthropological tools, and by exploring which prerequisites such an integration would need.

Chapter 2, "A medical operational perspective on anthropology in the setting of MSF", presents a medical operational perspective on the uses, benefits and challenges of anthropology in medical humanitarian operations and is a non-anthropologist's view of how anthropology has been applied in MSF operations. It addresses recent debates in MSF and the growing concern about how people and communities are associated in MSF's operational decisions and how anthropology could be a contributor to these debates. This chapter also delves into a concern from an operational perspective that anthropological expertise might displace project staff's own understanding of people and context. The following chapters, representing different anthropologists' perspectives, overturn these reservations: the sharing of anthropological tools and perspectives might be a drive to better understanding and a trigger for curiosity.

Chapter 3, "Ethical considerations and anthropology: the MSF experience", looks at ethics in the practice of social science with a focus on anthropology in humanitarian settings. We describe how anthropology is framed within the historical biomedical foundation for mediating ethics and methodological challenges in research. We discuss how the current ethical framework in MSF can be adapted further to better grasp the realities of social life, politics, power and value systems that social scientists encounter in their fieldwork. With examples, we share accounts of how ethics are navigated referring to the broader discourse on this topic in the social sciences and offer a way forward for how we can adapt to these challenges the context we work.

The subsequent eight chapters each present an experience of anthropology within an MSF project. Each one focuses on the assessment itself, its context and the ethnographic elements, as well as on general and operational contexts.

These eight ethnographic chapters start with Chapter 4, "Emergency in practice: doing an ethnography of malnutrition in South Sudan". This elucidates the unique experience of a year-long, multi-sited participant observation of a single medical humanitarian emergency, in real time. It is centred around 11 months of continuous anthropological participant observation of MSF activities in South Sudan. This chapter provides insight into the everyday operations of a medical humanitarian institution and, in the subfield of nutritional anthropology, provides details of how numerical measures, institutional structures and individual discretion contribute to the identification and response to acute mass starvation in the context of conflict. It details how, with adequate preparation, a long-term social research study can be carried out under adverse and rapidly changing conditions. This ethnography follows the evolution of an MSF response to nutritional emergency from its inception, through various levels of the MSF hierarchy, from headquarters to a country capital office to the project itself. It is vivid proof that rigorous anthropology can be done in emergency settings.

A study on reaching women with direct obstetric complications, and healthy women's health-seeking behaviour, in Afghanistan is the basis for Chapter 5, "The paradox of safe birth: the interaction between anthropology and medical humanitarianism – the dilemma of an MSF medical strategy versus health-seeking behaviour of Pashtun women in Khost province, Afghanistan". This chapter discusses the challenges of reconciling operational objectives with the local community's health needs and health-seeking behaviour. This can only be understood by carving out manifold issues – such as cultural and social (women's agency), institutional (health structure), financial (affordability), practical (availability, distance and equipment of the health structures), environmental (security) and empirical (former personal experience) factors – that leverage and sometimes restrict constructive solutions. This chapter therefore foregrounds ethical dilemmas, by discussing the local people's perception of, and access to, maternal health care services in Khost province, and its relationship with the MSF mandate and objective in a reproductive health care project.

Chapter 6, "Whose culture needs to be questioned? Access to HIV/AIDS treatment in Homa Bay, Kenya", looks at challenges seen in an operational research context and the researcher's methods to overcome them in order to improve the collaboration between medical anthropologists and MSF medical staff. In humanitarian contexts, the delivery of aid is constantly re-evaluated to obtain the most efficient delivery model. The research pointed out a large communication gap between health care providers and patients of the HIV programme. Health care providers did not take into consideration the daily realities of HIV patients, and their recommendations, while medically accurate, are poorly adapted to everyday life in Homa Bay. To reach a better impact of research results driven from anthropological evaluations on the delivery of humanitarian aid, the author looks at how to best translate anthropological research into operations, how to present their conclusions to multi-disciplinary teams, and how to consolidate this by reshaping and re-evaluating operational strategies.

Using research from seven different communities across Liberia, including interviews and focus group discussions with survivors and their families, traditional leaders and health care workers, Chapter 7, "Back to life – Ebola survivors in Liberia: from imaginary heroes to political agents", discusses the complexity of the Ebola survivor's identity as well as the programmes that have been put in place to offer support to them. The methodological contribution that anthropologists have made during the Ebola outbreak is described here; it discusses the increased exposure of the theoretical discipline, as well as the ethical and methodological challenges involved in fieldwork of this nature, highlighting the way in which anthropologists became some of the key actors in such an outbreak situation. This chapter looks at the Ebola survivor in Liberia through an anthropological lens, considering how shifts in survivor identity occur and how these are managed by the individual, as well as reflecting upon the benefits of an anthropological engagement for MSF operations.

Chapter 8, "Invisible dengue: epidemics and politics in Léogâne, Haiti", centres on a study involving qualitative and quantitative methods undertaken in a municipality with a high endemicity of dengue. It explores the conceptual dimensions of dengue 'invisibility' among health workers and the community in a location that has experienced recent major disease outbreaks. Through a perception-practices in-depth assessment with questionnaires, interviews and focus groups, involving communities, health centres and stake holders, this study shows that community and health workers' responses (in the context of previous major disease outbreaks) mobilised a far more complex set of anthropological parameters than just 'traditional culture', such as past epidemic social history and local and global political

Introduction **23**

and geopolitical relations. Health promotion programmes would benefit from understanding and integrating these parameters that affect health system response and health-seeking behaviour. The results of this study show that local ideological opposition 'against dengue' was more likely to contribute towards dengue unawareness than dependence on 'traditional culture'.

Chapter 9, "Revealing causes beyond culture: an MSF surgical project through the lens of anthropology and health promotion", features an anthropological study on the 'cultural aspect' behind the high number of patients leaving the surgical project in Abéché, Eastern Chad, against medical advice. This chapter demonstrates how anthropological findings can be put into the framework of an effective health promotion programme in a topic that usually works without standard health promotion materials. It also discusses how the study was perceived and received by international MSF staff. Finally, it demonstrates the key benefit of a grounded and reflexive applied medical anthropology, which does not look at people as cultural beings, but in their broader economic, political and ethnic context. The authors show how anthropologists have moved beyond the culture concept that sometimes masks significant structural factors such as social and political barriers to access to health care.

Chapter 10, "'Yaya hankuri da mutani?' (How is your patience with the people?): a medical anthropological inquiry into treatment challenges in the Anka Local Government Area, Zamfara Heavy Metal Treatment Project, Nigeria", details how MSF responded to an acute phase of a lead poisoning emergency in June 2010 in Nigeria. This chapter demonstrates how perceived treatment failures were a product of interactional dynamics between MSF and the local people, and how questions about cultural miscommunication have been explored by an anthropologist. It discusses elements of ethnography from a medical anthropological study carried out in an MSF project caring for children with acute lead poisoning in Zamfara state. The catastrophic event that prompted MSF assistance took place simultaneously in eight villages. Most people enrolled in the subsequent treatment program. However, in one village, MSF faced substantial challenges. The level of lead in the blood remained high in about 50% of the initial patients. The health promotion team struggled to keep patients in the treatment program and to motivate mothers to bring their children to clinic appointments. An anthropologist was called in to explore whether the challenges faced in this location could be related to what the medical team perceived to be specific 'cultural' issues. One important outcome from this anthropological assessment was to show that a single solution or a unilateral approach to treatment and care was unsuitable in this instance.

Chapter 11, "Dealing with the body social: an ethnography of dialogue in a health clinic, South Tehran, Iran", describes the situation in an MSF clinic in South Tehran. The clinic's location described in this ethnography is in a poor urban quarter where property and rental prices are among the cheapest in the Iranian capital. This study aims to present the use of ethnographic data in a cultural conflict – a context wherein social struggles are evident. In the MSF clinic in South Tehran, as well as in public and private hospitals and clinics, local staff often reflect community prejudice by refusing to accept members of certain minority groups (such as the Gorbat) as targets, while international staff and social workers insist on including them because they live in high-risk environments and are said to show high-risk behaviour. The results of this study bring to light the underlying logic of this 'rejection' as an anthropological object. This chapter shows how ethnographic data and anthropological insight helped to explain this situation, and suggests a more appropriate patient-oriented communication within this context.

The final chapter, Chapter 12, is an epilogue which frames the anthropology in humanitarian situations within post-humanist theoretical discourse. It looks at the main challenge to humanitarian action: humans themselves. The book concludes with a final consideration of the humanitarian agents that have appeared, although discretely in filigree, throughout the book. They are portrayed in an almost schizophrenic come and go between the ultimate medical procedures, technologies and pharmaceutical breakthroughs they have learnt as students, and the adapted, restricted and sometimes frustrating conditions of medical practice within a humanitarian crisis. They are also confronted by a severe cognitive dissonance. On one side, the post-humanist conquests of the 'augmented human' by prosthesis, computerised micro implants or gene therapy, and on the other, the sudden apparition of humans in highly vulnerable conditions reduced to bare survival. By locating the humanitarian situation at the interface between these clashing dynamics and realities, we intend to go back to the anthropologist's tasks of unfolding the premises on which 'humans' are built.

Notes

1 www.msf.org/sites/msf.org/files/msf_forced-to-flee-central-americas-northern-tri angle_e.pdf
2 www.theunion.org/what-we-do/courses/online-and-multimedia-training/sort-it; Methodshop mixed-methods blended learning, training brochure, Operational Centre Amsterdam. 2019.

References

Abramowitz, S. and Panter-Brick, C., (2015). Bringing life into relief: comparative ethnographies of humanitarian practice. In: S. Abramowitz and C. Panter-Brick, eds., *Medical humanitarianism: ethnographies of practice*. Philadelphia: University of Pennsylvania Press. 377–404.

Abu-Lughod, L., (1991). Writing against culture. In: R.G. Fox, ed., *Recapturing anthropology: working in the present*. Santa Fe, NM: School of American Research Press. 137–162.

Agamben, G., (1998). *Homo Sacer: sovereign power and bare life*. Stanford, CA: Stanford University Press.

Aron, R., (1981). *Le Spectateur engagé*. Paris: Julliard.

Atlani-Duault, L., (2007). Anthropologues et ONG: des liaisons fructueuses? In: *Humanitaire, Enjeux, pratiques, débats*. Hors série, No 4. Paris: Médecins du Monde.

Barth, F., (1969). *Ethnic groups and boundaries: the social organization of culture difference*. Boston, MA: Little, Brown and Co.

Beshar, I. and Stellmach, D., (2017). Anthropological approaches to medical humanitarianism. *Medicine Anthropology Theory*. doi:10.17157/mat.4.5.477

Bhabha, Homi K., (2012). *The location of culture*. 2nd ed. London: Routledge.

Boas, F., (1982). *Race, language, and culture*. Chicago: University of Chicago Press.

Boltanski, L., (2007). *La souffrance à distance*. Paris: Gallimard.

Bornstein, E. and Redfield, P., (2011). *Forces of compassion: humanitarianism between ethics and politics*. Santa Fe, NM: School for Advanced Research Press.

Cefaï, D. and Amiraux, V., (2002). Les risques du métier. Engagements problématiques en sciences sociales. Partie 1 (No. 47). *Culture & Conflits*. Centre d'études sur les conflits. doi:10.4000/conflits.829

Chakrabarty, D., (2008). *Provincializing Europe: postcolonial thought and historical difference*. 2nd ed. Princeton, NJ: Princeton University Press.

Chaumont, J-M., (2017). *La concurrence des victimes: génocide, identité, reconnaissance*. Paris: La Découverte.

D'Andrade, R. and Scheper-Hughes, N., (1995). Objectivity and militancy: a debate. *Current Anthropology*. **36**(3).

Das, V., (1996). *Critical events: an anthropological perspective on contemporary India*. Delhi: Oxford University Press.

Dreyfus, H.L. and Rabinow, R., (1983). *Michel Foucault: beyond structuralism and hermeneutics. Second edition with an afterword by and an interview with Michel Foucault*. Chicago: University of Chicago Press.

Erickson, P.A. and Murphy, L.D., (2003). *A history of anthropological theory*. Peterborough, Ont. and Orchard Park, NY: Broadview Press.

Fabian, J., (1983). *Time and the other: how anthropology makes its object*. New York: Columbia University Press.

Fassin, D., (2010). *La raison humanitaire: une histoire morale du temps présent*. Paris: Gallimard.

Fassin, D. and Pandolfi, M., (2010). *Contemporary states of emergency. The politics of military and humanitarian interventions*. New York: Zone Books.

Fox, R.C., (2014). *Doctors without Borders: humanitarian quests, impossible dreams of Médecins Sans Frontières*. Baltimore: John Hopkins University Press.

Haraway, D., (1988). Situated knowledges: the science question in feminism and the privilege of partial perspective. *Feminist Studies*. **14**(3), 575–599.

Harrell-Bond, B., (1986). *Imposing aid: emergency assistance to refugees*. Oxford: Oxford University Press.

Hemmings, C.P., (2005). Rethinking medical anthropology: how anthropology is failing medicine. *Anthropology & Medicine*. **12**(2), 91–103. doi:10.1080/13648470500139841

Hofman, M. and Au, S., eds., (2017). *The politics of fear: Médecins sans Frontières and the West African Ebola epidemic*. New York: Oxford University Press.

Kapferer, B., (2005). Situations, crisis, and the anthropology of the concrete: the contribution of Max Gluckman. *Social Analysis*. **49**(3), 85–122. doi:10.3167/015597705780275110

Kuznar, L.A., (1997). *Reclaiming a scientific anthropology*. Lanham, MD: AltaMira Press.

Lett, J.W., (1997). *Science, reason and anthropology: the principles of rational enquiry*. Lanham, MD: Rowman and Littlefield.

Mac Ginty, R. and Peterson, J.H., eds., (2015). *The Routledge companion to humanitarian action*. London: Routledge.

Maretzki, T.W., (1985). Including the physician in healer-centered research: retrospect and prospect. In: R.A. Hann and A.D. Gaines, eds., *Physicians of Western medicine: culture, illness and healing*. Dordrecht: Springer.

Mauss, M., (1936). *Sociologie et anthropologie*. Paris: Presses Universitaires de France.

MSF, (2018a). *Code of conduct*. MSF archives, Intersectional.

MSF, (2018b). *International activity report 2018*. MSF.

O'Driscoll, E., (2009). Applying the 'Uncomfortable Science': the role of anthropology in development. *Durham Anthropology Journal*. **16**(1), 13–21. Available from: http://commu nity.dur.ac.uk/anthropology.journal/vol16/iss1/odriscoll.pdf

Pool, R. and Geissler, W., (2005). *Medical anthropology*. Maidenhead, UK: Open University Press.

Riekje, E., (1996). "A discussion on Anthropology in Médecins Sans Frontières". MSF archives, Operational Centre Amsterdam.

Rosenberg, A., (1995). *The philosophy of social science*. Abingdon, UK: Westview Press.

Saint-Exupéry, A., (1943). *The little prince*. Trans. Katherine Woods. New York: Harcourt Brace & Co.

Sartre, J-P., (1972). Plaidoyer pour les intellectuels. In: *Situations, VIII*. Paris: Gallimard.

Schwartz, S.J., Unger, J.B., Zamboanga, B.L. and Szapocznik, J., (2010). Rethinking the concept of acculturation: implications for theory and research. *American Psychologist*. **65**(4), 237. doi:10.1037/a0019330

Shell-Duncan, B., (2001). The medicalization of female "circumcision": harm reduction or promotion of a dangerous practice? *Social Science & Medicine*. **52**(7), 1013–1028.

Shevchenko, O. and Fox, R.C., (1995). "Nationals" and "expatriates": challenges of fulfilling "Sans Frontières" ("without borders") ideals in international humanitarian action. *Health and Human Rights in Practice*. **10**(1), 109–122.

Singer, M. and Baer, H., (2011). *Introducing medical anthropology: a discipline in action*. 2nd ed. Lanham, MD: AltaMira Press.

Stellmach, D., Stringer, B. and Véran, J-F., (2017). *Cultural relativism is dead. Long live cultural relativism*. MSF archives, Operational Centre Amsterdam.

Strathern, M., (2004). Losing (out on) intellectual resources. In: A. Pottage and M. Mundy, eds., *Law, anthropology, and the constitution of the social: making persons and things*. Cambridge: Cambridge University Press. 204–209. doi:10.1017/CBO9780511493751

Streber, J., (2017). *The utility of medical anthropology in humanitarian action: the case of the Vienna Evaluation Unit of Médecins Sans Frontières*. MA Thesis, NOHA, University College of Dublin.

Taylor, C. and Gutmann, A., (1994). *Multiculturalism: examining the politics of recognition*. Princeton, NJ: Princeton University Press.

Ticktin, M., (2014). Transnational humanitarianism. *Annual Review of Anthropology*. **43**, 273–289.

Van Doorne, J.H., (1981). Situational analysis: its potential and limitations for anthropological research on social change in Africa. *Cahiers d'Etudes africaines*. **84**, 479–506.

Van Velsen, J., (2017). The extended-case method and situational analysis. In: A.L. Epstein, ed., *The craft of social anthropology*. New York: Routledge. 129–150. doi:10.4324/9781315131528

Véran, J-F., (2017). *Why is HIV prevalence so high in Homa Bay County?* MSF archives, Operational Centre Paris.

Weber, M., (2003). *Le Savant et le politique*. Paris: Éditions La Découverte.

1

CHANGING CONTEXTS IN HUMANITARIANISM

A challenge for anthropology

Tammam Aloudat and James Smith

Affirming the basis for anthropology in humanitarian contexts

An individual and collective desire to respond to situations of profound suffering and inequity has prompted a multitude of humanitarian initiatives worldwide. As the situations in which suffering and inequity are experienced continue to shift and change, so too do the resultant forms of humanitarian response. Large-scale and individual efforts adapt to changing realities.

It is now widely acknowledged that the success of humanitarian action, as measured by the delivery of culturally appropriate and effective assistance to people affected by crises, is predicated on an in-depth understanding of the context in which humanitarians attempt to achieve safe and timely access. This became particularly apparent to humanitarian organisations and their institutional financiers in the 1990s, following a string of widely publicised shortcomings in large-scale humanitarian response (Fustukian & Zwi, 2001; Minn, 2007; Pottier, 1996).

Almost every element of medical humanitarian action, incorporating the design, delivery, monitoring, evaluation and modification of programmes, requires a good understanding of affected people: their lived experiences and their multiplicity of perspectives, as well as the overarching socio-political context. While certain aspects of access and delivery may be predominantly logistical in both origin and solution, issues related to appropriateness, acceptance and security, and more fundamental concepts such as suffering, risk and vulnerability, clearly require a much deeper commitment to political, sociological and anthropological enquiry.

Imagine the recruitment of a health practitioner to a project in any one of a number of places as diverse as Iraq, the Central African Republic, Yemen, Nauru, Syria or the Democratic Republic of Congo. Médecins Sans Frontières staff have encountered, for example: displaced families living in schools in northern Syria who did not seek health care because of their distance from a facility; mothers in the Central African Republic who could not bring their children with severe malaria to nearby clinics because they had to care for others in the family; boys and men who did not seek care after being subjected to rape and other forms of sexual violence because they believed those services were only available for women; and women subjected to rape and other forms of sexual violence who did not seek care because they knew there were no female physicians and did not want to be seen by a male doctor. Each of these instances are incredibly complex, and heavily affect the ability to provide essential health services. Experience over time has informed medical teams that establishing a service intended to meet basic health needs is no guarantee of utilisation. Social, political, cultural and material factors beyond the immediate focus of medical assistance affect health and present additional challenges. This relatively recent appreciation of the social determinants of health, and by extension the multidimensional nature of health-seeking behaviour and the multiplicity of factors that determine a positive encounter with health professionals, has established a clearer basis for interdisciplinarity in humanitarian practice.

Far from a simple linear process that privileges the delivery of humanitarian assistance as an end-point, it is now widely recognised – and in large part due to insightful anthropological scholarship – that medical humanitarian action that engages with complex and often sensitive sociocultural issues can have unintended – often disruptive – consequences. Community acceptance of humanitarian responses,[1] particularly when delivered by an external entity, is dependent on whether they are perceived to be benevolent, accessible, non-discriminatory and sensitive to local histories, social relations and cultural experiences. Unfortunately, such considered humanitarian responses continue to clash with programmatic approaches that seek to prioritise interventions based on their medico-technical efficacy. This presents a challenge for medical humanitarian practitioners, who must navigate between what is considered technically optimal in principle, and what is acceptable in practice.

All forms of medical humanitarian assistance, from relatively simple medical procedures to complex responses including the management of undernutrition, mass vaccination campaigns, women's health programmes and, in particular, responses to sexual and gender-based violence, epidemics and situations of displacement, must be sensitive to social, cultural and political realities. Particular knowledge and skills are required to navigate the design and delivery of such varied programmes in order to identify, and subsequently meet, the needs of people affected by crisis.

Moreover, as humanitarians have gradually discovered, medical humanitarian programmes cannot be delivered solely in hospitals or clinics. Often in situations of crisis, many lives are lost, and much suffering is endured, before people reach a static medical facility. With this in mind, community outreach activities are now widely accepted as an essential component of medical humanitarian response. The form of such outreach varies widely from encouragement to follow better hygiene practices and increased community awareness of common medical problems to support for the diagnosis and community-based treatment of complicated diseases such as drug-resistant tuberculosis, or from nutritional screening and community-based feeding programmes to the management of outbreaks of cholera or Ebola. Recognising villages and neighbourhoods as sites of engagement has prompted many humanitarian organisations to prioritise long overdue interaction and cooperation with local people, and MSF has developed guidance to facilitate this changing relationship (MSF, 2016a). This trend has also led to recognition that the historical approach of interacting and negotiating almost exclusively with authorities and community leaders – 'over a cup of tea' – is not enough to achieve equity, acceptance and cultural sensitivity in the provision of medical humanitarian assistance that is inclusive and accessible to those in need (Roberts et al., 2014).

Meaningful interaction between humanitarian health organisations, their staff, patients and the communities in which they live is now widely considered a matter of both principle and utility. The principles of medical ethics – particularly autonomy – are applicable, insofar as people should be able to understand and choose their preferred means of receiving assistance. At the same time, patients, communities and influencers should also be engaged to ensure access, protection and the ability to safely deliver assistance (Roberts et al., 2014). More meaningful interactions have been progressively realised over the history of modern medical humanitarian action both in familiar and so-called 'classical' contexts (e.g. low-resource, rural settings, in refugee camps or following acute environmental disasters). Over time, solutions developed to address the challenges raised during such interactions, which were often dependent on negotiations to ease relations with national and local authorities, gain protection from attacks by belligerents or ensure access to local communities.

However, organisations such as MSF now have to respond to rapidly and ever-changing situations, which demand of humanitarian medicine a particular adaptability and depth of engagement that was under-appreciated in previous decades. Such contextual changes relate to the nature of conflict and other humanitarian crises, the diversity and typology of people engaged in humanitarian responses, the characteristics of people affected by crisis and their health and other needs. These changes are profound and necessitate a much wider and deeper engagement in order to understand people's needs and the terms of humanitarian engagement. This sort of response requires the participation of anthropologists at all stages in the life cycle of humanitarian projects (from design to evaluation), and the roll-out of anthropological tools for wider application by non-specialists.

Changing humanitarian contexts

It is now nearly 50 years since the formation of MSF, and the organisation has observed many changes to the contexts in which it operates, the people it seeks to help and the needs it intends to address. Such changes are already the subject of lengthy monographs and are too many to recount in this short chapter. However, some of these major trends are elaborated here to emphasise the challenges, and by extension, the opportunities for anthropological engagement.

Changing humanitarian architecture

The humanitarian sector has undergone phenomenal growth and is now represented by thousands of local, national and international organisations, financing and priority-setting consortia, think tanks, academic centres, civil society groups, community networks, government departments and international partnerships. Longstanding issues of coordination and collaboration are increasingly complex in such a diverse and often fragmented sector.

The growth and diversification of groups purporting to deliver humanitarian assistance has tended to undermine the principles of impartiality, neutrality and independence. In particular, the manipulation of the humanitarian imperative to meet political, security, economic and other objectives has long concerned those defending principled humanitarian action. In response to calls to better integrate humanitarian activities within a broader political, peacebuilding and economic development agenda in the early 2000s, MSF and a number of other international NGOs insisted that "Humanitarian action must not be a tool of political interests" (MSF, 2002). Seventeen years later, this call is no closer to realisation. Manipulation of humanitarian activities for military and other security-related ambitions is widespread, while the growing role of institutions such as the World Bank in financing and priority-setting for humanitarian action must be viewed with caution (Castellarnau & Stoianova, 2018). The 'ending needs' paradigm shaped by the 2016 World Humanitarian Summit, and the so-called 'new way of working', typified by the UN's triple nexus approach that seeks synergy between humanitarian, development and peace-building activities, threatens the space and funding for principled humanitarian action in favour of broader political and economic priorities. The pursuit of ambitious political goals – the triple nexus, universal health coverage and similar – must not lose sight of individual needs, and must remain attentive to those at risk of exclusion and neglect. MSF has highlighted systemic failures in achieving equitable access to care, and the importance of anthropological insights, at all stages in this process.

Changing armed conflict

Contemporary armed conflict has changed in a number of ways, which in turn affects the nature of medical humanitarian needs and the methods by which such needs can be met. These changes, which have intensified in recent decades, have had an inevitable impact on humanitarian and medical responses. Notably, the expansion of MSF operations throughout the Middle East and in parts of Europe is a result of changing trends in conflict and the subsequent displacement of people, which are far from temporary or geographically specific. Rather, such regional dynamics are the consequence of changes in conflict over the course of the last 20 years, the effects of which are now becoming more apparent.

Wars of the twentieth century were broadly characterised as "interstate tensions and one-off episodes of civil war" where belligerents were easily identifiable,

Changing contexts in humanitarianism **31**

and there was a certain linearity: "if a dispute escalates and full-scale hostilities ensue, an eventual end to hostilities (either through victory and defeat or through a negotiated settlement) is followed by a short 'post-conflict' phase leading back to peace" (World Bank, 2011). However, these linear conflicts are no longer the norm. Contemporary conflicts are diverse in character and duration, and are often more cyclical, punctuated by episodic periods of violence, and have been described collectively as the "New Wars" (Kaldor, 2013). Contemporary conflict involves new groups and alternative methods of violence, with armed groups often comprising a mix of regular and irregular armed forces, security contractors, mercenaries, warlords and ideological fundamentalists. The rise of new groups, and developments including the use of modern technologies such as drones and other forms of remote warfare, a proximity between combatants and civilians, and asymmetrical forms of warfare, have redefined conflicts and further complicated the delivery of humanitarian assistance.

These new – and only recently acknowledged – combatants include a wide range of non-state and non-national armed forces, which has significant implications for the way in which conflict is fought, and in turn, how people are affected. Perhaps the most significant contemporary examples include the Islamic State in Iraq and Syria (ISIS) and Boko Haram, two groups that have caused widespread suffering for civilians. Given the dynamic nature of both organisations, it has been difficult to engage or negotiate with either, which in turn has further compromised the delicate guarantees of safety on which humanitarian organisations often rely. More significantly, many such non-state armed groups actively disregard the legitimacy of nation-states.

The burden of these changing dynamics has fallen disproportionately on civilians. Contemporary conflicts are marked by: the targeting of civilians, as has been the case in Syria and Yemen; sieges and the intentional deprivation of basic needs for prolonged periods of time, as was the situation for civilians in ISIS-controlled regions; the impoverishment of civilians as a consequence of war economies and the degradation of wider economic conditions; and a lack of access to emergency and regular health care services due to a collapse of health infrastructure at a time of heightened health needs. Many international humanitarian organisations have faced severe barriers to accessing affected people under such circumstances, leaving local and regional organisations to deliver a greater proportion of essential health services (Aloudat & Abu-Sa'Da, 2017).

Yemen, one of the most complex humanitarian emergencies at the time of writing, is illustrative of many of the changing characteristics of contemporary armed conflict. MSF had managed projects in the country for many years prior to the conflict. However, escalating violence, the targeting of civilians and civilian infrastructure, the targeting of humanitarian and medical programmes, and the presence of a number of people unwilling to abide by international humanitarian law and other normative frameworks, has redefined the landscape for humanitarian response. While MSF's recent engagement in Yemen was intended to focus on the treatment of war injuries, medical staff at the local level were faced with different, and often unanticipated, problems resulting from the wider impact of the conflict on health infrastructure. Issues that were not regularly addressed by conventional humanitarian activities have included: the widespread decline of existing health infrastructure and services, including specialist services such as renal dialysis (MSF supplied dialysis renewables to ensure continued utilisation on an exceptional basis) and 'regular' services such as maternity, paediatric and neonatal care; the scarcity and high cost of medicines, with a shortage of supply in public hospitals; the imposition of patient fees in health facilities that were deprived of government funding; and outbreaks of communicable diseases such as cholera and diphtheria, requiring immediate management, prevention and sustained health promotion.

Changing people

Along with changes to the contexts in which humanitarian organisations intervene, the people who medical humanitarian activities ought to help have changed, as well. The first and most significant change over the last century has been life expectancy. The global average life expectancy at birth increased from fewer than 60 years in 1971 to more than 72 years in 2016 (World Bank, 2017), with some of the most dramatic changes observed in lower-income countries. Changes in life expectancy have altered the disease profile of people worldwide, including those affected by humanitarian crises. Lower rates of perinatal and neonatal mortality, and improvements in early childhood survival, along with increasing life expectancy, have challenged the automatic assumption that vaccination and the treatment and prevention of communicable diseases should be the principal medical humanitarian interventions, regardless of context. Practitioners of humanitarian medicine are now much more aware of the need to deliver services for the elderly, along with treatment for a diversity of non-communicable diseases, while remaining attentive to the ways in which needs are dynamic and multi-dimensional.

Urbanisation has also affected the people and places affected by humanitarian crises. 'Traditional' MSF projects were typically developed in very low resource rural settings, with humanitarian workers active during the 1980s frequently dispatched to work in remote villages and in small communities in parts of Sudan, Afghanistan or the Democratic Republic of Congo. It is now not uncommon to work with people in urban settings in a range of socio-economic settings, from the Kibera slums in Nairobi, Kenya, to the bustling cities of Beirut, Baghdad, Port-au-Prince or Kiev. Naturally, the experience and expectations of different people matter greatly and vary widely. This diversification of people and places has exposed 'one-size-fits-all' approaches as unhelpful. Instead, adapted interventions that take into consideration not only health needs, but also expectations and the wider context, are essential.

Another profound change relates to the displacement of people. A 2013 study on people affected by conflict found that refugees, the traditional target of many humanitarian interventions, might be less affected by conflict in terms of mortality and access to medical services than internally displaced people (CRED, 2013). Data from many recent MSF interventions in Syria show that accessing and providing medical care to displaced people inside Syria has been much more difficult and more risky than providing assistance to refugees who had reached the relative safety of neighbouring countries. Another change in displacement relates to the places of resettlement. While most refugees are still displaced to adjacent low- and middle-income countries, many no longer settle in refugee camps, which were the loci for intervention that had become familiar to humanitarian organisations (MSF, 1997). Refugees who are on the move for longer periods of time, or who settle within host communities, are more scattered, and thus often at a greater risk of neglect by humanitarian organisations whose practices have yet to adequately adapt to these changes.

Changing health needs

The epidemiology of disease has also changed in many contexts, comprising either a mix of communicable and non-communicable pathologies, or a rapidly rising prevalence of the latter. Although diseases such as malaria are still responsible for significant morbidity and mortality (MSF treated almost 2.4 million people with malaria in 2018; MSF, 2018), non-communicable diseases are widespread in several humanitarian projects across the Middle East, in Central Asia and Eastern Europe, among displaced people crossing the Mediterranean to Europe, and elsewhere. Such diseases, unlike many acute infections, require longer-term management, with a focus on adherence, follow-up and the adjustment of treatment over time. These management needs are all the more difficult to meet in humanitarian crises and in the context of ongoing displacement, when follow-up of patients on the move, and the application of conventional humanitarian approaches, is particularly difficult. Many of the management challenges now experienced with diabetes and cardio-vascular disease are reminiscent of the challenges faced trying to ensure patients with HIV benefited from lifelong treatment during the early 2000s. Together, MSF, a number of local and community-based organisations, and engaged anthropologists were able to generate valuable knowledge about the ways in which interaction with patients and their communities determines adherence to treatment and minimises patient lost to follow-up.

Additionally, the individual impact of certain diseases appears more pronounced. This is in part due to the emergence of resistant strains of infections, and to several large outbreaks in recent history. As the prevalence of many diseases that once caused regular large-scale outbreaks declined with the emergence of immunisation science and the roll-out of vaccination programmes, other diseases such as pandemic influenza and Ebola present a growing threat. The Ebola epidemics in West Africa of 2014–2016 and the Democratic Republic of Congo in 2018–2019 exemplified the devastating effect a disease can have on individuals and communities across several countries, and the massive and multi-faceted response required to contain outbreaks while simultaneously maintaining the dignity of individual patients.

Medical humanitarian organisations have also increasingly endeavoured to respond to health crises related to the neglect of specific diseases, driven in part by the global response to the HIV pandemic in the 1990s and early 2000s. The response to HIV has seen the emergence of new technical approaches to disease treatment and of diverse activist-driven responses in situations in which people have been neglected. Over the course of the last two decades, MSF has responded to new health threats including the rising impact of tuberculosis-related morbidity and mortality, particularly in Southern Africa and Eastern Europe, as well as widespread outbreaks of Ebola. MSF also continues to address the burden of 'old' and yet still neglected diseases, such as malaria, kala azar (visceral leishmaniasis), sleeping sickness, snakebite and meningitis.

What is common in the treatment of many of the diseases outlined here is that they require prolonged treatment, which can range from weeks to lifelong. For such treatment to be effective, management must address the drivers of adherence and acceptance, and the psychological, socio-economic and cultural aspects of illness, alongside ensuring access to health care and considering the clinical effectiveness of different treatments. Naturally, such approaches require a much closer engagement with patients and their communities. The complexity of management for certain diseases and conditions has highlighted the need for anthropological engagement. Similarly, the medical and public health sectors have increasingly come to appreciate the shortcomings of established biomedical practices, and thus have been prompted to re-evaluate the management of long-established issues such as the treatment of malaria and undernutrition.

Changes in humanitarian politics and practice

Changes to the contexts in which humanitarian organisations are pressed to intervene, the people they seek to help and the diversity of issues they seek to address, have established the need for nuanced approaches and contextual specificity, which amplifies the added value of anthropology.

Such changes broadly imagine anthropology as an enabling practice, which can be engaged to identify ways in which humanitarian responses can be delivered more effectively and in a manner that is socio-culturally sensitive (Stellmach et al., 2018). However, anthropology has demonstrated further value as a critical discipline, 'studying up' and thus interrogating the practices and perspectives that typify humanitarian action. Anthropology can direct a critical gaze towards institutions and the wider humanitarian sector, engaging with the structure and organisation of humanitarian programmes, the racialised and gendered politics that continue to shape humanitarian activities, the construction of exploitative power relations and other motivations, perceptions and assumptions that have shaped hegemonic 'Western' humanitarian discourse and praxis.

Beyond 'Western' humanitarianism

Pertinent to the emergence of anthropology both *of* and *for* a humanitarian response is a deeply ingrained belief in universalism in humanitarian practice; a recognition

Changing contexts in humanitarianism **35**

of our shared humanity, and an obligation and desire to relieve the suffering of strangers, irrespective of their social or cultural background (Calhoun, 2008; Malkki, 1996). Few would dispute a shared obligation to the wellbeing of others, but what has generated much consternation in recent decades is the way in which 'Western' humanitarianism, with its Eurocentric orientation, has come to monopolise humanitarian practice and narratives of humanitarian response. Despite the global distribution of staff working for MSF and other humanitarian organisations, the humanitarian is still widely personified as the white 'expatriate', who embarks to deliver assistance in the 'Global South'. Donini captures the complexity of this narrow conceptualisation of humanitarianism:

> Universal ethos, Western apparatus: Humanitarian ideals have the potential to unite, but humanitarian practice very often divides. . . . The humanitarian enterprise affirms that the core values of humanitarianism have universal resonance, but this is not the same as saying that such values have universal articulation and application.
>
> *(Donini, 2012, p. 186)*

Herein lies a challenge for humanitarians: how to promote and practice a universal humanity that "transcends any particularistic societal, political, or cultural claim" (Fox, 1995, p. 1608), while at the same time remains attentive to the ways in which the very same factors shape an individual's lived experience, and influence interactions with humanitarian organisations and their representatives.

The presupposition of a certain form of universalism in much of contemporary humanitarian response continues to undermine the pursuit of meaningful (i.e. true to a commitment to humanity, and thus to respect and dignity) humanitarian action because it suppresses experiences, actions and interpretations that diverge from a particular form of humanitarianism that can be characterised as a "top-down, externally driven, and relatively rigid process that allows little space for local participation beyond formalistic consultation . . . inflexible, arrogant, and culturally insensitive" (Donini, 2012, p. 187).

Thus, particularly important in relation to the use of anthropology in humanitarian action is the way in which humanitarian response by and large remains a reductive endeavour, predicated on the dehistorification, depoliticisation and homogenisation of people affected by crisis, and the creation of what Feldman describes as an "anonymous corporeality" (1994, p. 407). As such, individuals affected by crisis become objects of the humanitarian enterprise: entities to which assistance is given and must be passively received. This fracture of people affected by crisis from their histories and experiences may facilitate the delivery of humanitarian assistance, but ultimately undermines its quality and its ability to represent a genuine expression of solidarity or humanity. Such a tendency is captured in many of the visuals used to promote humanitarian work, which situate the nameless black child as the recipient of care from the named white nurse or doctor. This is neither ethically acceptable (Calain, 2013), nor representative of the fact that most humanitarian workers engaged with MSF in the delivery of humanitarian medicine are locally hired staff from the countries in which projects are established.

Shaping a new humanitarian discourse

An 'inversion of gaze' – i.e. a focus on humanitarian staff and their practices – holds promise, and is tantamount to the reimagination of humanitarian response as a collaborative project, rather than as a process of paternalistic imposition (Fassin & Rechtman, 2009, pp. 186–187). For as long as humanitarianism remains a cross-cultural endeavour (Hunt et al., 2014), it is imperative that humanitarian workers pay attention not only to local sociocultural dynamics, but also to the interplay between people affected by crisis and those local and international staff who seek to deliver support in the form of humanitarian assistance. To employ anthropological methods only to better understand people, behaviours and social networks is to tacitly imply that fault lies with local people, who simply do not *understand* what is best for them. Anthropology as a discipline has a tendency to explore power relations, and this enables a dual focus on local perceptions, desires and expectations on one hand, and on institutional approaches on the other, as well as on the various forms of power and influence that manifest in crisis contexts (Roberts et al., 2014).

More than 20 years have now passed since Benthall claimed that "anthropologists and the 'French doctors' seem as yet far apart" (1991, p. 3). Much progress has been made in the intervening period, with a far greater appreciation of the many ways in which anthropology can positively influence humanitarian response by re-centring individual experiences at the local level, and by casting a critical eye over dominant forms of humanitarian action. Contemporary anthropology is fundamentally concerned with respect and representation, and thus has much to contribute to the shift away from outdated forms of paternalistic medical practice. Medical humanitarian action will remain the subject of continuous and necessary critique, but with the greater involvement of anthropologists, we can expect a more genuine commitment to expressions of humanity and solidarity.

Future humanitarianisms

While anthropology is one discipline that has guided – and will continue to guide – the delivery of humanitarian assistance, political will and a desire for change are necessary in order to challenge the deeply ingrained perceptions that still permeate the humanitarian sector. Only with such change can humanitarian action be practised as both an empowering and a lifesaving endeavour.

The localisation agenda that emerged in the wake of the 2016 World Humanitarian Summit has potential, insofar as advocates have pushed for resources to strengthen local and national capacities (OCHA, 2018), which in turn may disrupt the sector's Eurocentric orientation and associated tropes of 'white saviourism'. Not only would such a move shift the political frame, but more practically, national and local organisations are more likely to have a deeper understanding of their local context. International counterparts will continue to play a role, assisting with technical support and additional logistical capacity, fostering a culture built around collaborative and collective action. However, despite a series of commitments to progressive systemic change (including localisation) in recent years, MSF's withdrawal from the World Humanitarian Summit less than three weeks before the event signalled a loss of faith in non-binding pledges, with these high-level sectoral events perceived as little more than "a fig-leaf of good intentions" (MSF, 2016b).

The desire for a radical reimagination of much of the humanitarian sector has been expressed widely, including by people who have been most affected by humanitarian crises. A humanitarianism is achievable that does not lose sight of the desire – and ability – to save lives, while acknowledging that such efforts should not come at the expense of dignity, empowerment and the meaningful engagement of affected people. Of the resources available to facilitate such a transformation, anthropology as a discipline is indeed capable of deepening our understanding of one another, and thus centring humanity as humanitarianism's guiding principle.

Note

1 It should be noted that 'acceptance' was elevated first and foremost as a risk management strategy, through which humanitarian organisations could mitigate the risk of security incidents during the delivery of assistance. Dependent on the context in which the term is used, an asymmetry of power in the relationship between giver and receiver may be presupposed.

References

Aloudat, T. and Abu-Sa'Da, C., (2017). A future for human dignity? The fragile perspectives of humanitarian assistance. *MTB*. **55**(1), 3–5.

Benthall, J., (1991). Le sans-frontierisme. *Anthropology Today*. **7**(6), 1–3. doi:10.2307/3033043

Calain, P., (2013). Ethics and images of suffering bodies in humanitarian medicine. *Social Science & Medicine*. **98**, 278–285. doi:10.1016/j.socscimed.2012.06.027

Calhoun, C., (2008). The imperative to reduce suffering: charity, progress, and emergencies in the field of humanitarian action. In: M. Barnett and T.G. Weiss, eds., *Humanitarianism in question: politics, power, ethics*. Ithaca, NY: Cornell University Press. 73–97.

Castellarnau, M. and Stoianova, V., (2018). *Bridging the emergency gap: reflections and a call for action after a two-year exploration of emergency response in acute conflicts*. MSF archives, Barcelona.

CRED, (2013). *People affected by conflict 2013: humanitarian needs and numbers*. Brussels: Centre for Research on the Epidemiology of Disasters. Available from: http://doi.org.cred.be/node/1329

Donini, A., (2012). Humanitarianism, perceptions, power. In: C. Abu-Sa'Da, ed., *In the eyes of others: how people in crises perceive humanitarian aid*. MSF archives, New York.

Fassin, D. and Rechtman, R., (2009). *The empire of trauma: an inquiry into the condition of victimhood*. Princeton, NJ: Princeton University Press.

Feldman, A., (1994). On cultural anesthesia: from desert storm to Rodney King. *American Ethnologist*. **21**(2), 404–418. doi:10.1525/ae.1994.21.2.02a00100

Fox, R.C., (1995). Medical humanitarianism and human rights: reflections on Doctors Without Borders and Doctors of the World. *Social Science & Medicine.* **41**(12), 1607–1616. doi:10.1016/0277-9536(95)00144-V

Fustukian, S. and Zwi, A.B., (2001). Balancing imbalances: facilitating community perspectives in times of adversity. In: H.A. Williams, ed., Caring for those in crisis: integrating anthropology and public health in complex humanitarian emergencies. *NAPA Bulletin.* **21**(1), 1–16. doi:10.1525/napa.2001.21.1.1

Hunt, M.R., Schwartz, L., Sinding, C. and Elit, L., (2014). The ethics of engaged presence: a framework for health professionals in humanitarian assistance and development work. *Developing World Bioethics.* **14**(1), 47–55. doi:10.1111/dewb.12013

Kaldor, M., (2013). In defence of new wars. *Stability: International Journal of Security and Development.* **2**(1), 4. doi:10.5334/sta.at

Malkki, L.H., (1996). Speechless emissaries: refugees, humanitarianism, and dehistoricization. *Cultural Anthropology.* **11**(3), 377–404. doi:10.1525/can.1996.11.3.02a00050

Minn, P., (2007). Towards an anthropology of humanitarianism. *The Journal of Humanitarian Assistance.* [online]. [viewed 20 September 2017]. Available from: https://sites.tufts.edu/jha/archives/51

MSF, (1997). *Refugee health: an approach to emergency situations.* London: Macmillan Press.

MSF, (2002). *Humanitarian action must not be a tool of political interests.* [online]. [viewed 29 April 2019]. Available from: www.msf.org/humanitarian-action-must-not-be-tool-political-interests

MSF, (2016a). *Involving communities: guidance document for approaching and cooperating with communities.* Vienna: Vienna Evaluation Unit, MSF. Available from: https://evaluation.msf.org/sites/evaluation/files/involving_communities_2016_online.pdf

MSF, (2016b). *MSF to pull out of World Humanitarian Summit.* [online]. [viewed 29 April 2019]. Available from: www.msf.org/msf-pull-out-world-humanitarian-summit

MSF, (2018). *MSF international activity report.* Geneva: Medecins Sans Frontieres.

OCHA, (2018). *Staying the course – executive summary.* Geneva: UNOCHA.

Pottier, J., (1996). Why aid agencies need better understanding of the communities they assist: the experience of food aid in Rwandan refugee camps. *Disasters.* **20**(4), 324–337. doi:10.1111/j.1467-7717.1996.tb01047.x

Roberts, K., Aloudat, T., Lockyear, C. et al., (2014). *It's not just about drinking tea. Dialogue between MSF, its patients, and their communities.* MSF archives, London.

Stellmach, D., Beshar, I., Bedford, J. et al., (2018). Anthropology in public health emergencies: what is it good for? *BMJ Global Health.* **3**, e000534. doi:10.1136/bmjgh-2017-000534

World Bank, (2011). *World development report 2011: conflict, security, and development.* Washington, DC: World Bank. Available from: http://hdl.handle.net/10986/4389

World Bank, (2017). *Life expectancy at birth, total (years.).* [online]. [viewed 31 January 2019]. Available from: https://data.worldbank.org/indicator/sp.dyn.le00.in

2

A MEDICAL OPERATIONAL PERSPECTIVE ON ANTHROPOLOGY IN THE SETTING OF MSF

William Hennequin and Kiran Jobanputra

On the need for social science in developing humanitarian health operations

In order to develop their medical programmes, organisations like Médecins Sans Frontières need to understand the social context and social relationships of the health needs they are targeting. Historically, this has been left to general coordinators and managers with different backgrounds, experiences and profiles, who rarely have expertise in social sciences.

Typically, the scope of these social context analyses is limited to matching the informational demands of operations and identifying gaps and needs for assistance from a provider's perspective. As such, we rarely take community perspectives fully into account, and our analysis remains 'operationally focussed' rather than 'community based'. While this may be enough in many programmes, we are often reminded of the limits of this approach. For example, a maternal child health (MCH) programme in Ethiopia, underpinned by an extensive needs assessment, received very few patients. Eventually a community-based assessment (by an external social scientist) concluded that women and children would only use the services if men did, too, and suggested that MSF offer chronic disease treatment to the male population. Once this was implemented, women and children started using the MCH services (Wright, 2017).

It is important that the ongoing contextual analysis of a public health objective (e.g. high vaccination coverage or quality services for complex diseases such as lifelong treatment for HIV) considers the beneficiaries' social environment. It may be that we need specific expertise – that is lacking in our standard teams – to make a deeper analysis, particularly of the relationship the community have with their health providers.

In other instances, we may recognise that we are trapped in a 'medical bubble', disconnected from a community due to the pressures of providing clinical care, and therefore seeing it mainly through the prism of people who are sick. Yet controlling infectious diseases such as HIV also means engaging with non-patients; for example, people who are seropositive and well, those who are seronegative, and those who do not know their status – in this way, we can detect and treat the first group early and better engage with the other two. When it comes to people turning up late to health facilities, we have to understand the community's relationship with its health system in terms of access and trust. We often rely on teams of community health or outreach workers, but rarely have people available with enough time, distance and know-how to analyse, interpret, adapt to and address community needs.

In these situations, social scientists, including anthropologists, can be extremely effective. More generally, we may reach for support from social scientists when we find ourselves struggling to manage the competing demands of delivering care and maintaining sound contextual knowledge. Reasons can include:

- Continuity in leadership and management. Today, senior field positions in MSF tend to be international staff on short contracts. This leads to loss of institutional memory, 'person-dependent' decision-making and difficulties in maintaining contextual understanding.
- New diseases and medical technologies. MSF increasingly offers care for chronic communicable and non-communicable diseases, including support for self-management. This requires an understanding of the patients' social and economic situations; for example, how they reveal their illness to their spouse or employers.
- Size of field projects. Over the past 20 years, MSF field projects have grown and have increasing internal management demands. As a result, it has become harder to fully understand and analyse the environment and internal issues of missions.
- Health systems integration. MSF often works in partnership with, or as part of, structures run by a Ministry of Health within existing health systems. In addition to the key partnership with the Ministry of Health, this implies a relationship with community leaders – teachers, health staff, religious leaders, elders – and with patients and their families.

The collaboration with anthropologists and other social scientists clearly will not eliminate these challenges, and may actually reveal them. Furthermore, few anthropologists have both operational experience and availability for long-term assignments, so their involvement may not help with continuity of engagement or solve our difficulties in embedding ourselves into a particular socio-economic environment.

What do operations typically require from social scientists?

The usual requirement for anthropologists in these settings is to help medical operational staff develop a deeper understanding of the social context than they could gain from their day-to-day work. The anthropologist has the expertise and experience to understand behaviour and discourses in their social context, taking into account the views of the community, as well as the organisation. With the help of an anthropologist, we may be better able to step outside our medical bubble and understand our blind spots, so that we can see where we need to go. Establishing the best relationship and mutual understanding with the community – beyond the trust built up by our quality medical care – may be hugely improved by the involvement of a skilled outsider encouraging community participation and acceptance.

Another, although less frequent, function of anthropologists in MSF is the ethnographic study of a target group of people. These studies often use practices not typical in ethnographic work, such as focus-group discussions and individual interviews, as these appear to be more acceptable to MSF medical programmes. These studies have tended to be undertaken at critical moments in a project's evolution in order to generate knowledge about the community and a context to inform programme choice (Burtscher, 2008; Burtscher & Velibanti, 2011; Burtscher et al., 2018).

Occasionally, the object of ethnographic study is MSF itself, to encourage critical self-examination and reflection on ourselves as an organisation. For example, a year-long ethnography of MSF, undertaken in operations in Europe and South Sudan, sought to understand the levels of knowledge and decision-making in humanitarian emergencies (see Chapter 4). The study found a dynamic tension between data-driven institutional logic and value-based decision-making by individuals (Stellmach, 2016). Studies like this have made critical insights into the organisational culture of MSF, highlighting areas for mitigating action or organisational change, as well as hidden strengths. But since the focus of this book is 'practising anthropology in humanitarian situations' rather than 'the anthropology of humanitarianism', we will not discuss them here.

Although the focus of this book is anthropology in humanitarian settings, we view anthropology as part of the broader social science current inside the organisation, and we accept that MSF has always needed social knowledge – particularly the socio-economic and cultural environment of patients – to be able to develop its humanitarian health programmes.

Anthropology in MSF medical operations – the example of a 20-year HIV project in Kenya

We share here a description of how anthropology has been applied in one MSF field project (Homa Bay). This is based on a review of historical documents (anthropologists' reports, end of mission reports, situation reports and planning meetings) and the direct experience of one of the authors of this chapter, who worked in Homa Bay from 2003–2005, and as head of the Kenya mission from 2012–2017. We chose to focus on this project because it is a long-term programme (even though strategy has generally been planned and reviewed every year), and it has been the subject of several interventions from social scientists, including four anthropologists. We do not claim here to provide a systematic and methodologically sound review of the

42 William Hennequin and Kiran Jobanputra

work of those anthropologists, although such an analysis would indeed carry merit; neither were we able to interview those involved. Nevertheless, the available information and experience permits a number of reflections on the role of anthropology in humanitarian programmes that we will discuss later.

1996–early 2000: project opens and is rapidly overwhelmed with very sick patients

The Homa Bay HIV/TB project was opened in 1996 and is still running today. It was opened as an emergency response to violent clashes between different Luo clans, during which the team uncovered the extent of the HIV/TB epidemic in the region. In her end-of-mission report, the head of mission at the time (who was also present in Kenya in the late 1990s when MSF reached Homa Bay) described the situation as follows:

> There was virtually no space in the medical wards, beside or under the beds, each space occupied by skinny, obviously AIDS terminally ill patients, or their carers. Overwhelmed and demoralised staff were encouraging families to take their loved ones home to die. The nearest HIV testing facility was located at the Adventist hospital close to Kendu Bay (1 hour's drive from Homa bay) at the rate of 500 KES/test and there was virtually no reliable tool to identify HIV infection prior to blood transfusions in the Hospital laboratory.
>
> *(MSF, 2007)*

The initial plan of the project in the absence of drugs to treat HIV/AIDS was to focus on sexually transmitted diseases, testing for HIV, care for patients with opportunistic infections in the wards, including tuberculosis (also in health centres in the district), and blood safety, hygiene and sanitation. In 2000, a dedicated HIV clinic was created. The first antiretroviral (ARV) treatment was initiated in November 2001 after early successes in bringing down the cost. The project was one of the HIV projects that MSF opened from early 2001 with the following objectives: 1) save the lives of patients registered in MSF HIV clinics, 2) demonstrate the feasibility of treating patients in poor resource settings and advocate for access to ARVs (breach strategy), and 3) provide impetus to others such as international institutions and governments to follow suit (MSF, 2007).

In June 2001, the first MSF anthropologist carried out an assessment "Chira ou la malédiction des ancêtres: tuberculose pulmonaire et sida chez les Luo et les Suba du Kenya" ("Chira[1] or the ancestral curse: pulmonary tuberculosis and aids among Luo and Kenyan Suba") (Rahem, 2001). The same head of mission referred to this study in her end of mission report as recommended reading under the chapter 'The Luo culture'. However, we could not obtain the original terms of reference or find any mention of this work in the archives; thus, it remains unclear how it was utilised.

The introduction of the anthropologist's report (p. 1) described the study's objectives as:

> 1) comprendre quelles étaient les représentations de ces maladies par les patients, quelles modalités dans la recherche des causes elles mettaient en branle, dans quels cadres nosologiques traditionnels s'inscrivaient les symptômes de ce qui pour la médecine dite moderne constitue la tuberculose pulmonaire et le sida (interview of people infected with HIV). Il s'agissait ensuite de 2) connaître les itinéraires thérapeutiques des malades, dans quelle mesure ils consultaient ou non des thérapeutes traditionnels, qui faisait le diagnostic, et comment. Nous nous sommes bien sûr penché sur les pratiques relatives à la sexualité, notamment en ce qui concerne l'usage des préservatifs parmi les jeunes du district. Et finalement 3) de repérer sur quels acteurs sociaux s'appuyer éventuellement pour la mise en place d'un système de distribution des médicaments, d'une politique d'information et d'éducation sanitaire, ce qui présuppose de connaître les structures sociales, leurs modes de fonctionnement, d'identifier les acteurs sociaux (chefs de clans ou de lignages, personnalités morales, personnalités politiques et administratives).
>
> 1) Understand the representations of those diseases by the patients, which methods they prompted in the research for the causes, in which traditional nosological frameworks lay the symptoms of what are, in modern medicine, pulmonary tuberculosis and AIDS (interview of people infected with HIV). 2) To establish the therapeutic journeys of the patients, to what extent they did or didn't consult traditional healers, who made the diagnosis, and how. Of course, we focused on practices related to sexuality, including the use of condoms among youth in the district. And finally, 3) to identify which social actors could be relied on in setting up a drug distribution system and a health information and education policy, all of which presupposes knowledge of social structures and how they function and how to identify the main social actors (chiefs of clans or lineages, moral leaders and political and administrative figures).

The introduction of this assessment states:

> Outre les aspects strictement médico-techniques, il est nécessaire de prendre en compte ces maladies dans leurs dimensions sociales, culturelles et anthropologiques. Ceci est d'autant plus important que les traitements proposés sont longs, fastidieux, et que leur diffusion massive sans suivi bien mené risque à terme d'entraîner des résistances aux conséquences désastreuses en termes de santé publique.
>
> In addition to the strictly medico-technical aspects, it is necessary to take into account the social, cultural and anthropological dimensions of these diseases. This is all the more important as the proposed treatments are long

and tedious and their widespread dissemination without proper monitoring could ultimately lead to resistance and disastrous consequences in terms of public health.

(Rahem, 2001, p. 1)

It then takes us through the history of people (the Luo and Suba) and their administrative and traditional organisations. It describes the traditional leaders, the people's representations of the world and human beings, the influence of Christianity, and diseases and curses. It also reveals how they see the HIV/TB epidemic and the traditional ways they treat the curse they call Chira (which shares HIV's symptomatology).

In its conclusion, "Les maladies et la médecine moderne" ("Diseases and modern medicine"), it explains that the health system at the time was unable to cope; the number of cases was greatly underestimated and solutions were needed to avoid catastrophe; health facilities did not offer the necessary testing and were seen as corrupt; the cost of transport was a major barrier, as few facilities offered crucial services; and people lacked information, despite being eager to learn about these diseases.

The report (p. 35) highlights the absence of information on these diseases at the time, particularly questioning the relationship between health care providers and patients:

> Les relations entre les personnels soignants et les patients sont, ici comme ailleurs, placées sous le signe de l'incompréhension mutuelle. . . . La qualité des informations délivrées . . . avoisine le degré zero.

> The relations between the nursing staff and the patients, here as elsewhere, fall under the banner of mutual incomprehension. . . . The quality of the information delivered . . . is close to zero.

The writer also comments (p. 36) on MSF's activities away from health facilities, and the impact this can have on access to health care for the population:

> Avant qu'X et Y, les deux infirmières de MSF, ne commencent, il y a peu, à établir des contacts directs avec la population, dont on ne soulignera jamais assez l'importance primordiale, les gens de Rusinga ne savaient pas que les médicaments pour la tuberculose étaient gratuits, ni les prix exacts des examens de dépistage.

> Before X and Y, the two MSF nurses, who had recently begun to establish direct contact with the population – the importance of which cannot be overemphasized – the people of Rusinga were unaware that Tuberculosis drugs were free and did not know the exact price of screening tests.

The report concludes (p. 41) that:

> A l'heure où l'on va proposer la mise sur le marché de médicaments géné-
> riques contre le sida, . . . on peut se demander l'intérêt de traiter les patients
> en aval, c'est-à-dire lorsqu'ils sont déjà à un stade avancé de la maladie, alors
> que la prise en charge en amont (éducation, informations sur la transmis-
> sion et les traitements, reconnaissance des premiers symptômes etc.) n'est
> pas faite! . . . Doit-on se contenter de poursuivre le travail dans les centres de
> santé kenyans. . . . Certes oui, mais au vu de notre étude cela est grandement
> insuffisant: nous ne touchons qu'une faible partie des malades et tardivement;
> ceux qui viennent jusqu'à l'hôpital ne pourront tous retourner ne serait-ce
> que pour des raisons financières. . . . Aussi, pourquoi vouloir . . . s'occuper
> de mettre en place des traitements lourds pour une minorité, alors que les
> gens vont continuer à se contaminer allègrement. Il y a là quelque chose qui
> heurte le bon sens!
>
> At a time when we are about to propose placing generic drugs for AIDS
> on the market . . . we can ask what is the point of treating patients down-
> stream, that is to say when they are already at an advanced stage of the disease,
> if early care upstream [education, information on the transmission and the
> treatments, recognition of the first symptoms, etc.] is not offered! . . . Should
> we be happy to continue the work in Kenyan health centres? . . . Yes, of
> course, but in light of our study, this is largely insufficient: we only reach a
> small portion of the patients and too late; those who come to the hospital
> will not be able to return there, if only for financial reasons. . . . Also, why do
> we want . . . to offer arduous treatment for a minority, while others cheerfully
> continue to infect themselves. It doesn't make sense!
>
> *(Rahem, 2001)*

As we will point out, the issue of providing earlier care (both primary and secondary prevention) would emerge ten years later when better tools and resources
became available. This report was perhaps far-sighted at that stage of the response to
the epidemic, and highlighted the enormous disparity between the health system,
health workers and the reality of people's lives. It is worth remembering, though,
that there was no access to treatment and testing, and the incredible burden on
health workers and MSF teams at the hospital would have made it almost impossible to implement any such recommendations. Testing and treating at village level
would simply have increased the demand for hospital services.

In fact, why increase the demand if we already can't cope with the numbers of
terminally ill patients on whom health workers would naturally focus their attention? From the head of mission's report (p. 75):

> In early 2002, the ART treatment initiation capacity was 30 patients per
> month. Yet 200 people were testing positive per month, and an average 80%

were eligible for ART according to WHO criteria (clinical staging or CD4 count threshold). By early 2002, MSF was already overwhelmed by patients and not in a position to cope with the ART demand.

(MSF, 2007)

At that time, MSF was the only organisation providing free treatment in public health facilities, and so adopted the rational approach of medics, coping with the existing demand at the hospital rather than creating more. We were also learning for the first time how to care for these chronic diseases, and doing so while the majority of the international scientific community opposed launching ART in Africa. We did not know how we were going to cope with such a high burden and growing numbers of patients, or how best to use the diagnostic and therapeutic tools we had, and we were constantly questioning how far to take this approach.

As a result, we can observe the role this anthropologist played in understanding the environment in which patients and their families lived, including the barriers they faced accessing care in the health system. He also described the poor relationship of patients with health staff and the inadequate information people received about the diseases and the treatment offered, as well as the difficulty health workers – including MSF teams – can have to extract themselves from health facilities. However, at that stage of the epidemic, it seems his recommendations, though justified, could not be taken into account when designing the MSF strategy. They differed too much from the pre-existing medical operational priorities of MSF health teams, which were directly related to the situation they were facing.

So, the first question for the anthropologist, and the timing of their involvement, are of great importance. Before commissioning such a study, we must ask whether we (Operations) have already decided how we want to proceed, or are we ready to change course in the light of the (as yet unknown) findings of the anthropologist? In this case, the anthropologist came up with operational proposals from his observation, but it seems that his work was used by Operations only as a "tool to better understand the Luo culture". This raises the question whether any objectives were agreed between Operations and the anthropologist at the start of the work. Given that the report is written in French, while the study was done in an Anglophone country, one can also ask who this report was aimed at, and what the expected outcome was.

2009: continuation – 'Access for more'

The following years were dedicated to addressing this overwhelming (pre-existing) need by increasing the hospital cohort (up to 150 new initiations per month by 2004), simplifying care, task shifting for nurses, developing patient counselling to encourage adherence, and decentralising HIV care to improve access.

When ART initiation rates stabilised, we focussed on neglected and vulnerable patients such as children and those with TB co-infection. When the Ministry of Health (MoH) started its ART project in Homa Bay (2005) and subsequently expanded care in other districts and facilities with its partners (2006/2008), MSF turned its attention to improving quality of care by developing approaches that would improve the lives of patients and health workers. This process was often referred to as 'simplification' – nurse-led patient care using simplified algorithm-driven consultations, integration of TB and HIV services and spacing out of appointments, for example.

This period also gave MSF an opportunity to test its capacity to work in partnership first with the Ministry of Health through integration of the two MSF cohorts in Homa Bay hospital and in peripheral health centres into MoH services, and also to adapt to the presence of other partners that MSF teams deemed to be "less quality focussed". For MSF, the question was how to embed itself in an existing and evolving health and social system, taking into consideration the different health agencies, and how to adapt its approach as a consequence.

In 2009, following significant developments in the global health context, the future of MSF involvement in the field of HIV was being debated at several levels within the movement. While some in MSF were in favour of disengaging from providing care for patients who were stable on first line ART or in pre-ART care, others were pushing for more to be done, as the situation was still precarious (MSF, 2009a).

The notion of 'Access for more' was introduced at the annual operational review of the Homa Bay project. The minutes of the annual review indicate that

> 'Access for more' is in effect a commitment by MSF to remain in Homa Bay for the short to medium term (3–5 years). The strategy is consistent with ongoing and future decentralisation activities. The goal is to identify the barriers to access (awareness, access to care providers, stigma, economics, etc.) and devise a plan that includes a target for an access percentage. 'Access for more' does not necessarily mean MSF would provide more care for people. It is about ensuring that the combined efforts of all parties (MoH, Aphia,[2] MSF, and others) achieve the access targets. In theory the goal is that all potential HIV-positive people have access to testing and care if they want it.
>
> *(MSF, 2009b, p. 10)*

At the national level, the Kenya National AIDS Strategic Plan III had been launched by the end of 2009 and, despite difficulty absorbing all the funding provided, had the ambitious coverage target of achieving universal access for prevention, care and treatment by 2013, as well as improving the outcomes of people on ART (MoH Kenya, 2009). It aimed to do so by increasing the percentage of facilities offering comprehensive ART services from 15% to 40%, and those providing Prevention of Mother to Child Transmission (PMTCT) services from 80% to 90%. Estimating that 83% of HIV-positive people had not been diagnosed, it recommended scaling up testing through door-to-door strategies with a focus on prevention that included medical male circumcision. Suffice to say that MSF field staff working in Kenya have regularly reported a significant gap between national

48 William Hennequin and Kiran Jobanputra

policies as written, and their implementation on the ground, the main issues being lack of staff and problems with resources.

It is in that context that the second anthropologist joined in 2010. According to the proposal presented at the annual operational review:

> Anthropological follow-up of a study done in 2001: 'Chira ou la malédiction des ancêtres: tuberculose pulmonaire et sida chez les Luo et les Suba du Kenya' (Rahem, 2001). It would be interesting to see, if years later perceptions/knowledge about HIV and TB have changed; perceptions of illness; health-seeking behaviour; impact of gender roles and cultural norms on women's access to PMTCT or other HIV related services. But should be more practical-communication-oriented than the first study.
>
> *(MSF, 2009b, p. 3) (see Table 2.1)*

This research was undertaken from March to December 2010. From the introduction to the final internal report, part I:

> The idea for 'Access for more' originates from the estimation that there are still between 13,000 and 29,000 HIV-positive individuals in Homa Bay district who are not accessing HIV/AIDS related treatment and care. The purpose of this research is therefore, to identify main barriers that prevent communities to fully make a use of available MSF and other health facilities that provide HIV/AIDS testing and care.... Ultimately, this research aims to contribute towards the development of strategies that are both, effective in accessing wider target community, and culturally and gender sensitive. Recommendations were developed in collaboration with the community.
>
> *(Kovačič, 2010-1, p. 6)*

In the research, denial and fear of stigmatisation, missed diagnosis at the formal health facility, preference for traditional treatments, and – to lesser extent – economic factors were found to be the principle barriers to early access to treatment. Men had been identified from the HIV database as seeking care later than women.

> In short: The formal health sector is the most important treatment option patients use when faced with HIV related symptoms. Poor diagnosing capacity results in treatment that does not bring desired relief of the symptoms. This causes great time gaps before the next visit to the formal health facilities and has an impact on choosing traditional treatment as an alternative.
>
> *(Kovačič, 2010-1, p. 13)*

Practical recommendations were made, such as strengthening testing capacity in the formal health sector, intensifying testing strategies including community-based and door-to-door approaches, encouraging men to undergo testing, testing families of HIV-positive patients, undertaking communication campaign strategies, improving

A medical operational perspective **49**

PMTCT by working with traditional birth attendants and focussing on prevention mainly by promoting condom use. The research looked closely at factors that helped patients to undergo early HIV testing, and compared their health-seeking behaviours with those of patients accessing care while in more advanced stages of the disease.

Many of these recommendations had already been identified as priorities by other health agencies. The need to extend the offer of care in order to increase access had already been integrated into national policies and into the thinking of MSF and other NGOs. Many of the recommendations were operational in nature and contained practical suggestions for health workers. Some were more visionary, concerning harder to reach populations such as men, the need to expand testing among widows, and encouraging disclosure to spouses.

Other recommendations were apparently more difficult for health workers to implement, such as those relating to the informal health sector and the links to the community. For example, they encouraged public dialogue about wife inheritance (the custom of re-marrying widows; see Chapter 6) in a 'culturally sensitive way' – not contradicting local customs but instead adapting biomedical approaches to the customs (such as advising the use of condoms during sexual cleansing and encouraging young religious leaders to tolerate condom use), and influencing behaviour changes through reducing stigma, getting traditional healers involved and encouraging cross-gender dialogue. Other recommendations included developing "alternative community oriented approaches, which would take into consideration African concepts of personhood as a social body and would decrease individual balancing between physical health with social integrity" (Kovačič, 2010-2, p. 22). Implementing such recommendations was not feasible for medical teams working on their own. The report, in its introduction, depicted recommendations as having been made jointly with the community; but had they also been discussed and agreed with the field operations and medical teams?

Some findings may have been helpful to medical teams, without being recommendations per se, particularly those touching on the social navigation of an HIV-positive individual. For example, realising the tension or fracture that could exist between what the health workers 'think is good' and what patients can accept or comply with.

> Despite all these benefits, it is impossible to ignore the fact that a positive result of the HIV test is a life-changing experience for the individual. HIV-positive individuals do not only become dependent on treatment providers, but are also expected to change their life in accord with what is biomedically considered as beneficial to their physical health. As observed in our study location this biomedical approach, however, often clashes with other determinants of health: mental and social well-being.
>
> *(Kovačič, 2010-2, p. 7)*

In this case, the anthropologist appeared to play the role of an observer outside the medical team, questioning the attitude of health workers toward patients, and helping reveal what they might have missed in their day to day interaction with them.

Subsequently, in the June 2011 planning meeting, MSF was struggling to position itself in an environment now occupied by several health agencies.

> We all agree that MSF does not have the medical/political space to define our program. We need to construct our role in collaboration with the partners (AphiaPlus[3] and MoH) on the ground – MSF needs to step back and position itself based on the others.
>
> *(MSF, 2011, p. 6)*

The report further highlights existing contradictory views on the project's future:

> Finally, it has been two years since the three levels (Desk, Coordination, Field)[4] have been struggling to be on the same page. Coordination and Desk pushed for the 'Access for more' strategy in 2009 and Field rejected it – then in 2010 Field pushed to prioritise PMTCT. We at Desk and Coordination believe that this approach should take a step back, frame our project based on the others, and then analyse whether this justifies MSF presence in the long term; this is the right approach.
>
> *(MSF, 2011, p. 7)*

It may seem surprising to ask an anthropologist to undertake research on how to increase 'Access for more', while MSF's political desire to do this remains uncertain. From the views attributed previously to Field, Coordination and Desk, it is unclear whether they all had the same understanding of what it meant to use an anthropologist for this work. Furthermore, many of these recommendations were either already in the MoH pipeline (which became clear in 2012) or would not be easily applicable for health workers unless the required field expertise was also available. With Operations already deciding to step back, this option may not have been discussed.

Once again, we must ask how much the initial question and the actual recommendations were worked on at the different levels of operations. And how can we ensure that such work actually becomes a reference document for teams and for future operational discussions, including identification of advocacy priorities?

2012: change of environment, change of approach, 'controlling the epidemic'

In 2012, the debate and disagreements over what to do next in Homa Bay continued. The environment had continued to change significantly. Access to treatment from the MoH and its partners had expanded, and mathematical modelling now suggested the possibility of reducing HIV transmission by extending ART

A medical operational perspective **51**

treatment to non-symptomatic HIV-positive people (Granich et al., 2010). In this context, MSF decided to hand over the Homa Bay hospital HIV project to the MoH (whose capacity had grown) and run a population-based incidence survey in Ndhiwa district to obtain an estimate of HIV incidence. This would underpin a people-based (as opposed to a facility-based) response to the HIV epidemic.

The report of the Ndhiwa HIV Indicator Population Survey states:

> Recent findings suggest that reduction of HIV transmission is now achievable through scale-up of testing, prevention (including voluntary male circumcision) and ART treatment programmes. . . . To assess the burden of HIV in the sub-county and provide baseline information prior to a joint MSF-MoH intervention, the study was one of the first which directly measured HIV Incidence, population viral load and coverage at each step within the cascade of care in late 2012.
>
> *(MSF, 2012, p. 7)*

We had now reached the point of implementing 'Access for more', but with the objective of curbing the epidemic by increasing not only the coverage of people in treatment, but also the number of HIV-positive individuals under virological control. We embarked on community-based approaches to test people in their homes, and we supplemented support from other NGOs to over 30 health facilities as HIV care was by then decentralised to dispensary level.

It is worth noting that the last anthropologist's report was not at that time part of the 'essential reading for the mission'; nor was it used to plan the project's next steps. It is also important to note that most of the health-system–related recommendations by the two previous anthropologists had actually been implemented by government and partners: free-of-charge HIV/TB care, care decentralised to dispensary level and systematic HIV testing, including home-based testing.

At that stage, we realised the new operational objectives would require us to take into account people's socio-economic and cultural environments much more, because we were now dealing with people in their villages and homes, where the majority were not sick. We also needed to target people who had problems following the treatment, including the socially vulnerable, adolescents and those with specific beliefs around HIV. Although the anthropologist's report provided relevant recommendations, implementation guidance on community engagement and culturally appropriate messaging was lacking.

The end of mission report by the head of mission (one of the authors of this chapter) states that:

> it is important to acknowledge a paradox: . . . to achieve an objective that is typically one of public health, strategies developed to diagnose, link, retain and keep healthy have to be multiple and we rather have to go back to individualised approaches since patients have a variety of personal reasons for not

adhering or not being in position to adhere to this concept. Looking at the care cascade the other way round may prove more useful – who are those not aware of their status? Who are those who have not linked? Those not retained? Not adherent? Those who are dying in the wards? And what are the different approaches we need to deploy to address these specific populations?

(MSF, 2017, p. 129)

Engaging in such intensive testing requires high levels of acceptance by the community. We may feel that such initiatives are justified from a biomedical or epidemiological perspective, but they confront us with socio-political challenges. How can we cover the great majority of the population who must 'get pricked' several times, begin lifelong treatment though not sick, and reveal their HIV status to their family?

We realised we needed to do extensive work on acceptance with the communities in Ndhiwa, particularly sharing with them an analysis of the Ndhiwa HIV Indicator Population Survey outcomes and their interpretation, deciding next steps together, jointly defining a message and actively engaging the community in the programme. This would evolve into the Community Mobile approach (COM-MOB), involving campaigns of testing and voluntary medical male circumcision (VMMC), but at that time, the field team did not have the expertise to carry this out. We requested an anthropologist, but none were available, and eventually we were connected to an epidemiologist with a degree in sociology who visited Homa Bay between October 2014 and August 2015. She had experience of VMMC campaigns in South Africa, and she worked with a team designed specifically for the community approach composed of social workers, health staff and community health workers.

Her end of mission report states:

> The COMMOB was designed with the support of the MSF medical, admin/HR, logistics and Monitoring and Evaluation (M&E) teams, the Ndhiwa sub-county health management team, the County AIDS Control Constituency (CACC) and other key local players in the HIV prevention and care field.
>
> *(MSF, 2015, p. 2)*

The community approach involved mapping sub-counties and listing all official divisions, locations, sub-locations and villages targeted for service delivery, an assessment of the condition of the road networks and establishment of the movement plan. It was underpinned by extensive consultation with stakeholders, partners, community leaders and gatekeepers (key community representatives such as teachers, religious leaders, elders, existing community groups, influential women, etc.) in counties, sub-counties, divisions, locations and sub-locations. These consultations lead to the creation of Community Health Advisory Boards (CHAB) in each division and location.

A medical operational perspective **53**

The CHAB terms of reference were defined and people elected to the boards. These were to be composed of "representatives from main community gatekeepers, partners and stakeholders", and were mandated:

> to promote community ownership, engagement, and support; act as a direct link between the mobile approach management team and the community; review and validate all programme activities, including communication plan, materials, and strategies of intervention delivery; determine the sites and modes of intervention delivery with MSF log management; inform on program activities and ensure community support; provide feedback and advise on community concerns; address challenges and issues with intervention delivery with the mobile approach management team; help organise community workshops and consultations (barazas).
>
> *(MSF, 2015, p. 8)*

For MSF, these teams were their interface with the community, approved by authorities from the different layers. The COMMOB team then worked on all aspects of service provision for testing and VMMC at village level, which later evolved into home-based testing.

However, questions remained about the content of the message, particularly the influence of the Luo people's sexual rituals on transmission, and about how to address the issue of sexual transmission in a context of high incidence. How could we develop a message that would be non-judgemental, factual and convincing enough for people to accept the situation and the risks and therefore take the test several times, and enroll into care if positive? Some research had been done on HIV and sexuality among the Luo, and on inheritance and cleansing. The Ndhiwa HIV Indicator Population Survey had also found that HIV prevalence among widows was above 60%, much higher than the 24% for the general adult population; that the incidence among young girls and among pregnant and breast-feeding women aged 15–30 was three times higher than other groups, and that men aged 40–45 had a prevalence that was double that of the general male population (38% vs 19%) (MSF, 2012).

The idea therefore was to adapt the message to the situation, and particularly to design an individual risk assessment that would help people identify their own risks of being infected, and so accept the idea of prevention through regular testing and treatment.

With this in mind, we discussed our need for support in Homa Bay with a third MSF anthropologist (who was running a survey on levels of violence and the health-seeking behaviour of people confronted with violence). Convincing people that our programme would benefit individuals and the community, without modifying or challenging beliefs around sexuality, was deemed to be key to its success (see Table 2.1). We agreed that the anthropologist would review the literature and make a quick assessment in Homa Bay, and then be replaced by another

54 William Hennequin and Kiran Jobanputra

anthropologist who would stay longer to help the COMMOB team to implement recommendations.

The objectives of this intervention were to:

> Develop messages used during testing and counselling and general communication/mobilisation adapted to the community that improve knowledge of HIV and of the intervention in order to:
>
> - Ensure the population understands HIV is a major public health issue for them and that there are biomedical approaches that can mitigate its impact, and how.
> - Ensure majority of the population accepts to be tested at least once a year with special focus on providing family approach (couple testing, children) that includes a component on disclosure – this addressing the issue on stigma.
> - Ensure that people found HIV-positive understand why they have to and accept to be linked to care and that we have access to all sexual partners for testing.
> - Ensure that people HIV-negative are provided with an accurate adapted risk assessment and improve their risk perception and their use of preventive methods (prep, VMMC, repeat testing).
>
> *(Véran, 2017, p. 1)*

In the conclusion of 'Why is HIV so high in Homa Bay County?', the anthropologist stated:

> No deep anthropological mystery, finally solved in this report, brings a definite answer to the question. . . . HIV in Homa Bay County builds on at the interface between a traditional system where sexuality is a key social organiser and a powerful symbolic significant (more than in many other societies), and the polarization of local economy towards fish business within a globalized market of Victoria Lake fish tank.
>
> *(Véran, 2017, p. 20)*

He thus reframed an issue that the MSF team had regarded as cultural in a wider socio-economical context, blurred by the Luo people's traditional relationship with sexuality.

> On the one side, the sex rites, the management by cleansing and inheritance of widow social integration, the existence of Chira itself with the same symptomatology as HIV, the virilocal patrilineal system, . . . all these elements did combine to make a favorable litter for HIV diffusion. On the other side, there is the destructuring impact of HIV itself and its inherent exponential multiplication of vulnerable widows struggling their way through the

only income-generating activity in the region, the fish business, at the exact moment of the insertion of this business within the globalized economic market. Meanwhile, young generations of vulnerable girls coming from families already deconstructed by HIV, getting contaminated as they are forced towards precocious independence within a system with no social nor economical space for them.

(Véran, 2017, pp. 20–21)

The report also explained that "organisations and institutions fighting HIV tended to feed those dynamics over time by fighting them on cultural grounds, instead of taking into consideration spiritual and economic pressures" (Véran, 2017, p. 21).

The report offered practical and operational recommendations for optimising the COMMOB approach, such as training negotiators, developing approaches and messages targeting specific groups such as men or adolescent girls, avoiding culturalism by providing facts, and targeting young girls who were identified as more vulnerable. All recommendations were discussed and agreed with the team in the mission before the report was released.

Subsequently, another anthropologist visited Homa Bay to help the team implement these recommendations over the next six months. Her end of mission report indicates her main task was: "technical support for community mobile approach" (Abi-Saab, 2017, p. 1). The report of the previous anthropologist became the foundation for her own work. She persevered with trying to identify and understand risky behaviour by linking with the Community Health Advisory Boards set up previously, and through other focus group discussions. She also worked on improving the negotiation skills of our team, developing Q&A materials from the list of concerns people were raising.

Finally, together with the team, she fine-tuned the door to door approach by:

designing targeted messaging for key population (men, young women, adolescents), make HIV make sense: Work in collaboration with medical coordination to elaborate accurate answers and workarounds, Elaborate a Q&A frequent 'complicated' topics or questions, establish differential diagnosis Chira/HIV and stop culturalism by telling the facts (No more moral lessons. No more cultural stigmatization).

(MSF, 2017b, p. 4)

All of this led to creating tools that would particularly help the testers achieve their tasks.

The study was requested by the field team within an agreed operational objective validated at all levels. Recommendations were agreed with the team, and followed up by another anthropologist for implementation. This meant that the team could present a number of recommendations that were highly operational, including the development of the message itself.

However, the team faced difficulties applying the message in a systematic way, including implementing the individual risk assessment. Teams were overwhelmed with the organisational aspects of such campaigns, such as the logistics and organising of the medical pathway for patients (linkage to care) and data monitoring. Furthermore, this approach was constantly and silently questioned by the testers, mainly community health workers from Ndhiwa sub-county, who were not used to these messages and did not utilise them. They were either unconvinced by them, or regarded them as clashing with their own beliefs. It would clearly take time to optimise this approach because, although the epidemic had already lasted more than 20 years, people's knowledge about HIV remained limited.

The time this work took was frequently questioned by some at headquarters, who deemed the approach too heavy and cost-intensive as it resulted in few new diagnoses of HIV. Indeed, a good proportion of the HIV-positive population had already been diagnosed. The tendency of medical teams was to focus on those patients and on testing by health facilities even though the new approach reached out to those who were untested or negative and used the test as a true 'moment of exchange' between health workers and local people. This difference of views led to the demise of this approach.

This latest intervention by social scientists, including two anthropologists, suggests that for such work to be effective, the field team and the target populations need to participate from the very beginning, from designing the questions to implementing recommendations. The fact that this technical support was available over a longer period was undoubtedly helpful, for as we see here, these analyses produce recommendations that often need time to implement, requiring substantial know-how and engagement with local people. The short-term perspective of medical operations struggles with this, and hence it struggles to incorporate a community-based perspective and analysis of the overall socio-economic environment in practice.

While it is clear that understanding our environment is vital if we want to provide adapted health services to communities, our will and capacity to look outside the medical bubble can be questioned. In this case study, anthropology helped teams adjust their understanding of local people. Each of these assessments challenged medical operations, from the first anthropologist questioning community non-involvement in prevention to the later ones reviewing the message delivered (Table 2.1).

Each assessment also improved our understanding of the epidemic. However, recommendations were not always timely or were not followed because of issues of staff capacity and continuity, and consistency of approach. Reports were not always easy to translate into programmes, and indeed Operations rarely reflected on how such work can be used afterwards. This raises the question of how anthropologists or other external staff interact with field teams, how their work is integrated within operations and how much understanding there is between Operations and anthropologists.

A medical operational perspective **57**

TABLE 2.1 Overview of the three anthropological studies undertaken in the MSF Homa Bay project

Year	Title	Main objective	Profile of anthropologist
2001	Chira ou la malédiction des ancêtres: tuberculose pulmonaire et sida chez les Luo et les Suba du Kenya	Community base assessment (baseline?); identifying barriers to seeking care (initial question not found)	Classical (cultural) anthropologist
2010	Anthropological follow-up of the study done in 2001(?)	Identifying barriers to access to services (to support a new strategy)	Mixed anthropology/health promotion, with prior MSF experience
2017	Why is HIV so high in Homa Bay County?	Developing messages around HIV and the new model of care; improving community understanding and acceptance	Academic (university) anthropologist with experience in operational MSF roles, followed by another anthropologist with MSF experience

How to better integrate social sciences with Operations

Most MSF programmes achieve their stated objectives without the input of social scientists. It is the role of Operations to analyse and understand the context in which it functions, but it often struggles to understand the perspective from the community's point of view. As a result, we tend to request the input of an anthropologist or other social scientist when we feel the need for such perspectives; for example, when we identify an issue that we do not know how to manage (often linked to the 'medical bubble' effect), or when the stated objectives of the programme are themselves in question.

It is essential from the start to clearly identify the issue that has prompted us to seek this external expertise. This will confirm whether we need an anthropologist, or some other social scientist, and the type of support the issue requires – long-term placement, distant support or a single short visit. We also need to reflect on how to integrate the programme into the operation, and communicate it before starting.

This case study and our broader experience emphasise the importance of achieving a strong shared understanding between Operations and anthropologists, both of the 'question' itself and the expectations each party has of the other. It further requires time to have the different level within the operation agreeing on the same, such as the work is thereafter being utilised. This requires time prior to initiation of any field study, and the ability to take on board the position of the other. The anthropologist must understand clearly what is being asked of them, in what timeline and with what constraints. They must try to speak the language of Operations, understand the situations medical teams face and offer technical support, while remembering that the value they bring is linked to their 'external' perspective. Operations must understand the anthropological approach; for example, that the choices or attitudes of Operations itself may be the object of analysis as much as the behaviours of a community. And they must be prepared to change direction on the basis of the results of the study (presuming they agree with the anthropologist's conclusions), or otherwise should not undertake the study at all. This can be partly achieved by allowing more time to prepare for anthropology visits and planning post-visit support from the anthropologist. In addition, Operations training could include an introduction to the social sciences 'mindset', not just its qualitative methodologies, and anthropologists should be encouraged to work in an operational role – for example, as a health promotion manager – before taking on anthropological research for MSF.

As seen in the Homa Bay case study, the issue of continuity – which is a challenge for our operations as a whole – poses a risk to successful implementation of recommendations from anthropological assessments. While the expertise and experience of an anthropologist can bring insights into what is happening away from the health facilities, the heavy workloads at those health facilities and changeable commitment at different levels from Headquarters to Field mean the anthropologist's findings may not receive the attention they merit. To increase the chance of such studies proving useful for programming, reports should be essential reading for new staff in that project, and longer-term social scientist field placements should be considered instead of one-off visits that produce only a single report.

Some MSF offices are starting to develop alternative ways of providing social sciences support, and this is to be encouraged. The field social scientist – who can be an anthropologist or have another social science profile (such as a qualitative health systems researcher) – could be part of a multi-disciplinary team that includes anthropologists and political scientists. This broader team can be based at Headquarters, other field settings, or other non-MSF institutions, and can deliver a broader range of expertise than that of a single social scientist.

We must also invest in developing knowledge of qualitative methodologies in field medical staff so that they can perform qualitative studies themselves with ongoing support from external social scientists. This brings significant advantages in terms of continuity, as those field staff will then maintain ongoing dialogues with the communities in question. As an example, in an MSF programme in the south of Chad, a nurse community activity manager and her team are currently receiving technical support from a health geographer based in Paris to administer a village-based analysis and dialogue on women and children's access to care.

As with any process of professionalisation, there is a risk that the consolidation of the anthropologist 'role' within MSF could result in our medical operational teams failing to listen to and understand the people they are there to assist. As an organisation, we have started to acknowledge that our model of operations-driven programming sometimes results in responses that are poorly centred around population needs.[5] Over the coming years, we are more likely to make use of the external perspective and expertise of social scientists. How, then, can we ensure that medical operational teams remain constantly curious and open to their environment, that they continue to reflect on who are our patients and who is 'the community', and that they retain the confidence to reach out to people to ask questions when necessary? Will the involvement of social scientists increase the distance between Operations and communities, or will the sharing of anthropological tools and perspectives trigger curiosity in our operational teams, a drive for a better understanding of MSF's role in that context, and the often unwitting part we ourselves play in local dynamics?

Notes

1 Chira is a disease of spiritual origins that people get from provoking the anger of the ancestors by not respecting seniority in general, and especially during sex rites. Symptomatology of Chira is equivalent to the one of HIV.
2 AIDS, Population, and Health Integrated Assistance – an NGO consortium financed by USAID.
3 AIDS, Population, and Health Integrated Assistance, including family health – an NGO consortium financed by USAID.
4 Different levels of MSF operations; the Desk is located in the headquarters, the Coordination team is in Nairobi and the Field is at the project level.
5 MSF international board (IB) internal paper: *A Call for Change: Challenging MSF's Status Quo on Evolution and Growth* (March 2018).

References

Abi-Saab, M., (2017). *End of mission report 2017*. MSF archives, Operational Centre Paris.
Burtscher, D., (2008). *"TB is a disease that is flying to the air". Traditional concepts and perception of TB and DR TB and the possibility of HBC, Shiselweni region, Swaziland*. MSF archives, Operational Centre Geneva.
Burtscher, D. and Velibanti, D., (2011). *"You see it, you know it, but you don't say it". Community based perception of HIV and AIDS Testing, counseling and ARV treatment Shiselweni region, Swaziland Patient*. MSF archives, Operational Centre Geneva.
Burtscher, D., Velibanti, D. and Bongekile, D., (2018). *"She is like my mother". Views and experiences of DR-TB patients and their treatment supporters regarding community-based DR-TB treatment. A PhotoVoice project in rural Shiselweni, Eswatini*. MSF archives, Operational Centre Geneva.
Genevier, C., (2007). *End of mission report 1996 to 1998 then 2003 to 2007*. MSF archives, Operational Centre Paris.
Granich, R., Crowley, S., Vitoria, M., Lo, Y-R. et al., (2010). Highly active antiretroviral treatment for the prevention of HIV transmission. *Journal of the International Aids Society*. **13**(1). doi:10.1186/1758-2652-13-1
Kovačič, V., (2010). *Access for more – overcome barriers to access to HIV/AIDS care in Homa Bay district, Kenya*. MSF archives, Operational Centre Paris.
MoH Kenya, (2009). *Kenya national AIDS strategic plan III*. Nairobi: Ministry of Health Kenya.
MSF, (2009a). *Maputo statement. A renewed vision for MSF on HIV/AIDS from the field*. MSF archives, Maputo.
MSF, (2009b). *Annual operational review*. MSF France, MSF archives, Operational Centre Paris.
MSF, (2011). *Planning meeting minutes*. MSF archives, Operational Centre Paris.
MSF, (2012). *Ndihwa HIV indicator population survey*. MSF Epicentre Paris.

MSF, (2015). *End of mission report.* Pascale Lissouba COMMOB manager, MSF archives, Operational Centre Paris.

MSF, (2016). *End of mission report.* Mariana Abi-Saab, MSF archives, Operational Centre Paris.

MSF, (2017). *End of mission report 2012–2017.* MSF France HoM, MSF archives, Operational Centre Paris.

Rahem, K., (2001). *Chira ou la malédiction des ancêtres: tuberculose pulmonaire et sida chez les Luo et les Suba du Kenya.* MSF archives, Operational Centre Paris.

Stellmach, D., (2016). *Coordination in crisis: the practice of medical humanitarian emergency.* PhD thesis, University of Oxford. Available from: https://ora.ox.ac.uk/objects/uuid:c81d8b4a-4e73-4bbb-b66f-7c84885ab9b8

Véran, J-F., (2017). *Why is HIV prevalence so high in Homa Bay County?* MSF archives, Operational Centre Paris.

Wright, R., (2017). *The rain. the milk, the drought, the death: an anthropological perspective. Dollo Zone, Somali region.* MSF archives, Operational Centre Amsterdam.

3

ETHICAL CONSIDERATIONS AND ANTHROPOLOGY

The MSF experience

Beverley Stringer, Renée Teernstra, Darryl Stellmach and Emilie Venables

How ethics in social science are framed

Ethical considerations and dilemmas are embedded in medical practice: what treatment will be best in this patient's situation? What can be done when someone refuses treatment? How can the harm of treatment be minimised? As patients and their carers may have vulnerabilities, it is the duty of the physician to protect the interest of the patient to the best of their ability.

Historically, the practice of ethics in medicine was the personal responsibility of a physician, to be informed about the ethical considerations affecting individual patients. Over time, the focus has shifted to designing and regulating generalised ethical frameworks and their corresponding constructs, such as protocols and review boards. Considerations have extended beyond individual patients to include, for example, medical samples (Brannan et al., 2012).

Many of the ethical agreements constructed are based for the large part on four basic principles as laid out by Beauchamp and Childress (2012): autonomy, non-maleficence, beneficence and justice (Sharif & Bugo, 2015; Rauprich & Vollmann, 2011). While there is continued discussion around these concepts (Cowley, 2005; Christen et al., 2014), a full review of which is outside the scope of this chapter, it is commonly agreed that the work physicians do should adhere to universal ethical standards, as this benefits not just patients, but society as a whole. As Cowley states:

> no relationship, no family, no institution, no society could ever hold itself together without an enormous amount of ethical agreement.
>
> *(p. 742)*

When looking at the broader field of medicine and clinical research, it follows logically that any researcher working with human subjects in a (para-)medical setting

62 Beverley Stringer et al.

should also uphold ethical standards (Maeckelberghe & Schröder-Bäck, 2017). The intention of the revised Helsinki Declaration (1964), and others that followed such as the Belmont Report (Great Britain, 1979), is to regulate ethics in this kind of research setting (World Medical Association, 2013).

While primarily known as an emergency humanitarian medical organisation, Médecins Sans Frontières also conducts in-house research to support medical field operations. The goal of MSF research is practical and immediate: studies must be of direct, demonstrable benefit to MSF's patients and operations. Most MSF research is clinical or epidemiological, and focussed on medical or public health practice. Thus, research in MSF is planned and undertaken in line with the norms and expectations of clinical and public health research. Almost all MSF research is conducted within this medical framework, and MSF social science research is expected to set goals, methods and outcomes according to the same expectations. So far, operational research has been driven by the need for continuous improvement and innovation in MSF medical programmes that can be measured and monitored:

> Historically, research was not seen as core to the mission of MSF. However, during its history, MSF has constantly developed innovative protocols and tools, in response to unmet field needs.
>
> *(Schopper et al., 2015, p. 1)*

The biomedical research model places heavy emphasis on the research protocol as the foundation and guiding document of the research process. The protocol exists, primarily, to ensure the welfare of the study participants, but also to ensure the integrity of the research process, the quality of data and the probity of the medico-scientific enterprise. Research institutions – and MSF is by no means an exception – tend to adopt a principle-based bioethical approach which places importance on the autonomy of the participant with equal emphasis on their voluntary and informed consent to join the study (Kingori, 2013; Simpson, 2011). As Kingori (2013) suggests, this approach makes it easy to answer and audit bioethical questions: "it allows researchers to produce (if called upon) signed consent forms from research participants as tangible evidence that ethics have been 'done'". For MSF, the duty of beneficence in research is keenly relevant, given that most research is conducted among acutely vulnerable subjects, in such times as mass conflict or disaster (Schopper et al., 2015; Tansey et al., 2017). However, the biomedical blueprint for research protocols, developed for lab-based or case-control studies, has a different purpose and effect when applied to field studies in an open setting. In these circumstances, a protocol can enumerate fixed procedures or routines, make clear the principles that guide the research, outline the standards that must be met to ensure research integrity, and establish contingency plans to be implemented in the case of a range of anticipated complications. From the point of view of a social science researcher, there are several issues to consider during the process of ethical reviews, which may occur at several stages of the research, and, as we discuss later in the chapter, these often involve multiple reviews from different institutions with varying frameworks.

There is criticism about the bureaucratic creep of ethical review boards (Haggerty, 2004), with critics equating ethics regulation to censorship and the restriction of researcher autonomy (Pollock, 2012). The multiple local, national and institutional ethics review committees and boards that have sprung up since the first Helsinki Declaration in 1964 create tensions due to the ensuing bureaucracy, overlap and subsequent lack of efficiency these review committees or boards then impose on researchers (Savulescu, 2017). Hammersley and Traianou (2011) summarise this by looking at ethical regulation creep and its association with funding in the context of British social science research, primarily citing the Economic and Social Research Council's research ethics framework established in 2005, and the framework for research ethics from 2010, as the moments that ethical guidance moved beyond codes of professional conduct to become the remit of institutional committees. Simpson (2011) shares a 'disquiet' among fellow anthropologists about this 'creep', not least because it distracts from the ethical complexities involved in ethnographic research, and the "fabric of relations that the anthropologist is setting out to engage, understand and describe" (p. 385).

Good ethical relations between people

A system primarily designed for medical research ethics governance will inherently be less able to effectively review social science research with regard to its potential harms and benefits, especially where emphasis on values and principles are not equally shared in the contexts where ethics apply. Social science in MSF (as is mentioned elsewhere in this book) has grown and multiplied as an important contributor in both critique and support of its operations. Those of us who do fieldwork and submit protocols for ethical review can relate to "a paramount concern for the human subject" and how this influences the way anthropological knowledge is shaped and validated (Simpson, 2011, p. 378). As Simpson (2011, p. 380) points out, a "failure to map out the ethics of the social" overlooks the day-to-day ethical realities that social scientists encounter in contexts where it is difficult to apply a categorised, predetermined outlook. This has practical consequences. A biomedical bias makes it difficult for medical colleagues to accept that social scientists can regulate themselves by following their own professional codes of conduct, which can be an alternative to external review. For this book, all ethnographic elements were overseen through the medical directors (who were overseeing research) as per the ethical framework at the particular time assessments were carried out. Many of the regulatory institutional frameworks, academic or otherwise, are based on a biomedical model, even though this may not be appropriate for anthropology and the social sciences. There is a tangible difference in the immediacy of harm a physician and their practice of medicine can cause to a patient (or research subject) from that a social science researcher can cause (Sheehan et al., 2017). While it is true

64 Beverley Stringer et al.

that social science is conducted with human subjects, this type of research does not involve making treatment decisions for a patient that can cause direct or lasting physical damage. Anticipation of harm in this instance hinges on relationships, trust and power – not only with the subject of research, but with their families, and with peers and colleagues, and with the wider social community and environment. We will look at why ethics should be different for anthropology later in the chapter, but research generally may be served better by considering human subjects in the context of their social day-to-day circumstances and, as Dingwall (2008) suggests, the extent of ethical regulation in this domain may be unjustified. While helpful differentiation has been addressed by many academic institutions through the application of high, low and, in some cases, minimal risk ethical review, this hasn't changed, overall, how reviews are traditionally framed. The discretion of the anthropologist is overlooked, and an intentional growth of moralism in research ethics persists (Hammersley & Traianou, 2011). The key point here relates to the problem the universal application of 'extrinsic values' has with regard to values specific to the place and the people involved in the research. Hammersley and Traianou suggest that "judgement has to be made, for example, about what degree and kinds of autonomy should be respected, as well as what 'respect' means in any particular context, and so on" (p. 386).

When looking at the social sciences within a humanitarian setting, this contrast becomes even larger, resulting in calls for an entirely different set of research ethics for disaster settings, because ethical challenges in clinical settings are not comparable to humanitarian settings (O'Mathúna, 2015). Historically, for MSF, research was not seen as a core task, but because of its pursuit of uniform procedures and a growing demand for standards in field research, in 2001 MSF established an external ethical review board or ERB (Schopper et al., 2009). Initially, this ERB used a framework designed by Emanuel et al. (2004), which was adapted by the then ERB in 2013 to accommodate practical applications of what is described as operational research, including an iterative and learning approach to planning research and ethical practice. This was an ERB attuned to the needs of the research community it works with and showing that, even with a specialised review committee like the MSF ERB, the focus moves beyond clinical research.

Though there are many good arguments to make against a 'one-size-fits-all' medical ethics research governance for social sciences, that is not to say that there should be no form of governance for social sciences research at all; if anything, research in humanitarian settings intensifies the ethical dilemmas (O'Mathúna, 2015). The revised ethical framework in MSF (2015) has, in part, contributed to this adaptation, because the researcher is encouraged to participate in a dialogue about ethical issues in more detail, rather than impose 'quasi-legalistic rules'. This, in turn, enables the researcher to reflect more deeply about their intentions. It takes into account how ethical issues are intertwined with methodological issues, and is sensitive to the social science approach. The framework describes the process as now "more of an active process, with the researcher as a participant, rather than the victim of an alien and abstract set of rules" (MSF Ethical Review Board, 2015, p. 5).

The new framework encourages a protocol that can enumerate fixed procedures or routines, make clear the principles that guide the research, outline the standards that must be met to ensure research integrity, and establish contingency plans to be implemented in the case of a range of anticipated complications. What this innovation does not calculate is the positionality of the researcher in both context and focus, and discussion is needed on what is required to achieve realistic, ethical responsibility and best practice in social science research, both from the bodies responsible for review and the researchers themselves. What is of most interest, and will be elaborated in the next section, is not only how researchers treat people participating in the research, but also what is happening as a consequence of doing the research with the diversity of people and settings involved (Hammersley & Traianou, 2011).

Why ethics are different for social science: a focus on risks and benefits

In the summer of 2015, Darryl Stellmach convened a workshop to bring together practitioners working with MSF with a mix of other field anthropologists to discuss the ethical complexities of crisis in their own field sites.[1] Later, a special issue of the *Journal of the Anthropological Society of Oxford* (2016) presented some of the papers from that day, highlighting a consensus that, for anthropologists working in humanitarian settings, ethical considerations are constant and implicate all subjects involved in the research, not least the researchers themselves. Together with an acknowledgement of what Nordstrom and Robben (1995) refer to as the improvisational practice of the anthropologist, fieldwork can remain a genuine endeavour, reflective of what is happening in a shifting world. As Wendy James argued on the day, anthropology practised in times of crisis is not about emergencies, but about understanding the contingencies people confront in the wider social context (James, 2016). It is in this ever-changing world that the practice of ethics plays out and where certain risks and benefits come to the fore.

Participants' accounts of carrying out fieldwork in humanitarian settings exposed several quandaries and ethical demands. Either the researcher is embedded within the aid system (as are the MSF anthropologists featured in this book), or those more peripheral to the aid system at times find themselves reliant on non-governmental organisations for logistics and security support (Felix da Costa, 2016). Such differences in how anthropologists do fieldwork has implications for how they are viewed in the field and how easy it is to make social connections. Technology can also make researchers less dependent on traditional anthropological practices such as local immersion, learning language and building networks; with phones and the internet, there is access to information about events as they occur (Duffield, 2010). In the workshop, Felix da Costa (2016, p. 39) shared her own experiences of the ethical reality of addressing hierarchies of knowledge: linked to "power and responsibility when telling a story . . . [as an anonymous colleague of hers noted] . . . it's rumour when 'they' say it but knowledge when 'we' say it".

66 Beverley Stringer et al.

Because of the concern about human vulnerability, suffering and the positionality of the research, Kunnath (2013) saw it to be important to admit that an anthropologist working with people affected by structural violence and inequalities is compelled to participate in the struggles together with people affected. Within anthropology and the social sciences, there is an emergence of new ethics to promote social justice, and this in turn highlights the limits of current guidance. On some occasions, it is not possible but to be partisan; where there is political polarisation, acting in a passive or neutral way makes it difficult to 'do no harm'. Equally, for issues of consent, it is often inappropriate to obtain an agreement to sign a written permission. Sariola and Simpson found this in Sri Lanka while looking at bioethics discourse among health workers involved in a clinical trial, which viewed ethics as "responsibilities and duties toward others rather than individual rights" (2011, p. 517). It is not consent that is disputed, more the application when international guidance assumes a universal understanding of the 'human research subject' model (Sariola & Simpson, 2011). Questions of disclosure in humanitarian contexts are compounded, especially when gathering politically sensitive data that may end up in the wrong hands. This is what Nordstrom and Robben (1995, p. 12) refer to as the transformation of "violent events into narrative accounts".

During the Ebola outbreak in West Africa, the embedded anthropologist was able to access operational knowledge – and therefore activate preferences linked to this. In such instances, observation of the suffering and the failures of biomedical responses to the outbreak is never an objective or straightforward process, but requires permanent ethical reassessment and improvisation. A constant concern can be what to do with anthropological knowledge in such instances. What happens to such information in highly politicised contexts? During the 2018 Ebola outbreak in the Democratic Republic of Congo, members of the community are described as 'resistant' to the heavily securitised biomedical intervention. Thus, anthropologists involved in this crisis have a responsibility to manage the fragility with which trust is engendered and lost due to communities being persistently disappointed and subjected to the biopolitics of the global health response.

Finally, what happens after the disaster or epidemic has passed, but there is still a scarcity of resources and poor health care? As Le Marcis (2015) found in an Ivory Coast clinical trial, the evidence of more effective and better tolerated treatment may end the trial, on the one hand, but on the other hand, open up the potential for inequities – especially in contexts where poor access to health and medicine affects everyone. This highlights the socio-political and ethical responsibility to commit to political engagement to address such inequities overall, and this is above and beyond reporting the results of research.

How MSF frames ethical review

From the outset, it was perceived to be essential to maintain the independence of the MSF ERB from MSF itself. To avoid a conflict of interest and ensure independence, ERB members cannot have a working relationship with MSF during their

Ethical considerations and anthropology **67**

tenure. Peopled by a variety of specialists from different technical backgrounds and geographical areas, the ERB acts to ensure ethical due diligence in field research across all MSF operational centres, linked to but independent from the institution itself. It is important to consider how far the MSF ERB allows institutional risk to be a factor in its approach. As Verhallen (2016) points out, often 'risk anxiety' and 'risk aversion' may sway ERB feedback. In principle, all MSF operational research conducted under the umbrella of the organisation should function with a protocol that has been reviewed and approved by the MSF ERB, in addition to a local ethical research board.

For social science and anthropology, there has been a growth in activities and an increase in mixed methods research, as mapped out in more detail in the introduction to this book. Most research projects undergo an ethical review unless they fulfil established exemption criteria – putting the onus on the medical directors in MSF to develop policy on an *a posteriori* analysis of routine data collection and to follow ethical guidance on prospective data that is descriptive or evaluative for certain activities. Ethical considerations in practice, such as confidentiality, minimising harm and acknowledging benefits and relevance of local collaborations, should be included as standard (Schopper et al., 2015). Elaborating on this guidance, we would suggest that people involved in operational research in MSF consider the type of studies, assessments and research that need ethical review. We would maintain that all researchers should be alert to the ethical problems they encounter day to day, and make decisions on how to resolve them through the research process. Consent is not dealt with as a one-off event, but is repeatedly checked as the research develops; anthropologists, like those in other professions, refer to their code of conduct and associated professional guidance. This centres on issues to consider that may include variations of informed consent, the degree of confidentiality and anonymity that can be assured, anonymisation procedures, protection from harm, right to withdraw at any time, and the management and storage of sensitive data (Association of Social Anthropologists of the UK and Commonwealth, 2011). While these things are useful to debate, it is essential to recognise the importance of ongoing review by researchers involved in the work (Kunnath, 2013; Verhallen, 2016). For the ethnographies presented in this book, ethical approvals followed the MSF framework in place at the time.

The example in Box 3.1 highlights the potential for modifying ethics in MSF and why we need to look at social science and anthropology differently. At the moment, a marked attention to methodological challenges is actively combined with ethical considerations, so for example, the techniques for collecting, analysing and presenting information gathered by anthropologists are approached in the same way as our survey-oriented colleagues. The improvisational nature of ethnographic fieldwork, its participatory form and the need to blend with the context in which we do our fieldwork, all make reviewing more complex, so increasing the dialogue and engagement on such issues is seen to be beneficial for ERBs and researchers. There is much more potential for considering how best to accommodate the considerations characteristic of anthropology to allow for both reviews and research

68 Beverley Stringer et al.

to take place. The ethical framework for research lists exemptions from the ERB and nutritional and vaccination surveys are good examples of this because they rely on techniques as the skills of the ethnographer do, to make relationships based on "trust, respect and avoidance of delimiting the subject" (Simpson, 2011, p. 385). There is value in creating a 'hotline' for a dialogue about ethics whereby we are able to register an 'ethics of the social' shifting the emphasis to principles of justice (Simpson, 2011).

The profiles of members on the ethical review board increasingly include social science experience, and at the same time, their practice of reviewing this type of work has contributed to clearer understanding of areas of concern with such research from the perspective of reviewer and researchers. As shown previously, the iterative approach, highlighted in the most recent MSF guidance for researchers seeking ethical approval, should lend itself to improved reviews.

How ethical issues for social science are navigated within MSF

The contexts in which social science research takes place – such as ethnographic fieldwork, or, more often in an MSF context, the application of anthropological practice that simply dialogues with communities – pose ethical challenges of their own. One of the most frequent, and fair, comments asked by ethical review boards in many different contexts is whether the researcher has considered the risk of therapeutic misconception that may occur when someone working within an MSF project and providing a medical service is also a researcher asking questions. This has been asked on several occasions in relation to proposed research with patients of mental health services, in which the psychologist or counsellor working on the project is also the researcher, as well as in relation to patients being recruited for research studies from clinical waiting lists.

Anthropological research within MSF usually happens in two settings: first, within the confines of a health care facility in which MSF is working, whether a hospital, clinic, rural health post or Ebola Management Centre, and secondly, in the wider community. This wider community encompasses venues such as schools, church halls, gathering spaces used by traditional leaders, village meeting points and, in some instances, people's homes.

Conducting fieldwork in people's homes often raises a red flag for ethical review boards, as it could be considered an invasion of privacy or raise additional questions about the security of the researcher, depending on the context. If someone was living with HIV and had not told their family, for example, the presence of an MSF car in an area where MSF is known for its work with people living with HIV could cause accidental disclosure and community gossip. However, this risk can be mitigated by asking the individual where they would prefer the interview to be held, and only coming to their home if invited and checking in advance about the presence of an MSF car or other identifying information. In other cases, the person may prefer to be interviewed at home, for example, because they want to reduce the number of visits they make to a health care facility associated with HIV, as this in turn reduces the number of chances they have of being seen by someone

Ethical considerations and anthropology **69**

they know while they are there. Due to the nature of social science research, the content of data observations or text narratives is difficult to predict until later in the process, so issues such as harm, intrusion and sensitive disclosures are better managed as well-thought-out probable scenarios such as those described. Equally, the relationship between researcher and participant requires a personal interaction that is fundamental for data gathering, and this includes reflection that ensures coercion and power do not undermine trust.

An example of gaining ethical approval for ethnographic fieldwork in South Sudan is shown in Box 3.1.

BOX 3.1 EXAMPLE OF GAINING ETHICAL APPROVAL: SOUTH SUDAN (STELLMACH, 2013)

In line with this standard, after my research concept note was provisionally accepted, the next step was to work the proposal into a research protocol for review by MSF's ERB. This process ended up taking much longer than I anticipated, because the aim was to have the strongest possible document before review. Once the document had been submitted to the ERB, the approval of the protocol, with minor revisions and clarifications, took a further six weeks. I achieved final approval in late October 2013 (see Stellmach [2013] for the final protocol).

This was not the end of the ethics process. One of the stipulations of the MSF protocol review was that I should seek local ethics approval in my destination country. Since I would not know my destination country until midway through the study, this could not be undertaken in advance. I would have to work through the ethics process at the time. In South Sudan, this was not straightforward. The absence of functioning government research structures in the country meant that I would need to seek an informal approval through a protocol reading by local academics and, in Leer, discussion with members of the community.

Thus, over the course of my research, I pursued three different ethics clearance processes: Oxford's anthropological ethics approval, protocol development through the MSF ERB and a local ethics review in South Sudan. Each process was aware of the other processes, and each sought to address ethical and methodological concerns unique to a specific constituency. Each ensured (to a degree) that I had the support and approval of those constituencies within my study: the university and professional anthropologists, aid workers and medical researchers, and South Sudanese people themselves.

Of the three processes, the university process was the shortest and most straightforward. A committee reviewed a short form detailing my proposed research. It sought evidence of a feasible, safe and well-thought-out research programme, while simultaneously recognising the – at times – improvisational process of anthropological fieldwork. Since my participant observation would be conducted in an institutional framework, under the umbrella of MSF, focussed primarily on 'elites' (aid workers, as opposed to aid recipients) and would not interfere directly with the health and wellbeing of my subjects, it was considered a straightforward plan. The time from application to approval took less than a month.

The short Oxford review would contrast sharply with the MSF protocol document, which ran to 30 pages with annexes, and took most of a year to draft. The different weight placed upon these two institutional processes was telling. Oxford focussed only on ethical due diligence, leaving the nuts and bolts of study objectives and methods to the academic supervision process. MSF's ERB required a formal protocol to actively assess feasibility and make stipulations or suggestions on multiple aspects of the planned study. For example, the ERB expected explicit policies for participant consent, data management and a disclosure procedure should I observe malpractice. Project outcomes and potential benefits were weighed against risk. The protocol became the project's central referent document. The development of the MSF protocol was similar to a project proposal or major application for institutional research funding (which, effectively, it was: a request for research sponsorship). As part of the process, I would also draft and sign a research agreement and data management agreement. Thus, the concept and role of 'ethics review' expanded to a wider scrutiny of project feasibility. The MSF process was exacting, but – once completed – conferred a great degree of legitimacy on the research, particularly among members of the institution itself. In addition to protecting patients and the agency itself from risk, the MSF practice implied that inefficient research was unethical research. To be ethical in an emergency setting, where time and other resources are scarce, research should impose a minimal burden on host populations and MSF alike.

The third process, the ethics review within South Sudan, was difficult to obtain, since there were no functioning research ethics committees in the country. Ultimately, a South Sudanese academic facilitated an informal in-country review, as he agreed to read through and comment upon the protocol. This review helped to situate the research within the local context, and in particular, to highlight local sensitivities. In South Sudan, there were two key sensitivities. First, sensitivities of local communities that, among other things, often experienced research fatigue. Given the ethics and security protocols of foreign agencies and universities, only a handful of regions or communities were readily accessible to researchers (i.e. considered safe and secure from an institutional risk management perspective, which often implied day trips within an easy drive of a reliable airport or other amenities). So, the same communities were typically visited by a variety of researchers, asking similar and often intrusive questions, and occasionally making promises about the changes that would materialise from the research. Community members saw little practical impact from their participation in a parade of interviews, surveys, questionnaires and focus groups (for more on this phenomenon, see de Waal [1989] and his discussion of 'disaster tourism'). The second sensitivity in South Sudan was even more serious: sensitivities of the national security services, who viewed researchers with suspicion – as potential spies or reporters who could compromise national security. South Sudan's record on press freedoms and transparency in its security services is well documented. Fortunately, in my case, since my study was primarily focussed on MSF as an institution, it did not aggravate either community or security sensitivities. Nevertheless, when I arrived at my Leer field site, I sought local approval from both these constituencies.

Local ethical reviews have been sought for some of the MSF projects anthropologists are currently involved in – with mixed results. In some cases, reviews have had a positive influence on collaboration and understanding. Often, the capacity for social science research at a local level is limited, but this is not necessarily a limiting factor, because training has been welcomed and carried out both formally at local institutional levels and more recently through training local field researchers who work as principal investigators for social science and anthropological research. In other places, there may be no local ethical review board in the country in which the planned research is to be conducted, or anthropologists may try to submit their protocols to a local university ethical review board – only to be told that the committee can only review clinical protocols, is unable to accept submissions from researchers based outside the country or, in some cases, that a local co-investigator (who may have a political interest in being part of the study) is required to act as main investigator – but in name only. This last point raises an important question about the code of practice for anthropologists in terms of relationships outside the immediate research subject: with colleagues, the discipline itself and with host governments and officials. It is essential for the visiting anthropologist to acknowledge the presence of local researchers already working in the same setting, with a view to include them. Conflicts of interest, both professional and political, are a key consideration, especially in humanitarian settings. Insistence on officials participating who may not be accepted by participants in the study will present problems, as will an inadequate collaboration – for example, despite good intentions, a visiting researcher may fail to team up with a local researcher, or vice versa.

Now that demand has increased for anthropological and social science research in MSF, the following points have arisen to be considered by researchers and the MSF ERB:

1   Relations with research participants: there needs to be an emphasis on trust and coercion, power imbalance and scenarios for disclosure. Consent from

72 Beverley Stringer et al.

participants for both conversations and observations would first and foremost be concerned with participants being made aware of the presence of the researcher and the purpose of the study. Consent needs to be continuously checked and, in most cases, confirmed verbally, due to either political sensitivities within the setting for research or contextualised practice. It should also take into account the family as a decision-making unit, as argued by Sariola and Simpson (2011). They show how in Asia, bioethics differ with notions of ethics that are perceived "holistically in context of the life situation" (Sariola & Simpson, 2011, p. 517). In addition, we nominate that all aspects of information will need to be approved by the study subjects; how it is presented, stored, identified and used. Intrusion and privacy should be a central marker when developing scenarios of potential harm for participants and the wider social environment and community.

2   Relations with colleagues and host governments: there should be a reflection on potential conflicts of interest, non-harmful collaborative partnerships and the significance of local laws and wider societal politics and the bearing this may have on the research. Irresponsible actions by a researcher or research team may put access at risk for others. Covert research that undermines trust and openness should be acknowledged as problematic.

3   Methods: an improvisational approach and a diversity of methods may mean that tools are not well developed until research begins. Research may need to adapt to the setting, so repeated visits and feedback to acknowledge the relationships with research participants should be part of the ethical considera-tion – an ethics of social interaction related to moral obligations toward, for example, a political engagement with health systems for increased access to care during and after a research process.

4   Funding: impartiality of funding is a fundamental principle in MSF; due dili-gence will be applied to ensure certain priorities are not imposed, and fair representation is maintained.

There is a current assumption that ethics are inherent to the act of research, but for anthropology and social science, we need ethical guidance that develops this sup-position. A good start would be to avoid a biomedical lens and focus instead on the participants in the research, the context of the research and the role of researcher. In MSF, the request would be for ethics committees to support not only a contextualised approach to ethics that takes into account subject matter and details, but also a form of engagement with social science researchers that extends the open dialogue and itera-tive intentions toward the development of new paradigms that can adopt an 'ethics of the social'. The ethical process in research is continuous, and the values and principles that steer the ethical focus are not always given the same level of importance by the people in the places where we do 'ethics' (Sariola & Simpson, 2011; Le Marcis, 2015).

A way forward

Anthropologists and social scientists doing research in humanitarian settings are well placed to guide responses to ethical dilemmas as they emerge in fieldwork.

Ethical considerations and anthropology **73**

Drafting specific and nuanced local guidance for conducting social science research in these situations and discussing transferable professional codes of conduct would be a useful addition (Lowton, 2016). Within MSF, we would propose that research should incorporate an organisational ability to accommodate how people within a community may perceive the research within its own modes of analysis, giving importance to how the information collected and the findings will be represented. Similarly, the *postcolonial–decolonial* nexus between knowledge and power should help underline how a principled based ethics approach is limited when applied in such circumstances (Bhambra, 2014). In other words, we should avoid imposing external categories and be open to co-definitions of the study content and process so that we can also consider how people want to participate and what they want to know. Use of participatory approaches that engage in social relations and issues of power, inequities and justice put emphasis on how to navigate an "ethics of the social subject" (Simpson, 2011, p. 380). For the Ebola crisis in the Democratic Republic of Congo (2018–2019), this has been critical to negotiating the fragile nature of trust with people when trying to prevent the risk of illness and death in a context where there is no faith in the health care system or the response to the outbreak. Similarly, frontline data collectors in Kenya demonstrate through their day-to-day encounters of social inequities a preference in their bioethical practice for justice, beneficence over autonomy (Kingori, 2013). Preparing protocols in the local context, and training those conducting the research in the process, would help address these concerns (Wood, 2006, p. 374).

Changing the way that ethical reviews occur may allow for more direct dialogue with reviewers (a kind of reviewer-meets-reviewed situation). Some committees ask researchers to present their studies in person in front of a board, allowing the chance for immediate clarifications and instant responses instead of a lengthy back-and-forth written procedure that can take weeks or months. A face-to-face dialogue can help researchers respond to questions from the ERBs, and vice versa. For example, certain questions and answers can be anticipated in light of what may or may not be contextually acceptable; the issue of sensitivities around consent could be emphasised to enable ERB members to understand more fully the context in which researchers are working. It allows, as Lowton puts it, the possibility to "show our competence in our research planning and why their ethical framing may be limiting" (2016, p. 52). Such dialogues should include power relations analysis, and moderation of this should be a systematic consideration within the processes of the ERB itself and for ERB approvals, not only for social science, but for all research.

The provisional, adaptive nature of anthropological research can be a problem for ERBs, but this can be addressed by considering different scenarios and making plans to accommodate them. An ethics 'hotline' – or, as Simpson (2011, p. 389) suggests, "mentors as ethical consultants" – could also facilitate discussion on urgent dilemmas faced in contexts especially related to disclosures, answerability and preferred actions. Additionally, for particularly sensitive research – such as a study on sexual and gender-based violence – it has been proposed that separate stages of ethics approval or responses to ethical concerns could be developed to analyse nuances of contexts at local level more easily. Such local-level exchanges

74 Beverley Stringer et al.

will promote adaptation of a pluralistic ethical approach that is able to integrate non-Western epistemology, as well as virtue and relational ethics alongside those that are principled based.

For anthropologists working in difficult or emergency situations, it is important to share their incremental experiences of where and how ethical conflict and dilemmas occur in their practice. The ethical limits of the humanitarian relationship, the pervasive presence of power and the positioning of MSF are considerations that are not discussed enough. Anthropologists recognise that the vast majority of people working within MSF are continuously checking their practices to maintain the trust of the people they are working with and to ensure they do no harm, so ethical considerations are not therefore solely reliant on or limited to a review committee. Anytime MSF responds, there are ethical dilemmas of what response is appropriate, who to work with or not, whether to open a project or not. To improve the way humanitarian organisations react to local situations, more effort should be made to help fellow professionals improve their practice by describing dilemmas previously faced and resolved. At the same time, field-based anthropologists and other social science practitioners should be nominated to be part of ethical review boards.

Note

1 *Fieldwork Ethics in Crisis: Practical Considerations for Ethnographic Research in Complex Emergencies,* a workshop supported by the School of Anthropology and Museum of Ethnography (SAME) and Wolfson College, University of Oxford (Stellmach & Beshar, 2016).

References

Association of Social Anthropologists of the UK and the Commonwealth, (2011). *Ethical guidelines for good research practice.* Available from: www.theasa.com

Beauchamp, T.L. and Childress, J.F., (2012). *Principles of biomedical ethics.* 7th ed. Oxford: Oxford University Press. doi:10.1136/jme.28.5.332-a

Bhambra, G.K., (2014). Postcolonial and decolonial dialogues. *Postcolonial Studies.* **17**(2), 115–121. doi:10.1080/13688790.2014.966414

Brannan, S., Sommerville, A., English, V. and British Medical Association, (2012). *Medical ethics today: The BMA's handbook of ethics and law.* Chichester, West Sussex: BMJ Books, John Wiley. doi:10.1002/9781444355666

Christen, M., Ineichen, C. and Tanner, C., (2014). How "moral" are the principles of biomedical ethics? – a cross-domain evaluation of the common morality hypothesis. *BMC Medical Ethics.* **15**(47). doi:10.1186/1472-6939-15-47

Cowley, C., (2005). The dangers of medical ethics. *Journal of Medical Ethics.* **31**(12), 739–742. doi:10.1136%2Fjme.2005.011908

de Waal, A., (2005). *Famine that kills: Darfur, Sudan.* New York City: Oxford University Press.

Dingwall, R., (2008). The ethical case against ethical regulation in humanities and social science research. *Twenty-First Century Society.* **3**(1), 1–12. doi:10.1080/17450140701749189

Duffield, M., (2010). Risk-Management and the fortified aid compound: everyday life in post-interventionary society. *Journal of Intervention and Statebuilding.* **4**(4), 453–474. doi:10.1080/17502971003700993

Ethical considerations and anthropology **75**

Emanuel, E., Wendler, D. and Grady, C., (2004). What makes clinical research in developing countries ethical? The benchmarks of ethical research. *Journal of Infectious Diseases*. **189**(5), 930–937. doi:10.1086/381709

Felix da Costa, D., (2016). The ethics of researching in conflict: personal reflections from Greater Pibor and South Sudan. *Journal of the Anthropological Society of Oxford*. **8**(1), 31–43.

Great Britain, Department of Health Education and Welfare, (1979). *The Belmont report: ethical principles and guidelines for the protection of human subjects of research*. London: Office for Human Research Protections. Available from: www.hhs.gov/ohrp/regulations-and-policy/belmont-report/read-the-belmont-report/index.html

Haggerty, K.D., (2004). Ethics creep: governing social science research in the name of ethics. *Qualitative Sociology*. **27**(4), 391–414.

Hammersley, M. and Traianou, A., (2011). Moralism and research ethics: a Machiavellian perspective. *International Journal of Social Research Methodology*. **14**(5), 379–390. doi:10.10 80/13645579.2011.562412

James, W., (2016). The innocence of fieldwork lost in the shifting landscapes of war: a case study from the Upper Blue Nile (1965–2015). *Journal of the Anthropological Society of Oxford*. **8**(1), 16–30.

Kingori, P., (2013). Experiencing everyday ethics in context: frontline data collectors perspective and practices in bioethics. *Social Science and Medicine*. **98**, 361–370.

Kunnath, G.J., (2013). Anthropology's ethical dilemmas: reflections from the Maoist fields of India. *Current Anthropology*. **54**(6), 740–752. doi:10.1086/673860

Le Marcis, F., (2015). Life promises and failed family ties: expectations and disappointment within a clinical trial (Ivory Coast). *Anthropology and Medicine*. **22**(3), 1–14. doi:10.1080/13648470.2015.1081671

Lowton, K., (2016). The inner workings of an ethics review board for social science research: reflections on research in difficult contexts. *Journal of the Anthropological Society of Oxford*. **8**(1), 44–54.

Maeckelberghe, E.L.M. and Schröder-Bäck, P., (2017). Ethics in public health: call for shared moral public health literacy. *European Journal of Public Health*. **27**(4), 49–51. doi:10.1093/eurpub/ckx154

MSF Ethical Review Board, (2015). *Exemption criteria document no. 1. Retrospective analysis of routinely collected clinical data from pre-existing established programmes*. MSF archives.

Nordstrom, C. and Robben, A.C.G.M., eds., (1995). *Fieldwork under fire: contemporary studies of violence and culture*. Oakland: University of California Press.

O'Mathúna, D., (2015). Research ethics in the context of humanitarian emergencies. *Journal of Evidence Based Medicine*. **8**(1), 31–35. doi:10.1111/jebm.12136

Pollock, K., (2012). Procedure versus process: ethical paradigms and the conduct of qualitative research. *BMC Medical Ethics*. **13**(25). doi:10.1186/1472-6939-13-25

Rauprich, O. and Vollmann, J., (2011). 30 years principles of biomedical ethics: introduction to a symposium on the 6th edition of Tom L Beauchamp and James F Childress' seminal work. *Journal of Medical Ethics*. **37**(8), 454–455. doi:10.1136/jme.2010.039222

Sariola, S. and Simpson, B., (2011). Theorising the 'human subject' in biomedical research: international clinical trials and bioethics discourses in contemporary Sri Lanka. *Social Science and Medicine*. **73**(4), 515–521. doi:10.1016/j.socscimed.2010.11.024

Savulescu, J., (2017). The structure of ethics review: expert ethics committees and the challenge of voluntary research euthanasia. *Journal of Medical Ethics*. **44**(7). doi:10.1136/medethics-2015-103183

Schopper, D., Dawson, A., Upshur, R., Ahmad, A., Jesani, A., Ravinetto, R., Segelid, M.J., Sheel, S. and Singh, J., (2015). Innovations in research ethics governance in humanitarian settings. *BMC Medical Ethics*. **16**(10). doi:10.1186/s12910-015-0002-3

Schopper, D., Upshur, R., Matthys, F., Singh, J.A., Bandewar, S.S., Ahmed, A. and van Dongen, E., (2009). Research ethics review in humanitarian contexts: the experience of the independent ethics review board of Médecins Sans Frontières. *PLoS Medicine.* **6**(7). doi:10.1371/journal.pmed.1000115

Sharif, T. and Bugo, J., (2015). The anthropological approach challenges the conventional approach to bioethical dilemmas: a Kenyan Maasai perspective. *African Health Sciences.* **15**(2), 628–633. doi:10.4314/ahs.v15i2.41

Sheehan, M., Dunn, M. and Sahan, K., (2017). In defence of governance: ethics review and social research. *Journal of Medical Ethics.* **44**(10). doi:10.1136/medethics-2017-104443

Simpson, B., (2011). Ethical moments: future directions for ethical review and ethnography *Journal of the Royal Anthropological Institute.* **17**(2), 377–393.

Stellmach, D., (2013). *Research protocol: the practice of medical humanitarian emergency: ethnography of practitioners' response to nutritional crisis.* Operational Centre Amsterdam: University of Oxford/Médecins Sans Frontières-UK. Available from: http://hdl.handle.net/10144/323862

Stellmach, D. and Beshar, I., (2016). Introduction: the ethics of anthropology in emergencies. *Journal of the Anthropological Society of Oxford.* **8**(1), 1–15.

Tansey, C.M., Anderson, J., Boulanger, R.F., Eckenwiler, L., Pringle, J., Schwartz, L. and Hunt, M., (2017). Familiar ethical issues amplified: how members of research ethics committees describe ethical distinctions between disaster and non-disaster research. *BMC Medical Ethics.* **18**(1), 44. doi:10.1186/s12910-017-0203-z

Verhallen, T., (2016). Tuning to the dance of ethnography: ethics during situated fieldwork in single-mother child protection families. *Current Anthropology.* **57**(4), 452–473. doi:10.1086/687356

Wood, E.J., (2006). The ethical challenges of field research in conflict zones. *Qualitative Sociology.* **29**(3), 373–386. doi:10.1007/s11133-006-9027-8

World Medical Association, (2013). World medical association declaration of Helsinki: ethical principles for medical research involving human subjects. *Journal of the American Medical Association.* **310**(20), 2191–2194. doi:10.1001/jama.2013.281053

4

EMERGENCY IN PRACTICE

Doing an ethnography of malnutrition in South Sudan

Darryl Stellmach

Introduction

In the autumn of 2012, I approached the Medical Director of Médecins Sans Frontières' Operational Centre Amsterdam with a proposal for a PhD anthropology project. I suggested something that hadn't been tried before in MSF, or any other agency, as far as I was aware; a year-long, multi-sited participant observation of a single medical humanitarian emergency, in real time. I would wait at the agency headquarters for something to happen, then follow the emergency teams as an anthropologist, seeing through the lens of aid agency structures and operations, at the headquarters and in the field, as events unfolded over time.

Embedded with MSF's teams, my research focus would be the agency itself; how members understood the nature and extent of the crisis as a coherent and emergent narrative. The research would go where the organisation went in its pursuit of emergency. From the headquarters to the field, my methods, protocols, arrangements and agreements would be preconfigured as much as possible. This would make for a flexible, mobile study capable of following incident and response as they emerged. Metaphorically, just as MSF might prepare a cholera kit – all the material components needed to combat an epidemic, stored in a container ready to dispatch anywhere in the world – I would be a living anthropology kit: a mobile researcher, my head and laptop full of research methods and theory, with as many as possible administrative arrangements prepared ahead of time. A pre-approved research protocol and ethics clearance would make participant observation of emergency feasible, maintaining the most rigorous research practice possible under the circumstances.

It was an ambitious proposal, but I had strong credentials. A Commonwealth Doctoral Scholar and student at Oxford's Institute of Social and Cultural Anthropology, I was also an aid worker with ten years' field experience in medical humanitarian interventions. I developed the research plan with the intention to capitalise

78 Darryl Stellmach

on my experience and connections in the aid sector. These would help me access an institution and set of conditions that were, under normal circumstances, difficult for anthropologists to enter. Thus, I hoped my emergency management experience would allow me to be an anthropologist of emergency management – to be present as members of a medical humanitarian institution came to grips with acute life-and-death crisis.

In seeking a field site for my doctoral study, I could have approached any one of several aid agencies. But to take full advantage of my professional network, my goal was to do the research with the institution where I have spent most of my career – MSF – and, specifically, the headquarters office I was most familiar with: Operational Centre Amsterdam. There I could draw upon on my existing institutional knowledge and network of colleagues. I was aware my role as anthropologist would test old friendships (for example, see Mosse, 2006), but I also hoped my research could benefit those same colleagues who I had worked beside for so long. It would be an original and meaningful reflection on humanitarian action as a life and enterprise.

When I approached MSF in late 2012, I followed its standard procedure for research proposals. I submitted a research concept note that outlined the potential study. Then I waited. I sent a follow-up enquiry. I waited again. It would be two months before I had a reply. I learnt that the proposal had spent time in limbo; medics within the organisation were uncertain about the potential contribution the study would make. The purpose, methods and potential findings were out of synch with MSF's usual (clinical) research agenda. Eventually, I was directed to Beverley Stringer, at that time one of MSF's health policy and research advisors. She would assess the merit and potential of the proposal. Based in the London office, Bev is a nurse practitioner, former field medical coordinator and a trained anthropologist. Following a long phone conversation to review the concept note, Bev was convinced of the potential value of the research. She would become my advocate and key research contact within the organisation. This began a ten-month process of protocol development before the study gained operational and ethics approval.

When the protocol was accepted, in October 2013 (Stellmach, 2013), I started work in the Amsterdam headquarters, making short research visits to the organisation's offices in London, Paris and Brussels. In December 2013, South Sudan exploded into violence. Over the next six or eight weeks, the hostilities worsened, resulting in mass displacement and looming starvation. The emergency was clear, and, for a variety of reasons, MSF's South Sudan mission was a site that could accommodate my research as an anthropologist. I would shift my field site there, first to the nation's capital in Juba and then to the rebel-controlled enclave of Leer. My research was interrupted for one month when MSF requested that I act as interim Emergency Coordinator in government-controlled Bentiu.

I concluded the field portion of my study in September 2014. This was not because events had reached a logical conclusion. South Sudan's war and resulting humanitarian emergency continue to the present. Rather, I left because my field

Emergency in practice **79**

notes had grown to indigestible proportions, I had personal issues calling me back home and I had been present long enough to accomplish my research objectives. I had managed to be a participant observer for nearly one year in the life of a medical humanitarian agency, and had enough ethnographic notes to keep me writing many years more. In total, I spent four months with MSF in Europe, and seven months in South Sudan. In this time, I took three breaks of 10–14 days away from the field to rest and catch up on notes, academic matters, visas and other approvals. Thus, the resulting ethnography can be considered an accurate, if highly individualised, documentary account of the opening months of South Sudan's war and the humanitarian response. Perhaps more importantly, it provides a more general insight into the nature, character and values of aid workers and their interventions. This ethnography, including the theory and findings of the project can be read elsewhere (Stellmach, 2016).

This chapter examines some aspects of this complex research project and how it was actually accomplished, and, through a short ethnographic vignette, gives some insight into the findings and potential value of the approach. The intent is to outline the practicalities, and the practice, of ethnographic fieldwork in emergencies. In the context of the whole book, this contribution functions a bit like a methods chapter; it describes some administrative and preparatory challenges, tools and techniques used to accomplish the research, along with an ethnographic example of the work in practice. I hope that this chapter demonstrates that ethical, valuable, long-term ethnographic research can be undertaken in complex emergencies – and, as such, I hope it can be a guide for similar studies in the future.

Before the field: study design and preparation

As noted previously, my study faced some challenges to its acceptance largely because of people's understanding or misunderstanding of what anthropologists do. Before I was able to begin work as an ethnographer for MSF, I had to address these issues in full. I was lucky – although not everybody involved in the approvals process understood the purpose and methods of the study, all acted with goodwill. Thus, the challenges I faced were of three types:

1   Helping people understand the nature of the research and the question I was pursuing.
2   Helping people understand the research method, and how participant observation in a humanitarian emergency could be conducted in a manner that was both methodologically and ethically sound.
3   Passing biomedical ethics approval (a process designed for clinical, not social, research).

After these three obligations had been met, the research began in earnest and additional challenges arose. These were in the technical or ethical aspects of research management, and also in the management of people's expectations.

80 Darryl Stellmach

The remainder of this chapter is broken into three subsections. The first section discusses study design, and some of the concerns, challenges and opposition addressed in the design phase. The next section examines the execution of the research plan – the practical administration of the study in the field. Both of these touch on the interpersonal dynamic between anthropologist and participants. This provides an argument for the importance of anthropology in a crisis zone and shows how it can be done. Finally, I share elements of an ethnographic description exploring the practice of medical humanitarian emergency aid.

Study design: questions of focus, objectivity and neutrality

As a former MSF field manager, my résumé helped position me in relation to other aid workers; in particular, those MSF colleagues who were gatekeepers and facilitators for the research. People regarded me as someone with considerable experience. My record and achievements were solid but unremarkable in the aid world. I fit somewhere in the middle of MSF's loose hierarchy. My history did not come close to that of the elders – career humanitarians of 25 or more years' work – but my ten years in the field put me in a respected tier among aid professionals. My authenticity, credibility and insider status were established in advance of the research. This had implications for my position as a researcher, both positive and negative.

Questions of project workability were the first source of friction. In the very early phases of research planning, a senior Oxford academic objected to my proposal's feasibility. An aid worker studying emergency would, he insisted, be pulled into the action. I would become embroiled in crisis response to the detriment of research. His concern seemed reasonable. Emergencies make twin demands on our psyche: there is, first, the practical need to mobilise all available resources to address the situation, and second, there is the emotional pull: human crisis is emotive. Confronted with mass destitution or extreme hunger, most researchers might feel an imperative to put down the notebook and do something – anything – to address the immediate situation. Compassion might lead one to suspend research in favour of doing something more immediately practical.

This concern, however, was founded on popular perceptions of emergency. In practice, several factors work to make participant observation possible, even in crisis. Importantly, responses to complex emergencies by established institutions are largely template-based. In the face of chaos, intervention is made predictable by necessity. To cope with uncertainty, there are rituals, rhythms and routines. Responders' roles and responsibilities must be clearly defined and adhered to. I would not enter a vacuum to be pulled in any direction. Rather, my presence could be enabled by pre-defining a purpose and role within the institution, and then making space within an emergency response that was already being adequately addressed.

This pre-definition was made explicit in the research protocol and in discussions with key managers at each level of the hierarchy. As noted previously, I did take up the role of emergency manager for a period of one month during the fieldwork. Yet this possibility was accounted for in the research protocol, with a clearly delineated procedure for the agreement of MSF and my department at Oxford. There was a rapid round of consultations when the request occurred; my intervention was agreed to be short term, to cover a gap in staffing. I was put on a contract for a fixed period. When my replacement arrived, that contract ended on time and I resumed my duties as an anthropologist. The experience enriched the ethnography, as I gained new insight and appreciation for the dimensions of the conflict. Managed well, my dual role became a strength, not a weakness.

Early scepticism about the project's feasibility was not limited to academics. Midway through my field research, a senior MSF manager confided that their initial scepticism was phrased more colourfully. Thus, concerns about how to do an anthropology of emergency were common, but they could be addressed through shared management of a clear protocol.

Research management in the field

This subsection describes some of the process of the field study, and some of the techniques used. It will briefly cover how I introduced the study to people on the ground, how I managed expectations and my daily routine.

The research was planned and budgeted to take place across at least three locations (the aid agency headquarters, the capital coordination office and the field base) over a period of approximately one year. By observing events from three different locations at different times, it was hoped that I could scrutinise at least three different perspectives – their similarities and differences.

My first field site was MSF headquarters in Amsterdam, where actual and potential humanitarian crises are tracked globally. This phase of the study focussed on the practices, techniques and mechanisms that attempt to understand early warnings of crisis. The trigger for the next phase would come from this project surveillance, as the large-scale crisis began to emerge. It is important to emphasise that, at the start of my study, I did not know which country I would end up in. Because emergency response is – by its nature – unpredictable, the study framework was designed to incorporate the debate and choice of the crisis location as a part of the research itself. The pathway for this decision-making process was written into the research agreement with MSF, structured as a collaborative endeavour between myself, key managers and the field teams. The site chosen would be deemed to balance key factors of high acuity and feasibility (from the perspective of access, personal and organisational security, and team and government permissions). When a certain crisis came to the foreground as more acute and more feasible than others, the research planned to move to the MSF country office, where the team attempts to pinpoint crisis on a national or regional scale, and then to the field project, where the daily work of monitoring, surveillance and treatment is carried out at the local level.

Key to this plan was the kind of emergency I would study: nutritional crisis. I focussed on nutrition for good reason. While the timing of other forms of disaster is harder to anticipate, nutritional crisis is recurrent and predictable. Caused by people's inability to produce or access a decent quality or quantity of food, nutritional crisis

82 Darryl Stellmach

follows seasonal patterns of sowing and harvest. Hunger gaps (as they are called) are predictable to the month. Nutritional crises are also exacerbated by political conflict, economic inequality, desertification and other climate and resource stressors. This grim combination of factors exists at present in parts of the Sahel, central Africa and the Horn of Africa; certain MSF project locations within these regions are regularly affected by acute hunger. This made it possible to plan a research timeline. While not assured, it was a safe bet that some degree of nutritional crisis would happen somewhere in these regions in the early part of 2014. Indeed, this was borne out when MSF began response to several nutritional crises by late 2013.

My final field location of South Sudan came as a surprise to me. Around August 2013 (harvest time in much of sub-Saharan Africa), and well before the start of the research, weather and conflicts in Chad and the Central African Republic had already pushed these two nations forward as potential hunger hotspots in 2014. They would remain the countries of my primary concern for the coming months, along with Syria. The surprise eruption of hostilities in South Sudan on 15 December 2013 did not immediately trigger warnings of food crises; at that time the nature and extent of the fighting was unclear. Through late December and all of January, as fighting spread – along with reports of mass displacement, atrocities, looting and destruction of property – the possibility of a localised food crisis entered MSF's general consciousness. By February 2014, widespread food shortage – and even the potential for famine – were foremost concerns.

South Sudan met the criteria for acuity. It would also prove to be the most feasible of project sites. Since South Sudan was the largest of MSF Amsterdam's missions, it boasted a large operational carrying capacity that could accommodate my presence without disruption. It was also a country well accustomed to international researchers, so my presence would raise no significant concerns among staff, authorities or the people. On top of that, the agency's in-country chief – the Head of Mission – was a former academic and sympathetic to the needs and aims of research in emergencies. He opened the door for the study, and provided material support and a very welcome degree of personal and institutional transparency. Thus, by early March 2014, I was on a plane to Nairobi, then onward to Juba.

I would be in South Sudan from March to September, most of that time in Juba, with one month in Bentiu and six weeks in Leer. The month in Bentiu was operational. Faced with a desperate situation, MSF asked to put me on contract as the country's emergency coordinator. A mass displacement led 40,000 people to sit in a United Nations camp without clean water or sanitation. I would travel there to take over the MSF response to the situation. I headed MSF's emergency operation for a month before my replacement arrived, after which I resumed my anthropological duties. The time spent in Bentiu was intensive and deeply moving on a personal level, but due to the extremity of the crisis, the ethics of conducting participant observation in a UN camp and obvious time constraints, I made no official field notes from the period. I did, however, keep a personal diary, to document personal reflections, key events and conversations, and some of those reflections featured in my doctoral thesis.

Emergency in practice **83**

With Bentiu as the obvious exception, most of my field research was spent peaceably seated in offices and, later, in hospital wards. I conducted interviews, wrote observations and typed notes. I spent a good deal of time working on research administration – the essentials of organising interviews, data archives, visas and ethics approvals. At a casual glance, I was indistinguishable from other desk-dwelling denizens of the MSF site – those people who run the machinery of any aid agency apparatus. I was happy to blend in.

Observation and interview techniques

I spent most of my time in the field as a participant observer; this was the primary research method and consisted of taking notes based on passive observation and informal exchanges. In keeping with the expectations of people who anticipated that I should enact the role of researcher, I also conducted formal interviews.

As noted previously, the study was planned, and occurred in three phases: beginning at the level of the MSF headquarters in Amsterdam, then moving to an MSF country office in a crisis-affected country (Juba), and finally moving to an MSF project site within that country (Leer). Each of these three locations was an anthropological field site, and I followed the same procedures in each place – introducing the research, asking for consent and settling into unobtrusive observation. The particular focus of the observation was on meetings, discussions and care practices where acute hunger was conceptualised, monitored and treated.

In each location, I introduced the study in several ways. Immediately on arrival, I would post a research note for participants, explain who I was and what the study was about, and arrange to give general presentations about this to the staff. In the Amsterdam headquarters, where I began my research, I arranged for the project to be featured on the intranet news banner, a web-based scrolling headline on every office computer. I put the project documents on the shared file server in a web-based wiki format, including project information and Frequently Asked Questions. This allowed viewers to click and read only the areas of the study that interested them and find answers to specific questions. The format was designed to be accessible, familiar and easily digestible – a style that suited the fast-moving pace of an emergency organisation. I could easily refer employees to the site in conversation. In addition to posting written materials, in each of the three study locations, I gave one or more verbal presentations soon after arrival. The verbal presentations introduced me as the anthropologist and familiarised the community with the aims of the study. The presentations varied in length and nuance, depending on the audience. In such a large, fast-paced environment, it was impossible to get consent from everyone individually. I sought explicit consent from group leaders and for individual interviews, while my presentations and information notes ensured that the largest possible number of people were informed about the nature and purpose of my presence.

In my daily routine, I would choose a strategic place to sit and listen to the chatter around me. I would interject and ask questions. These would often result

84 Darryl Stellmach

in short discussions that might further clarify some aspect of the current action. I spent a lot of time like this, but people expected to see me doing something different. Several asked when I was going to start doing interviews, because that was their impression of what an anthropologist does. So, in addition to observation and casual exchange, I would take care to formalise the process and sit down one-to-one with people, notebook in hand. I did this despite a preference for less ritualised forms of interview, but it fulfilled expectations and often was the only way to speak with busy, over-scheduled senior managers. Formal interviews – by journalists, specialist advisors, visitors and others – were a common sight in the headquarters and the field. They were a known phenomenon, and the interviewer had a role and classification within that space. So, I did sit-down interviews to be seen to be doing the job of an anthropologist – rather than just sitting around the clinic or spending time in the office on a computer.

In the headquarters and the country office, I would change desks and departments every two to three weeks to gain an impression of activity in each sphere of the organisation. In Amsterdam, I sat for an extended period at the Emergency Support Desk – the hub of emergency response activities – before moving to a desk in the medical department. In addition to these obvious locations, I sat variously in the human resources, finance and media departments. This gave me a broad exposure to people and issues. Aware of my purpose, members of each department would often talk to me to learn more about my project. Some would highlight events they though would be of interest, while others would ask for my thoughts on departmental issues. Whenever asked for advice or an opinion I would be careful to phrase my response in a neutral way. This would give me a further role or identity in people's eyes as an impartial sounding board.

The research was conducted almost exclusively in English, the operational language of the MSF movement. I very occasionally drew upon Spanish and French. During my time in Leer, I studied some of the Nuer language (N'aath) with the help of MSF local staff. This was amusing for everyone involved, but I never managed to achieve conversational fluency.

Because descriptive anthropological accounts of emergency situations are scarce, I thought that detailed narrative accounts could be one of the more immediate contributions that my thesis could make to the discipline. Thus, in my field notes and narrative, I focussed as much as possible on long-form, detailed description and direct quotes from participants. My intent was to capture in detail the events and mood of the moment and, wherever possible, to portray it in participants' own words.

My focus on direct quotations served several purposes. First, obviously, to represent the participants in their own voices. Further, to reflect multiple voices; to convey the words – and thus, the perspectives – of many actors in a given situation, not just those in key positions of authority. Participant voices lend authenticity, multiplicity, immediacy and a succinct clarity to the account. A participant's elegant turn of phrase can substitute for a paragraph of explanation. Finally, since my own background both enabled and potentially biased the study, there was a risk that my

Emergency in practice **85**

personal reading of events could overwrite those of other participants. Participants' own words are a partial antidote to this problem. To this end, I carried a notebook everywhere and attempted to record specific statements and turns of phrase in the moment. It was not an obtrusive technique in this context; MSF people are used to reporters and their jottings. I would often preface my scribbling by asking: "that's an interesting thought; do you mind if I write it down?" No one ever refused, and no one seemed bothered by my notebook. It helped to situate my research as reportage.

The practice of humanitarian emergency: an ethnographic vignette

This subsection showcases a short ethnographic vignette that was first used as part of an operational research report to MSF. The vignette introduces and describes some key findings from the research: the importance of insider knowledge, the collaborative and provisional nature of knowledge, numbers as a focus and currency of debate, the improvisational and chancy nature of intervention, and notions of 'care' and 'action' as central to MSF's worldview. It highlights some of the techniques and subject matter of ethnography in emergencies, and some of the insights that can emerge as a result.

★★★

BD: "In nutrition you're OK."
MH: "Yes, OK."
VF: "OK. But there is measles."
BD: "How is the market?"

This cryptic exchange is cut and pasted from my field notes (entry 00184D/2014– 05). It comes from an operational meeting in Juba of MSF's Country Management Team: the Head of Mission, two Deputy Heads of Mission and two Medical Coordinators, plus coordinators of Human Resources, Finance, Logistics and all their deputies. In total, there are about 20 people in the room. South Sudan is a big mission.

The group sits in a crisp, air-conditioned cargo container in the tiny orange-dirt parking lot of the MSF Juba office. They face each other across a vast table – five tables, actually, bumped together to make one enormous table. They speak rapidly, business-like. There are too many people for deep discussion; this is an update meeting, to bring everybody onto the same page, let people put in their two cents and make quick decisions on overarching issues. That's what the Head of Mission says. The Head of Mission says this meeting is strictly limited to one hour and a half, or as close to one hour and a half as can be managed. Any issue that takes too long is put aside, passed to another agenda for another, smaller meeting that only the issue's key people will attend.

There are not enough chairs. I sit on the vinyl floor, cross-legged. I scribble notes fast, but not fast enough to take it all down verbatim. A little more is said,

86 Darryl Stellmach

a little elaboration given, but not much. The team is talking about a place called Lankien. The exchange lasts 25 seconds, perhaps 30, no more:

BD: "In nutrition you're OK."
MH: "Yes, OK."
VF: "OK. But there is measles."
BD: "How is the market?"
       There is some discussion. BD asks: "if you compare this year to last year what is the situation?" VF doesn't have those figures at hand, but she can get them from GY.
BD: "Can we ask GY to develop an overview specifically for Lankien?", looking at population versus malnutrition.
VF: "OK." They'll do measles and polio for 17,000 U15s.

And that is the end of the matter (in my notes, at least). The conversation turns to another topic.

Three hours later, I sit at a temporary desk in the Financial Coordinator's office, typing up these meeting notes. I re-read those first four lines, and sit upright. I re-read them again. The lines strike me. They're exactly the sort of thing I've been looking for because they illustrate the thing I'm in South Sudan to study: insider knowledge and insider decisions in crisis situations. Those four lines are verbatim; they were said just like that in the meeting. Any outsider reading those four lines, or hearing them spoken, would be hopelessly confused. The rest of the passage would not do much to clear up the outsider's confusion. But insiders reading this page have already understood. If insiders were momentarily confused by the first four lines, the rest of the passage puts it into perspective.

For those who know, this exchange should tick all the boxes. It tells us what we know, and don't know, and what we need to find out about nutrition in Lankien at the present moment (that is to say, for this week and maybe next week). It's an executive summary of the situation. It raises key questions and takes a decision on the next action needed. It's done in 30 seconds, and all in telegraphic code. Insiders – people who know about these things – can read this typed code (79 words, 428 characters) and say yes, the team did OK on this one; good enough for now.

During my time with MSF, people often complained they got no work done in meetings; meetings were just a lot of talk. Afterwards, people went away to do real work separately, sitting alone at individual desks or on patient wards. But this short dialogue opens a window on just how much work is done in a meeting, with a few seconds of conversation.

In order to appreciate precisely how much work is done and how much insider knowledge matters, I want to look closely at this short exchange, to break it into its component parts. There is a risk of over-analysing this tiny text, attributing too much weight to it, but what happens during and after these 79 words is potentially very important. It has implications for people, processes, budgets and strategic commitments.

Emergency in practice **87**

These 79 words aim to clarify a vast series of concerns, hopes, assumptions and questions into a single, concrete assertion ("in nutrition you're OK"). That assertion is the basis for what comes next. It will help determine the next action and the action after that – the multiple chains of decisions, acts and consequences that make any MSF programme.

Said a different way, this exchange is the creation of factual knowledge. Facts guide action for MSF, much of the time. In the context of an MSF meeting, to make an assertion, state a fact or raise a concern ("in nutrition you're OK") implies a plan for action. Statements of fact and statements of concern impel action; each fact and each action are composed of a chain of previously considered facts and actions.

In this case, the process starts with three very different things: food, a virus (measles) and market economics, juxtaposed against each other and linked together. Where these individual concerns intersect, they make a joint concern. To this, the team adds other considerations: the 'population' (people), this year, last year, a place (Lankien), another virus (polio) and 17,000 things called U15s.

This is a strange assortment of people, things and numbers. Why do they matter, and why do they go together? One needs insider knowledge to know why. To understand this exchange, it is necessary to be aware of dozens of facts and assumptions about medicine, human nutrition, geography, politics, MSF people, operating principles and values – things that people who work in or study humanitarian action would know, but an outsider would not know or would only vaguely understand.

Some of these facts and assumptions are listed in Box 4.1. These are some key assumptions that underpin MSF's insider knowledge. It's important to note this can only ever be a partial list, and each numbered statement is composed of its own lengthy sub-list of facts and assumptions, themselves composed of sub-sub-lists, and so on. It is not necessary to read the whole discussion in detail; it is only to give some idea of how many things are taken for granted in 79 words of MSF discussion. In 30 seconds, all of these factors were put on the table and taken into consideration in order to answer one concern: "in nutrition, you're OK".

BOX 4.1 STATEMENTS, KNOWLEDGE AND ASSUMPTIONS

"In nutrition you're OK."

1 Lankien is a town in South Sudan, site of a large MSF hospital.
2 South Sudan is in widespread civil conflict.
3 The conflict has resulted in displacement and loss of food stocks.
4 As a result, people around Lankien probably don't have enough to eat.

88 Darryl Stellmach

5 Children under the age of 5 years are generally the first to be physiologically affected by hunger.
6 Acute hunger and starvation are defined medically as 'malnutrition'.
7 Starvation (malnutrition) can be measured and recorded on an individual basis through the use of number scales (indicating 'nutritional status').
8 Individual measures from children can be aggregated to form population data.
9 The nutritional status of children is a bellwether for the nutritional status of entire populations.
10 Population data ('nutrition') can be extrapolated to indicate roughly how many people in the population are starving.
11 Population nutrition is quantified in percentages and thresholds.
12 Above a certain threshold, mass mortality is likely.
13 Mass mortality is unacceptable.
14 The nutrition situation in Lankien is currently below the threshold, and gives little indication of approaching the threshold.
15 Therefore, mass mortality is unlikely at present.
16 Therefore, we can conclude that the nutritional situation in Lankien is currently acceptable ("OK").

"Yes, OK."

17 Correct: mass mortality is unlikely at present.
18 Therefore, the nutritional situation in Lankien is currently acceptable ("OK").

"OK. But there is measles."

19 There is evidence of a measles outbreak in Lankien.
20 Children under 15 years (U15s) are the group most vulnerable to measles.
21 Measles and other infections can quickly and dramatically affect individual and population nutritional status.
22 Therefore, the nutritional situation is acceptable at present, but subject to rapid change.

"How is the market?"

23 The price and availability of food on the market are good indicators of near-future prospects for hunger.

There is some discussion [etc.]

The conversation continues. It covers the following points in a few more seconds:
24 The price and availability of food on the market are uncertain.

> 25 Other things (such as the status and results of food surveys or the planned action of other actors) are uncertain ("There is some discussion.").
>
> 26 Hospital nutrition data from last year can be compared to hospital nutrition data from this year.
>
> 27 Data from past years can indicate what an expected rate of malnutrition would be in any given year.
>
> 28 An epidemiologist (GY) is capable of making this calculation.
>
> 29 Therefore, a decision on whether the situation is acceptable at present will be deferred until GY's calculation is available ("an overview specifically for Lankien").
>
> 30 A vaccination for measles is available.
>
> 31 Vaccination for measles can help prevent a dramatic deterioration of people's nutritional status.
>
> 32 There are 17,000 children in the under-15 age group in Lankien.
>
> 33 This number is based on a) a World Food Program survey that counted 38,000 people in Lankien, and b) the calculation that U15s make up 45% of the population in sub-Saharan Africa.
>
> 34 The measles vaccination can be combined with another vaccination (for polio), which prevents another risk to the health of U15s.
>
> 35 Therefore, MSF will do a vaccination campaign for 17,000 U15s in Lankien.

The chain of reasoning is strong – logical – and composed of many very small links, each one a fact, value, assumption or shared understanding. Each link is itself composed of a similar molecular chain of logic and values. The analysis reveals some of the uncertainties and dependencies that underwrite our knowledge of crisis situations. An assumption proved wrong can put all subsequent assumptions and decisions into question. So, too, the introduction of a new factor ("But there is measles.").

As we can see from the example, this process – the process of coming to know and understand the dimensions of crisis – is not a passive process of assessing facts and reasoning to a conclusion. The facts do not speak for themselves. It was insider knowledge and insider action that brought certain facts and certain concerns (and not others) to the table. These disparate things would never be considered together (what does the market have to do with measles?) if a very specific, specialist knowledge had not brought them together in the first place. Specialist 'ways of knowing' influence what one sees and how one acts.

Specialist knowledge allows a privileged insight into the world, but is bound by its own set of norms and values. In the example here, empirical statements (about the way the world is) mingle with value statements (about the way the world ought to be). They are intertwined. These values influence not only what facts we bring to

90 Darryl Stellmach

the table, but also how facts come to be known in the first place. Values are inherent in measures. The existence of an empirically measurable percentage threshold for population malnutrition implies that starvation and mass mortality are wrong, and must be prevented.

In crisis, factual knowledge is not written on the wall, but an interpretation brought to the table for debate and clarification. The action composes the knowledge, which informs subsequent action, and so on. It is the action of the people around the five tables (and tables like it, in Lankien and Amsterdam) that brings the dimensions of the crisis into being. How we interpret the crisis implies and pre-configures the action we will take. Our definition of crisis contains the seeds of our response.

These shared networks of knowledge and values are what permit rapid action in crisis. In this case, the conclusion of the process, at the end of the short exchange, was a decision that more information was needed: in order for us to know if we're OK, give us a comparison of Lankien's population size versus malnutrition rates over the years. All of the factors, interpretations, debates and discussion were compressed into 30 seconds and 79 words. The meeting that day ran 1 hour and 45 minutes (5,400 seconds, logged in my notes at 3,088 words). During my field research with MSF, I attended around 100 meetings, as any professional does over a period of weeks and months. Thus, the meeting minutes in my field notes run to tens of thousands of words, each its own capsule of assumptions.

This vignette introduces some of the key themes that emerged through the larger study and consequent thesis. It draws out the collaborative nature of knowledge and the importance of insider knowledge. It implies that our knowledge of a crisis is provisional and iterative – it is never fixed, but always in process – knowledge and action are rarely conclusive, only 'good enough for now'. The vignette also highlights numbers as a focus and currency of debate. Numbers are everywhere in MSF. In situations of chaos and uncertainty, numbers provide a foothold on which other questions and decisions can form. The vignette also shows the often improvisational and chancy nature of MSF's action and intervention, where so much depends on individuals – individual knowledge and individual reactions (what if VF had not been in the room on that day?). Yet at the same time, the response is collective. There are shared concerns and shared ways of seeing – a collaborative, co-created understanding of the situation.

MSF's key concern, the collaborative understanding that unites MSF people, is a focus on making an appropriate response to human suffering. This response is enacted through a common (historically European) framework for aid. That framework sees the reduction of suffering and assertion of individual autonomy as the goal, and structured medical care as the means to achieve that goal. There are many assumptions (some of them problematic) within this framework; many things are taken for granted that would be invisible to outsiders. Thus, the vignette also indicates why aid action may at times appear absurd or incomprehensible to outsiders, or even paternalistic and exclusionary.

At the heart of MSF's model are a couple of key concepts. The notions of 'care' and 'action' are key to the MSF worldview. It is a worldview that asserts that political injustice can, at least partially, be addressed through the physical act of care (Redfield, 2013). Politics are inscribed on the patient's body – their wounds and diseases tell us a story of who the individual is and how power and politics worked on them. Injustice, aggression and neglect are given physical form through and upon the body of a patient. Medicine can be a means (although imperfect and unsatisfactory) to redress injustice and neglect. In attending to the health of a single human being, the patient becomes a proxy upon which an individual or institution can assert, through medicine, a desire for an ethical life and world.

Conclusion

I left South Sudan in September 2014 with regret and hesitation. The crisis continued unabated. Though my field research had reached a logical conclusion, I could have stayed on to contribute to the emergency response as an aid worker. However, though the fieldwork was done, the research itself was far from over. My field materials needed analysis, the insights needed writing up, and the results needed to be disseminated, both within MSF and academically. The horizon of the research is longer than that of the emergency itself.

My study had academic value because it provided insight into the everyday operations of a medical humanitarian institution and, in the subfield of nutritional anthropology, provided further detail on how numerical measures, institutional structures and individual discretion contribute to identification of, and response to, acute, mass starvation in the context of conflict. In addition, I hope its insights may make for better aid agency response. For operational purposes, this research project demonstrates how, with adequate preparation, a social research study can be carried out under adverse and rapidly changing conditions. This ethnography – to date, probably unique in terms of its duration and depth of immersion in a frontline humanitarian crisis response – indicates that rigorous anthropology can be done in emergency settings. More important than proof of concept, however, the study showcases the unique strengths of anthropology. As a form of research, the anthropological method may be amenable to settings where other forms of investigation are impossible. It also has a unique longitudinal potential: a particular kind of insight that comes from prolonged presence and focus over time.

References

Mosse, D., (2006). Anti-social anthropology? Objectivity, objection, and the ethnography of public policy and professional communities. *Journal of the Royal Anthropological Institute.* **12**(4), 935–956. doi:10.1111/j.1467-9655.2006.00371.x

Redfield, P., (2013). *Life in crisis: the ethical journey of Doctors without Borders.* Berkley and Los Angeles: University of California Press.

Stellmach, D., (2013). *Research protocol: the practice of medical humanitarian emergency: ethnography of practitioners' response to nutritional crisis.* Available from: http://hdl.handle.net/10144/323862

Stellmach, D., (2016). *Coordination in crisis: the practice of medical humanitarian emergency.* Doctoral thesis, University of Oxford. Available from: https://ora.ox.ac.uk/objects/uuid:c81d8b4a-4e73-4bbb-b66f-7c84885ab9b8

5

THE PARADOX OF SAFE BIRTH

The interaction between anthropology and medical humanitarianism – the dilemma of an MSF medical strategy versus health-seeking behaviour of Pashtun women in Khost province, Afghanistan

Doris Burtscher

Introduction

The working day of Ava (name changed by the author), a 28-year-old midwife working in the Médecins Sans Frontières maternity clinic in Khost, Eastern Afghanistan, is marked by the challenges that pregnant women living in rural areas face in cases of complications during pregnancy or premature delivery. It is very difficult for these women to find a maternity clinic when they need it for many different reasons, as Ava explains during one of our conversations tucked away in a quiet corner of the ward. Sometimes, visits to the hospital are delayed because the woman's family first tries to solve the problems at home, with paracetamol or homemade drugs, or because the decision-making process within the family takes too long. Additionally, treatment is expensive for impoverished rural people, so they need to borrow money from relatives or neighbours before they can travel. All these factors – and many others – often lead to obstetric complications, and Ava and her colleagues sometimes have to watch pregnant women die.

Maternal death is a well-known feature in resource-poor settings, and much dreaded. However, interventions have shown that it can be prevented if women suffering from complications during pregnancy or childbirth receive emergency obstetric care in a timely manner (Paxton et al., 2005), usually provided in hospitals or health centres. Yet this is difficult in the context of Afghanistan, where well-trained staff for emergency obstetric care is scarce and most of the health care institutions are located in the bigger towns. A major reason for this lack of skilled health personnel is "the dearth of qualified female medical workers living in or willing to relocate to Khost" (MSF, 2014). For many years, the ongoing armed conflict in the country, accompanied by security issues and various other factors, have additionally been limiting women's access to public health facilities, including obstetric care (Porignon & Hennart, 2002). Consequently, maternal mortality remains high

94 Doris Burtscher

in Afghanistan and is one of the highest worldwide; according to the WHO, 396 women out of 100,000 live births are likely to die (WHO et al., 2015).

Another remarkable factor in this area of Afghanistan is the socio-cultural features of the Pashtun communities – the dominant population in Khost province. They are marked by strong gender boundaries and gender segregation, close family bonds with tight decision-making control over its members, and marital relationships with restricted privacy (Sanauddin, 2015). The Pashtun ethical and moral code, *Pashtunwali*, forges the daily life of its people and determines how they conduct their lives (Grima, 1992; Rzehak, 2011). However, health-seeking behaviour and access to health care have only partly to do with socio-cultural determinants and dynamics. It is also about security concerns, as well as practical, financial and economic factors which prevent patients and carers from getting to clinics and hospitals in time (Park & van der Geest, 2010; MSF, 2014). Access to health care in general, and to a safe delivery facility in particular, represent enormous challenges in this context. As in other resource-limited settings, few women are able to reach a medical facility in time when labour starts. They are either too far away or too scared to come (Van Schoor, 2010). The experience of Khost shows that women are able to come to a health facility in time when they are supported by their family members and when they appreciate the quality of care delivered. As will be shown in this chapter, in the case of the MSF Khost maternity clinic, this has even led to a paradoxical situation: it was receiving too many women for 'normal deliveries' and therefore introduced a referral system to the Khost provincial hospital, a government structure whose maternity ward is not well appreciated by local people.

This chapter therefore seeks to focus on the subsequent ethical dilemma, by discussing local perception of, and access to, maternal health care services in Khost province, and the relationship between the maternity clinic and the MSF mandate and its objective in a reproductive health care project. Numerous other studies have reported factors leading to maternal mortality in Afghanistan (Bartlett et al., 2005; Hirose et al., 2011; Khorrami et al., 2008; Kim et al., 2012; Lin & Salehi, 2013; Todd et al., 2015; van Egmond et al., 2004; Vogel, 2014; Izquierdo et al., 2016), the role of delay (Pacagnella et al., 2012) and health-seeking behaviour related to maternal morbidity and mortality in neighbouring contexts (Fikree et al., 2004; Khan, 1999; Mumtaz & Salway, 2005). The fieldwork presented here aimed to identify and understand why women with a high risk of obstetric emergency do not reach the maternal facilities of an MSF program with a focus on maternal mortality. It examines what appears to be contradictory results for the MSF team. On the one hand, MSF has successfully socialised the concept of safe birth so women do seek medical assistance at delivery, and on the other hand, this is precisely when safe birth is at stake. For cases that really need it – i.e. direct obstetric complications (DOCs) – certain social aspects (for example, bleeding in public) prevent women from seeking assistance when it is most urgent. It will be shown that for women, 'safe birthing' goes beyond the biomedical notion, and the meaning of the 'safe space' has a highly symbolic connotation within a context of warfare and insecurity. This study builds on a previous MSF report (2014) that discussed the ongoing struggle to access health care in Afghanistan, and it comes to similar conclusions, for example, with regard to the impact of security concerns and the scarcity of well-trained medical personnel in rural areas.

The findings presented here are derived from an anthropological study, which was carried out in March and April 2016 in Khost province at an MSF project on sexual and reproductive health. The study analysed how MSF responds to the ethical and humanitarian challenges of having to send women away to other (government) health facilities knowing that in almost all cases, women and their carers categorically reject a referral. However, these other places not only do not reach MSF's quality standards, but also do not match women's expectations of good and 'welcoming' care in a safe place. MSF's actions are guided by medical ethics and the principles of independence and impartiality. One of MSF's principles states that:

> MSF's actions are first and foremost medical. We carry out our work with respect for the rules of medical ethics, in particular the duty to provide care without causing harm to individuals or groups. We respect patients' autonomy, patient confidentiality and their right to informed consent. We treat our patients with dignity, and with respect for their cultural and religious beliefs. In accordance with these principles, MSF endeavours to provide high-quality medical care to all patients.[1]

According to this principle, MSF promotes safe births by providing quality secondary care for women with DOCs in an emergency obstetric maternal and neonatal care hospital in Khost city. However, the MSF maternity clinic faces a high number of women *without* birth-related complications trying to access it for their delivery. This leads to the uneven situation that despite being filled to capacity since its opening in 2013, the maternity clinic has been struggling to reach its target population – women with DOCs in Khost province. In 2015, MSF treated roughly only 20% of the total expected deliveries with DOCs in the region, instead of the 60% that had been set as an objective in the annual revision of operations in 2014 (MSF, 2016a).[2] At the same time, the target of providing skilled assistance for 35% of the expected deliveries in the province was vastly over-achieved. In the first six months of 2015, about 45% of the expected deliveries in the province took place in the MSF clinic, thus resulting in a crowded hospital, difficulties in maintaining a high quality of care and no capacity to increase the number of DOCs treated in the project. Hence, MSF faced the situation that patients came in high numbers but did not correspond to the intended target group. However, the high influx of women without complications might have indirectly contributed to reducing DOCs in the area to a certain extent, because women came to the clinic instead of waiting at home, where complications may arise.

The continuing burden of the conflict in Khost province

Khost province is situated in the east of Afghanistan, bordering Pakistan. The provincial capital, Khost city, is located 150 kilometres southeast of Kabul. The province

96 Doris Burtscher

is grouped into 13 districts, and has a population of approximately 1.5 million (MSF, 2016c).

After almost 35 years of war, the standard for health care in Khost province remains particularly affected by the conflict, and ongoing violence and insecurity determine everyday life. Khost is of high strategic value for the armed opposition groups, hence also for the government. The intensity of the conflict in Khost has ebbed and flowed over the years, reaching its peak in 2011. With the downsizing of US forces, the conflict indicators for Khost demonstrate a reduction in Armed Opposition Group incidents. Nevertheless, 2013 was one of the most violent years since the US-led NATO military intervention started in 2001. An MSF study conducted in 2013 in Kabul, Khost, Kunduz and Helmand found a severe impact from violence and uncertainty on the lives of Afghan people. Many had either experienced violence themselves or had a family member or friend who had experienced violence. Others had a family member or friend who had died as a result of violence (MSF, 2014). The great majority of violent incidents and deaths were caused by the continuing armed conflict. After the 2014 elections and the creation of the National Unity Government, instability and lack of governance again contributed to an increase in security incidents throughout the province. While border districts with Pakistan are often the theatre of clashes between Afghan national forces and armed opposition groups, the Matun district in Khost province faces the highest number of improvised explosive device explosions, targeting armed opposition group members as well as Afghan national forces. In June 2015, a new governor was appointed by the president to reinforce the government's effective control of the province; however, in 2016, more security incidents were witnessed than in previous years.

The MSF Khost maternity clinic

In 2011, before the opening of the MSF Khost maternity clinic with its focus on maternal and child health, MSF conducted an assessment and met various stakeholders. It was found that women and children in Afghanistan face a distinctly high burden of illness and death, with a high mortality rate in women mainly related to difficulties during pregnancy and childbirth. Additionally, women and girls face specific obstacles to accessing health care, including shortages of qualified female staff, especially in rural areas. Also, the restricted opening hours of clinics poses severe difficulties for women in labour, as most clinics are open only in the morning and "do not fit with the medical reality of childbirth" (MSF, 2014, p. 46).

The MSF maternity clinic in Khost started in March 2012 and reached a volume close to maximum capacity during 2013. As outlined previously, the project's objective was to focus on assistance to women with DOCs, relying on a referral system from comprehensive health centres (CHCs) to MSF, and from MSF to the Khost Provincial Hospital (KPH). Since the opening of the MSF clinic, deliveries in the provincial hospital had dropped from 660 to an average of 500 births per month in 2014 (MSF, 2016b). Another 300 deliveries per month were attended in

CHCs and basic health centres (BHCs), while MSF accounted for 1,265 births per month. This number further increased, reaching a peak of more than 2,132 deliveries in May 2018 (MSF, 2018). However, it is known informally that many deliveries, especially with DOCs, take place in the private health sector and at home. According to MSF estimates, only around two-thirds of the deliveries in the province are attended by skilled medical personnel. With regard to the missing third, the main concern for MSF are the deliveries with expected DOCs. As mentioned earlier, in 2015 only 20%, in 2016 roughly 40%, in 2017 about 32% and in 2018 28.6% of the total expected deliveries with complications were received at the MSF clinic (MSF, 2018). The question thus arose: where and how did all the other women with DOCs gave birth, and did they survive?

Therefore, in November 2015, the project team requested anthropological assistance to adapt the medical strategy for the Khost maternity clinic. The anthropological study was intended to help generate operational recommendations on how MSF could reach and serve more women with DOCs, and how MSF could encourage women without complications to go to other health care institutions such as the CHCs and the provincial hospital in Khost. Besides these two main objectives, the study set out to analyse patients' and carers' perceptions of the MSF Khost maternity clinic and the community perception of the maternal health care services provided by the Khost provincial hospital, CHCs, BHCs, private clinics and other informal services. MSF expected this study to present a 'medical anthropological diagnosis' of the challenges related to the number of admissions, along with recommendations for how to go about dealing with these challenges.

An ethnography of women seeking safe birth

The discussion of women's sexual and reproductive health and their perception of and access to 'safe' maternal health care services draws upon ethnographic fieldwork data collected during a stay in the MSF maternity clinic in Khost. The study applied an exploratory approach (Pope & Mays, 2006) to understand the health-seeking behaviour of pregnant women and their families, the decision-making process and influencing factors. The study team consisted of the author (a female medical anthropologist), a male and a female interpreter, and a male study assistant from the Pashtun community in Khost for the transcription of the interviews.

Due to the precarious security situation, the great majority of interviews were conducted at the MSF compound, either in or outside the maternity clinic or in the office area. Two external visits, one to a comprehensive health centre in Gurbuz (a 30-minute drive from Khost) and one to the provincial hospital in Khost, allowed us to talk to health personnel there. Open-ended in-depth interviews were carried out with patients (female only), carers (male and female), and midwives and doctors (gynaecologists), as well as health promoters, cleaners and other people attending the maternity clinic. Additionally, members of the health *shura*[3] of three different districts and community health workers from several districts were invited and interviewed at the MSF office. Observations consisted of being present when

98 Doris Burtscher

women arrived at the hospital, identifying general behaviour patterns among parturient women during delivery or while they were caring for and feeding their
newborn baby, analysing the interaction between women and their female carers –
mainly mothers-in-law – and between male carers and female carers, as well as reactions towards health personnel, particularly during health promotion sessions. This
method was applied in order to account for what people say compared with what
they actually do (Burgess, 1984), and to describe the "mundane and unremarkable
[for participants] features of everyday life" (Green & Thorogood, 2018, p. 174).

Pashtun society in the context of war and insecurity

Two main themes emerged throughout the study process: 'safe birthing' and 'lack
of women's autonomy and agency', which are sometimes intertwined in people's health-seeking behaviour. While 'reaching a safe delivery place' is the first
and main goal of the women and their families, 'lack of women's autonomy and
agency' sometimes hinders them from reaching it. To better understand how much
these gendered agencies of power relations influence Pashtun families' decisions
on where to go to give birth, it is important to understand the Pashtun ethical and
moral code, *Pashtunwali*, and family dynamics based on it.

Contemplating the issue of 'shame', a limited yet unavoidable explaining factor

The Pashtun ethical and moral code, *Pashtunwali*, is so essential to people's identity
that there is no distinction between practising *Pashtunwali* and being a Pashtun
(Rzehak, 2011). Pashtuns describe *Pashtunwali* as the ideal way of life, "the ideal
of honourable behaviour" (Rzehak, 2011, p. 1). Key *Pashtunwali* concepts for this
study are *nang* (honour), *sharam* (shame) and *purdah* (gender boundaries). In the
MSF Khost maternity clinic, *purdah* translated into segregation of women and men
within the hospital compound and a total ban on men inside the clinic. The honour
element, *nang*, is related to gender boundaries: if someone offends the rules of the
gendered order, then there is reason to act in defence of one's honour (Sanauddin,
2015). "While masculinity is judged by a man's honour, femininity is judged by the
concepts of *haya* (modesty) and *sharam* (shame), which epitomise the ideal virtues of
femininity for Pashtun culture" (Sanauddin, 2015, p. 143). In the presence of men,
women exhibit *sharam* by silence, subservience and obedience (Grima, 1992), and
by maintaining physical distance from male colleagues in a working environment.
While its comprehension for men is symbolic, for women, shame materialises its
virtue in the *hijab* and the *burqa* (Abu-Lughod, 2002), the symbol of oppression
during the Taliban era (Dorronsoro, 2001). The main rule of conduct is how one's
behaviour (both male and female) is evaluated in the eyes of others. Women are
restricted in their freedom of movement and autonomy when they decide where
and when they want to go to hospital for childbirth. Women have to be accompanied not only by female but also by male family members. Their mobility depends
on the *burqa* and *mahram*;[4] however, *mahram* was not only practised in restrictive

ways. Rostami-Povey explains that many men bravely accompanied their women to secret schools and organisations, risking punishment and death[5] (Rostami-Povey, 2007). Reaching a 'safe birth place' may pose serious problems when women face DOCs while giving birth at home or in a nearby health facility and then need to be transferred to a hospital. In such a case, the family has to rent a car and a driver, and it is unavoidable that men and women are mixed. Such experiences represent the reality of pregnant women and are linked to the dichotomy of honour and shame – transporting a bleeding woman enters this sphere.

Traditionally, clans live in a joint family system and practice patrilocal residence; married sons live with their parents in one household. Women move to their husbands' home and live with their family-in-law. In most cases, the extended family forms a social unit that not only lives together, but also supports and – most importantly – protects each other. As in many other countries in the region, the preference for boys is widespread among Pashtuns (Arnold et al., 1998; Arnold & Zhaoxiang, 1986; Bairagi & Langsten, 1986; Khan & Sirageldin, 1977). Giving birth to a boy is more rewarding than bearing a girl; by contrast, giving birth to a girl can provoke men – and sometimes their mothers-in-law – to beat the woman if she has only given birth to girls before. The two major reasons for preferring sons over daughters are economic and social. Sons can assist in agricultural production, earn wages and provide security. Additionally, derived from the kinship and descent system, sons provide the family with social status and strength. In Khost province, the preference for boys is mainly explained by giving strength and security to the family in an insecure environment. Furthermore, sons guarantee inheritance of land and its defence. As one woman explained, "If you have more men, it means you have more power in our country".

Getting married – a bride's silence is her consent

Marriage is mainly agreed within the same clan or kinship group, and is often arranged between cross-cousins.[6] Girls are given to 'unseen' men (men they have not seen before), and in their powerless situation remain silent on the day of their marriage. This is well captured in the following proverb: "A bride's silence is her consent" (Sanauddin, 2015, p. 142). Girls become engaged after their first menstruation, when they are between 12 and 14 years old. They will be married when they reach 17 or 18. Not getting married is desirable for many women at first, because they remain with their mother in the security of their natal home, but when their parents die, unmarried women endure fights and submission to their brothers' wives, who are often hostile (Grima, 1992; Schütte, 2014). A woman's 'muteness' starts with her marriage. Limitations on movement and restrictions on behaviour become more severe.

Pregnancy – a time for happiness and cheering?

In Pashtun society, fears of maternal mortality overshadow pregnancy and delivery. It could be a normal healthy state that most women aspire to at some point in their lives, yet it carries with it serious risks of death and disability (Berg et al., 2001).

100 Doris Burtscher

A first pregnancy is often a traumatising experience for a young woman. She has no power over her body; marital intercourse takes place when the husband desires. A woman is expected to become pregnant within the first months of the marriage. Mothers-in-law control their daughters-in-law by counting their menstruation days and observing if they are still praying, because Muslim women do not pray during menstruation. Women feel strong pressure from their family-in-law to get pregnant soon after marriage. If pregnancy fails, the young bride is accused and has to endure defamation.

Participant: My mother-in-law was following me, and she followed my menstruation.
Researcher: And how did she know that you are pregnant?
Participant: She is asking that you are praying or not. I was not pregnant up to the eighth month.
Researcher: But the mother-in-law was asking you?
Participant: Yes, she is counting the days; it means the mother-in-law is counting the days for the menstruation.
Researcher: And what was she saying to you?
Participant: My mother-in-law told me what is going on with you, you are not an old woman and you also get the menstruation on time, so why you can't get pregnant.

(Mother, 22 years, delivered of twins)

As emotions are seen to be gender-specific and highly socially shaped, many events in a Pashtun woman's life are interpreted as sorrow and sadness (Schütte, 2014). Women construct their life stories as a series of sorrows. While male life begins with the shooting of guns, cries of joy, days of visiting and congratulations and gifts to the mother, the life of a girl starts with a sigh or even tears. The birth of a daughter is perceived as sadness, and a girl may even be referred to as a shame for her family (Grima, 1992). This cycle of sadness starts again for the woman when she bears a baby girl and does not end.

When a woman gets pregnant, she does not tell anyone but her husband. In some cases, younger women talk to their mothers-in-law, but in many cases, they don't. Pregnancy is a state of shame, because it is the result of sexual intercourse. A young woman's pregnancy can proceed unnoticed by the members of her family-in-law. If the new bride in the family is not under the constant observation of her mother-in-law, the family will recognise her pregnant state only when labour starts. In rural areas, this factor still influences health-seeking behaviour for deliveries and access to health care in case of complications.

Some of them [young women] are very shy, they are trying to hide the pregnancy; some of them are telling the pregnancy to their mother-in-law or to the sister-in-law. I was also shy when I was first pregnant. When I delivered then I tried to hide the child from my father. I was hiding my daughter from my father. I was feeling shame so much. Some women nowadays they show their babies to the others and say look this is my baby. The past people were feeling more shame, but nowadays the people don't feel so shy anymore. We are Pashtuns. From mother and father, they feel ashamed because mother and father will say she slept with her husband and now she has a baby.

(Female carer, 50 years)

In rural and remote areas, antenatal care (ANC)[7] is not widespread and services are not much used, so any DOCs during pregnancy might go unnoticed. As pregnancy is a state of shame, women neither want others to know that they are pregnant nor seek ANC, unless it is really needed. People from Khost city and Khost Matun,[8] as well as people who are educated or well-off, will seek ANC in private or government clinics during pregnancy, and this means that DOCs can be discovered earlier and treated in a timely way. ANC is a question of affordability. Going for a check-up at a private clinic during pregnancy means that expensive tests will be done.

When 'danger signs' appear

Health-seeking behaviour for delivery is influenced by a large number of factors, as well as knowledge and awareness of the so-called 'danger signs', an expression used in the Khost maternity clinic during health promotion sessions to refer to DOCs. Particularly in the rural communities, this behaviour is a complex outcome of many factors operating on individual, family and community levels, including socio-cultural background, past experiences with health services, influences at a community level, and the availability of (alternative) health care providers – including elder women who help during delivery, security and restrictions on freedom of movement – as well as perceptions regarding efficiency and the quality of services.

Although at first sight, male elders are the decision-makers in the family, when it comes to childbirth, it is the pregnant woman's mother-in-law who decides where to go for delivery. She is the one who informs the male elders of the family, who then give their approval. Apart from this authority of the mother-in-law, health-seeking behaviour depends very much on the financial situation of the family, the location of the family's dwelling (remote village, in the mountains or in the town) and the district. Further main factors that influence the decision are distance and transport issues, the time when the contractions start (for example, if it is night time) and security concerns.

Many complicated deliveries take place at home because of adverse circumstances. The majority of women would like to deliver in a health facility with trained midwives and health care staff (either at a private clinic or at the MSF maternity clinic) with the agreement of the family (mother-in-law and male elders). However, if women 'realise' that they have the so-called danger signs, it is often too late to reach a health facility. Excessive bleeding during pregnancy or after delivery accounts for a great number of maternal deaths. Families who do not have

102 Doris Burtscher

the financial means, or women who do not get permission from their family-in-law, are not able to go to any health facility and the women will die.

As mentioned previously, another difficulty is women's lack of agency over their bodies within their homes and marriage. As described by Schütte, women are well aware of the subordination that constrains their agency when it comes to decision-making power. This becomes even more important when women's agency is affected by gender relations (Schütte, 2014). Within their homes and marriages, women lack agency to talk about their health issues, and in the interviews this was expressed as 'feeling shame' (*sharam*). It is seen as inappropriate for a woman to discuss health problems with her mother-in-law. Women living in urban areas and in educated families might see this differently, but younger women hesitate to talk about health conditions with their mothers-in-law. A daughter-in-law is not allowed to have problems. She has to be obedient, respectful and hard-working, and any expression of health issues is considered a complaint. Complaining about her life and health to the family-in-law is inappropriate and disrespectful.

> I was 16 when I became the first pregnancy; when I was 3 months pregnant, then I did heavy works on the kitchen and I did not know that the heavy work is dangerous for me, after that then I lost a lot of white water, then the doctor said that you should rest and you should not work, when I was in the rest then the sisters-in-law asked me that you are not shy [feel ashamed], that you are the new woman in the house and you don't work, so then again I had to start my work; but my husband was nice with me, he said to me you should rest.
>
> *(Midwife working in a CHC, 37 years)*

A wife can speak to her husband about her problems – restrictions within the couple are not so severe – but in most cases the husband cannot talk about female health issues with his mother because he is constrained by gender relations. Some women have the support of their husbands, but within the limitations of the Pashtun behavioural codes. These do not allow the man to show his sentiments towards his wife in front of others. However, numerous husbands support their wives by encouraging them to talk to other female family members who can then inform the mother-in-law.

> There are many problems, when they become pregnant, the women cannot talk freely about their problems to their husbands. Sometimes they feel shame and sometimes they cannot talk due to the cultural issues they hide their problems inside them and they work a lot during the pregnancy, they cannot, e.g. if she is too tired she cannot say anything to her husband or the mother of her husband, because the mother of the husband is like the king of the family.
>
> *(Male health care provider, 48 years)*

The paradox of safe birth **103**

Given all these limitations, it is essential that women make the danger signs visible. If the mother-in-law 'sees' them (for example, bleeding, vomiting, anaemia or weakness), then the chance is greater that she will acknowledge them. Women do recognise several DOCs during pregnancy like bleeding, losing 'white' water, low and high blood pressure, weakness, anaemia, belly pain, swollen body and diabetes. Heavy work is considered the cause of these conditions, but heavy work is unavoidable, and so are its consequences on pregnancies. Women seek treatment for these problems first within the family and at home, for example with decoctions of herbs or sugar water to stop bleeding. Sometimes, a *Mullah* – a local Islamic cleric – is consulted when the problems are attributed to the evil eye.[9]

Delivery at home or at a hospital – the big dilemma

Women perceive giving birth at home primarily as an emergency solution. However, women face situations where a delivery at home is unavoidable; for example, when contractions start at night time, when the closest health facility is too far away, when security is a concern or when financial problems and lack of transport prevent families from going to a private clinic. Other families might perceive the health facility as being inappropriate, or in-laws tell the woman to deliver at home. Some mothers-in-law argue that their daughters-in-law should deliver at home because they delivered at home themselves. However, for some individuals, it is also out of shame – others should not see the pregnant woman or the woman at all. Unlike other societies, Pashtuns do not have a system of traditional birth attendants who learn and inherit their profession from their mothers and grandmothers; in most cases, elder women from the same family or mothers-in-law assist women during delivery. They are referred to as 'elder', 'famous', 'experienced' or 'intelligent' women. Many of these elder women started to help during deliveries because they were 'forced' to assist when a delivery happened suddenly in the night.

If contractions start during night time, and women do not want to deliver at home, they have to resort to private clinics. Free health care facilities like the CHCs are only open during the day until noon or 2 p.m.; then the midwives continue in their private facility. They are busy during the night, but during the day, those clinics mainly provide ANC services. Khost city boasts several private clinics, and referrals from these health facilities to the MSF maternity clinic work very well. Sometimes, private facilities are consulted when complications arise during birth at home and the hospital is too far away. In other cases, women who come to the MSF maternity clinic and who still have time until delivery, are sent away to come back later or will be referred to the provincial hospital in Khost. In such situations, they search for a private clinic in Khost because they don't want to go to the provincial hospital or back home because they are afraid that they will not be able to get back to Khost again in time. In private clinics, labour-inducing medication like oxytocin and misoprostol is easily dispensed. Both women and health professionals consider them an essential part of the delivery procedure; they are given to virtually every woman before or during labour, and can be bought everywhere. They

104 Doris Burtscher

are often administered by insufficiently trained health care workers, as also happens in Pakistan (Shah et al., 2016). According to widespread perception, it is considered the most important treatment for women when they come to give birth. Labour-inducing medication is widely perceived to be essential – and sometimes even magic – so women request it. However, oxytocin abuse has a huge and often negative impact on women's health and health-seeking behaviour. Women think they need oxytocin for their delivery because so many health care workers use it, be it trained or untrained midwifes, medical doctors in government or private institutions or elder women in the rural areas. Oxytocin is called 'hot injection' because it makes the contractions 'hot' and 'hard'; they are reinforced. It is seen as the 'guarantee' for a quick delivery procedure. Therefore, women are disappointed if they come to the MSF maternity clinic and do not receive an injection of oxytocin. Women who are overdosed with oxytocin and manage to reach the MSF maternity clinic frequently present with a uterine rupture. In extreme cases, if those women do not get timely professional care, the uterine rupture can result in the death of the baby or the mother – or both.

If a family cannot afford any other option and has decided that they want to go to a health care institution, they choose comprehensive health centres (CHCs), known as government 'clinics'. However, it is seen to be inappropriate for women to deliver there because there is no 24/7 service and no midwife is available after 2 p.m. – and sometimes not at all. Most midwives are not well trained and often there is no electricity, or only on request. The local perception is that it is not a 'safe' place in terms of quality and human resources, and not appropriate in terms of the location of the delivery room, because it is separated only with a curtain from the male area. People do not trust the health care providers there and note the lack of equipment and drugs. Also, it is not easily reachable because of security and checkpoints, a river to cross and, in winter, snow.

The Khost Provincial Hospital (KPH) appears to be a solution only for logistical reasons for people who live in the neighbourhood and people who have their homes close to the hospital. Everyone else who can afford the transport and knows about the MSF maternity clinic will try to reach it. The provincial hospital lacks equipment, medication and staff. The quality of care is not on the same level as the MSF maternity clinic, and people are well aware of this. Compared to the MSF clinic, the midwives are fewer in number and have a greater workload, as they are responsible for several wards and not only for the maternity ward. When the MSF clinic is overloaded with normal deliveries, it refers people to KPH, which frustrates the midwives there because of the additional work. Health care providers acknowledge that the KPH lacks guidance and supervision in general, but mainly in the maternity ward, where doctors systematically urge women to come to their private clinics. Women are sent for tests, but when they come back, the doctors have left and they are forced to go to the doctors' private clinics. "The doctors have made the KPH like their business centre", as one health care provider frames it.

The MSF Khost maternity clinic represents a place of safety and security, both physically and symbolically, for the people of Khost province. It is seen as an environment where women can move and act more freely and give birth with health care personnel they trust. People appreciate both the high quality of the care and the fact that it is free of charge. The medical quality is demonstrated by drugs and medical services, human resources, location, security and safety. The MSF Khost maternity clinic is *the* place to go for the majority of respondents. Everyone who knows it, and is able to reach it, will come to deliver there. Since the beginning of the project in 2012, the local population understood that 'foreign' doctors were working there and that the treatment and drugs were of good quality. The MSF clinic is also highly appreciated for its neonatology and for the behaviour and attitude of its international staff – called 'foreign' people by the population and 'experts', adapted from the word 'expats',[10] by their national colleagues. The MSF maternity clinic is also valued for MSF's principle of impartiality. Everyone is treated in the same way, and no one is favoured. However, with the overcrowding of the hospital and the referrals to KPH, nepotism started to play an important role in admission and avoiding referrals. MSF changed its admission criteria to avoid congestion. But unlike MSF's own evaluation, people do not consider the MSF maternity clinic to be overcrowded or having reached its capacity. One birthing mother said to the midwife "we agree to deliver in the MSF yard or in the door or outside in the sand, but we don't want to go to KPH".

The referral system – trading trust for quality?

Because of the steadily rising numbers of deliveries in the Khost maternity clinic, MSF started a referral system from the clinic to Khost Provincial Hospital and from the CHCs to the MSF clinic in case of direct obstetric complications. The 2016 project document (MSF, 2016b, p. 9) for the Khost project states:

> Since the MSF maternity target of total deliveries is set at 1,200 deliveries/ month, it is expected that about 300 patients/month (10 patients/day) will be referred to KPH. A standard package of drugs and consumables ('referral kit') will be provided to every patient referred to KPH.

Meanwhile, MSF has reached more than 2,132 deliveries per month as of May 2018 (MSF, 2018).

When the study was conducted, the objective of the referral system was to reduce the number of normal deliveries assisted in the MSF clinic and to keep to a high level of quality standards. If the MSF clinic accepts too many women with normal deliveries, this stretches the clinic's capacities in terms of quality of care. This poses an ethical dilemma: should MSF refer patients to a hospital that people do not want to go to and is known for providing a lower quality of care than the overcrowded MSF maternity clinic? Patients prefer to lie on the floor or share beds rather than going to KPH. They see referrals to KPH as something negative. Most of them made a long journey specifically to reach the MSF maternity clinic in Khost, and already spent a considerable amount of money (1,000–3,500 rupees,

106 Doris Burtscher

about 10–35 USD) only to be sent somewhere else again, where they don't want to go and where they know that they will have to pay again. People come because they trust MSF. Moreover, the unwanted referral to KPH impacts negatively on their trust in MSF as an organisation, in the MSF maternity clinic in Khost itself and in the people working with MSF – both national and international staff.

Another aspect to consider is the security issue. According to the MSF principle of impartiality, any individual is treated as a patient, regardless of his or her political orientation. Families might be disappointed or astonished when their women get referred to KPH, which could result in a security concern for MSF. People do not understand why MSF refers them to other facilities. They don't perceive the reasons given by MSF in the same way MSF does – that the MSF clinic assists too many normal deliveries and neither has the space nor the capacity to provide the appropriate level of quality of care for an increased number of people. In the patients' eyes, they are not admitted to the MSF clinic and are referred to a place where it is even more crowded and where the quality of care, equipment and drugs are all worse. To reach the KPH, the MSF ambulance takes the women and their female carers. Male carers have to rent a private car to follow the ambulance. It is unacceptable for the women to go alone. If the delivery takes place on the way in the ambulance, it brings dishonour to the woman and her family because the driver is present (he cannot leave the car). Additionally, upon arrival at the KPH, it might happen that no one takes care of the women at all, and some women deliver at the entrance of the hospital. Often, the MSF referral kit with some drugs is taken from them and people are asked to buy medication from outside in the private pharmacies that are spread around the entrance of the hospital.

All these experiences result in many patients trying to hide inside the MSF maternity clinic in the waiting tents and in the in-patient department in order not to be referred until it is late afternoon, or, when the cervix opening is more than 6 centimetres to match the MSF admission criterion. As a consequence, nepotism has started to become an issue; whoever knows someone inside the clinic tries to contact them to try to arrange being accepted. The ones who are referred to KPH and can afford other options try to find a private clinic in Khost city. On top of this, the referrals bring an additional workload to KPH, despite MSFs intention not to weaken the existing health system. The KPH staff feel pressure when receiving patients from the MSF maternity clinic, as these patients expect to receive the same care they would have received at the MSF clinic, but KPH is not able to offer it. Apart from that, patients come with a negative attitude, as they have not chosen to go to KPH, but were forced by MSF to go there. They would have gone to KPH, if they had wanted to, but they chose the MSF clinic. Being rejected is humiliating and impairs MSF's reputation. Families of MSF employees receive phone calls from community members who complain their daughters are not being helped to stay in the MSF clinic. This is considered 'shame' for the whole family, as was also found in a study on understanding Afghan health care workers (Arnold et al., 2015). Additionally, experience has shown that a referral can add to the damage done to the moral code of honour if a woman delivers on the way to hospital. All of this results in misunderstandings, mutual distrust and frustration among patients, KPH staff and MSF staff.

The interaction of medical anthropology and humanitarian work – a crucial alliance

Anthropology and MSF's operations both try to achieve the same objectives, but by different paths. The humanitarian imperative aims to reduce human suffering, while the medical anthropologist moves into this space of humanitarian work by taking a holistic approach and looking at diverse aspects to find new solutions. In recent years, anthropologists have shown a growing interest in humanitarian assistance, which has developed into an anthropology of humanitarianism. Recognition and discussion of the collaboration between anthropology and humanitarian action has emerged, with some anthropologists specifically focussing on MSF (Pool & Geissler, 2005; Redfield, 2005, 2006, 2012, 2013, 2015; Fassin & Pandolfi, 2010; Abramowitz & Panter-Brick, 2015; Wagner, 2016).

This chapter enters the discussion of humanitarianism and anthropology from a different angle. It is not an anthropology of humanitarianism, but it elaborates on an anthropological intervention with the objective of supporting MSF's humanitarian paradigm to alleviate human suffering, postulated as the least common denominator of anthropology and humanitarianism by Ticktin (2014). It adds to previous field studies where similar findings of various factors influencing health-seeking behaviour helped to understand people's everyday life and reality. The Afghanistan experience was exceptional in that, as a (female) medical anthropologist, I faced an ethical dilemma with MSF's referral of parturient women to KPH to reduce the number of normal deliveries in the MSF maternity clinic.

While the assignment was to find out the reason why women with direct obstetric complications came in fewer numbers than women with uncomplicated deliveries, I was more concerned with how to avoid referrals to the provincial hospital at all, since I knew from the interviews that women categorically objected to giving birth there. To fulfil my mission with MSF, I elaborated how concepts of 'safe birth' and 'lack of women's autonomy' influence people's health-seeking behaviour in Khost province and how it shapes their perception of 'a safe place' for childbirth. The paradox of these two concepts: looking for a 'safe birth' while 'lacking autonomy' associated with security concerns, as well as practical and economic factors, illustrates how humanitarian interventions are challenged by local conditions. It also exemplifies how MSF's principles as a medical humanitarian organisation and the particular medical strategy for Khost resulted in frustration among women and their families who came to use MSF services they valued.

Multiple stakeholders, together with the Ministry of Public Health, have been trying to reduce the high maternal mortality rate in Afghanistan by improving access to proper health care. Although the number of health facilities has increased over the years, study results confirmed that rural and less-accessible areas lack functioning and affordable clinics more than urban areas. Poor health care provision can

108 Doris Burtscher

be attributed to insufficient equipment and medication, as well as to the absence of trained medical staff in government structures (Trani et al., 2010). Furthermore, as has been shown by dismantling the influence of women's lack of agency, women feel uncomfortable being pregnant and do not talk about complications related to pregnancy and childbirth within their homes. This is highly intertwined with structural factors impeding access to health services, such as distance, cost and security issues. Safe access to health care is difficult to achieve in a volatile conflict zone like Afghanistan, where pervasive insecurity dominates everyday life. The unstable context not only hinders people from accessing health care, but at the same time impedes MSF in providing its services outside the 'bunkerised' institution of the Khost maternity clinic. However, this protective situation inside the walls of the clinic has a critical symbolic meaning for the people. In an unpredictable environment, giving birth in a safe place is a question of survival and a moment of reassurance – not only for the mother and the child, but for the whole family.

As seen throughout this chapter, MSF and the local community have differing perceptions of the humanitarian space provided by MSF. For MSF, the humanitarian space is first of all characterised by the strict adherence to its principles of neutrality, impartiality and independence, while providing good quality medical care to save lives and reduce suffering by decreasing morbidity and mortality. Orbinski states that "our imperative is to create a strong humanitarian space that acknowledges the humanity of 'the other'" (quoted in Paupst, 2000).[11] According to Orbinski, another feature of the humanitarian space is the freedom to move and act, to access people, assess their needs and to reach those who are in need. In Afghanistan, these features apply only partly. MSF cannot move, and does not have as much access to people as it would wish. MSF is able to assess needs and provide a humanitarian space in a limited environment – in this sense, the MSF Khost maternity clinic responds to local need. For the people – and especially for the women – in Khost province, the humanitarian space means to be able to reach a place where they can safely deliver their babies. Khost maternity clinic is this humanitarian space.

However, this study's analysis has shown that the MSF clinic faces an ethical dilemma because the humanitarian imperative of reducing suffering and saving lives is challenged. People often reach the clinic under the greatest difficulties; they risk their lives to receive health care (Vogel, 2014). Nevertheless, MSF refers some patients to another institution like KPH, while being aware of the inferior quality of care there and local perception that it is an 'unsafe' place.

Although the MSF clinic is confronted with an increasing number of deliveries, only some of the women with direct obstetric complications are reached – and even then, not according to the project's objective. While structural barriers such as economic constraints and security concerns apply for all situations, in the context of DOCs, women's lack of agency comes into play. Because of the critical and sometimes fatal condition of women with DOC, their families often decide that they would rather deliver at home. In other cases, where the condition was initially ignored (because it is not approved of if a woman 'complains' too much), it is sometimes too late to rush to a clinic after realising the severity of the situation. Additionally, it is considered a dishonour, because the family took the wrong decision and had to travel with a bleeding woman. However, the family will try everything to save the pregnant woman's life and will first of all try to 'fix' the problem close to where they are; with female elders attending the birth, or in private clinics – which often worsen the situation due to the unregulated use of labour-inducing medication.

Solving the dilemma – health promotion and adapted services

To come back to the dilemma of how to respond to the high number of women coming for delivery, and to encourage more women with direct obstetric complications to reach the MSF maternity clinic in a timely manner, taking into account women's lack of agency, this anthropological study helped MSF to adjust its objectives. The study confirmed that it is important to bring sexual and reproductive health care closer to the people and to step out of the 'bunker' situation.

While the referrals to Khost Provincial Hospital were maintained, MSF has, since 2017, provided training, human resources, financial and logistic support to KPH in order to improve its maternal health care services. In 2016, MSF had already started supporting two health centres in the peripheral districts of the province; in 2017, this support was extended to three other facilities with the main goal of increasing their capacity, allowing them to remain open 24/7 and assist more simple deliveries without needing to refer women to MSF's maternity clinic. Health promotion was scaled up by visiting rural communities and by taking into account the various factors shaping health-seeking behaviour.

However, while the support to the five health centres worked quite well, support for KPH did not lead to an improved acceptance of referrals by KPH. Advocacy and health promotion activities were additionally expected to help MSF draw attention to the fact that KPH and CHCs are supported by MSF to perform normal deliveries. In a new project, MSF has built two maternity facilities of 200 square metres in Lakhan and Sabari and, by the end of 2017, turned another small clinic in Nadir Shah Khot into a facility equal in size.

To encourage more women with DOCs to come to the MSF maternity clinic in a timely manner, MSF reaches out to the communities with a tailored health promotion programme on DOCs during pregnancy, in separate sessions for men and women. Other messages inform people about MSF support of the CHCs, and this has improved the image of CHCs and the provincial hospital, as well as promoting the importance of travelling early to somewhere near the MSF Khost maternity clinic. Radio programmes aimed at families are broadcast twice a day, and there is a special programme dedicated to MSF once a week. If men are convinced of the importance of these messages, they will ensure their family members listen to them. In this way, men are given an important way of using their power within the family to benefit everyone. There is a tradition among Pashtun female elders of talking about sad events in their life – the sadder the story and the better told it is, the more

110 Doris Burtscher

she is appreciated and consoled by the others. This is one of the features that work well in the radio programmes (Grima, 1992; Schütte, 2014). With the community health promoters, MSF has workers going into women's homes, and this increases the uptake of services, as was found in Pakistan (Mumtaz & Salway, 2005). First and foremost, targeting mothers-in-law encourages women to negotiate their own care during pregnancy and delivery. The advice of women who said "Tell it to my mother-in-law; it is not my decision", is taken into account in the construction of the entire health promotion strategy. As a result, almost one-third of all expected DOC cases in Khost province were treated in the MSF maternity clinic in 2018, compared with only 20% in 2015 (MSF, 2018).

One challenge still remains, however: the number of deliveries in the MSF Khost maternity clinic is still increasing, even though the new strategy of decentralisation and health promotion positively influenced access to safe deliveries for many women in Afghanistan.

Anthropology's main endeavour is to gain a better understanding of people and their ways of living in different socio-cultural settings. Anthropologists are mediators in the broadest sense. This study about the health-seeking behaviour of Pashtun women in Khost province required listening, understanding, mediating and negotiating. It meant hearing voices like those of Ava and her colleagues, who are distressed about avoidable maternal deaths. But it also meant listening to women and their families who did not want to deliver at Khost Provincial Hospital and reacting to the challenges of reconciling operational objectives with local people's realities.

This study expanded its scope to include larger structures and rules in this particular society, such as *Pashtunwali* and its influence on daily lives, and it took into account the critical security situation during conflict and war. In this specific setting, it was crucial to find common ground between MSF's medical strategy, critically hampered access to health care and the decisions of Pashtun men and women about where to find help for normal and complicated deliveries. This particular experience has shown how anthropological investigation and analysis can help operations to reach – at least partially – a specific concrete objective. This study has shown once again the vital importance of understanding and listening to the community when aiming to reduce morbidity and mortality – in this case, by improving prenatal and obstetric conditions for Pashtun women.

Notes

1 www.msf.org/en/msf-charter-and-principles (accessed 6 September 2016).
2 By the end of 2016, MSF reached the objective of 60% for the first time.
3 A *shura* is a process of decision-making by consultation and deliberation.
4 *Mahram* means to be accompanied by a male person; the husband or a male blood relative.
5 Referring to the years 1996–2001 when the Taliban held power over a big part of Afghanistan.
6 A cross-cousin is either the child of the mother's brother (maternal uncle's child) or of the father's sister (paternal aunt's child).
7 MSF was not involved in antenatal care to avoid interference with the private sector.

8 The nearest district to Khost city.
9 The evil eye is a curse believed to be cast by a malevolent glare, given to a person when they are unaware. Receiving the evil eye will cause misfortune or injury.
10 Expat derives from 'expatriate', meaning international MSF staff.
11 www.msf.org/en/article/a-meditation-on-evil (accessed 29 September 2016).

References

Abramowitz, S. and Panter-Brick, C., (2015). *Medical humanitarianism: ethnographies of practice.* Philadelphia: University of Pennsylvania Press.

Abu-Lughod, L., (2002). Do Muslim women really need saving? Anthropological reflections on cultural relativism and others. *American Anthropologist.* **104**(3), 8. doi:10.1525/aa.2002.104.3.783

Arnold, F., Choe, M.K. and Roy, T.K., (1998). Son preference, the family-building process and child mortality in India. *Population Studies.* **52**(3), 301–315. doi:10.1080/0032472031000150486

Arnold, F. and Zhaoxiang, L., (1986). Sex preference, fertility, and family planning in China. *Population and Development Review.* **12**(2), 221–246. doi:10.2307/1973109

Arnold, R., van Teijlingen, E., Ryan, K. and Holloway, I., (2015). Understanding Afghan healthcare providers: a qualitative study of the culture of care in a Kabul maternity hospital. *BJOG: An International Journal of Obstetrics and Gynaecology.* **122**(2), 260–267. doi:10.1111/1471-0528.13179

Bairagi, R. and Langsten, R.L., (1986). Sex preference for children and its implications for fertility in rural Bangladesh. *Studies in Family Planning.* **17**(6 Pt 1), 302–307. doi:10.2307/1966907

Bartlett, L.A., Mawji, S., Whitehead, S., Crouse, C., Dalil, S., Ionete, D. and Salama, P., (2005). Where giving birth is a forecast of death: maternal mortality in four districts of Afghanistan, 1999–2002. *Lancet.* **365**(9462), 864–870. doi:10.1016/S0140-6736(05)71044-8

Berg, C., Daniel, I., Atrash, H., Zane, S. and Bartlett, L., eds., (2001). *Strategies to reduce pregnancy-related deaths: from identification and review to action.* Atlanta: Centers for Disease Control and Prevention.

Burgess, R.G., (1984). *In the field: an introduction to field research.* London, Boston and Sydney: George Allen & Unwin. doi:10.1177/144078338502100227

Dorronsoro, G., (2001). Après les Taleban: fragmentation politique, hiérarchie communautaire et classes sociales en Afghanistan. *Cultures & Conflits.* **44**, 153–172.

Fassin, D. and Pandolfi, M., (2010). *Contemporary states of emergency. The politics of military and humanitarian interventions.* New York: Zone Books.

Fikree, F.F., Ali, T., Durocher, J.M. and Rahbar, M.H., (2004). Health service utilization for perceived postpartum morbidity among poor women living in Karachi. *Social Science & Medicine.* **59**(4), 681–694. doi:10.1016/j.socscimed.2003.11.034

Green, J. and Thorogood, N., (2018). *Qualitative methods for health research.* London: Sage.

Grima, B., (1992). *The performance of emotion among Paxtun women: 'The misfortunes which have befallen me'.* Karachi: Oxford University Press.

Hirose, A., Borchert, M., Niksear, H., Alkozai, A.S., Cox, J., Gardiner, J.K., Osmani, K.R. and Filippi, V., (2011). Difficulties leaving home: a cross-sectional study of delays in seeking emergency obstetric care in Herat, Afghanistan. *Social Science & Medicine.* **73**(7), 1003–1013. doi:10.1016/j.socscimed.2011.07.011

Izquierdo, G., Trelles, M. and Khan, N., (2016). Reducing maternal mortality in conflict areas: surgical-anesthetic experience in Boost hospital – Afghanistan. *Revista Colombiana de Anestesiología.* **44**(1), 13–16.

112 Doris Burtscher

Khan, A., (1999). Mobility of women and access to health and family planning services in Pakistan. *Reproductive Health Matters*. **7**(14), 39–48. doi:10.1016/S0968-8080(99)90005-8

Khan, M.A. and Sirageldin, I., (1977). Son preference and the demand for additional children in Pakistan. *Demography*. **14**(4), 481–495.

Khorrami, H., Karzai, F., Macri, C.J., Amir, A. and Laube, D., (2008). Maternal healthcare needs assessment survey at Rabia Balkhi Hospital in Kabul, Afghanistan. *International Journal of Gynecology & Obstetrics*. **101**(3), 259–263. doi:10.1016/j.ijgo.2007.11.022

Kim, Y.-M., Zainullah, P., Mungia, J., Tappis, H., Bartlett, L. and Zaka, N., (2012). Availability and quality of emergency obstetric and neonatal care services in Afghanistan. *International Journal of Gynecology & Obstetrics*. **116**(3), 192–196. doi:10.1016/j.ijgo.2011.10.017

Lin, A. and Salehi, A.S., (2013). Stimulating demand: effects of a conditional cash transfer programme on increasing maternal and child health-service utilisation in Afghanistan, a quasi-experimental study. *The Lancet*. **381**(Suppl S84). doi:10.1016/S0140-6736(13)61338-0

MSF, (2014). *Between rhetoric and reality: the ongoing struggle to access healthcare in Afghanistan*. Brussels: MSF.

Mumtaz, Z. and Salway, S., (2005). 'I never go anywhere': extricating the links between women's mobility and uptake of reproductive health services in Pakistan. *Social Science & Medicine*. **60**(8), 1751–1765. doi:10. 1016/j. socscimed.2004.08.019

Pacagnella, R.C., Cecatti, J.G., Osis, M.J. and Souza, J.P., (2012). The role of delays in severe maternal morbidity and mortality: expanding the conceptual framework. *Reproductive Health Matters*. **20**(39), 155–163. doi:10.1016/S0968-8080(12)39601-8

Park, R. and van der Geest, S., eds., (2010). *Doing and living medical anthropology: personal reflections*. Diemen, The Netherlands: AMB Publishers.

Paupst, J., (2000). *A meditation on evil*. Available from: https://www.msf.org/meditation-evil

Paxton, A., Maine, D., Freedman, L., Fry, D. and Lobis, S., (2005). The evidence for emergency obstetric care. *International Journal of Gynaecology & Obstetrics*. **88**(2), 181–193. doi:10.1016/j.ijgo.2004.11.026

Pool, R. and Geissler, W., (2005). *Medical anthropology*. London: McGraw-Hill Education.

Pope, C. and Mays, N., eds., (2006). *Qualitative research in health care*. 3rd ed. Oxford: Blackwell, BMJ.

Porignon, D. and Hennart, P., (2002). Reconstruction of health care in Afghanistan. *The Lancet*. **359**(9311), 1071–1072. doi:10.1016/S0140-6736(02)08084-4

Redfield, P., (2005). Doctors, borders, and life in crisis. *Cultural Anthropology*. **20**(3), 328–361. doi:10.1525/can.2005.20.3.328

Redfield, P., (2006). A less modest witness: collective democracy and motivated truth in a medical humanitarian movement. *American Ethnologist*. **33**(1), 3–26.

Redfield, P., (2012). The unbearable lightness of expats: double binds of humanitarian mobility. *Cultural Anthropology*. **27**(2), 358–382.

Redfield, P., (2013). *Life in crisis: the ethical journey of Doctors without Borders*. Berkeley: University of California Press.

Redfield, P., (2015). A measured good. In: S. Abramowitz and C. Panter-Brick, eds., *Medical humanitarianism: ethnographies of practice*. Philadelphia: University of Pennsylvania Press. 242–253.

Rostami-Povey, E., (2007). Gender, agency and identity, the case of Afghan women in Afghanistan, Pakistan and Iran. *Journal of Development Studies*. **43**(2), 294–311. doi:10.1080/00220380601125149

Rzehak, L., (2011). *Doing Pashto: Pashtunwali as the ideal of honourable behaviour and tribal life among the Pashtuns*. Kabul: Afghanistan Analysts Network.

Sanauddin, N., (2015). *Proverbs and patriarchy: analysis of linguistic sexism and gender relations among the Pashtuns of Pakistan*. PhD thesis, University of Glasgow. Available from: http://theses.gla.ac.uk/6243/

Schütte, S., (2014). Living with patriarchy and poverty: women's agency and the spatialities of gender relations in Afghanistan. *Gender, Place & Culture.* **21**(9), 1176–1192. doi:10.108 0/0966369X.2013.832661

Shah, S., Van den Bergh, R., Prinsloo, J.R., Rehman, G. et al., (2016). Unregulated usage of labour-inducing medication in a region of Pakistan with poor drug regulatory control: characteristics and risk patterns. *International Health.* **8**(2), 89–95. doi:10.1093/inthealth/ ihv051

Ticktin, M., (2014). Transnational humanitarianism. *Annual Review of Anthropology.* **43**, 273–289. doi:10.1146/annurev-anthro-102313-030403

Todd, C.S., Mansoor, G.F., Haider, S., Hashimy, P. et al., (2015). A case-control study of correlates of severe acute maternal morbidity in Kabul, Afghanistan. *International Journal of Gynaecology and Obstetrics.* **130**(2), 142–147. doi:10.1016/j.ijgo.2015.02.035

Trani, J.F., Bakhshi, P., Noor, A.A., Lopez, D. and Mashkoor, A., (2010). Poverty, vulnerability, and provision of healthcare in Afghanistan. *Social Science & Medicine.* **70**(11), 1745–1755. doi:10.1016/j.socscimed.2010.02.007

van Egmond, K., Naeem, A.J., Verstraelen, H., Bosmans, M., Claeys, P. and Temmerman, M., (2004). Reproductive health in Afghanistan: results of a knowledge, attitudes and practices survey among Afghan women in Kabul. *Disasters.* **28**(3), 269–282. doi:10.1111/j.0361-3666.2004.00258.x

van Schoor, V., (2010). We came, we saw, we misdiagnosed: how medical anthropology can enhance emergency medical relief programmes. In: R. Park and S. Van der Geest, eds., *Doing and living medical anthropology: personal reflections.* Diemen, The Netherlands: AMB Publishers.

Vogel, L., (2014). Afghan people risk their lives to obtain health care: MSF. *Canadian Medical Association Journal.* **186**(6), 411. doi:10.1503/cmaj.109-4751

Wagner, U., (2016). Der Stellenwert der Anthropologie in der humanitären Hilfe am Beispiel von Ärzte ohne Grenzen. *EthnoScripts.* **17**(2). Available from: http://nbn-resolving.de/ urn:nbn:de:gbv:18-8-9067

WHO, UNICEF, UNFPA, World Bank Group and United Nations Population Division, Maternal Mortality Estimation Inter-Agency Group, (2015). *Maternal mortality in 1990–2015 Afghanistan.* Available from: www.who.int/gho/maternal_health/countries/afg.pdf

Médecins Sans Frontières archives

MSF, (2015). MSF Khost Medical Strategy 2015.
MSF, (2016a). MSF Khost Medical Strategy 2016.
MSF, (2016b). MSF Khost Project Document 2016.
MSF, (2016c). Population Figures Khost 2016.
MSF, (2018). MSF Khost Situation Report 2018.

6

WHOSE CULTURE NEEDS TO BE QUESTIONED?

Access to HIV/AIDS treatment in Homa Bay, Kenya

Vanja Kovačič

Introduction

The context of HIV/AIDS in Homa Bay, Kenya

Homa Bay county stretches along the lakeshore of Lake Victoria in western Kenya and has a population of approximately one million (NACC, 2016). Due to the extremely high HIV/AIDS prevalence, this county has received special attention from national and international HIV control programmes. HIV prevalence in Homa Bay (at 26%) is nearly 4.5 times higher than the national average (5.9%), and accounts for more than 10% of the total number of people living with HIV in Kenya. The consequences of this epidemic are still severe: in the area of Homa Bay in 2015, over 500 children and 2,700 adults died of AIDS-related conditions.

The obvious question about the causes of such a concentration of HIV cases remains unanswered, despite much speculation. It has been suggested that the specific lifestyles of traditional fishing communities contribute to the spread of HIV (Asiki et al., 2011; Kwena et al., 2010). Some authors observed high HIV related risk behaviour and associated it with the tolerance fishermen develop to the risk of drowning as a part of their daily occupation (Asiki et al., 2011). Multiple sex partners, low condom use – even with partners known to be HIV infected – transactional sex and sex under the influence of alcohol or drugs were observed in these communities (Asiki et al., 2011).

It has also been suggested that interactions between fishermen and fish traders, food vendors, alcohol brewers and other service providers have furthered the HIV epidemic (Asiki et al., 2011). Fish trading does not require any initial capital or specific skills. This attracts women, particularly economically vulnerable individuals, to the business. Exchange of fish for sex (e.g. fishermen offering free fish to female fish traders in exchange for sexual favours) has been documented in the area

Whose culture needs to be questioned? **115**

of Homa Bay (Kwena et al., 2010), as well as in other fishing settings in developing countries, particularly in lake fisheries (Béné & Merten, 2008). Women who sexually engaged with fishermen reported having specific benefits, such as greater access to fish and a better price for them compared to their counterparts who did not engage in such trade.

Gender and power imbalances related to economic inequalities have also been suggested to help account for the spread of HIV in settings similar to Homa Bay. Hence, multiple reasons – such as attitudes towards risk-taking among fishermen, economic pressures, gender relations and attitudes towards sexuality – have been considered in attempts to explain the HIV epidemic in Homa Bay.

Luo ethnic group

The Luo ethnic group, which predominantly occupies the area of Homa Bay, has also been examined under the lens of the HIV epidemic. Luos are Nilotic speaking and are traditionally fishermen and cattle keepers (Ocholla-Ayayo, 1976). Cultural practices and traditions, such as polygamy, sexual cleansing rituals and wife inheritance (more details in Box 6.1), as practised by the Luos, have commonly been used to explain the spread of HIV. Let us have a closer look at the social mechanisms related to these practices.

BOX 6.1 WIFE INHERITANCE

Wife inheritance refers to the custom of re-marrying widows. The new husband is supposed to be a brother of the deceased husband or, if the deceased did not have a brother to take on this role, another male relative is chosen. Children in many African settings 'belong' to the male family lineage. Remarrying of widows within the same family clan is considered to be a social measure to protect children and widows; the male family clan is responsible for their welfare.

Polygamy is common, and in 2010, it was estimated that one in four marriages in the Luo community are still polygamous (KNBS, 2010). Polygamous marriages were traditionally regulated and the order of seniority among co-wives played a major role. For instance, if the husband died, the first wife enjoyed greater privileges in matters of land inheritance, children's marriage and lineage leadership, compared to her co-wives. There are additional rules associated with the order of sexual engagement of the husband with his co-wives (Ocholla-Ayayo, 1976). In HIV debates, sex with multiple partners, even within the same marriage, is considered 'risky' in terms of the spread of HIV.

Two other traits often associated with high HIV prevalence among Luos are sexual cleansing rituals and wife inheritance. Both practices, like polygamy, follow a strict social order (Ayikukwei et al., 2007). Sexual cleansing occurs on particular occasions that are considered 'sensitive' for the individual or with regard to the community. An example of such a sensitive occasion is a period of transition, perhaps to a different social status or a new planting period. Sexual intercourse among married couples is therefore used to mark such periods, and planting the fields cannot occur before family members confirm to each other that this custom has been fulfilled. In relation to HIV, a ritual that breaks a mourning period for widows includes the sexual engagement by widows of a 'cleanser'. A cleanser is usually someone who does not belong to the clan of the deceased husband and sometimes does this 'professionally' in exchange for money or goods. The widow, who potentially contracted HIV from her deceased husband, as well as the cleanser, who has a history of multiple sexual partners, serve as potential sources of new HIV infections. Furthermore, a cleansed widow is traditionally expected to re-marry, ideally to the brother or another male member from the husband's clan, consequently transmitting the infection yet again to a new person (Ayikukwei et al., 2007).

These socio-cultural issues have been used to explain why the medical targets for HIV control have not been achieved in Homa Bay. I will, using my research findings, examine and challenge some of these assumptions.

MSF involvement in the control of the HIV/AIDS epidemic in Homa Bay

An extremely high number of HIV cases drew the attention of Médecins Sans Frontières to the Homa Bay area in 1996, which is when a referral centre for HIV cases was established there (Bradol, 2011). A year later, MSF began operations in Homa Bay district hospital. This was still a difficult time for HIV patients as antiretroviral therapy (ARV) was too expensive and not available for mass use in Africa, and patients were strongly stigmatised and discriminated against. The pioneering achievement happened in 2001, when MSF provided the first patient in Kenya with free ARV in a public health institution. During the following decade, MSF, in collaboration with the Kenyan Ministry of Health (MoH), actively engaged in decentralisation of care, re-construction of the district hospital, (which received a new section dedicated to HIV treatment, Clinic B) and the expansion of their programmes to include tuberculosis (TB) treatment, nutritional support and care for HIV-positive pregnant women. Over time, MSF built a professional capacity (training medical doctors, nurses and counsellors) and established medical protocols that became standard for HIV treatment. In 2009 (a year before the start of this research), over 9,000 patients were registered in MSF's HIV programme (Bradol, 2011).

These huge achievements engendered confidence in MSF, and so more ambitious plans emerged. MSF's target at the time was to control the HIV epidemic by increasing the coverage of HIV testing and treatment. According to the statistics, an alarming number of HIV-positive individuals in the Homa Bay district, between 13,000 and 29,000,[1] were still untested and untreated, and this was causing serious concern. But in the light of various socio-cultural issues and assumptions, the need for an anthropological perspective on the situation was recognised, and I was invited to carry it out.

An anthropological study to address the late arrival of patients to MSF-run Clinic B

The main operational focus was to increase enrolment by HIV-positive individuals into the MSF HIV control programme. The severe consequences of the HIV epidemic in the area led to the question: what prevents people from accessing HIV testing and treatment? Or in other words, what are the barriers people experience in accessing HIV testing and care? Considering that testing and treatment were provided free of charge, the issue was more complex than being merely about economic constraints.

With this focus in mind, I needed to define what was expected from health providers. With the understanding that the medical management of HIV is much more complicated when patients arrive at Clinic B with advanced symptoms, the consensus was that the desirable situation would be to test and treat patients early. Achieving this would have a second benefit – HIV treatment largely reduces the risk of passing on HIV; hence, a more successful control of the HIV epidemic could be achieved.

On this basis, I started examining what would be a threshold between 'early' and 'late' management of the disease. This threshold has been medically defined by staging HIV infections based on the number of so-called CD4 cells (a type of white blood cell) and the use of laboratory techniques. The higher the CD4 count, the better the abilities of the body to fight infections including HIV (AIDS.gov n.d.). In contrast, a low number of CD4 cells – for example, a count below 100/mm^3 – indicates that the immune system is compromised and a progressive number of secondary infections can occur, which defines HIV stages 3 and 4 (WHO, 2005). This means that patients with HIV stage 3 or 4 are the most severely ill. The physical health of these patients is severely compromised, because (at least in theory) they have not received testing and treatment early enough to repress the HIV in their bodies. This was the group that I was interested in studying, to understand what prevented them from accessing treatment earlier.

Conducting fieldwork in Homa Bay

A nine-month ethnographic study was carried out, which comprised observations within MSF Clinic B, as well as home visits and interviews with the patients who were late arrivals to Clinic B.

Field setting

Homa Bay town is relatively small in size, but it serves as an administrative and business centre for the area. All essential services are available in the town, including a couple of banks, a district hospital (where Clinic B is located), small shops, a fish processing factory, a number of guesthouses and an orphanage. The area attached to Lake Victoria is known as 'Shauriako slum', and it can easily be spotted by the dense concentration of wooden structures covered with iron sheets, and running sewage through the settlement. The area outside the town is rural and has the typical feel of African countryside: round clay-built huts, dirt roads cutting through the villages, people gathered in conversations in front of the huts, plantations of cassava, maize, beans and sorghum surrounding settlements, and goats, cattle and chickens wandering around.

The main hospital in the area is Homa Bay district hospital, but smaller health centres and dispensaries serve villages located nearby. HIV testing is supposed to be available in all these public health centres, as well as in numerous private centres run by charities. As in other rural African settings, alternative health providers such as traditional and spiritual healers are common.

Methods

The main data collection method was in-depth interviews[2] (Richie & Lewis, 2003). In total, 86 interviews were conducted between April and May 2010. Numerous informal interviews and observations, however, were also conducted throughout the nine-month period I was working in Homa Bay. The main participants were patients who were categorised as 'late arrivals' to Clinic B. The selection criteria used was their stage of HIV related symptoms (stage 3 or 4, CD-4 count below $100/mm^3$)[3] (WHO, 2005). I obtained this information from the medical records stored in Clinic B. Those who fit the criteria and were scheduled for routine checkups in Clinic B were approached with an invitation to participate in the study. We (my interpreter and myself) interviewed, in total, 56 patients. The interviews were predominantly focussed on: 1) different treatment options that patients had accessed, prior to arrival at Clinic B, 2) the reasons for their choice, and 3) the timeframe of their health-seeking. This timeframe was defined as the time they suspected that they could be HIV-positive (either their partner disclosed their HIV-positive status to them, or their symptoms became persistent) to the time they received HIV testing and treatment in Clinic B.

In addition, we interviewed 15 key members of the community who influenced patients' health-seeking behaviour. These included traditional and religious authorities (village chiefs), traditional healers and patients' relatives. To obtain a broader perspective, we also interviewed some other members of the community (patients' relatives, religious leaders, traditional healers) who were not directly linked to the patients' social network (a further 15 interviews).

In-depth interviews were conducted in the language native to the participants (Luo or Kiswahili) using probes, which were pre-tested and back-translated to avoid errors and inaccuracies. A short questionnaire was also used to elicit information on the socio-economic background of the patients. Conversations were recorded on a digital voice recorder and were simultaneously translated into English by a

Whose culture needs to be questioned? **119**

trained interpreter. We transcribed audio recordings and analysed transcripts using a theoretical framework of health-seeking pathways (Good, 1987). Different treatment options and sequences of using them were identified for each participant. We used this information to draw patients' health-seeking pathways (see Figure 6.1).

Participant observation[4] (Richie & Lewis, 2003) was an important element of the methodology, and was used to gain insights into the interaction of HIV-positive individuals with their social environment inside and outside treatment centres. The research team (author: VK and interpreter: JA) therefore spent extended periods in the villages where the patients selected for interviewing originated, as well as in Clinic B alongside the medical staff during their daily routine work.

Results: blaming patients, but the formal health care sector was failing them

Fieldwork: experiences and challenges

Conducting fieldwork in Homa Bay was a unique experience, and some aspects may be useful to understand for researchers and programme implementers working in similar settings. Interacting with patients outside the hospital context gave us the opportunity to engage with each other in a more informal manner. This led to some important insights and a better understanding of their daily lives and realities.

It soon became evident that despite HIV infection reaching epidemic proportions, and that "everybody knew somebody infected or affected", this topic still required a great deal of sensitivity. What was later confirmed by the interviews was that many of my participants had not shared their HIV-positive status with anybody, not even with their closest family members, and they were keen to keep this unchanged. Surprisingly, when approached with an invitation for the study, most patients felt comfortable with the idea of home visits. This indicates that they were confident they would be able to manage the reasoning behind our visit within the family context. Some, however, requested to meet in a neutral location of their choice: a church, a wooden bank on the side street or in the school yard.

We made every possible effort to protect patients' confidentiality, and we carefully thought through each step of the data collection. Our association with MSF, for instance, which is well known to the community for the provision of HIV care, could have brought some negative consequences for the patients who would be seen talking to us. We therefore made home visits as discreet as possible: our participants were informed by phone a day before the visit, an MSF car was parked at the entrance to the village and the house was approached on foot by myself and my interpreter only. My interpreter received enquiries about me – who I was, why I came to the village – but she had a ready response. She usually identified me as "her friend from abroad" (which in Homa Bay is quite likely, considering that there are many international charities and missionary stations) and she explained that we were coming to visit her relatives, who lived in the village. This was a socially acceptable response, and, to the best of our knowledge, it prevented any unwanted

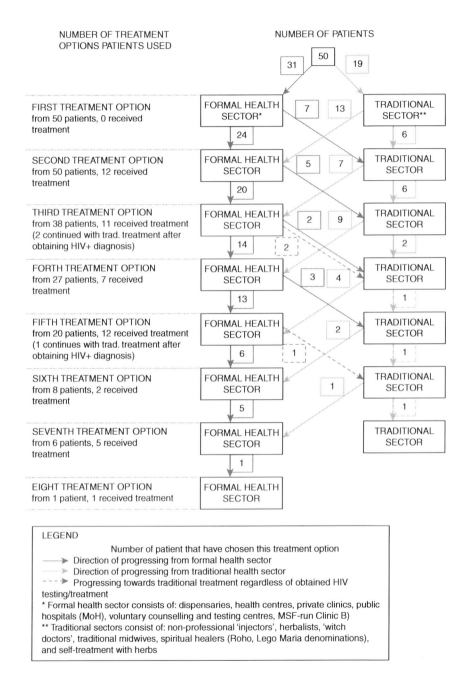

FIGURE 6.1 Patients' health-seeking pathways

Source: Adapted from Kovačič and Amondi (2011)

rumours later. We also made sure that we were wearing no visual signs associating us with MSF (such as T-shirts with MSF logos). After we were greeted by all the family members who were present at the home with a handshake (the usual etiquette when receiving guests), we entered the house and asked for "some privacy" with the patient. Other people then left the house without any hesitation.

Occasionally, however, we were faced with challenges in our attempts to ensure participants' confidentiality caused by the participants themselves. One of them, for instance, tried to 'use' us to disclose his HIV-positive status to his wife. He insisted that his wife should sit through the interview with us. We asked her if that was her wish, as well, but she clearly disagreed. We then conducted the interview with the patient only, during which we learnt that he had not disclosed his HIV status to his wife.

Another observation was that, reassured of our confidentiality, participants were extremely open to sharing their life stories, regardless of the distressing details. Aware that I had no professional capacity to support patients affected by psychological trauma, I made an arrangement with the counselling supervisor at Clinic B: all participants who discussed traumatic events (for example, the death of their child, gender-based violence or abuse) were informed about the free professional counselling services they could access after the interview in case they felt any emotional distress.

Overall, participants' openness, transparency and ability to verbalise their experiences helped us to develop a rich data set and to reconstruct their individual narratives, including the history of symptoms, their attempts to seek health care and the various coping mechanisms they concurrently developed.

Patients' health-seeking pathways

Of the 56 interviews, 50 (25 female and 25 male participants) provided enough information to trace patients' health-seeking pathways (Kovačič & Amondi, 2011). These pathways, the diagnostic and treatment options patients used before finally being diagnosed as HIV-positive, are illustrated in Figure 6.1. The boxes on the left side indicate the number of treatment options patients used (from one to a maximum of eight), with explanations on how patients filtered out at each stage as soon as their HIV-positive diagnosis was made. The arrows and boxes positioned central left show how patients moved between formal health care options and between formal and traditional health sectors. The arrows and boxes on the right indicate patients' movements through traditional health care options and from the traditional back to the formal health sector.

Let us have a closer look at the diagram. The formal health sector, comprising dispensaries, private clinics, district hospitals, etc., are the most important and the most frequently used choice in patients' health-seeking behaviour. More than half of the patients (62%) began searching for care in the formal health care sector where they could potentially be tested for HIV. None of them received an

HIV-positive diagnosis during the first visit, which made them all continue the journey to obtain 'better' health care.

Failure to diagnose patients with HIV (there was no test for HIV in the visited health facility) continued and during the first four visits to a health care facility was on average 74% (first visit, 100%; second visit, 68%; third visit, 59%; fourth visit, 74%; fifth visit, 40%; sixth visit, 75%; seventh visit, 17%; eighth visit, 0%). Furthermore, over half (57%) of the patients had to take at least four different stages before receiving satisfactory treatment. The maximum number of stages reported before receiving appropriate treatment was no less than eight.

Furthermore, it emerged that the formal health care sector was the preferred path to health-seeking in comparison to traditional treatment; patient flow is considerably higher (on average, 19 patients per health-seeking stage) compared to the traditional sector (on average, seven patients per stage). More than one-third of patients (34%) turned to traditional health systems as a second option after becoming disillusioned with the ineffective treatment provided at formal health care facilities. But, of the 19 patients who began with the traditional health care sector, 68% turned to the formal health care sector as their next treatment option.

In summary, the formal health care sector is the leading treatment option chosen by patients when confronted with HIV-related symptoms. Poor diagnosis results in treatment that does not relieve symptoms. This leads to substantial intervals before the next visit to a formal health care facility and affects opting for traditional treatment as an alternative. Hence, failure to successfully diagnose patients at the formal health care units results in delays to their access to treatment, and consequently contributes to the poorer state of their health once they eventually reach HIV-positive diagnoses.

I primarily focussed on patients' health-seeking behaviour; however, the in-depth interviews helped to also explain the pattern we observed through mapping patients' pathways. Some sub-themes, which shed light on patients' decision-making, also emerged in the process. I therefore describe some of the most influential factors and illustrate them with examples of patients' quotes, in the following subsections.

Institutional denial: poor diagnostic capacity of the formal health sector

Despite HIV/AIDS being generally recognised as one of the main public health problems in the area of Homa Bay in Kenya, many of the interviewed patients reported not being offered an HIV test even though their symptoms were persistent and HIV specific. The most commonly treated conditions in the first visits to the health facilities (early in health-seeking behaviour) were malaria and typhoid. Some of the participants explained that during several visits no other diagnosis was made, despite persistent complaints to the formal health sectors, and there was no improvement in their symptoms. For example, a patient with persistent diarrhoea was treated in the district hospital for typhoid for a period of two years. Another patient had a couple of repeat visits to another district hospital for 'serious malaria' before an HIV test was offered. It is also important to mention that even if patients themselves suspected they were HIV positive, they went with a doctor's diagnosis of 'serious malaria' instead of asking for an HIV test; this indicates that they did not feel ready to accept a positive HIV diagnosis or empowered enough to question or influence decisions made by medical personnel.

In theory, all health facilities in the Homa Bay area, even the smaller ones, should be capable of performing HIV tests. According to participants, smaller health facilities were often not equipped with HIV testing kits, and patients were advised to get tested elsewhere. A common belief that they may need to wait for the results of the test for days further reduced their motivation to get tested, and in most such cases, they decided to do HIV testing much later, at which point their health was already severely compromised.

Missed diagnosis fuels the use of traditional treatment

As illustrated in Figure 6.1, traditional treatment is very common and accessed by more than two-thirds of the interviewed patients (72%). There was not much difference between urban and rural areas in this regard (urban 75%, rural 71%), but we observed some differences in the type of traditional treatment accessed. While in urban areas, buying herbs at the market was reported more commonly; in rural settings, people preferred to visit one of the traditional healers (a 'witch doctor', or spiritual healer). Women also tended to use traditional treatments slightly more compared to men (76% and 68%, respectively).

Interviews further revealed that patients who were disillusioned with ineffective treatment received in the formal health sector used traditional methods as an alternative, and it took them a long time before a decision about another visit to the formal facility was made. This is also related to traditional beliefs about diseases, as one of the participants explained: "If one suffers from Luo diseases, tests in the hospital do not show anything in blood". This is especially important with regard to the window period in HIV (the period before HIV specific antibodies became detectable) and during TB sputum testing, which can often be a false negative. One of the traditional healers particularly mentioned negative results of the x-rays as an indicator for 'traditional disease': "So those in the hospital, who get a picture [x-ray], and don't find any results [any disease] . . . those are the ones who have *chira* [traditional disease] and are treated here. For *chira*, there will be no [medical] diagnosis" (Lego Maria healer). Hence, negative test results in the formal health sector, which are not sufficiently explained to patients, promote the use of alternative routes; that is, traditional treatment. On the other hand, many participants who suspected that they might have HIV, because their spouses had already disclosed their HIV-positive status, have not sought traditional treatment. This also confirms that once a clear medical diagnosis is given, the possibility of 'traditional disease' is ruled out.

The most commonly mentioned traditional diseases (*Luo diseases*), which, according to participants, have some overlapping symptoms with HIV/AIDS are *chira* and witchcraft. It is important to understand that there is a very clear logic in this interpretation of symptoms. In local terms, both categories differ in: 1) causality, 2) symptoms and 3) estimated time before the patients' death. Both are caused by 'disruption of the social order', either by the breaking of traditional taboos (*chira*) or by the medium (witch), who is motivated by jealousy and performs witchcraft to hurt the victim. Symptoms of *chira* are described as "thinness that progresses slowly and eventually kills the patient". This describes well the progress of some HIV-related symptoms. The witchcraft was described as more acute ("it kills a patient faster") and with a more complex set of symptoms. These, it was explained, depend on the "type of witchcraft used". Abnormalities of legs (swellings, wounds), skin abnormalities and severe stomachache and vomiting were described, which again correspond with some HIV symptoms (more details in Box 6.2).

BOX 6.2 TRADITIONAL LUO DISEASES

Chira is reported to be caused by breaking traditional Luo customs or taboos. These customs are related to interpersonal relations between the younger and older generations (parents/sons) and inter-marital relations (husband/wife, co-wife/co-wife, widow/new husband). Commonly, they are associated with sexual intercourse, which is not only associated with fertility, but also with recovery from traumatic events and with celebration. As one of the participants stated: "We Luos, we use sex as healing" (male, Homa Bay, 2010). There are many occasions when Luo rites involve sexual intercourse: during celebrations of marriage, after funerals, after a birth in the family, before planting and harvesting, among others. However, these rituals are regulated by a strict order that determines the sequence of sexual acts within the family. Parents must have sexual intercourse first. They communicate this to their married sons by saying: "Home is opened now", which signals that the firstborn son is the next one to have intercourse with his wife, followed in turn by younger brothers. If these rituals are not followed in this particular order (for instance, if children have sexual intercourse before parents), children are not allowed to eat food produced on the parents' farm, and this will result in *chira*.

Witchcraft is understood to be caused by a member of the community who is jealous of another's well-being (progress at work, material well-being, education of children). There are three ways of bewitching: 1) leaving herbs by the path that effect specific people who come by (symptoms include any abnormality of legs: swellings, wounds, etc.), 2) bewitching by an evil eye looking at a particular part of the body (symptoms include abnormal skin conditions on that part: face, feet, etc.), and 3) bewitching by food by an evil eye (symptoms include severe stomach ache, vomiting). Effects of witchcraft can be sudden, and can quickly cause death if not treated traditionally.

If traditional disease is suspected, traditional treatment is provided by traditional healers ('witch doctors', herbalists, traditional midwifes) and religious healers (Roho and Legio Maria denominations were mentioned). Traditional healers who we interviewed explained that while 'witch doctors' and religious healers have spiritual powers, traditional midwives and herbalists only have 'technical' skills; that is, knowledge of herbs and abnormal body conditions. Traditional treatment, it was explained, involved different methods such as drinking herbal infusions, licking dried herbs, using herbs for bathing, superficially cutting skin and applying herbal mixtures on the cuts. Spiritual healing was explained differently, entailing use of prayers, sprinkling of blessed water over the patient and drinking blessed water. Another category of healers that operates in the villages are 'injectors', who were said to be lay people with limited medical skills (sometimes they have private drug shops) and who use injections and sometimes combine them with herbal treatment.

The participants expressed high trust in some of the well-known traditional healers whom they approached "in search for help" when challenged by symptoms. None of the healers interviewed claimed to be able to treat or cure HIV/AIDS. As one of the herbalists commented: "No, we don't have any kind of herbs, which could treat HIV!" or "AIDS, I cannot pretend I can cure it using blessed water. For that particular disease, whether it is [affecting] a man or a woman, that person needs to go to the hospital" (Lego Maria healer). In short, healers were very clear that HIV-related treatment is the domain of the formal health care sector ("hospital disease", as they call it). Some of them, when they saw their clients' symptoms, even said they had suggested to them the possibility of HIV and referred them to the nearest health care facility. Therefore, in some circumstances, the local culture works in collaboration with, rather than against, the formal medical institutions.

Patients' fear of defaulting from medical recommendations

Another interesting finding was patients' denial and fear of receiving an HIV-positive diagnosis. This was reported even in cases when patients already suspected they could be infected with HIV. Some patients explained that this fear was by no means associated with the lack of information. One of the participants, who was even involved in campaigning for HIV testing, illustrated this clearly: "I was advocating and campaigning about HIV test. But [when it came to test] myself it was like a devil [stopping me]. I don't know why, I have so many brochures and books about HIV, I know everything about HIV! But for myself to go there [for a test], it was a problem" (HIV-positive man).

A vast majority of my participants were clear that they were thinking 'irrationally' and were overwhelmed with fear when they thought of the prospect of an HIV-positive diagnosis. This fear, as expected, was commonly associated with the fear of dying, as well as being recognised as an HIV-positive person and therefore being stigmatised. Surprisingly, fear of defaulting on medical instructions and being labelled as 'non-compliant' by medical treatment centres was also reported to have a huge impact on patients' decision-making.

126 Vanja Kovačič

The idea of taking drugs every day, twice a day, at exactly the same time, without fail, for the rest of one's life, was described as a chilling reality by the patients who took treatment. Most participants described the treatment regime as being "strict" and "requiring inner strength". Adherence to prescriptions was an issue that came up during my interviews, most often in a hesitant, painful tone. Most of the people I interviewed were terrified of being labelled 'defaulters' (people who refuse to take drugs either partially or completely). Their fears that defaulters ended up dying "before their time" were so strongly embedded in their minds that they were reluctant to even start treatment. As one of the participants stated: "I know somebody should not default! I saw somebody on the other side [of the river]. She was admitted [to the hospital] and then she was given drugs, but she hid them. She didn't take the drugs! And that lady has been already buried; she is already dead" (HIV-positive woman). Hiding drugs, or throwing drugs away, was also mentioned as a strategy for those who did not feel ready to start life-long treatment. Not surprisingly, this fear was also associated with the notion that the health facilities might refuse to provide antiretroviral drugs (ARVs) to defaulters.

In addition, participants also mentioned the fear of side effects and an assumption that pills are difficult to swallow because of their size – they "could cause choking". The large amount of drugs per patient, which was sometimes assumed to be equivalent to the box that patients carry back from the hospital (a box containing a bed net, a water purification kit and other items not related to treatment) also caused concerns.

The lifestyle changes and adjustments that HIV patients who were in treatment programmes would need to make were also described as problematic. Eating a 'balanced diet', which was recommended along with ARVs, was thought to be expensive and unaffordable. According to participants, this diet should include meat, fruits and commercially available fruit juices. Another recommendation patients received at the treatment centres which caused some concern was "to work moderately". Patients thought that this was unrealistic and could compromise their capacity to survive and support their families. One of them, for example, told us: "Where we normally go for medication [to the treatment centre] they [health workers] tell us . . . that we need to work in a temperate manner, not over-stretch. When we get such [information], some people get frustrated: how shall I survive? Now this may make us feel that in few years [from] now our community may be swept [away due to poverty]" (HIV-positive man).

Thus, when patients think of the prospect of HIV-positive diagnoses, they experience immense emotional pressure and fear, which is not only associated with stigma and discrimination, but also with the fear of being unable to fulfil medical recommendations.

An interaction of multiple barriers

As discussed so far, multiple barriers hamper access to HIV-related testing and treatment in Homa Bay. These barriers, in all probability, do not work in isolation, but are inter-connected and reinforce each other. I therefore attempted to examine them as interactions between the formal health sector and patients, with the aim of illustrating how these interactions ultimately lead to fewer individuals being tested and treated for HIV. Figure 6.2 is a conceptual framework, which summarises these barriers. The upper half of the diagram corresponds to the identified barriers which originate in the formal health sector (ellipses with boxes indicating details). The lower half of the diagram represents patients and barriers that originate from their side (ellipses and boxes). Arrows show interactions between different barriers (in which direction the barrier is likely to push towards).

Poor diagnostic capacity at the formal health centre, for instance, is pushing towards interpretation of symptoms as 'traditional disease' and the use of traditional treatment. A formal health sector does not approve of traditional treatment (it is considered a part of 'Luo culture'), so patients who approach traditional and spiritual healers are likely to be blamed for their lack of adherence to the formal health sector.

Missed opportunities to diagnose and treat HIV early result in multiple consequences. The progression of HIV-related symptoms affects both medical services and patients. From the medical providers' viewpoint, it is more complicated to treat patients who are already in the third or fourth stages of HIV (different combination of drugs, more side effects, etc.). This gives treatment centres additional reasons to 'blame' patients who arrive 'late' for testing. From the patients' viewpoint, advanced symptoms are an indication of an HIV-positive status, which causes fear of lifelong treatment with ARVs and associated changes in their lifestyle. This creates further concerns about defaulting medical recommendations and ultimately hinders patients from making decisions to enrol in the programme. Patients hence appear 'non-compliant', which results in another opportunity to 'blame' them, and thus a vicious cycle of fear and 'non-compliance' repeats itself.

Advanced symptoms of HIV also become more visual (skin abnormalities, deterioration of physical strength, loss of weight), which increases the likelihood of patients being recognised as HIV-positive. This then makes them fearful of being stigmatised, which causes more reluctance to get tested for HIV (and to have their fears confirmed). All these interactions then lead towards sub-optimal use of HIV-related medical services.

In reality, the different interactions are much more complex, and Figure 6.2 only partly illustrates the situation. However, this summary stresses how important the relationship is between patients and health providers; so, to improve access to HIV treatment in Homa Bay, a major focus will need to be on how to improve these interactions and communications. It also appears that the formal health sector creates barriers to reaching HIV testing and treatment goals, but often places the blame for poor utilisation of medical services on the patients.

Discussion

Working with beneficiaries, not working on them

Let us return to the main operational questions, which were framed as: "what prevents people from accessing HIV testing and treatment in Homa Bay?" and "why do HIV-positive individuals present themselves for HIV testing 'late', when their

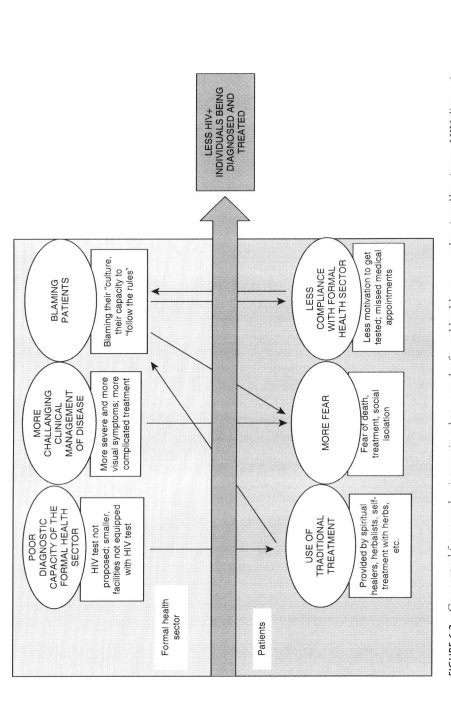

FIGURE 6.2 Conceptual framework – interactions between the formal health sector and patients' barriers to HIV diagnosis and treatment

physical health is severely compromised?" Both questions indicate that the focus of attention was placed on patients, and their inability to carry out what seemed to be an obvious course of action: accessing medical facilities to receive treatment early. This framing suggests that providers of health care had in mind what was a 'desirable' behaviour, and they intended to influence behavioural change for their beneficiaries without critically examining the nature of care on their part, which, according to research results, would be the way forward.

This opens up debates on how narrowly medical programmes, even in humanitarian settings, perceive their patients. Patients can be considered to be passive recipients of aid and it is expected that they follow what medical establishments recommend, regardless of the consequences. The issue of unequal power relations in the provision of health care (Rifkin, 1996, 2014; Cooke & Kothari, 2001; among others), as well as in the delivery of humanitarian aid (Farmer et al., 2013), have both been widely debated in social science theory. In addition to examining the situation in Homa Bay through this lens, a parallel reality, which is the patients' agency and motivation to manage their own health, needs to be acknowledged.

The active search for health care, as reported by my participants, certainly indicates that they are not in any way 'passive'. Furthermore (and as we have already discussed elsewhere, in Kovačič & Amondi, 2011), HIV-positive individuals also came up with different strategies to help themselves manage expectations from the medical care system and their own social environment. We called this process a 'social navigation', and it was most evident when it came to issues of discussing HIV-positive status with their spouses and starting ARV therapy. Male interviewees in particular reported that they did not engage in direct discussion with their wives, but often used more indirect strategies, such as deliberately leaving their health facility registration card (with the HIV-positive option ticked) in the house or in their clothes so that their wives would find it when going about household chores like cleaning and washing. Interviewees from polygamous marriages have more options for social navigation, since they could choose to disclose their positive status to just one wife. This removed the pressure from the health care providers ("Yes, I told my partner"), and gave them room to manoeuvre through their marital affairs. Additionally, some of those participants, who were not ready to start ARV therapy, reported ignoring the first positive test and throwing away their medical card. When their symptoms worsened, they got re-tested, making it out to be their first test (Kovačič & Amondi, 2011).

Patients' agency and innovative thinking show that they evaluate and act upon what they perceive as being beneficial for their physical, mental and social wellbeing, and this cannot be ignored. If they were treated more as equal partners and empowered to make decisions that influence their own lives, this could lead to original and more effective strategies to provide HIV care to those in need of it, while also meeting the health sector's HIV control programme goals.

Whose culture needs to be questioned?

When examining the HIV situation in Homa Bay, Luo culture was commonly not only blamed for the spread of HIV, but also for the failure to achieve medical targets

130 Vanja Kovačič

and control the epidemic. Polygamy, wife inheritance, sexual cleansing rituals and the use of traditional and religious treatment have all been mentioned in this regard. It is important to stress that these notions were extremely widespread among scientists (Ayikukwei et al., 2008; Dilger, 2006; Ogoye-Ndegwa, 2005) and health care providers, including MSF (End of Mission report, Kenya: 2003–2007, unpublished), at the beginning of my research.

In the light of the results I have presented, let us re-examine these arguments. If we explore the notion of polygamy, it is straightforward to conclude that this custom is not specific to Luos, but is very common across Africa (Senegal, Cameroon, Zimbabwe, Tanzania, Uganda, South Africa, to name a few) and among many other ethnic groups (Tsoaledi & Takayindisa, 2014). These ethnic groups have diverse rates of prevalence of HIV, so no evidence exists to date which would directly link polygamy with high HIV prevalence.

The much debated so-called cultural drivers of HIV among Luos, such as sexual cleansing rituals and wife inheritance, are often associated with promiscuity. Ayikukwei et al. (2007), for instance, presented an assumption that both customs "encourage men and women to have multiple partners". These simplistic views are supported by quoting as an example the commercialisation of cleansing rituals, which are reported to be sometimes performed by commercial cleansers (Ayikukwei et al., 2007). New HIV infections, however, could only occur if one of the people involved in such actions was HIV negative. Considering that both parties (a widow and a cleanser) are perceived as a high risk group (Ayikukwei et al., 2007), the risk for new HIV transmission is not, even in theory, higher compared to the rest of the population. Hence, these culturalistic explanations appear too superficial to explain the high prevalence of HIV among the Luo community, and using them is not only disrespectful, but also results in diverting attention from the real problem.

These cultural critiques are not new to public health. Anthropologists have been criticising culturalistic explanations of disease control for decades. For example, anthropological research brought to attention the tendency to apply dualistic thinking; 'us' (health providers) and 'exotic other' (recipient of care from another culture) (Vaughan, 1991). My research in Homa Bay provides another example of how the old stereotypes have not died out yet, and how this type of dualistic thinking causes barriers for effective implementation of HIV care. Diverting attention to the local culture perhaps reduces the ability to critically question our own culture; i.e. that of health providers, and their capacity to deliver health care. Hence, a lot of work still needs to be done to completely break racial and cultural taboos in medical care provision, and the humanitarian field is no exception to this.

Assumed supremacy of formal health care in pluralistic health settings

The use of traditional treatment among my participants was also considered as part of the Luo culture and held partly responsible for the poor utilisation of medical services in Homa Bay. This phenomenon, however, is common among HIV/AIDS patients. On Mfangano Island, for instance, 70% of people living with HIV/AIDS had used medicinal plants after their HIV diagnosis (Nagata et al., 2011). Thus, as in many other settings in the developing and developed world, multiple treatment systems coexist with Western biomedicine,[5] just as they do in Homa Bay.

This coexistence of 'local traditional' and outsiders' Western viewpoints often prompts conflict and results in the assumed supremacy of the formal health care system when it comes to the treatment of HIV/AIDS (Puoane et al., 2012). Medical staff providing HIV-related care in Homa Bay often positioned themselves against traditional healers, but the reverse does not occur – traditional healers, who participated in my research, have never expressed any criticism of formal health care. Furthermore, they demonstrate their collaborative spirit by referring patients whom they believed would not benefit from their skills to the formal health sector. Considering that many patients approach traditional healers at some stage in their health-seeking behaviour, the window of opportunity is open. Actively involving healers and linking them to the formal health sector could have a positive impact on increased access to HIV treatment. This has already been successfully implemented in the treatment of many diseases in other places, including HIV/AIDS (Furin, 2011; Audet et al., 2013).

For such collaborative processes to occur, a mutual trust and recognition that both health care systems carry the potential to improve the quality of patients' lives is essential. Patients who were interviewed described overwhelming feelings of fear when they dealt with the prospect of an HIV-positive diagnosis. These strong emotions were, according to them, an important influence on their decisions. The emotional support they received when they "were prayed for" and the absence of guilt "because they were suffering from Luo disease" are sufficient reasons to approach traditional healers and so should not be ignored. Furthermore, their choice indicates that their emotional needs have not been met within the formal health sector. Traditional healers in the Homa Bay area thus need to be recognised as partners in the provision of HIV-related care. Medical anthropologists, who have insights into both medical systems, could greatly contribute towards connecting all the beneficial aspects that medical pluralism can offer.

Conclusion

The impact of anthropological research in Homa Bay and other humanitarian settings – a critical view

Despite HIV/AIDS being a major public health issue in the area of Homa Bay and that patients regularly accessed formal health care facilities, the ability to diagnose an individual with HIV in these facilities was extremely poor. Strengthening diagnostic capacity, ranging from improving the rate of clinicians' ability to detect HIV infection to upgrading the technical capacity of all health facilities in Homa Bay, were essential steps to increase access to HIV-related care.

This research also pointed out a large communication gap in the HIV programme between health care providers and patients. Health care providers did not take into consideration the daily realities of HIV patients, and their recommendations, while medically accurate, were poorly adapted to everyday life in Homa Bay. Discussion panels consisting of representatives of both groups could be established, as a first step to a regular dialogue, and to shift the perception of HIV patients from passive receivers of aid to equal partners in the programme.

More broadly, the example of my research in Homa Bay points to many opportunities for the involvement of anthropologists in efforts to move the provision of humanitarian aid towards more targeted and needs-based programmes. From my observation of and communication with some other authors (Abramowitz et al., 2015), this process is not straightforward, and the results of anthropological research often remain 'on the paper', rather than benefiting our participants. Ethical obligations, as humanitarian workers, drives us to change this tendency, especially because we often personally witness human suffering.

Anthropologists involved in the evaluation of humanitarian programmes are often brought in when programmes are already running. As with this research, the need for evaluation is usually recognised only when operational challenges occur, which poses a certain degree of risk. In such situations, there is little space to introduce changes, especially if programmes have already elicited resistance from patients and their communities. Once the trust between communities and the providers of aid is lost, it may take a long time and be difficult to regain it. For instance, interviews with elders from the endemic sleeping sickness area of Uganda showed that memories of control interventions, particularly if they are traumatic, remain a part of collective memory for several decades (Kovačič et al., 2016). If the humanitarian field was aware of such long-term consequences, more attention might be paid to careful planning from the beginning of the programmes with the involvement of medical anthropologists. Anthropologists, particularly those experienced in applied anthropology, have a set of unique skills such as building and maintaining trustworthy relationships with patients and their communities, evaluating needs from a user perspective and the questioning of mainstream delivery models, among others. All these skills, if used to their full potential, could revolutionise delivery of humanitarian aid.

Furthermore, translating the results of anthropological research into practice is a demanding process which is often met with resistance and a lack of institutional support. Several challenges have been debated among anthropologists in this regard. First, anthropologists are often critical of established programmes, and disseminating results more broadly causes concerns that this would reduce the success of humanitarian organisations (Henry & Shepler, 2015). Some authors, such as Bradol (2011), recognised the importance of professional independence, which anthropologists commonly lack when trying to respond to specific organisational needs. Second, the time frames available for fieldwork is determined by our employment institutions, but is often too short (Napolitano & Jones, 2006; Henry & Shepler, 2015). Consequently, instead of focussing on a larger picture, anthropologists often

Whose culture needs to be questioned? **133**

choose to study narrow and previously covered areas of research, such as secondary 'social factors' (Henry & Shepler, 2015), which may have little to contribute to the development of humanitarian programmes. Third, the communication of the results of research to programme management and implementation team members, who may be unfamiliar with anthropological methods and terminology, is often taxing and received with reluctance (Napolitano & Jones, 2006). All these challenges and compromises reduce the depth of understanding of the benefits that anthropological research could deliver, and ultimately contribute towards a lack of impact in the humanitarian settings where we work. Only if research results are translated into practice can the role of anthropologists in the delivery of humanitarian aid become better recognised.

Notes

1 This calculation is based on estimated HIV prevalence recorded in anti-natal care units (between 15% and 24%), the number of people actively enrolled in the programs (13,000 patients) and the estimated number of people aged between 15 and 50 years living in the district (175,000) (Kovačič,V., MSF Report 1, unpublished).
2 Due to the sensitive nature of the research and the vulnerability of our participants in terms of potential stigma, in-depth interviews which provide confidential face-to-face interaction (Richie & Lewis, 2003) were chosen as the primary research method.
3 WHO clinical stages 3 and 4 are characterised by severe immunosuppression, and advanced and severe symptoms (WHO, 2005).
4 Participant observation is one of the principle methods in anthropological research, which are joined under the term 'ethnography'. It is characterised by direct observations and other techniques applied by researchers to study specific phenomena.
5 The term 'medical pluralism' (Leslie, 1973) is used in medical anthropology to describe this co-existence.

References

Abramowitz, S., Marten, M. and Panter-Brick, C., (2015). Medical humanitarianism: anthropologists speak out on policy and practice. *Medical Anthropology Quarterly.* **29**(1), 1–23. doi:10.1111/maq.12139

AIDS.gov., (n.d.) [online]. [viewed 18 April 2017]. Available from: www.aids.gov/hiv-aids-basics/just-diagnosed-with-hiv-aids/hiv-in-your-body/stages-of-hiv/

Asiki, G., Mpendo, J., Abaasa, A., Agaba, C., Nanvubya, A., Nielsen, L., Seeley, J., Kaleebu, P., Grosskurth, H. and Kamali, A., (2011). HIV and syphilis prevalence and associated risk factors among fishing communities of Lake Victoria, Uganda. *Sexually Transmitted Infections.* **87**(6), 511–515. doi:10.1136/sti.2010.046805

Audet, C.M., Salato, J., Blevins, M., Amsalem, D., Vermund, S.H. and Gaspar, F., (2013). Educational intervention increased referrals to allopathic care by traditional healers in three high HIV-prevalence rural districts in Mozambique. *PLoS One.* **8**(8). doi:10.1371/journal.pone.0070326

Ayikukwei, R., Ngare, D., Sidle, J., Ayuku, D., Baliddawa, J. and Greene, J., (2007). Social and cultural significance of the sexual cleansing ritual and its impact on HIV prevention strategies in western Kenya. *Sexuality and Culture.* **11**(3), 32–50. doi:10.1007/s12119-007-9010-x

Ayikukwei, R., Ngare, D., Sidle, J., Ayuku, D., Baliddawa, J. and Greene, J., (2008). HIV/AIDS and cultural practices in western Kenya: the impact of sexual cleansing rituals on sexual behaviours. *Culture, Health and Sexuality*. **10**(6), 587–599. doi:10.1080/13691050802012601

Béné, C. and Merten, S., (2008). Women and fish-for-sex: transactional sex, HIV/AIDS and gender in African fisheries. *World Development*. **36**(5), 875–899. doi:10.1016/j.worlddev.2007.05.010

Bradol, J.H., (2011). AIDS: from initiating treatment to fostering patient loyalty. In: J. Amondi, J.H. Bradol, V. Kovačič and E. Szumilin, eds., *AIDS a new pandemic leading to new medical and political practices*. Paris: CRASH/Fondation – Médecins Sans Frontières. 23–66.

Cooke, B. and Kothari, U., (2001). The case for participation as tyranny. In: B. Cooke and U. Kothari, eds., *Participation: the new tyranny?* London: Zed Books.

Dilger, H., (2006). The power of AIDS: kinship, mobility and the valuing of social and ritual relationships in Tanzania. *African Journal of AIDS Research (AJAR)*. **5**(2), 109–121. doi:10.2989/16085900609490371

Farmer, P., Kleinman, A., Kim, J. and Basilico, M., eds., (2013). *Reimagining global health: an introduction*. Berkeley: University of California Press.

Furin, J., (2011). The role of traditional healers in community-based HIV care in rural Lesotho. *Journal of Community Health*. **36**(5), 849–856. doi:10.1007/s10900-011-9385-3

Good, C.M., (1987). *Ethnomedical systems in Africa: patterns of traditional medicine in rural and urban Kenya*. New York: The Guilford Press.

Henry, D. and Shepler, S., (2015). AAA 2014: Ebola in focus. *Anthropology Today*. **31**(1), 20–21. doi:10.1111/1467-8322.12156

KNBS, (2010). *Kenya demographic and health survey 2008-09*. Calverton, MD: Kenya National Bureau of Statistics.

Kovačič, V. and Amondi, J., (2011). Cultural stereotypes and the health seeking behaviour of HIV/AIDS patients in Homa Bay, Kenya. In: J. Amondi, J.H. Bradol, V. Kovačič and E. Szumilin, eds., *AIDS a new pandemic leading to new medical and political practices*. Paris: CRASH/Fondation – Médecins Sans Frontières. 67–78.

Kovačič, V., Tirados, I., Esterhuizen, J., Mangwiro, C.T.N., Lehane, M.J., Torr, S.J. and Smith, H., (2016). We remember. . . elders' memories and perceptions of sleeping sickness control interventions in west Nile, Uganda. *PLOS Neglected Tropical Diseases*. **10**(6), doi:10.1371/journal.pntd.0004745

Kwena, Z.A., Bukusi, E.A., Ng'ayo, M.O., Buffardi, A.L., Nguti, R., Richardson, B., Sang, N.M. and Holmes, K., (2010). Prevalence and risk factors for sexually transmitted infections in a high-risk occupational group: the case of fishermen along Lake Victoria in Kisumu, Kenya. *International Journal of STD & AIDS*. **21**(10), 708–713. doi:10.1258/ijsa.2010.010160

Leslie, C., (1973). The professionalising ideology of medical revivalism. In: M.B. Singer, ed., *Entrepreneurship in South Asia*. Durham: Duke University Press. 16–42.

Nagata, J.M., Jew, A.R., Kimeu, J.M., Salmen, C.R., Bukusi, E.A. and Cohen, C.R., (2011). Medical pluralism on Mfangano Island: use of medicinal plants among persons living with HIV/AIDS in Suba District, Kenya. *Journal of Ethnopharmacology*. **135**(2), 501–509. doi:10.1016/j.jep.2011.03.051

Napolitano, D.A. and Jones, C.O., (2006). Who needs 'pukka anthropologists'? A study of the perceptions of the use of anthropology in tropical public health research. *Tropical Medicine & International Health*. **11**(8), 1264–1275. doi:10.1111/j.1365-3156.2006.01669.x

National AIDS Control Council (NACC), (2016). *Kenya HIV county profiles*. [online]. [viewed 1 February 2017]. Available from: http://nacc.or.ke/wp-content/uploads/2016/12/Kenya-HIV-County-Profiles-2016.pdf

Ocholla-Ayayo, A.B.C., (1976). *Traditional ideology and ethics among the Southern Luo*. Uppsala: Scandinavian Institute of African Studies.

Ogoye-Ndegwa, C., (2005). Modelling a traditional game as an agent in HIV/AIDS behaviour-change education and communication. *African Journal of AIDS Research.* **4**(2), 91–98. doi:10.2989/16085900509490347

Puoane, T.R., Hughes, G.D., Uwimana, J., Johnson, Q. and Folk, W.R., (2012). Why HIV positive patients on antiretroviral treatment and/or cotrimoxazole prophylaxis use traditional medicine: perceptions of health workers, traditional healers and patients. A study in two provinces of South Africa. *African Journal of Traditional Complementary and Alternative Medicines.* **9**(4), 495–502.

Richie, J. and Lewis, J.E., eds., (2003). *Qualitative research practice: a guide for social science students and researchers.* London: SAGE.

Rifkin, S.B., (1996). Paradigms lost: toward a new understanding of community participation in health programmes. *Acta Tropica.* **61**(2), 79–92.

Rifkin, S.B., (2014). Examining the links between community participation and health outcomes: a review of the literature. *Health Policy and Planning.* **29**(Suppl 2:ii), 98–106. doi:10.1093/heapol/czu076

Tsoaledi, D.T. and Takayindisa, F., (2014). An exploration of polygamous marriages: a worldview. *Mediterranean Journal of Social Sciences.* **5**(27), 1058. doi:10.5901/mjss.2014. v5n27p1058

Vaughan, M., (1991). *Curing their ills: colonial power and African illness.* Oxford: Polity Press and Basil Blackwell. Available from: http://doi.org/10.1017/S002185370003382X

WHO, (2005). *Interim WHO clinical staging of HIV/AIDS and HIV/AIDS case definitions for surveillance, African Region.* WHO/HIV/2005.02. Geneva: WHO.

7

BACK TO LIFE – EBOLA SURVIVORS IN LIBERIA

From imaginary heroes to political agents

Umberto Pellecchia and Emilie Venables

Introduction

In its February 2017 edition, New York-based *Time* magazine informed its readers of the death of a Liberian nurse named Salome Karwah on the 21st of the same month, from complications during childbirth. A picture on the same page as the article portrays the grave face of the unfortunate woman when she was alive, wearing a white apron, her arms folded across her chest and an intense stare on her face (Baker, 2017). Why is such a prestigious magazine that normally covers stories of political leaders, tycoons and celebrities so concerned by the death of an African woman? Why was she specifically chosen to be 'glamourised', when maternal mortality in Africa is among the highest in the world, and hundreds of unnamed women still die every month despite decades of targeted programmes and international engagement (WHO, 2018)?

What makes Salome special is not really the cause of her death, but rather what kept her alive. The Liberian nurse was a survivor of EVD – Ebola Virus Disease – and she had previously featured on the front page of *Time* magazine in 2014 when she was nominated, along with others, as Person of the Year and appointed as an Ebola Fighter. Salome worked for Médecins Sans Frontières' Ebola Management Centre (EMC) in ELWA 3, Monrovia, during the dramatic months of the epidemic's spread. She worked as a nurse, and after overcoming EVD herself, decided to keep caring for those who were still affected. In fact, like others surviving the disease, Salome was immune and therefore considered potentially very helpful in dealing with infected patients. As *Time* tells us, Salome had the dream of using her 'superpowers' to help others in a private clinic beyond her assignment with MSF. In parallel, she started a new life, had children and then tragically passed away. Yet the magazine skims over the cause of death:

complications in childbirth, they write, but also a "lingering social stigma" and a "broken medical system" – two phrases that, in short, capture the essence of the tragic EVD outbreak.

The story of Salome was a typical example of the experience of most 'survivors', apart from appearing on the front-page of *Time*. Many people in Liberia, Sierra Leone and Guinea experienced the critical stages of the infection, and for reasons that are still under investigation, were cured even without treatment and survived. As of June 2016, 42 days after the last recorded cases of Ebola in Guinea and Liberia, the outbreak had caused 11,310 deaths out of 28,616 cases worldwide (WHO, 2016). Apart from the medical component, some common social features that Ebola survivors experience can also be analysed. The long-term effects of Ebola on the health of survivors also remain relatively unknown but include ophthalmological problems, as well as mental health challenges (Christie et al., 2015; Deen et al., 2015, 2017; Mate et al., 2015; Sprecher, 2015; Harries et al., 2016).

The social experience of Ebola survivors, and their connection to the global and national response to the outbreak, constitute a particular and little-explored anthropological subject in which theoretical implications intertwine with practical approaches.

Anthropology in the time of outbreak

This chapter focuses on the identity and perceptions of Ebola survivors in Liberia, and how anthropological insight can help to understand their experiences better and therefore support them. We discuss how the survivor's body can take on new meanings – public and private – after experiencing Ebola, and how the label of 'survivor' is as problematic as it is celebratory, with many survivors feeling stigmatised and ostracised upon returning to their communities.

In reflecting upon what it means to be a survivor, the authors also consider the complexity of conducting research within an Ebola outbreak involving six different communities across Liberia, including ethnographic fieldwork, interviews and focus group discussions (FGDs) with survivors and their families, traditional leaders and health care workers. We discuss the methodological contribution that anthropologists can make in the context of Ebola, and how anthropologists become key during an outbreak.

The fieldwork forming the basis of this chapter was conducted in the same MSF project in Monrovia, Liberia, by the two authors in three different phases: September–October 2014, October–November 2014 and January–March 2015. Fieldwork took place in six neighbourhoods across Monrovia and in Grand Cape Mount County in the northwestern region of the country. Interviews and FGDs were facilitated by three local Liberian research assistants who also helped with recruitment of participants, translation and transcription. Owing to the security and movement restrictions put in place at this time to protect MSF staff in Liberia, it was not possible to conduct in-depth, long-term ethnographic fieldwork,

138 Umberto Pellecchia and Emilie Venables

to spend long periods in local communities or to observe daily activities because of the heightened risk of infection from crowds forming. As a result, data collection was more formalised than typical field ethnography and relied mostly on planned interactions and observations and, when possible, participation in routine activities.

Interviews and FGDs took place outdoors – under trees in local community gathering areas or on people's porches – to avoid people crowding together in restricted spaces and spreading the virus through touch. In some cases, FGDs were held in empty school classrooms when lessons had been cancelled because of the outbreak and no pupils were present. Hand-washing measures were put in place before and after interviews and FGDs, and people were asked to follow the 'no touch' policy which was being promoted across the region at the time to prevent further infections. In addition, to allow safety regulations to be met, FGD participants sat further apart than usual, creating a somewhat artificial environment. In one FGD, a female participant became very emotional discussing the impact that Ebola had had on life in her community, and one of the research assistants was left frustrated as he was unable to go to her and comfort her by touching her hand.

Interviews with survivors were also conducted at the Ebola Management Centre (EMC), as this was a place that they were familiar with and where the heart of MSF's medical and psycho-social activities took place. Some survivors were concerned about the research team visiting their homes after they had left the EMC, fearing that being seen with people recognisable as MSF staff could lead to increased stigmatisation, so they preferred to meet the researchers outside their own community. Others did not want to travel and preferred the research team to visit their home where interviews took place on terraces or in open areas outside their houses.

Data was collected during the routine activities of the ongoing emergency MSF project in Liberia, and concentrated not just on survivors but on perceptions of quarantine (Pellecchia, 2017), understandings and perceptions of Ebola in Monrovia, particularly in relation to the EMC, and how communities reacted to MSF's Ebola response.

Anthropologists' participation in MSF's projects is not new, as seen elsewhere in this book, but they became increasingly involved in MSF's Ebola projects in West Africa, along with strong health promotion teams focussing on community engagement (see excerpts from blog, Box 7.1). Anthropologists were usually established inside the medical teams to provide in-depth insight into community beliefs, perceptions and understandings of Ebola, its transmission and the support offered by MSF (Venables & Pellecchia, 2017; Venables, 2017; Pellecchia, 2017). While it was not always possible to answer the operational questions inside the timeframe allocated because of the emergency situation with its strict security measures, anthropologists – including the authors of this chapter – were able to provide a deeper insight into community life beyond the walls of the EMC within which many staff were confined.

BOX 7.1 EXCERPTS FROM MSF BLOG – EMILIE VENABLES, DECEMBER 2014

https://blogs.msf.org/bloggers/emilie/caffeine-and-reflexivity

I have been in Liberia for almost a month now, working as an anthropologist in Monrovia. During these last four weeks I have talked to endless people, asked question after question, scrawled down replies and queries and thoughts. I wake up in the night with the voices of the people I spoke to running through my head, thinking 'I should really write this down.' . . .

So now I am going to try to write it down and explain part of my role as an anthropologist in an Ebola outbreak. One of my tasks has been to find out what people think about MSF's Ebola treatment centre: what do people imagine happens inside and how can MSF help to demystify it? This is a work in progress – every time I find a new piece to the puzzle or a new research path to follow, I risk losing sight of the original objectives and need to stop and reel in my thoughts before they become too far from home.

When the outbreak began, before people had any information, they made sense of it using the frameworks and snippets of information that they had. I would do the same thing. In the same way that I Google my symptoms if I am sick, and try to out-smart and question my doctor with my own knowledge and proposed diagnosis, I would absorb every bit of information about Ebola that was available to me, whether its source was reputable or not.

This is why health promotion and the background understanding of Ebola are an essential part of responding to the outbreak. The more accurate, accessible information that can be given to communities, the more empowered they are and the more they can begin to make sense of (and prevent) Ebola.

All FGD and interview transcripts, notes from interviews and notes from observations were coded manually by the two authors and discussed with the research assistants. Common themes were then identified from the data and discussed among the wider team members including the medical team. In addition, regular feedback was given to the medical, health promotion and psycho-social teams and where possible, practical recommendations were made that could be easily and rapidly implemented in project activities. Practical examples of this included a focus on burials in the first phase of fieldwork, specifically how the local community rejected the idea of cremation; and later on, the importance of informing people about what was happening *inside* the EMC in order to dispel many of the myths and rumours that were circulating in the community. Also, traditional and community leaders were invited to the EMC to see what happened inside, and – as discussed in this chapter – understand the experiences of survivors in order to better define support for them.

Surviving in the time of outbreak

If people surviving Ebola were alive and physically restored, the social components that make a human a *person* – relationships, position and status in the community, belongings, emotions and opinions, rights and duties – were completely altered, if not eliminated, by the epidemic itself. Many survivors, after the actual process of surviving, fell into a social vacuum. In this emptiness, or "bare life", to borrow Giorgio Agamben's concept,[1] complicit with the needs of international aid actors (including MSF) and global media communication logic, the survivor gained an ephemeral status of 'hero' thanks to their ability to touch infectious patients without the need of protection. However, caught between a social emptiness and a provisional heroic status, the effect on daily life was, for many survivors, a crisis of personal and social identity. Even so, most of them did not give up and sought political recognition (and often material and financial support) by regrouping themselves under a newly created social label – the Ebola survivors. This went a long way to countering any characterisation of victimhood indirectly reproduced by charities, non-governmental organisations and the media, and showed a capacity for agency in the fragmented landscape of a post-epidemic (and post-war) Liberian society.

Back to life: the rite of passage from death to life

The word 'survivor' is normally understood to mean a person remaining alive after an event in which others died. Yet, a complete list of definitions broadens this meaning. According to the Oxford Dictionary,[2] a 'survivor' is also "the remainder of a group of people" and "a person who copes well with difficulties in life". The etymology is also quite illustrative; the English word survive comes from the Latin *supervivere*, which means 'to live beyond'. In a sense, the concept of 'survivor' has a quality of exceptionality, uniqueness and extraordinariness.[3] The survivor is a special entity – a stayer, a remainer, someone 'beyond' – but not so special as to be supernatural or other-worldly. The survivor is still a person, but has been through a process that has led to acquiring (or accomplishing) a renewed status.

In the 2014–2016 EVD outbreak in West Africa, survivors were those who had been infected by the deadly virus but had recovered and were no longer in an EMC. In most cases, this was due to their own body's natural defences and their tenacity in undertaking the palliative care offered in designated EMCs. Indeed, with the absence of curative treatment, EVD survivors could be considered to have beaten the virus on their own. EVD was believed to be incurable and untreatable, at least during the first phase of the epidemic, and awareness messages were spread throughout the three most affected countries, stating the very real risk of death in the case of infection.

Local populations were constantly reminded to apply preventive measures – avoid bodily contact; not to perform traditional funeral rituals; report symptoms when they are first observed – all with the subtle threat of certain death. Ebola was portrayed as a 'killer' and personified as a menace to community solidarity, family harmony and the slow process of rebuilding the post-war Liberian State. Liberians were invited to 'fight'; the imagery of war was used by the media, international agencies and governmental bodies, as well as being replicated by local populations, as we see in some of the following examples (Figure 7.1). Nevertheless, from August–December 2014, despite efforts to contain the spread of the virus, the number of deaths continued to rise and the messages that circulated were often inconsistent.

In this scenario, people who survived acquired a quality that could not be explained. The virus was framed by the coordinates of death, in which a few people of different ages, genders and social status survived. Local communities sought a social understanding of this phenomenon using the cultural and conceptual tools available to them. Indeed, the ethnography shows that for some, survivorship was a matter of magic or miracle. For others, it was a clear example of the conspiracy theories and rumours surrounding Ebola, in which Western powers were spreading the virus to curb local populations with the ultimate aim of exploiting resources. Then, towards the end of the outbreak (during the first months of 2015), a different approach was taken towards communication, and gradually a scientific explanation of the reasons for survival appeared. Yet, at that point, beliefs based on the initial understanding were deeply grounded and communities were starting to shift from

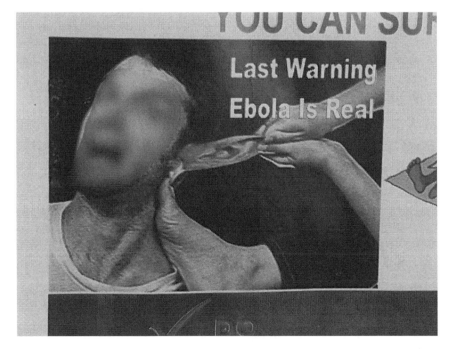

FIGURE 7.1 An example of harsh messages spread among the population

Source: Umberto Pellecchia (2015)

a sense of disappointment with their government to a self-managed approach to containing the virus.

The idea of the survivor as a new figure emerged in a very dynamic social landscape. The absence of scientific explanations for survival and the local interpretations of the experience were not the only factors. Another important influence was the way survivors took on the features of an actual *rite of passage* (Van Gennep, 1960; Turner, 1969). The stage for this ritual was the EMC, where many of those showing symptoms were brought by ambulance or family members or they arrived by themselves. Normally, sick people reached the EMC in a very advanced state of the disease, often almost unconscious. Once at the gate, they were taken by health personnel fully covered by personal protective equipment (PPE), the cars transporting them were sprayed with chlorine and their carers were asked to leave. At that point, the sick person entered the EMC, whose functioning and logic were generally unknown to local people, especially at the beginning of the outbreak, and this contributed to an initial climate of mistrust. In this sense, whoever entered that space were understood to be leaving forever.

Inside, the EMC was structured into tented passages. People – now considered as suspect cases – entered through a gate, were triaged and then moved to a 'suspect' area, where they waited for the diagnosis of the presence of the virus. If positive, the case became confirmed and the patient moved to another area for palliative care. In this last tented passage, the patient was often facing their own destiny, along with the health personnel who were acutely aware of the limits of the care they were providing. The tragic result of arriving in the 'confirmed' area was often death.

The bodily remains were then handled by special personnel, who were in charge of loading the corpses into trucks and transporting them to a crematorium. Accordingly, the visible outcome of entering the EMC was, for communities observing from outside, dead bodies being sent to an incinerator. If the family wished, a photo was taken of the deceased person and then shared with them. The remainder of the events occurring inside were a matter of secrecy, symbols (PPE), unexplainable actions (spraying) and special performers (the foreign, often white, personnel from international agencies). The process was, in sum, a ritual, whose phase of *liminality* took place inside the EMC – a 'betwixt place' where a change of status occurred (Turner, 1969). The exceptionality of the survivors was that they defied the normal outcome by staying alive. Communities were seeing people who were once sick and fated to die coming back to life, a reverse process that seemingly could not be explained. In addition to this, as described later in this chapter, these people were applauded as heroes by the personnel of international agencies.

Building the survivor's identity

Photographs of survivors leaving the dressing room, sometimes in the act of hugging an international staff member, spread throughout the media, gradually forming a fundamental part of the flow of information around Ebola. Normally, as part of the process of being discharged, the survivor was asked to place their handprint on a board beside the huge plastic tents used in the EMC. Throughout the epidemic, many handprints in different colours decorated the board. Other pictures of survivors and MSF staff were taken with the board as a backdrop and posted on the organisation's official websites and blogs. This circulation of images became global. The survivor became an identity, a crucial part of the Ebola experience, reaching its peak in the coverage by *Time* magazine.

The 'Certificate of Discharge' was the representation of the newly acquired identity and was issued after a test revealed the absence of the virus. As a sort of new identity card, the organisation's headed paper declared in a few lines the transformed status of the holder:

> On the date of issue of this document, the carrier of this certificate is declared to be cured from Ebola and does not present the risk to contaminate other people. His/her health condition does not cause a danger for the community. For this reason, he/she can return back to his/her home and working environment to continue the daily activities.

Then, in conclusion, foreseeing possible problems in acquiring a new status:

> The family, community and authorities are requested to facilitate his/her social insertion.

This certificate became, in itself, a valuable means for individuals to 'prove' their status; being formally recognised as a survivor could lead to additional support from various associations and organisations. Evoking this shared identity could also provide a link to new forms of collective assistance, and, as in the example in Box 7.2, could help to reassure others.

BOX 7.2   DISTRUST

Yes, the community . . . some of them used to pass by to speak to us, talk to us, but they did not contribute anything towards us. Nobody used to pass here, they were on that side, just like that. I was feeling bad because you could at least come round and say 'oh my brother, hello,' but there was nothing.

We brought these documents [certificate stating he was Ebola negative] and all these kinds of things so some of them started coming round and this and that. . . . Some of them want to make sure.

But as long as you've been infected with that thing and then you are free, it's hard for you to give it to someone except through sexual intercourse. This is how we've been talking to people and through these papers they started getting brave enough to come closer to us.

> But even my children or my very close friends say they are still in doubt of this thing.
>
> *(Verbatim quote from male survivor in the Chicken Soup Factory neighbourhood of Monrovia)*

The survivors were used as an asset in the community-oriented efforts to curb the epidemic. At times, they were called 'ambassadors', granted representation powers by international agencies and even governmental authorities, as in Sierra Leone (Kabba, 2014). Survivors were selected by reason of possessing an intrinsic and unquestionable feature: being a positive messenger of hope. Neither a competency nor a skill, this alleged positivity was communicated as being literally embedded in survivors' bodies. It was not a matter of social experience linked to a pathway through illness: the survivors were *in se*, in their natural bodies, a good thing.

In many professional and informal occasions, conversations with members of the communication department of MSF and other journalists suggested that the most commonly held opinion was that survivors undoubtedly gave a positive message.

Those who considered the argument further pointed out that the survivors' life was anything but easy, especially after severe family losses, as well as loss or damage to property and goods. Yet the negative personal aspects of being a survivor, such as the stigma shown previously and the loss of family and property, were seen to contrast with the positivity of the message given to the communities, which focussed around hope and welcoming people home.

"The Liberians need a message of hope, and the survivors give it", a Health Promoter Officer, part of MSF's operations in Monrovia in 2014, said to one of the authors during their fieldwork. Liberian society as a whole was regarded as a body in need of distilled positive messages. And indeed, from this standpoint, throughout the epidemic, Liberians only received bleak information alerts, phrased with negative keywords such as 'war' or 'killers'. In this landscape, the impact of the allegedly positive messages of hope was overstated and contradicted by the actual experience of survivors within their communities. In conversations held during the various periods of ethnographic fieldwork, survivors reported experiencing stigma from their neighbours on top of finding on their return home that they had lost family members, their possessions and in some cases, their jobs.

Revival of associations and agency

Particularly at the beginning of the outbreak, agencies and governmental authorities did not consider the re-integration process to be important. Given the traumatic conditions of an uncontrolled deadly epidemic, the act of surviving was assumed to be a positive experience. It was only in late 2014 and early 2015 that questions were raised about how to deal with the increasing numbers of survivors and their medical, ophthalmological and psycho-social needs. This was surprising because the health consequences of surviving EVD soon emerged, despite most clinics in the field believing that the medical process would finish after the infectious period. On the other hand, the survivors themselves soon became aware of the necessity to unite in a communal bid to get recognition of, and support for, their needs.

The divide between the portrayal of survivors and their reality started to take on a political nuance. Socially neglected and suffering rejection by stigma, many continued their search for identity and membership of a community (Bolten, 2014). As if wishing to create a new group or even a new kind of nation (Anderson, 1983), they expressed the traditional claims needed to conjure up an imagined community, including the demand for a monument.

Their political claims arose from being increasingly used as health care workers or blood donors, and from their potential involvement in clinical trials using survivors' plasma (Ebola Response Anthropology Platform, 2014; Emergency Ebola Anthropology Network, 2015; van Griensven et al., 2016).

Their role as unpaid community workers for NGOs was also scrutinised. Some members of the association in-the-making were developing the idea of being a 'resource' that many organisations, media and commentators had built around the function of the survivors (Abramowitz et al., 2015). They believed that their work as volunteers was often driven by the organisations themselves and that, in the long run, their needs extended beyond simply a set of clothes, a new mattress and some mobile phone credit.

During a gathering organised in the Pentecostal School at the gates of Monrovia, some of the survivors expressed their disappointment at having been used for many months to create awareness in their communities or as helpers in local clinics without proper compensation. Others, without calling into question the importance of helping others and insisting on the value of solidarity, were nevertheless asking for additional support from organisations and the government in terms of training or material goods such as identification documents. In both cases, the bottom line was the search for a different kind of recognition. Either through money, goods or immaterial benefits, the Ebola survivors eventually pushed for a shift in identity – from being a resource to be used, to being a resource to be recognised and compensated.

The unstable and short-term programmes of many NGOs and charities, which, like MSF, were working in an ever-changing, emergency context, also contributed to the difficulties facing survivors trying to rebuild a new life (Mukpo, 2015).

Stigmatisation of survivors

The survivor identity was not just an individual one, but something – despite the confusion and intrigue surrounding the EMC and what happened in the liminal period behind the fences – that was publicly consumed, discussed and judged. Survivors took on a role in local society – the role of hope – but at the same time, they

146 Umberto Pellecchia and Emilie Venables

were feared and stigmatised after leaving what, for many, had become the protective space of an EMC.

The survivor was often the subject of stigmatisation from family, friends, community members and the general population due to a misunderstanding about EVD and their newly acquired status of survivor (De Roo et al., 1998; Arwady et al., 2014;Venables, 2017).While survivors were portrayed as bringing hope to the nation – and the world, as stories of EVD spread through the global press – they were simultaneously feared closer to home.

In communities across Liberia, much of the anger and discrimination aimed at survivors at the time of our fieldwork appeared to be directed towards men.The belief that they could transmit the Ebola virus through sexual intercourse incited the language of war and battle (discussed previously), and in one focus group discussion, they were even described as 'atomic bombs'. Those survivors who had previously provided communities with hope because they were the 'miracles' who survived, became, in the language of battle, people who needed to be fought against, kept at a distance and protected from (Box 7.3).

BOX 7.3 RELATIVISM

We want to bring safety to the community and to the nation because one person in the nation can cause desperation for the whole nation. One man can become an atomic bomb for the whole nation: feelings are not important here! If we have to feel for x, y and z and think of their trauma their sickness will not go away . . . so let them be there. We want to keep you in here.

(Verbatim quote from an FGD participant in ELWA 3, Monrovia)

The stigmatisation of survivors, and the discourse of threat and danger around the elimination of Ebola, was at times amplified by constantly changing health promotion messages, which made it difficult for people in Liberia to understand the actual – if any – risk that survivors posed.At times, it felt as if health promotion messages from a multitude of local and international organisations confused people, particularly around the potential for the sexual transmission of EVD by male survivors.This was in part due to the body of knowledge that was growing daily as new evidence surfaced. Even as we write, three years after the worst of the outbreak, new findings and new literature are still emerging which lead to the constant need to change and adapt health promotion messages and guidelines (Deen et al., 2015, 2017).

The most recent WHO guidelines state that "the Ebola virus can persist in the semen of males for a year or more after acute infection . . . it is not clear for how long the virus is still infectious" (WHO, 2016, p. 22). The WHO thus recommend that "all EVD survivors and their sexual partners should receive counselling to ensure safe sex practices until their semen has been determined to be free of Ebola virus" (WHO, 2016, p. 22). At the time of the authors' fieldwork in 2014 and 2015, however, earlier WHO guidelines stated that "no formal evidence exists of sexual transmission, but sexual transmission from convalescent patients cannot be ruled out" (WHO, 2015).

Since we conducted this fieldwork, there have been several research studies from Ebola-affected countries demonstrating the persistence of Ebola RNA in semen for long periods of time for some Ebola survivors (Keita et al., 2017; Soka et al., 2016; Fischer & Wohl, 2016; Sissoko et al., 2017). One study in particular has suggested the need to implement semen testing programmes for EVD survivors (Deen et al., 2017). The authors of this clinical trial highlight the importance of involving survivors in such research, as well as ensuring that it is carried out soon in order to better inform policy and response efforts. Another recently published study developed an 'Ebola Virus Persistence Risk Reduction Behavioural Counselling Protocol' to provide guidance to mitigate the risk of transmission of EVD from survivors in Sierra Leone (Abad et al., 2017). The protocol was based on previously developed HIV counselling guidelines and has been shared with and adapted by EVD survivor bodily fluid testing programmes and studies in countries affected by Ebola. What was interesting to note in the study was that during the developmental stages of the protocol, female survivors in particular discussed their experiences with stigma, as well as their fears of resuming sexual activity and concerns about condom use. This suggests that stigmatisation is an ongoing issue that needs to be addressed for those surviving EVD and, in such cases, we would stress the need for the involvement of anthropologists in such research.

One of the ways in which anthropologists engaged in MSF projects in the West African region was working with the health promotion teams responsible for community outreach to contribute to the messages they were developing and ensure that any information was culturally sensitive and appropriate (Manca, 2017). However, MSF was not working in a vacuum, and many communities were targeted by other organisations with their own, slightly different, messages, despite the creation of a common attempt to harmonise the emergency response.

Health promotion messages about survivors and the potential for sexual transmission of Ebola were often misunderstood, and some communities requested a separate 'camp' to 'quarantine' men for an additional 90 days to reduce what they felt was a threat to the wider community. Understanding the meanings and sources of such stigmatisation – particularly the fear and mistrust aimed at men – is vital to be able to work with and support survivors through psycho-social care and health promotion activities.

During stigma awareness training run by one of the authors with the mental health team working in the EMC in Monrovia during November 2014, issues surrounding survivor identity – and indeed, survivor fear – were discussed with staff. While these were trained psycho-social personnel who were working with EVD daily, this did not prevent them from having their own questions and concerns about EVD survivors. Staff themselves experienced daily stigmatisation from their families, taxi drivers, churches and neighbours because of their work, and many believed that their contact with survivors could exacerbate this.

The main questions they asked concerned their own risks, especially in relation to the survivors who were employed in the EMC. As described previously, survivors could be considered 'useful' if able to take on roles that other staff could not, and were able to empathise with current patients based on their own experiences in a similar way that 'expert clients' in HIV projects share their experiences with others to promote HIV testing and adherence to treatment. Survivors working inside the EMC did not have to wear the same level of PPE as the rest of the staff, because they were no longer at risk of becoming infected. Instead, they wore what was referred to as 'light' PPE, which gave them a degree of protection but meant that they were not restricted by hot, heavy PPE and goggles, and could thus engage more easily with patients and offer them support and reassurance. Some staff questioned this practice in relation to themselves; they wanted to know whether a survivor who carried the virus on their own skin, although not becoming re-infected themselves, could pose a risk to the rest of the staff.

Ongoing support for survivors

What do the anthropological data just presented mean for survivors, for MSF and for other organisations' activities with survivors? How does an understanding of survivors' voices, feelings and complex and shifting identities lead to support during the transition to life outside the tented confines of the EMC? MSF closed its last project for survivors in October 2016, after supporting survivors with medical and psycho-social care in Liberia, Guinea and Sierra Leone. Before its closure, the survivors' clinic in Monrovia provided more than 11,500 consultations between January 2015 and August 2016 as a result of ongoing need. In addition, a clinic in Conakry, Guinea, cared for 330 survivors and their relatives, and a clinic in Freetown, Sierra Leone, assisted more than 400 survivors and their families by providing individual and group psycho-social sessions. Ongoing psycho-social support has since been handed over to local organisations.

In providing an anthropological understanding of the multiple meanings of being a 'survivor' and the impact this has upon individual lives after discharge from the EMC and reintegration into their 'before' lives, we also stress the importance of such a gaze when designing and implementing programmes for survivors (Figure 7.2). We also highlight the importance of including survivors themselves, whether through formal research studies, observation and participation in community events where survivors are present or simply listening to people's individual experiences. Ensuring that survivors and survivor organisations continue to be heard is challenging, particularly in a climate where the international presence has been significantly reduced and activities have been handed over to local actors, but it is essential for the sustainability and continuity of programmes providing

FIGURE 7.2 An MSF health promotion activity: celebrating the return of survivors at home

Source: Umberto Pellecchia (2015)

psycho-social support. In addition, the presence of structures to monitor and evaluate locally run survivor assistance programmes are crucial to ensure that people's ongoing needs are met.

Conclusion

This chapter has studied the Ebola survivor in Liberia through an anthropological lens, considering how shifts in survivor identity occur and how these are managed by the individual, as well as reflecting upon the advantages of an anthropological involvement in MSF operations.

The concept of survivors as heroes per se, and success stories framed around the status of being biologically alive, led MSF and other organisations to use them in the public arena without questioning the social foundations and political meanings of survivors' newly gained identity. This represented a divide between the organisation's idea and the reality, but it also showed the limits of embedding a purely biomedical vision of the person (equivalent to Giorgio Agamben's "bare life") into MSF's approach. As much research confirms, MSF's medical mandate is challenged by the socio-political implications of every form of life within a given context: the survivors' experience in Liberia represents a good example of the risks of viewing

150 Umberto Pellecchia and Emilie Venables

medical action as un-anchored from its social dimensions (Fassin, 2012; Redfield, 2013). For the patient, the social dimensions are profoundly associated with their experience of illness.

Knowledge gained through the anthropological fieldwork of the two authors was employed directly in the day-to-day running of project activities and contributed to a wider discussion on the role of anthropology in situations such as the 2014–2016 Ebola outbreak. MSF was not the only organisation to employ anthropologists in its work in West Africa, and the scale of anthropological insight – and development of a specific anthropological approach to sharing experiences and providing recommendations – was larger than in previous, smaller outbreaks such as in the Democratic Republic of Congo (Abramowitz, 2015; Minor, 2017; Marí Saéz, 2015).

This research showed the practical value of involving anthropologists as early as possible in an outbreak, so that their findings could be acted on as quickly as possible. This is even more significant in a rapidly changing environment such as Ebola's spread across Liberia and its neighbouring countries. While not always possible, and always dependent on the skills, experience and availability of staff, anthropological intervention has been widely approved and has been recommended in different reports and evaluations of the response (MSF, 2016).

Anthropologists cannot work in isolation, and another lesson gained from the outbreak in West Africa was the importance of linking anthropological work to that of health promotion teams, medical personnel and psycho-social staff. This ensures that anthropological findings have a practical application, can be used in project activities and ultimately will improve the situation of the people and patients who are at the heart of any MSF programme. Practical recommendations included sensitive management of traditional burials and deaths that occurred at the EMC, communication about the inner workings of the EMC to outside communities through the engagement of local leaders, and acknowledging the importance of community engagement when considering implementing clinical trials. Findings can also be used to create practical training tools and information, such as the stigma awareness workshop, which can in turn be utilised by health promotion teams working in local communities (Change Project, 2003). While field-based anthropological involvement in MSF projects finished after the outbreak was declared over, further anthropological research could be conducted for several more years to understand how survivors continue to live and manage their identities and to establish what kind of ongoing support they still require, particularly in light of the ongoing Ebola responses in the Democratic Republic of Congo.

Notes

1 Philosopher Giorgio Agamben's use of "bare life" refers to his theories on biopower and state of exception (Agamben, 1998). Agamben refers to the Greek distinction between *bios* (the form and manner in which life is lived) and *zoe* (the mere biological fact of life) that the modern term 'life' overshadows. He sees that in the modern system of sovereignty (to a certain extent framed within Michel Foucault's idea of governmentality, see Foucault, 2009) emphasis is given to the sheer biological facts of life over the *ways* that life is lived

(socially, culturally, politically). Being merely biologically alive, for the current system of power, becomes merely a sufficient condition for life. Rather, Agamben sees the necessity to broaden the concept of life to include social aspects, legal rights and political agency.

2 https://en.oxforddictionaries.com/definition/survivor
3 www.etymonline.com/index.php?term=survive&allowed_in_frame=0

References

Abad, N., Malik, T., Ariyarajah, A., Ongpin, P. et al., (2017). Development of risk reduction behavioral counseling for Ebola virus disease survivors enrolled in the Sierra Leone Ebola Virus Persistence Study, 2015–2016. *PLoS Neglected Tropical Diseases.* **11**(9). doi:10.1371/journal. pntd.0005827

Abramowitz, S., McLean, K.E., McKune, S.L., Bardosh, K.L. et al., (2015). Community-centered responses to Ebola in urban Liberia: the view from below. *PLoS Neglected Tropical Diseases.* **9**(5). doi:10.1371/journal.pntd.0003706

Agamben, G., (1998). *Homo Sacer: sovereign power and bare life.* Stanford, CA: Stanford University Press.

Anderson, B., (1983). *Imagined communities: reflections on the origin and spread of nationalism.* London: Verso.

Arwady, M.A., Garcia, E.L., Wollor, B., Mabande, L.G., Reaves, E.J. and Montgomery, J.M. and Centers for Disease Control and Prevention, (2014). Reintegration of Ebola survivors into their communities: firestone District, Liberia, 2014. *Morbidity and Mortality Weekly.* **63**(50), 1207–1209.

Baker, A., (2017). Liberian Ebola fighter, a TIME person of the year, dies in childbirth. *Time Magazine.* Available from: http://time.com/4683873/ebola-fighter-time-person-of-the-year-salome-karwah/?iid=sr-link1

Bolten, C.E., (2014). Articulating the invisible: Ebola beyond witchcraft in Sierra Leone. *Hot Spots, Cultural Anthropology Online.* (7 October). Available from: https://culanth.org/fieldsights/596-articulating-the-invisible-ebola-beyond-witchcraft-in-sierra-leone

Change Project, (2003). *Understanding and challenging HIV stigma: toolkit for action.* Washington, DC: The Change Project.

Christie, A., Davies-Wayne, G.J., Cordier-Lasalle, T. et al., (2015). Possible sexual transmission of Ebola virus – Liberia, 2015. *Morbidity and Mortality Weekly.* **64**(17), 479–481.

Deen, G.F., Broutet, N., Xu, W., Knust, B. et al., (2015). Ebola RNA persistence in semen of Ebola virus disease survivors – preliminary report. *New England Journal of Medicine.* doi:10.1056/NEJMoa1511410

Deen, G.F., McDonald, S.L.R., Marrinan, J.E., Sesay, F.R. et al., (2017). Implementation of a study to examine the persistence of Ebola virus in the body fluids of Ebola virus disease survivors in Sierra Leone: methodology and lessons learned. *PLoS Neglected Tropical Diseases.* **11**(9). doi:10.1371/journal.pntd.0005723

De Roo, A., Ado, B., Rose, B., Guimard, Y. et al., (1998). Survey among survivors of the 1995 Ebola epidemic in Kikwit, Demographic Republic of Congo: their feelings and experiences. *Tropical Medicine and International Health.* **3**(11), 883–885. doi:10.1046/j.1365-3156.1998.00322.x

Ebola Response Anthropology Platform, (2014). Available from: www.ebola-anthropology.net/wp-content/uploads/2014/11/Anthro-Brief-Identifying-and-Enrolling-Survivors-to-Donate-Blood-10Nov14.pdf

Emergency Ebola Anthropology Network, (2015). Available from: www.ebola-anthropology.net/wp-content/uploads/2015/01/Emergency-Ebola-Anthropology-Network-Culture-and-Clinical-Trials-ADVISORY-BRIEF-FINAL1.pdf

Fassin, D., (2012). *Humanitarian reason: a moral history of the present*. Berkeley: University of California Press.

Fischer, W.A. and Wohl, D.A., (2016). Confronting Ebola as a sexually transmitted infection. *Clinical Infectious Diseases*. **62**(10). doi:10.1093/cid/ciw123

Foucault, M., (2009). *Security, territory, population. Lectures at the College De France, 1977–78*. London: Palgrave.

Harries, J., Jacobs, M. and Davies, S.J., (2016). Ebola survivors: not out of the woods yet. *BMJ*. 2016 Jan 22: 532.

Kabba, M.,(2014). Ebola survivors are our ambassadors-Pres. Koroma. *Sierra Leone News*. [online]. 27 February. Available from: https://awoko.org/2014/10/29/sierra-leone-newsebola-survivors-are-our-ambassadors-pres-koroma/

Keita, A.K., Toure, A., Sow, M.S., Raoul, H. et al., (2017). Extraordinary long-term and fluctuating persistence of Ebola virus RNA in semen of survivors in Guinea: implications for public health. *Clinical Microbiology and Infection*. **23**(6), 412–413. doi:10.1016/j.cmi.2016.11.005

Manca, M.C., (2017). 'Yassaba' or the fear of being abandoned: adapting health-promotion messages to incorporate local meanings in *Guinée Forestière*. *Anthropology in Action*. **24**(2). doi:10.3167/aia.2017.240202

Marí Saéz, A., Weiss, S., Nowak, K., Lapeyre, V. et al., (2015). Investigating the zoonotic origin of the West African Ebola epidemic. *EMBO Molecular Medicine*. **7**(1), 17–23. doi:10.15252/emmm.201404792

Mate, S.E., Kugelman, J.R., Nyenswah, T.G., Ladner, J.T. et al., (2015). Molecular evidence of sexual transmission of Ebola virus. *New England Journal of Medicine*. **373**(25), 2448–2454. doi:10.1056/NEJMoa1509773

Minor, O., (2017). Ebola and accusation: gender dimensions of stigma in Sierra Leone's Ebola response. *Anthropology in Action*. **24**(2), 25–35. [online]. [viewed 6 November 2018] doi:10.3167/aia.2017.240204

MSF, (2016). Stockholm evaluation unit. MSF archives. *OCB Ebola Review*.

Mukpo, A., (2015). Survivor guilt: former Ebola patients struggle with virus' legacy. *Al Jazeera*. 12 April 2015, 05:00. Available from: http://america.aljazeera.com/articles/2015/4/12/ebola-survivors-liberia-struggle-to-cope.html

Pellecchia, U., (2017). Quarantine and its malcontents: how Liberians responded to the Ebola epidemic containment measures. *Anthropology in Action*. **24**(2), 15–24. doi:10.3167/aia.2017.240203

Redfield, P., (2013). *Life in crisis: the ethical journey of Doctors without Borders*. Berkeley: University of California Press. doi:10.1080/17441692.2013.859721

Sissoko, D., Duraffour, S., Kerber, R., Kolie, J.S., Beavogui, A.H. et al., (2017). Persistence and clearance of Ebola virus RNA from seminal fluid of Ebola virus disease survivors: a longitudinal analysis and modelling study. *Lancet Global Health*. **5**(1), 80–88. doi:10.1016/S2214-109X(16)30243-1

Soka, M., Choi, M., Baller, A., White, S., Rogers, E., Purpura, L. et al., (2016). Prevention of sexual transmission of Ebola in Liberia through a national semen testing and counselling programme for survivors: an analysis of Ebola virus RNA results and behavioural data. *Lancet Global Health*. **4**(10), 736–743. doi:10.1016/S2214-109X(16)30175-9

Sprecher, A., (2015). Handle survivors with care. Editorial. *New England Journal of Medicine*. **377**, 1480–1482. doi:10.1056/NEJMe1512928

Turner, V., (1969). *The ritual process: structure and anti-structure*. Harmondsworth: Penguin.

van Gennep, A., (1960). *The rites of passage*. London: Routledge and Kegan Paul.

van Griensven, J., Edwards, E., De Lamballerie, X., Semple, M.G. et al., (2016). Evaluation of convalescent plasma for Ebola virus disease in Guinea. *New England Journal of Medicine*. **374**(1), 33–42. doi:10.1056/NEJMoa1511812

Venables, E., (2017). 'Atomic Bombs' in Monrovia, Liberia, 'Atomic Bombs' in Monrovia, Liberia: the identity and stigmatisation of Ebola survivors. *Anthropology in Action*. **24**(2), 36–43. doi:10.3167/aia.2017.240205

Venables, E. and Pellecchia, U., (2017). Engaging anthropology in an Ebola outbreak: case studies from West Africa. *Anthropology in Action*. **24**(2), 1–8. doi:10.3167/aia.2017.240201

WHO, (2015). *Sexual transmission of the Ebola virus: evidence and knowledge gaps*. Geneva, Switzerland: World Health Organization. Available from: http://www.who.int/reproductivehealth/topics/rtis/ebola-virus-semen/en/

WHO, (2016). *Clinical care for survivors of Ebola virus disease: interim guidance*. Geneva, Switzerland: World Health Organization. Available from: https://www.who.int/csr/resources/publications/ebola/guidance-survivors/en/

WHO, (2018). *Maternal mortality*. Geneva, Switzerland: World Health Organization. Available from: www.who.int/mediacentre/factsheets/fs348/en/

8

INVISIBLE DENGUE

Epidemics and politics in Léogâne, Haiti

Jean-François Véran

Introduction

> I first heard of dengue with the CDC [Centers for Disease Control and Prevention] study (2012). As far as I'm concerned, in Haiti, we didn't have it until then. It is like cholera. They wanted us to believe that we had it all here. But it is wrong. We studied every epidemic disease that exists here. I don't want to hear that it is our fault. From a scientific perspective, I can believe that the vectors were indeed present. But it [dengue] never came out. If we didn't study it, it is because it didn't exist.
>
> *(Senior national MSF doctor)*

This somewhat exasperated and bitter quote comes from an Médecins Sans Frontières Haitian doctor while being questioned on why dengue[1] was never diagnosed in his hospital, even though there was considerable laboratory and entomological evidence for both the disease's high endemicity and for the vector's presence in the region. Later, a local medical authority[2] confidentially told me that this doctor had been withdrawn from a dengue training programme because he was "ideologically against dengue". How can a medical doctor be – or be accused of being – ideologically opposed to a clinically well-documented disease?

It is a fact that dengue wasn't diagnosed in the region of Léogâne until numerous foreign staff working in Haiti in the aftermath of the 2010 earthquake began to be infected – some returned with severe (haemorrhagic) forms. Since then, alerted by this, the international NGOs present in the region began to raise the concern that dengue was dramatically under-diagnosed. A meeting held locally by the US Centers for Disease Control and Prevention (CDC) in 2012, which was attended by all local medical authorities, provoked a blast of discontentment. The CDC was presenting epidemiological evidence of dengue's extremely high prevalence, as

Invisible dengue   **155**

well as entomological evidence that mosquito presence was 'above acceptable levels'. Participants left the meeting split between scepticism and open accusations of manipulation. Meanwhile, dengue remained invisible among the local people, and this presented a problem for international medical organisations, since invisibility meant no vector control, no adequate health-seeking behaviour, no diagnosis and no treatment.

The anthropological assessment described here was expected to somehow 'solve the puzzle'; that is, to unveil the reasons why dengue was subject to such resistance (from now on, we will refer to this phenomenon as 'dengue resistance') and invisibility, and propose ways to reach better awareness. The underlying assumption of the assessment was that culture was at play in a context marked with recent catastrophes and their cortège of fears and prophecies among a notably traditional and superstitious people. And that assumption included the medical staff themselves.

Between November 2010 and March 2011, during the great cholera outbreak that followed the earthquake, I was an outreach health promotion coordinator, and as a consequence, I was already familiar with the spontaneous narratives that international actors produce when confronted with perceived 'cultural obstacles' to adequate health-seeking behaviour: "they contaminate because of their funeral rituals", "they still prefer their traditional healers", "they believe cholera is a curse", etc. All these notions usually resulted in two messages spread widely as key health promotion messages: "cholera is not voodoo", and "*lavé main nou*" (wash your hands). By this, international agents were, albeit unintentionally, practising cultural relativism: "cholera is not voodoo", as they were advocating, is different from saying "voodoo is a superstition, it does not exist", as would probably have been the message 50 years ago. "Cholera is not voodoo" implies that voodoo might be something, but cholera is not. Culture was indeed understood in its respectable otherness, yet it was still held accountable for cholera's dazzling expansion, and dengue's persistent invisibility. In this latter case, the anthropological component of the dengue assessment was precisely to capture those cultural elements that fostered the curse of invisibility.

This chapter intends to elaborate on how cultural relativism permeates humanitarian interventions, even though international actors express a concern to be more receptive, respectful and efficient while dealing with local people. It is out of this concern that the anthropologist makes their way through the fields of humanitarian action, until then reserved for skillful doctors and logisticians. However, what should be celebrated as a success of anthropology – to make 'culture' the core paradigm – where it's most needed, rapidly turns into a concern and a call for responsibility – the responsibility, in humanitarian settings, to monitor the uses and abuses of culture, and to constantly remind us that culture is not a panacea to fix community engagement strategies. Culture itself must be relativised among the many factors, sociological, economic, political, etc., that are also at play. This is what this essay on dengue 'invisibility' in Haiti is about.

This study was fieldwork undertaken as part of the project: 'Dengue: Surveillance and Rapid Assessments in Haiti', initiated by the Innovation Unit from

Médecins Sans Frontières (MSF) in collaboration with the Brazilian Medical Unit (BRAMU).[3] The objective was to conduct a perception/practices in-depth assessment involving community, health centres and stakeholders. The data presented here were collected during two research periods: the first one (November 2010–March 2011) at Léogâne focussed on the MSF response to the cholera outbreak that followed the earthquake (12 January 2010).[4] The second one (during May 2014), also at Léogâne, was more specifically dedicated to the dengue assessment. During that second period, activities were strongly affected by a major chikungunya outbreak in Léogâne that hit an estimated 50% of the population in three weeks.[5] It turned out to be an excellent opportunity to reveal and analyse the large invisibility surrounding dengue in contrast with the hyper-visibility chikungunya acquired in just a few days.

The community element of the study involved 224 adults and their families (approximately 1,500 individuals), selected by the convenience criteria of their living locally. This was in contrast to previous sampling that had included people from the coastal areas, the lowlands and the mountains. Using a questionnaire and semi-structured interviews, the following issues were investigated: 1) awareness of dengue and belief in or denial of its existence, 2) beliefs around the cause(s) of fever and other dengue symptoms and 3) health-seeking behaviour in the case of a fever, and the understanding of biomedical and traditional treatments for dengue.

For the health workers, semi-structured interviews and focus groups were undertaken with 17 MSF national staff, 30 government-run health centre supervisors and four voodoo specialists and natural healers. Previous dengue training and clinical experience, and the ideological background to the participant's belief in or denial of dengue were the focus of the study.

Dengue resistance: a biomedical perspective

A differential diagnostic, with dengue as the last option

For MSF doctors at Léogâne hospital at the time the study was conducted (May 2012), dengue came last in common medical practice and differential diagnostics – if it was ever mentioned. Heavy fever was likely to be diagnosed as malaria or typhoid and, when laboratory tests were negative, the symptom was usually classified as 'indeterminate fever'.

When associated with cephalalgia (headache), most of these indeterminate fevers were effectively treated as malaria. As dengue viremia and symptoms usually regress within four to eight days, the treatment was perceived as functional and the malaria diagnosis was retroactively confirmed: dengue invisibility was therefore reproduced. As an MSF doctor concluded: "we can't ignore that we have a lot of fevers of unknown nature. We do a lot of therapy against malaria even if the tests turn out negative, and it always ends up working".

The overall lack of laboratory tests for dengue was indeed a main factor for its invisibility. The cost was considered to be prohibitive: no medical institution in post-earthquake Haiti would have had the means to implement it, anyway. Additionally, low demand for medical intervention logically derived from the perceived inexistence or low impact of dengue within Haiti.

As reported by MSF staff and the Medical Coordination of the Ministry of Health (MoH) in Léogâne, doctors who attended medical school in Haiti received no instruction on dengue, and consequently could not diagnose it. The argument was circular. Haitian doctors were trained only for existing infections in Haiti and, as no training was given on dengue, it surely did not exist:

> We studied every epidemic disease that exists here. I don't want to hear that it is our fault. From a scientific perspective, I can believe that the vectors were indeed present. But it [dengue] never came out. If we didn't study it, it is because it didn't exist.
>
> *(Senior MSF Haitian doctor)*

As clearly shown by this quote, Haitian MSF doctors themselves believed dengue was not an issue in Haiti. One of them, with first-hand experience of a dengue epidemic and who had received clinical training on dengue in Cuba, would maintain that dengue was not a serious issue in Haiti despite his experience.

The main observation supporting the case for the nonexistence of dengue was the lack of any diagnosed severe case of the disease. While reporting mortality associated with 'indeterminate fever', the absence of haemorrhagic symptoms strengthened this conviction. Even in an MSF hospital, with adequately trained personnel, differential diagnostics only marginally included dengue. And even then, the diagnosis was difficult to sustain in front of sceptical colleagues:

> When I returned from Cuba, nobody here talked about dengue. One colleague of mine, also trained in Cuba, once wrote on a medical file 'dengue suspicion'. His tutor humiliated him publically. "Don't you know Haitians don't get dengue?" And everybody was advised not to get anywhere near this doctor. He even got relocated to another health centre. But there is no case because there is no test. And we can't open the debate. Coming from Cuba, we can't argue. And there is no protocol, no laboratory to support us.

During the study period, I followed the case of a ten-year-old boy with haemorrhagic symptoms and a positive dengue test, who also had pneumonia. Yet, no reference to dengue appeared in the medical records. This particular case of 'active invisibilisation' confirmed that, beyond the lack of training and laboratory support, there was a confrontation around the disease between international and Haitian MSF staff, which mirrored broader issues.

The inconclusive laboratory 'evidences'

Given that this whole issue hinges on the presence or not of a disease caused by a mosquito-driven virus, the dispute seems to be a simple one to settle: can the virus and the vector be found in the Léogâne area?

Some 20 years ago, Paul Farmer had already written about his clinical experience as a founder of a hospital in Centre Haiti. He stated that the three years after the military coup of 1991 were a: "sanitary disaster . . . with epidemic outbursts of dengue" (Farmer, 2003, p. 26). This means that the presence of dengue with significant morbidity had already been established. Between 2011 and 2013, the Notre-Dame University Haiti Programme studied dengue with a sample of 61 children aged 2–10 years in Ça-Ira, a coastal village near Léogâne. The research was based on a Polymerase Chain Reaction multiplex protocol. Results were 62.3% positive in 2011 and 80.3% positive in 2013, with identical results for serology 2–4 and 1–3 (Poirier et al., 2016).[6] They confirmed an undeniable and extreme exposure to the virus. However, the study contained no clinical data, neither on the symptomatic/asymptomatic ratio, nor on morbidity/mortality; it showed people had been infected, but not that they were sick.

In October 2012, the Haitian Ministry of Health and the CDC were notified of 25 recent dengue cases among non-governmental organisation (NGO) workers. On this notification, the CDC conducted a dengue investigation in Port-au-Prince and Léogâne. It revealed that 10% of the participants (both international and Haitian workers) had been infected between September and November 2012. However, the study also reported that "only one Haitian with a recent dengue infection reported dengue-like symptoms, and no Haitians reported symptoms of severe dengue" (p. 8). The authors also reported that "in our investigation, some Haitian NGO staff said that dengue was not a health threat to Haitians and therefore declined to participate", and they outlined this refusal as a limitation in the interpretation of the results; i.e. the sample was biased because of the resistance of national staff. They finally acknowledged that "while our investigation and previous studies collectively provide strong evidence for dengue endemicity in Haiti, questions remain about the clinical course of dengue among Haitians" (Salyer et al., 2014, p. 8).

Laboratory studies were insufficiently crossed with clinical reports to either confirm or refute the Haitian resistance hypothesis. In other words, because they failed to establish a clear pattern of local dengue symptom and morbidity experience, the Haitian medical staff systematically doubted and criticised these studies. This is why even clear laboratory tests establishing the prevalence of the virus did not result in better dengue visibility. For the national medical staff, the resistance against dengue was not 'irrational'. It simply expressed the insufficiency of the laboratory results to account for the clinical lack of evidence.

Yet, in the case previously mentioned of the doctor accused of being 'ideologically against dengue', this doctor was perceived – together with all those doctors who did not acknowledge, or insufficiently acknowledged, dengue – as displaying incomprehensible and idiosyncratic behaviour. Although medical practice is fundamentally evidence-based (clinical and laboratory), those doctors were allegedly irrational, and therefore bad doctors. Between the 'superstitions' and 'cultural traditions' of the people in general and the 'ideology' of those doctors in particular, a continuum was established, trickling down to the false proposition that ignorant locals must be educated because they lack proper knowledge about health issues even when they are health professionals.

Indeed, the simple fact that an external agency, the CDC, arrived in 2012 and gathered the local doctors to 'reveal dengue' to them upon laboratory 'evidences', instead revealed the absence of correct diagnoses and necessarily implied a confrontation between national doctors and international organisations.

Faced with the tacit accusation that the local doctors were failing to apply a simple principle of causality (here is the vector, here is the reservoir and here is the virus; therefore, here is the disease) and the explicit challenge to their medical authority, these doctors reacted by making their case on the basis of rational and clinically based elements, and sustained their scepticism about CDC's revelation that dengue had a high prevalence in the region. If it is true that: "Medicine's position today ... has an officially approved monopoly of the right to define health and illness, and to treat illness" (Good et al., 2010, p. 56), the medical national staff were competing for this monopoly.

> In 2012, CDC came with that dengue story because expats got sick. So they made a study. The doctors from Léogâne were shocked because here there is no dengue. But the expats also were circulating in the Dominican Republic and Guadeloupe. This is where they contracted the disease. Just like that, by chance, it was the MSF staff that was sick. The CDC in its study never got the courage to bring about this relation with the expats. I wanted the researchers to explore this hypothesis of imported dengue. In France, when dengue is talked about, it is mentioned that it's imported dengue. Why not here? The direction [MSF] thought that I was hostile to dengue. They tried to convince me. But I only wanted the truth, and the studies are more than doubtful.
>
> *(Haitian medical doctor)*

Maladiblan *and the racial argument*

There is a widespread notion among medical staff that Haitians do not get dengue, or, if they do, it is asymptomatic and never severe. This notion is centred on the 'afro-descendant hypothesis'. In 2001, Halstead showed that the annual dengue infection rate among school children in Port-au-Prince was high (30%). However, the study could not identify a single case of severe dengue fever (haemorrhagic fever). The author concluded that this finding provided "further evidence of a dengue resistance gene in black populations" (Halstead, 2001, p. 180). The same hypothesis was consistently upheld in nearby Cuba, where race was presented as a risk factor for dengue haemorrhagic fever:

> Cuban Dengue Hemorrhagic Fever (DHF) outbreaks have provided evidence of a reduced risk of people of Negroid race for DHF compared to those of Caucasoid race. These observations from Cuban dengue outbreaks have significant epidemiological interest, as the differences in susceptibility to

DHF among racial groups in Cuba coincide with that reported in African and Black Caribbean populations.

(Sierra et al., 2007, p. 533)

In a highly racialised environment, and in a context where biomedicine historically struggled within a 'dialectic of healing powers' never far from the shadow of colonial power itself (Brodwin, 1996), the racial hypothesis was known, widespread and popular among medical staff. It was a good argument why 'Haitians don't get dengue'. The fact that dengue existence was revealed upon the infection of white people confirmed the racial perspective and gave the full meaning to what quickly became dengue's nickname among the hospital staff: *maladiblan* (white's disease).

Aside from dengue, the argument that there are racially based diseases was not only upheld by local health professionals, but also by international medical workers themselves. For instance, they frequently stressed that black women had very low haemoglobin rates (between five and eight) and argued forcefully that sickle cell anaemia was indeed a 'black disease'. An international midwife even stressed that under such low haemoglobin conditions, any haemorrhagic fever would be quite noticeable. Returning to the argument: if there were 'black diseases', then there could also be 'white diseases', and dengue was one of them. The racial argument appeared all the more sustainable since it matched everyday clinical experience; all medical staff that were consulted affirmed they had never met a single case of haemorrhagic dengue in their whole career. Aside from the white internationals, that is.

Finally, this argument converged with the hypothesis that dengue is endemic in Haiti (Salyer et al., 2014), but was also compatible with the assertion of its innocuousness. The reasoning ended in a perfect tautology: there was no haemorrhagic dengue because (black) Haitians didn't develop these symptoms, even when they were infected with the virus. And because Haitians didn't develop it, it was never diagnosed.

The taxonomic trap of dengue fever

At this stage of the assessment, it became relevant for the MSF's project to understand how the resistance of the medical staff towards the recognition of dengue was affecting local people's knowledge of the disease, its vector and its symptoms, and health-seeking behaviour. The underlying assumption was that since laboratory results showed such high infection levels and no case was diagnosed, then dengue was a disease neglected by the national doctors, and people with dengue were left untreated. Dengue would then be a 'gap', gaps being central arguments for the development of MSF projects or for the extension of existing assistance packages.

As part of the anthropological assessment, we conducted a quick quantitative study (n = 224) among the people living in the coastal areas, the lowlands and the mountains. That left no doubt: only 1.8% of respondents spontaneously mentioned dengue as an example of a febrile infection. When dengue was mentioned by its name, 88% of participants had never heard of it. It is noteworthy that 45.8% of those who knew about dengue were concentrated in a coastal village where MSF had previously done a health promotion assessment. Among the dengue-aware group, respondents reported one single case of dengue, diagnosed by an NGO. The survey participants never mentioned dengue as auto-diagnostic for fever symptoms. This data logically mirrored weak medical recognition, under-diagnosis and an overall deficit of health promotion; invisibility was systemic.

By contrast, the population had a long experience with malaria and typhoid. The survey established that spontaneous notoriety was comparatively high (59% for malaria, 40% for typhoid, 34.4% for chikungunya and 27% for common flu), and medical health-seeking behaviour was well established. This notoriety was logically correlated with routine medical diagnosis, as 35.5% of fever symptoms reported by participants over the previous six months were diagnosed as malaria by a medical facility, 16.1% were diagnosed as chikungunya and 11.3% were diagnosed as typhoid. It is also noteworthy that reported malaria cases over the previous six months were equally distributed throughout most of the studied areas, with lower occurrences in the mountain region. Malaria was a consistent experience in the whole region.

The semi-structured interviews complementing the quantitative study revealed that the two diseases – malaria and typhoid – coexisted with fevers of 'spiritual' origin. Within the local taxonomy, there was no such a thing as 'indeterminate fevers'. Fever symptoms can have a clear medical identification, like malaria, or have a clear spiritual one. For example, children are taught not to kick empty cans or bottles lying on the floor, as they may contain a zombie that will provoke *corcho* (literally, 'hot body'). In this case, the family is likely to seek spiritual and/or traditional healing. According to the type of fever, the cure is attained by means of pharmaceutical drugs and/or a large natural pharmacopoeia. It mainly consists of local herbs and teas, mostly *assorossie* (*Momordica charantia*), a renowned natural fever reducer, *lila* or *laloi* (*Aloe vera*) used for superficial skin infections, and *mombinbata* (*Trichiliahirta sp.*). A mixture of Clairin, a local rum, and starch sometimes relieves itching of the rash provoked by fever. Bathing in cold water is a widespread practice. Sometimes, a headband containing plants is tied to the forehead. Paracetamol is by far the most popular pharmaceutical drug, followed by diclofenac.

In summary, the community assessment showed that although there was a clear taxonomy and a set of practices for heavy fever, dengue was invisible. Its symptoms were therefore likely to be caught in a classificatory trap between malaria-like fevers and spiritual affections. The weak symptom specificity and fast self-recovery of most infected individuals probably reinforced this invisibility. Furthermore, 65% of the fever cases reported in the quantitative survey (referring to the previous six-month period) were self-medicated, and therefore, they had never been seen by a medical doctor. This weak medical health-seeking behaviour, correlated with restricted access to medical care, reinforced dengue invisibility. Finally, at the community level, people ignored dengue-related mortality – no one dies of a disease that nobody knows about.

162 Jean-François Véran

Yet over the previous six months, 6.1% of the participants, or someone in their family, experienced the blood in the gums, nose, vomit or urine associated with a febrile condition. This, of course, did not prove that haemorrhagic dengue was implicated, but it surely kept the hypothesis open and showed the need for further investigation.

'Take care of your mosquitoes'

Based on the CDC revelation that the mosquito was present 'above acceptable levels', largely due to the lack of vector control, the NGOs working in Léogâne (including MSF) launched a health promotion campaign on dengue carried out by their health promotion teams. Dengue began to be 'revealed' to the local people, with a message combining the importance of vector control and the necessity for individual protection. Avoiding infection by a disease nobody had heard about until then suddenly became the responsibility of the local people: "it's a community work, we all have to fight the mosquito" was the motto of the health promotion. This message proved difficult to get through local resistance. There was reluctance because of the innocuousness of the message. How was it possible to fight the mosquito in a place where there was no wastewater treatment and the sewers were open? How can contamination be prevented if prevention tools like mosquito nets or repellents were not available?

Within a few weeks, the scepticism of national doctors had extended to the general population. During the health promotion sessions, hostility was palpable as the people felt as if they were being blamed for 'not taking care of their mosquitoes', while the real responsibility was not addressed: *maladiblan* was sent by the whites.

> The expats travel a lot in countries like in Africa. So this kind of idea progresses: it's the expat who infect the mosquitoes. They say they have registered dengue cases amongst Haitians. But the fact that there hasn't been an epidemic like chikungunya now makes it hard to believe because we don't see anything. So we just say it's the expats who have it. We didn't have it here before.
>
> *(Community leader)*

An anthropology of modern epidemics in Haiti

The 'community' assessment established a clear correlation between the medical resistance to acknowledging dengue and ignorance of the disease in the community. Dengue resistance was more than simply a confrontation discourse between international and national medical staff around symbolic and material issues, as MSF had experienced in many settings (Shevchenko & Fox, 2008). The assessment confirmed that dengue had never been considered and treated as a public health problem at a regional level because local people were largely unaware of it. This establishes the good faith of the national doctors when they were saying that dengue only became an issue after the arrival of the international NGOs and their workers, but it does not explain why such a resistance continued after its 'revelation'. Why were the laboratory results doubted in the first place? Independently of whether Haitian people were racially resistant to dengue or not, why was dengue so hard to acknowledge and integrate within medical practice?

'We will always believe in sent diseases'

Faced with the 'racial' argument sustained by national staff, the international staff would invoke Haitians' culture as the key explanation for the resistance to the proper diagnosis and treatment of dengue. Eager to distance himself from his 'ideological' colleagues, a local doctor explained: "the Haitians will never renounce to attribute diseases to witchcraft. Maybe differently from the 70s [and] 80s. But we will always believe in sent diseases". In the hospital, in their practice as nurses, midwives or doctors, some international workers would maintain this exact cultural argument to account for the generally inadequate health-seeking behaviour of their patients for all sorts of afflictions, or for the lack of professionalism of their national colleagues. Within that critical mindset, 'dengue resistance' was just one more atavistic superstition impairing proper understanding of complex modern epidemics. 'Culture' had become a recurrent discursive disclaimer between international and national staff since the 2010 earthquake and the great cholera outbreak that followed in 2011. It became obvious that a visiting anthropologist was expected to sort things out and appropriately blame 'culture' for the MSF project's difficulty of introducing dengue as a legitimate medical issue within its own hospital. The question indeed could not be sidestepped: to what extent, and in what terms, was 'dengue resistance' related to culture?

The prophecy made by the Haitian doctor: "we will always believe in sent diseases" was a good starting point. Anthropologists who studied the voodoo religion in Haiti, such as Alfred Métraux in the 1950s, reported that a disease is never internal, something that someone *has*, but instead something that someone receives from the outside, something that is sent. Disease is therefore associated with evil, evil is associated with bad intentions, and bad intentions with witchcraft (Métraux, 1958). In his study of the emergence of AIDS in the 1980s, Paul Farmer investigated how the representation of the disease evolved from a variant of tuberculosis in 1983–1984, to an ill-defined blood disease in 1986, to a Duvalier[7] conspiracy in 1987, and finally as a 'sent disease' related to voodoo (Farmer, 1994). This is why, as stressed by Françoise Héritier, it is always necessary to understand the cause of the evil's striking, because to any identified cause, there necessarily corresponds an antidote (Héritier, in Farmer, 1996). Paul Farmer, similarly, stresses in his ethnography that: "the treatment of a 'sent illness' requires that wizards be identified . . . sorcery is never the result of chance, it is sent by enemies, most often people envious or who consider themselves victims of dark magic" (Farmer, 2013, p. 37). And because of that, his interviewees are: "less obsessed with the evolution of the disease than with its origin" (Farmer, 2013, p. 34). AIDS became the 'envy sickness'; i.e. a sickness sent by magical means to selfish people who came to be economically successful at the expense of others without sharing the profit. As a result, the idea that 'an AIDS dead', that is, a zombie, was sent to the infected person dominated perceptions of the disease and challenged biomedical narratives.

I found the same thing in my fieldwork during the 2010 cholera outbreak. Cholera was frequently believed to be a sent disease in a post-earthquake context where social relationships were fractious and tense. At the very beginning of the outbreak, 40 houngans[8] were lynched with machetes and stones by their neighbours when they were accused of spreading the disease with a powder.[9] In the MSF Centre for the Treatment of Cholera (CTC), part of my assignment as a health promoter was to understand the causes for late arrival (with severe dehydration) and treatment refusals. This is how I met a young woman who did not believe in cholera: she was being punished because she had refused to take over the voodoo temple of her dead father. Similar scepticism was displayed by a man who had not honoured his promises as a widower and believed he was being haunted by his deceased wife. A young woman ridiculed the oral rehydration solution for cholera, convinced that her problems lay elsewhere: "a place you white people can't understand". In each of these instances, cholera was thought to be just a detail that was only given importance by those who did not really grasp the broader issues. And what was important was that cholera had been sent.

BOX 8.1 SEND THE DISEASE: FIELDWORK NARRATIVES FROM LÉOGÂNE, 2012

Powder. One common way to send a disease is to send a powder or poison. To cast a spell, it can be a poison left at a threshold, for example. "Then it just takes to cross the door. Sometimes, it is under the fence. You get cursed just by going out. At times, a houga, a 'package', is dedicated to one specific person. There also are malefic things that are transmitted by body contact. One husband who feels his wife has been unfaithful, can 'arrange' her sex in such a way that if she has sex with somebody else, her partner will die if he doesn't consult a houngan. There also is the powder sowed in the front door. It provokes inflammations like filariasis and swollen testicular. Another powder will give rash with pustules. If the neighbour has all the ingredients to make this powder, he will be accused" (MSF staff).

Koutlè (blown air). "Muscle aches and stiff neck can be transmitted by bad souls. This is the way it works. You can transmit the poison by an electric lamp projected at night to the victim, or by an empty bottle left on the floor. Or you can do it by *Koutlè*. You capture fetid air from a graveyard. You just aspirate it from a little hole you drill in a grave. This

> contaminated air associated with other things provokes stiffness. In this case, tension will be normal, glucose will be normal. Besides high fever, all the clinical tests will come out normal. If the patient stays at the hospital, he will die" (MSF staff).
>
> **Zombification.** "This is a phenomenon where the victim is given the appearance of a dead person. The pupil is closed, the heart stops, the pulse falls, the doctor declares him deceased and delivers the death certificate. But in reality the person is not dead. It is very common in Haiti. If a deputy loses the sense of what he's saying, he might be zombified. If you want to eliminate a rival better than with a gun or a knife, you zombify him. If you kill him, it will be deliverance for him. But if you really hate him, because he persecuted you at work for example, you kill him for his parents, but you use him as you wish. He can be your slave and work for you in a corn field, or you can put him in a cage and whip him. It's better pretending to kill him. And take profit at will" (MSF staff).

As the field notes in Box 8.1 show, ethnographies since the 1950s, and my own observations, were converging towards the conclusion that, indeed, the belief in sent diseases was a strong component of people's perception of illness and that this perception may have been at play when dengue was 'revealed' in 2012. This certainly contributed to the understanding of some of the international staff. It was also what the Haitian doctor implied when, referring to dengue, he said that Haitians will always believe in sent diseases. Yet, this element needs to be nuanced for the following three reasons.

First, Haitian ethnologists and intellectuals, such as Jean-Price Mars, have ever since the 1920s denounced the way that voodoo is stigmatised and reduced to the myths of human immolation, sorcery and zombies (Magloire & Yelvington, 2005). While conceding that the superstitious beliefs in voodoo are indeed prevalent, Price-Mars dedicated his work to the rehabilitation of voodoo as a religion (Price-Mars, 1973). He was already denouncing the anti-superstition campaign launched in 1912 by the Catholic Church that was supported by the local elites, while a presidential circular ordered the repression of voodoo (Clorméus, 2012). Exactly a century later, I was able to observe that international organisations were also launching an anti-superstition campaign by adopting the slogan for health promotion that 'cholera is not voodoo'. Given this pattern, even though the concept of 'sent disease' is partially responsible for 'dengue resistance', this would be less because of 'cultural belief' and more about a political resistance to stigmatisation.

The second reason why caution should be exercised when examining the cultural argument is that, even if we assume that belief in witchcraft was at play, attributing a cultural causality to 'dengue resistance' was not compliant with the basic anthropological principle of double causality. In his classic 1937 work on witchcraft among the Azende, a people of the Upper Nile (South Sudan), Evans-Pritchard pointed out that if a house's roof caved in, the cause would be attributed to witchcraft. The Azande were aware that termites were the natural cause of the incident, but the 'socially relevant' question was why it had happened at that particular moment, when some specific people gathered in the house (Evans-Pritchard, 1937). Although a pragmatic direct causality was correctly identified and acknowledged, it was the spiritual origin of evil that really mattered. I experienced this in Léogâne. An old man had just received his medical discharge and, as he was leaving the CTC, I congratulated him on his recovery, but he shook his head in disagreement: "Yes, I got away this time, but the sender is still there, and next time, he may succeed". He, too, would have readily admitted that the treatment for cholera was oral rehydration salts, but the cure did not eliminate the true origin of his affliction. Medical anthropology has long established that there is no such thing as a 'cultural obstacle' to the integration of biomedicine – except possibly from the biomedical establishment itself. The phenomena of rejection or resistance can conveniently be blamed on otherness and culture, but such phenomena are usually rooted in contemporary power relations (Sindzingre, 1985).

The third reason why the cultural argument itself needed to be relativised was that the national doctors and, later, the hospital staff at large, were not invoking witchcraft, but instead a plot hatched by international organisations to preserve their power over the country. In the MSF hospital at Léogâne, as dengue was 'revealed' in 2012, a rumour began to spread that *maladiblan* was an attempt by MSF itself to contaminate its patients. Evil still came from the outside and disease was still sent; however, it was not about traditional culture but modern politics.

These are the reasons why the representation of dengue as a sent disease cannot be trapped in a culturalist analysis where 'traditional superstition' would be the cause of an inadequate understanding and management of the infection. If a disease is about who sent it and why, then it is not about unveiling a witchcraft plot, but about understanding the complex geopolitics of epidemics and the multiple accusations Haitians have been charged with in the first place. To try to understand, we shall now reconsider the argument of Paul Farmer that the complex repertories of accusation that arose during the emergence of AIDS needed to be understood within a broader 'geography of blame' and within a historicised perspective. We shall pursue Farmer's argument by showing how 'dengue resistance' among the national doctors feeds on previous AIDS and cholera experiences.

'4H to AIDS': a devastating charge

A high mountain village, only accessible by climbing a rocky path for four hours, was included in the quantitative study on dengue notoriety. I had already visited this village in 2010 as part of the cholera containment plan. When asked about health-seeking behaviour related to febrile syndromes, the people would tell me of a severe disease provoking fever, persistent skin infections and diarrhoea. The person infected would lose weight and finally die. During the interviews, I suggested

Invisible dengue   **167**

that maybe they might have heard of HIV/AIDS, and that it seemed to me that was exactly what they were describing. They told me it was not. They explained that it was similar to AIDS, but unlike AIDS, the disease had a spiritual origin and bio-medicine had no explanation nor solution for it. This is why it has a different name, a name that they would reveal in a low voice, almost whispering: "katrach, katrach".

> Katrach, katrach, Haitians use this word, I don't know why. When someone has a lot of diarrhoea, we say he has katrach. I was ashamed just by the word when I was a little girl. Then it gained meanings.
>
> *(Senior MSF nurse)*

In 1982, a doctor from the United States Cancer Institute declared about the AIDS virus, "we suspect that it might be a Haitian epidemic virus transmitted to the US homosexual population" (Farmer, 1996). By mid-1982, the CDC warned, "Physicians who care for Haitian patients should be aware that opportunistic infections may occur in this population" (Pitchenik et al., 1983, p. 176). The *Journal of the American Medical Association* published in 1986 an article entitled 'Night of the Living Dead', questioning if necromantic zombiists transmit HTLV-III/LAV during voodooistic rituals (quoted by Cantwell, 1988, p. 129). Others proposed, "Haitians may have contracted the virus from monkeys as part of bizarre sexual practices in Haitian brothels" (Sabatier & Tinker, 1988). On 4 March 1983, the CDC labelled Haitians as a 'high risk' group, completing the 'club' of the four Hs (4H): homosexuals, haemophiliacs, heroin users and Haitians. In the early 1990s, the USA began to quarantine Haitian migrants at Guantánamo Bay naval base in Cuba. The practice didn't end until 1993. Haitians were released from CDC risk groups in 1985, but the information was not broadly publicised. Meanwhile, the 4H theory had spread, and the damage had been done.

The impact on tourism, the second largest source of foreign earnings in the country, was "immediate and devastating. . . . Haiti´s economy never recovered" (Beyrer et al., 2008, p. 673). The Haitian Bureau of Tourism estimated a decline in the flow of foreign visitors and tourists of as much as 86% in one year (Farmer, 2006). In 1983:

> already suffering from an image problem, Haiti has been made an international pariah by AIDS. Boycotted by tourists and investors, it has lost millions of dollars and hundreds of jobs at a time when half of the work force is jobless. Even exports are being shunned by some.
>
> *(Chaze, 1983, p. 41)*

In the USA, the large Haitian population suffered severe discrimination. The US Food and Drug Administration barred Haitians from donating blood. Some were forced to leave their neighbourhoods and sell their houses, kids were removed from schools after parents' protests and cab drivers began to lie about their origins. An overwhelming stigma was built, directly proportional to the fear of AIDS contamination (Farmer & Kim, 1991).

The local health community reacted strongly to such accusations. In 1983, at its annual convention, the Haitian Medical Association claimed that "the United States Public Health Service officials made a serious mistake, and that researchers used faulty and sometimes prejudiced methods". The president of the association, Dr. Saidel Laine, denounced those methods, and claimed that they were "racist" and the findings had "left a whole nation of people unduly alarmed and unfairly stigmatized" (Altman, 1983, p. 226). Haitian doctors counterclaimed that AIDS originated in the USA and was taken to Haiti by homosexual tourists who transmitted the disease to male Haitian prostitutes.

It was the beginning of decades of Haitian medical research aiming to reverse CDC accusations. And this was not the first time the Haitian medical establishment had faced stigma. During their training as doctors, Haitians also had to learn about the myth that syphilis was contracted in Haiti by members of Columbus' crew who later joined the army of Charles VIII of France and participated in the siege of Naples. There again, the syphilisation of the world had its origins in Haiti (Luger, 1993; Holcomb, 1937). The new generation of doctors trained in Haiti, those who were hired by international organisations after the earthquake, were carrying the burden of the stigma of their people.

Indeed, the stigma was not just a matter of medical controversy or the sole experience of Haitian migrants living in the USA. It had trickled up to the remote mountain village visited during our dengue study. It was only a few weeks later that I understood where the name of that mysterious disease people called katrach had come from: it was the phonetic transcription of '4H' in French-based creole. Thirty years later, the '4H' theory of the CDC was still there. The stigma had become the disease itself. Indeed, katrach was something white people couldn't understand.

Cholera: reversed accusation

In this context where, historically, epidemic and accusation were tightly bound together, is it surprising that the sudden arrival of cholera in 2010 would quickly be processed by the community in narratives ranging from sorcery to international conspiracy? *Kolera se yon politic* (cholera is politics) was an omnipresent graffiti in the urban environment of Porto Principe. The tagged word 'politics' was eventually replaced by the name of the candidate to the presidential elections or by the chief coordinator of the MINUSTAH (*Mission des Nations Unies pour la Stabilisation en Haïti*). There were variants of this conspiracy theory: cholera was not a real disease, but a tool to control through fear; or the disease was indeed real, but it had been sent to keep the country occupied by 'the republic of NGOs' (Schuller, 2017), as commonly mocked, and/or to justify financial aid.

In Léogâne, many young people who attended the MSF health promotion sessions remained reticent and frequently asked, "shouldn't we be asking about the origin of this disease?" The one response the MSF health promotion team gave, alongside other NGO partners, was that the origin of the disease did not matter; what did matter was knowledge of the transmission modes and proper health-seeking behaviour. The community health workers hired by NGOs were required not to engage with the issue of the origin of the disease, because it was politically saturated. This silence turned out to be an obstacle to prevention. Many late arrivals to the centre for cholera treatment in Léogâne were people who, although familiar with prevention discourses, did not follow its recommendations because they were believed to be biased or incomplete.

Meanwhile, health promotion messages relied on individual responsibility: *lave main nou, lave main nou* (wash your hands). The lack of hygiene was taught to be the source of infection; i.e. the people's fault. Cholera was 'the dirty-hands disease'. But the responsibility was all the harder to bear because the means of protection were not available in post-earthquake Haiti. How could one expect hygiene in Léogâne, where there was one latrine for every 250 people in the camps, and where these few existing latrines were full due to lack of pumping devices? How was one supposed to wash fruits with treated water in a place where there was no access to treated water? In such a context, placing the responsibility for the disease on people's lack of hygiene was seen as a scandalous accusation.

In 2012, seven expert teams concluded that cholera had been introduced into Haiti: "Molecular-genetic evidence points to the United Nations peacekeeping troops from Nepal as the source of cholera in Haiti, following their troop rotation in early October 2010" (Frerichs et al., 2012, p. 158). Although cholera is endemic in Nepal and at the time the soldiers left their country, there was a cholera outbreak, these soldiers had not been tested. The expert reports also proved that pipes from the camp leaked faecal waste into the river and that a septic pit on a hilltop near the UN camp allowed waste fluids to seep down into the nearby river, the Artibonite, Haiti's main river. Three years later, there were 635,980 reported cases (6.3% of the population), 1.2% of those resulting in death (7,912). The cholera drama strongly reinforced local conviction that unfair accusations made towards the Haitian people in regard to AIDS and cholera should be reversed to rightful accusations of bad intentions and incompetence on the part of the international community. Yes, diseases could indeed be sent, by others to Haitians.

In 2014, a class action lawsuit of 5,000 victims and families of victims was filed against the UN in New York under the charge of negligence. The UN invoked immunity (Freedman, 2014).

And then came chikungunya

The first cases of chikungunya were reported in Léogâne at the beginning of May 2014. In the absence of specific tests in Haiti, the first two international workers with suspected infections had samples sent to Barbados, and they were positive. By 28 May, 241 of the 400 staff of MSF Châtulay hospital had been infected (60%), while emergency attendance rose by 61% in two weeks and neonatal by 26%. This resulted in a serious shortage of human resources. We conducted a quick assessment that established that, in two weeks, 52% of the population had already been infected. The chikungunya outburst in the Léogâne region had been spectacularly fast and virulent. As the field notes in Box 8.2 testify, the first clinical observations pointed at heavy symptomatology and morbidity.

BOX 8.2 AN OUTREACH AT BEAUSSAN (9 KM FROM LÉOGÂNE)

At the first home visited, a 40-year-old man who spoke good French welcomed me: "the end of times has come". Quoting the Apocalypse, he saw, in the multiple epidemics hitting the region after the earthquake, the signs of the prophecy.

In the next house, five out of seven members of a family were infected. They referred to the fever as *KrazeZo* (breaking bones). One man, shivering and vomiting, complained he was unable to eat. He said it hurts so much it could only be the devil: "it is the devil eating me". His son said the disease was very different from anything else they had ever seen before, as it caused a lot more suffering. "I'd rather be beaten up by an enemy", he concluded.

In a home nearby, an old man – approximately 70 – was also infected. He was so weak he could not go to the bathroom himself. His family installed his mattress outside, in the courtyard, attempting to give him fresher air to breathe. As we engaged in conversation, his daughter was massaging his joints. He appeared to be in a lot of pain. Another daughter was squatting, unable to stand up. A neighbour walked by. She was also infected and said she couldn't sleep all night because her whole body was itching. "I'd rather give birth twice than suffer what I'm suffering now", she concluded. Twenty metres away, sitting on a chair, an old man was sweating and shivering. He said he couldn't move his fingers and had swollen and very sore testicles. Two kids passed by and whispered to one another, "it is the whites who give the disease". A teenage girl said that at Portail Ça-Ira, she heard that eight people had died of chikungunya last week. The health promotion agent replied that it couldn't be, as chikungunya doesn't kill people. She replies, "yes, it does". The general climate was hostile. A 35-year-old man at the next house said he worked at civil security and knew chikungunya was not about mosquitoes, but indeed about politics. Another one said it was provoked by Chinese nuclear experiments.

In three weeks, chikungunya acquired far more visibility and notoriety than dengue had in the two years since the beginning of the health promotion campaigns. In the quantitative survey, when questioned if they knew the name of the fever, 60% spontaneously answered 'chikungunya', while 25% mentioned its quickly acquired nickname: *KrazeZo*. Infected informants were unanimous in reporting the symptoms to be clearly distinct from anything they had previously experienced,

Invisible dengue **171**

especially from other fevers like malaria. Most reported exceptional pain as the main distinctive symptom.

Not only did people immediately produce and transfer information about the new fever, but they also promptly found ways to adapt and respond to it. This operational pragmatism, however, coexisted with a strong feeling of incredulity and irritation regarding the vector and the origin of the new epidemic. The transmission theory did not convince. The mosquito was indeed blamed by 50% of the participants, while 22% believed air or water was the contaminant factor and 30% did not know. Following the pattern observed during the cholera outbreak, local witchcraft accusations eventually emerged. Only two weeks after the beginning of the outbreak, drug resellers in the markets had to give up supplying paracetamol because prices had gone up so much up that they were being accused of originating the epidemic to profit from it. Some were beaten up by their clients. However, according to our study, a majority was still speculating about the origin of the epidemic and admitted they did not know (65%). But for the others, the origins were less in local sorcery than in international settings or even plots. For 9%, 'whites' were responsible, alongside the MINUSTAH. For another 9%, Africa was the source. For yet another 9%, China was responsible because of its exported plastic or nuclear tests. Russia, India, Brazil and the Dominican Republic were also mentioned. For many people, the symbolic weight of past epidemics had driven away the causes of the disease from voodoo to globalisation and whoever profits from it.

In such a context, dengue's invisibility was reinforced by the overwhelming presence of chikungunya. No denial was possible there; the symptoms were too specific and strong, and the epidemic too virulent. In their persistent attempts to raise awareness on dengue, the NGOs were losing the battle. Chikungunya had imposed its reality, and there was no room for two infections with similar symptoms: one that nobody had ever heard about, and one that hit half the population in two weeks. Finally, the medical staff saw in chikungunya's spectacular diffusion the retrospective proof that dengue was never an issue in Haiti. If the vector and the environment were the same, then why would one never 'come out', while the other one hit so quickly? An old man concluded with a bitter tone: "every year, it's a different disease. Here it's an 'entrance-exit' country. All these diseases are imported".

> Chikungunya is politics. I hear a lot around me that it's a plot. We always tend to think that we the Haitians, other peoples don't like, and that everything is done to eliminate us. So they inject us all kind of diseases. See, after cholera, this new catastrophe. And with cholera, we already thought that it was a plot to eliminate us.
>
> *(Community leader)*

Conclusion

In the light of the epidemiological and political history of AIDS and cholera, 'dengue resistance' gains a new perspective. It was neither about atavism, nor superstition, nor a lack of scientific rationality, but it was about an ethos of resistance forged over the previous four decades against systematic blame.

It is a plausible hypothesis that the opposition in Léogâne was particularly strong because it was a CDC study, conducted in Léogâne, of all places, that 'revealed' the disease. This happened to be the same organisation that attributed a Haitian origin to AIDS in the first place. At that time, 40 years previously, the CDC had become, "for many Haitians, the principal architect of the AIDS stigma" (Farmer & Kim, 1991, p. 210). In the light of this hypothesis, it becomes more understandable why, during the 2012 presentation of the CDC study in Léogâne, the doctors expressed such scepticism and hostility.

> How can they trust such an organism as CDC? From 1980 till today, they do everything they can to destroy us. To destroy a whole population. This is not correct. If they are here to make things worse, then they should go. Everything that is spent for information campaigns returns to the funders. And the Haitians have nothing to do with that, they die anyway.
>
> *(Nurse)*

As Paul Farmer stressed in his study on AIDS in Haiti, there are three ways to perpetrate an accusation: moral condemnation, sorcery and conspiracy. Extended to three more epidemics, this analytic framework still proved to be fully functional. Sorcery can be seen locally to account for a pattern of catching disease and for specific coping mechanisms. An infection always follows a movement from the outside to the inside, and this movement is induced by the intention of the sender to the receiver. This is exactly the way AIDS, cholera and chikungunya were subjectively experienced and socially constructed. Infection has an external cause that needs to be identified for adequate treatment to take place. The bad intention is generally sought within a complex network of competing relationships for access to scarce resources within the neighbourhood and the family. Systematic accusation and sorcery cannot be understood here as voodoo atavisms from long ago. They reflect an overall dysfunction of contemporary society in addressing people's basic needs. It is a projection of Haiti's harsh socio-economic conditions at the interpersonal level.

Yet, if sorcery is locally so powerful to explain people's contamination, it is because moral accusation has definitely been the dominant pattern used to make Haiti internationally responsible for the modern world's most tragic epidemic, AIDS. Let's recall that in American medical journals, voodoo and sexual rituals were described as contaminating factors. Thirty years later, cholera's spectacular outburst was attributed to the lack of hygiene of a people that supposedly needed to be taught how to wash their hands: *lavé main nou, lavé main nou*. Meanwhile, international organisations kept trying to convince Haitians to renounce their 'cultural superstitions' – cholera is not voodoo! – which supposedly accounted for poor health-seeking behaviour. Two years later, the medical staff were indirectly accused of incompetence by failing to acknowledge an infection that was silently killing its people: dengue. And again, two years later, chikungunya was perceived

Invisible dengue **173**

to be overwhelming because mosquitoes were present 'above acceptable levels' and because people were unable to practice elementary vector control.

This systematic moral accusation of Haiti's sexuality, religion, hygiene and medical competence resulted in a strong collective stigma that projects onto Haitians an unwanted shadow that looms before them. It is significant that in 2012, it only took the first few hundred Haitian migrants coming to Brazil to immediately provoke a huge propaganda campaign against the risks of AIDS, cholera and even Ebola contamination that their presence was said to be driving (Véran et al., 2014).

Believing in 'sent diseases' is therefore less about traditional culture than about the necessity of reversing the stigma by inverting the accusation. Haitians claimed that foreigners brought all four epidemics, not because of voodoo, but because of their dubious moral and political intentions. Accordingly, AIDS is a consequence of sexual tourism. Cholera was proven to be brought in as a consequence of MINUS-TAH's carelessness. Dengue only affects international staff and came with them, and chikungunya was recently imported.

These reversed accusations express doubts and conjectures about the sender's intention. A third form of accusation, the conspiracy, then surges and irrigates all the other accusatory fluxes. As told by an MSF doctor, it often dives deep into Haiti's history. To win over Napoleon's army, Toussaint was thought to have sold his soul to the devil and Dessalines by agreeing to pay a fee to the French and so prove that independence was indeed a bargain. During the Duvalier dictatorship, rumour spread that a torture camp was set up exactly underneath the grave of the Unknown Maroon, a terrifying mix of physical and symbolic violence. Another doctor believes that in the early 1980s, the Haitian government falsified HIV tests. Haiti would endorse AIDS responsibility in exchange for international financing. Once more, the people's souls were being sold. In the same vein, cholera was sent at the very moment NGOs were beginning to withdraw from Haiti. Cholera came opportunely to inflate funding and give legitimacy for an extension of the assistance programmes. Dengue is a failed attempt to keep up the epidemic industry and business. An MSF nurse even believed that MSF international staff voluntarily inoculated themselves with dengue and chikungunya to convince local staff and foment suspicion.

> The Haitians feel that the international community wants to destroy them. We know they don't like us. And our territory has not been exploited yet. We are rich and they want our mines. The Americans are behind this all. They want to destroy our population. But the government should take over the situation.
>
> *(MSF nurse)*

Last but not least, the racial dimension overlaps the accusation patterns. It is not only about senders and receivers, perpetrators and victims, but also about blacks and whites in a context where the racial dimension is always held as a very strong analyser of Haiti's international situation when compared, for instance, with the

Dominican Republic. In other words, Haiti is kept in poverty because its people are black. This racial framework gives a deeper understanding of the meanings within the accusations. AIDS was believed to be brought by black people to a predominantly white country and infected white people. Symmetrically, cholera was sent by a white organisation and infected black people. As a matter of fact, many Haitians wondered why white international staff were not getting cholera. 'Invisible dengue' was seen as another attempt to accuse blacks of infecting white people, since it is in Haiti that the whites got sick. But a resistance formed against this new ideological assault and dengue became *maladiblan*, brought by the whites, and the blacks don't get sick from it. A continuum was established between the 'racial resistance' of physical bodies to the virus, and the racial resistance of the national medical staff to endorse dengue as an issue they should be dealing with, since it is wrongly believed not to affect Haitian people. Finally, chikungunya infected both whites and blacks equally. It was indeed quite an experience to work in villages telling people that I myself was also infected. People would immediately smile, happy to be finally sharing some kind of common destiny. Many would spontaneously comment, "*Chikungunya li se pa rasis; li afekte tout moun*" (chikungunya is not racist; it affects everybody). But then, who sent chikungunya? The Chinese? As a woman concluded after a visit to her home, "only the whites know what they want to do with the Haitian people".

> The international organizations have long made of Haiti a 'guinea pig' country. We are all guinea pigs, on who are practiced countless health experiences. But we believe it's different about dengue. They said we are resistant, protected against dengue. They say it's a disease for white people only.
>
> *(Senior national MSF doctor)*

The final conclusion of the anthropological assessment on 'dengue resistance' was that the medical discourse held by international organisations (including MSF) suffered from a serious lack of credibility and legitimacy. Unless a rehabilitation of the medical discourse takes place, there will be no significant change regarding dengue awareness. Therefore, in order "to improve dengue care and management in MSF projects" in Haiti, as stated in the terms of reference of the assessment, the first step is to open the discourse on dengue in particular and epidemics in general.

Since 'dengue resistance' is mostly a consequence of false accusations and hidden facts during previous epidemics, both the CDC's regrettable '4H' mistake and MINUSTAH's protection failures with cholera need to be fully acknowledged and widely diffused. NGOs should be able to tell the truth, and advocate that the actors involved need to tell the truth. Following that logic, with chikungunya, we tested a clear communication line whereby the question of origins was no longer avoided, but answered with world diffusion maps of the epidemic and simple epidemiological information. By simply avoiding any kind of cultural imputation and acknowledging that, historically, chikungunya came from abroad, we had their full attention. The health promotion strategy was able to be redefined in this way.

The final report also stressed the hopelessness of recommending prophylactic practices that are not applicable in local contexts. The use of treated water during cholera outbreaks or mosquito repellent during chikungunya creates an unnecessary stress on health promotion credibility, since people cannot be held responsible for not using solutions they do not have access to. Ultimately, this is about devolving responsibility to the place it truly belongs.

Notes

1 Dengue fever is a mosquito-borne tropical disease caused by the dengue virus. Dengue is spread by several species of mosquito of the *Aedes* type, principally *A. aegypti*. "In a small proportion of cases, the disease develops into the life-threatening dengue haemorrhagic fever, resulting in bleeding, low levels of blood platelets and blood plasma leakage, or into dengue shock syndrome, where dangerously low blood pressure occurs" (Wikipedia).
2 In conformity with the terms of consent of this study, anonymity will be preserved. For that purpose, any information liable to establish a direct link with the informant will be obscured.
3 BRAMU, Brazilian Medical Unit. Created in 2007, the BRAMU of the MSF-Brazil office specialises in neglected tropical diseases, such as dengue, Chagas and other infectious diseases, in contexts where violence is not directly related to armed conflicts, and with focus on the impact of disease on the health of the people.
4 I was at that time a member of the Outreach Health Promotion staff as a volunteer.
5 Estimate based on the quantitative survey conducted as part of the activities of the dengue assessment and presented later in this chapter.
6 There are four known serotypes of dengue, and therefore, an individual can be infected up to four times.
7 Jean-Claude Duvalier, nicknamed 'Baby Doc', was the president of Haiti from 1971 until he was overthrown by a popular uprising in 1986. He succeeded his father, François 'Papa Doc' Duvalier. Thousands of Haitians were killed or tortured and hundreds of thousands fled the country during his presidency.
8 Houngan is the term for a male priest in Haitian voodoo.
9 Haïti Press Network, 'Haïti-choléra: des sorciers tués au nom du choléra' at http://hpn haiti.com/site/index.php/nouvelles/19-haiti–cholera/1676-haiti-cholerades-sorciers-tues-au-nom-du-cholera (accessed 26 October 2017).

References

Altman, L.K., (1983). Debate grows on US listing of Haitians in AIDS category. *New York Times*, 1–50.
Beyrer, C., Davis, W. and Celentano, D.D., (2008). *Public health aspects of HIV/AIDS in low and middle income countries: epidemiology, prevention and care*. Berlin: Springer Science & Business Media.
Brodwin, P., (1996). Medicine and morality in Haiti: the contest for healing power. Vol. 3. Cambridge: Cambridge University Press.
Cantwell, A., (1988). *AIDS and the doctors of death: an inquiry into the origin of the AIDS epidemic*. Los Angeles: Aries Rising Press.
Chaze, W., (1983). In Haiti, a view of life at the bottom. *US News and World Report*. **95**(18), 41–42.

Clorméus, L.A., (2012). La démonstration durkheimienne de Jean Price-Mars: faire du vodou haïtien une religion. *Archives de Sciences Sociales des Religions*. (3), 153–170.

Evans-Pritchard, E.E., (1937). *Witchcraft, oracles and magic among the Azande*. Vol. 12. Oxford: Clarendon Press.

Farmer, P., (1994). AIDS-talk and the constitution of cultural models. *Social Science & Medicine*. **38**(6), 801–809.

Farmer, P., (1996). Social inequalities and emerging infectious diseases. *Emerging Infectious Diseases*. **2**(4), 259.

Farmer, P., (2003). Haïti, l'embargo et la typhoïde. *Le Monde Diplomatique*. (7), 26.

Farmer, P., (2006). *AIDS and accusation: Haiti and the geography of blame, updated with a new preface*. Oakland: University of California Press.

Farmer, P., (2013). "Envoyer la maladie". Entre sorcellerie et politique, l'évolution des conceptions du sida dans les zones rurales d'Haïti [1990]. *Genre, sexualité & société*. (9).

Farmer, P. and Kim, J.Y., (1991). Anthropology, accountability, and the prevention of AIDS. *Journal of Sex Research*. **28**(2), 203–221.

Freedman, R., (2014). UN immunity or impunity? A human rights based challenge. *European Journal of International Law*. **25**(1), 239–254.

Frerichs, R.R., Keim, P.S., Barrais, R. and Piarroux, R., (2012). Nepalese origin of cholera epidemic in Haiti. *Clinical Microbiology and Infection*. **18**(6).

Good, B.J. et al., eds., (2010). *A reader in medical anthropology: theoretical trajectories, emergent realities*. Vol. 15. Hoboken: John Wiley & Sons.

Halstead, S.B. et al., (2001). Haiti: absence of dengue hemorrhagic fever despite hyperendemic dengue virus transmission. *The American Journal of Tropical Medicine and Hygiene*. **65**(3), 180–183.

Héritier, F., (1996). Préface. In: P. Farmer, *Sida en Haïti, la victime accusée*. Paris: Karthala.

Holcomb, R.C., (1937). *Who gave the world syphilis? The Haitian myth*. New York: Froben Press.

Luger, A., (1993). The origin of syphilis: clinical and epidemiologic considerations on the Columbian theory. *Sexually Transmitted Diseases*. **20**(2), 110–117.

Magloire, G. and Yelvington, K.A., (2005). Haiti and the anthropological imagination. *Gradhiva*. (1), 127–152.

Métraux, A., (1958). *Le vaudou haïtien*. Vol. 14. Paris: Gallimard.

Pitchenik, A.E., Fischl, M.A., Dickinson, G.M., Becker, D.M., Fournier, A.M., O'Connell, M.T. . . . Spira, T.J., (1983). Opportunistic infections and Kaposi's sarcoma among Haitians: evidence of a new acquired immunodeficiency state. *Annals of Internal Medicine*. **98**(3), 277–284.

Poirier, M.J., Moss, D.M., Feeser, K.R., Streit, T.G., Chang, G.J.J., Whitney, M. . . . Barry, A.K., (2016). Measuring Haitian children's exposure to chikungunya, dengue and malaria. *Bulletin of the World Health Organization*. **94**(11), 817.

Price-Mars, J., (1973). *Ainsi parla l'oncle*. Montréal: Leméac.

Sabatier, R. and Tinker, J., (1988). *Blaming others: prejudice, race and worldwide AIDS*. London: Panos.

Salyer, S.J., Ellis, E.M., Salomon, C., Bron, C., Juin, S., Hemme, R.R. . . . Desormeaux, A.M., (2014). Dengue virus infections among Haitian and expatriate non-governmental organization workers – Leogane and Port-au-Prince, Haiti, 2012. *PLoS Neglected Tropical Diseases*. **8**(10), e3269.

Schuller, M., (2017). Haiti's' republic of NGOs'. *Current History*. **116**(787), 68.

Shevchenko, O. and Fox, R.C., (2008). "Nationals" and "Expatriates": challenges of Fulfilling "Sans Frontières" ("Without Borders") ideals in international humanitarian action. *Health and Human Rights*. 109–122.

Sierra, B.D.L.C., Kouri, G. and Guzman, M.G., (2007). Race: a risk factor for dengue hemor-rhagic fever. *Archives of Virology*. **152**(3), 533–542.

Sindzingre, N., (1985). Présentation: tradition et biomédecine. *Sciences sociales et santé*. **3**(3), 9–26.

Véran, J.F., Noal, D.D.S. and Fainstat, T., (2014). Neither refugees, nor migrants: the arrival of Haitians to the city of Tabatinga (Amazonas). *Dados*. **57**(4), 1007–1041.

9

REVEALING CAUSES BEYOND CULTURE

An MSF surgical project through the lens of anthropology and health promotion

Paul Grohma and Ursula Wagner

Introduction

In January 2014, Médecins Sans Frontières Holland started a project in Abéché's general hospital in eastern Chad operating a surgical trauma ward in cooperation with the Chadian Ministry of Health (MoH). Prior to that, the International Committee of the Red Cross had a similar arrangement with the same hospital to treat war-wounded trauma patients in the larger context of the Darfur crisis. Soon after its deployment, the MSF project faced problems with patients' treatment adherence and called for an anthropologist to shed light on this situation and provide recommendations.

This chapter depicts the step-by-step progress of the Abéché project – from evident difficulties to an anthropological analysis and its implications for subsequent health promotion activities and operational decisions. The anthropological study (Grohma, 2014), which forms the basis of this chapter, was commissioned because of obvious problems with patients' compliance in the surgical ward supervised by MSF. It was initiated about six months after the start of medical activities. Interviews and discussions with patients, carers, staff and community members were carried out to establish patients' and carers' perceptions and the patients' reasons for leaving the facility against medical advice. Contrary to the expected outcome that 'cultural perceptions of diseases and biomedical treatment' were the causes, structural problems seemed to account for patients' doubts about the medical performance, and about the quality of treatment delivered by the cooperation between MSF and MoH. Socio-cultural differences (for example, education, language, ethnicity) between medical staff from the south of the country and patients predominantly from the north were also a factor. The findings served as an important working basis for the development of tailored health promotion activities, which started six months after the anthropological study was conducted.

Hence, this chapter contributes to an understanding of an 'anthropology in humanitarian settings', of its advantages, contributions, challenges and restrictions. At the same time, it serves as an example of the potential for linking anthropology and health promotion in order to contribute to an amelioration of services offered in humanitarian contexts. Moreover, this chapter aims at outlining the distinction between anthropological analysis on the one hand and its implementation within the field of health promotion activities on the other. This is especially important, as both are rather 'exotic' positions in many MSF projects and tend to be lumped together, while their methods, objectives and use are distinct (see Wagner, 2015).

Challenging the notion of 'culture'

From a theoretical point of view, this chapter aims to contribute to an 'anthropology beyond culture' (Fox & King, 2002) without discarding the importance of 'cultural competency' for humanitarian aid (Abramowitz et al., 2014). As will be shown, it can be for seemingly trivial and practical reasons that people do not accept services or that patients leave against medical advice. The anthropological study on patients' perceptions of treatment in the surgical ward can be read in the same light as failures in the health care for migrants in the Netherlands – as van Dijk (1998) described in his article 'Culture As Excuse'. Instead of acknowledging structural deficiencies, failures are blamed on the 'culture' of the people. The culture concept applied in the first place is a static one: "culture is seen as a patient-bound variable with roots in a distant past" (van Dijk, 1998, p. 244).

Anthropological debates have acknowledged for decades that culture is a vexed and complicated term. Starting with Abu-Lughod's (1991) critique of 'othering' and Daniel's (1996) warning of the essentialising connotation of culture, no unified answer to what culture actually is has been found. The concept has not been completely discarded (see Randeria and Karagiannis [2015] for an overview of the debate), but it has become obvious that other concepts might be more fruitful for an anthropological analysis. Here, the concept of 'ethnicity' as the perceived difference between (often culturally close) groups (Eriksen, 1993) seems to deliver more insights, as will be shown by the important finding of the ethnic conflict between 'Southerner' medical staff and 'Northerner' patients and carers in the Abéché setting.

When anthropologists are requested, they are expected to provide "the social, cultural, and psychological characteristics" (Foster, 1976, p. 3), and "thereby the explanations", for patients' and carers' behaviours. But it is exactly this approach that has been denounced in critical medical anthropology (Witeska-Mlynarczyk, 2015). This field, which emerged in the 1990s, displays a "strong criticism of culturalist anthropological interpretations, which emphasize health practices and techniques, while turning a blind eye towards the social and political dimensions at the root of problems of illness, as well as of the absence of solutions" (de Oliveira Nunes, 2014, p. 3). Anthropologists are not only trained to analyse 'culture', although this is often seen as the centre of their competences, but also – and more importantly – it is their task to take the context into account and to analyse social and power relations.

Project setting

Abéché is the fourth biggest town of Chad, the capital of the Ouaddai region and located in the Sahel zone, 60 km from the border of Sudan. Due to its vicinity to the war-ridden Darfur region, it served as a major hub for humanitarian assistance to refugees from this conflict zone who were sheltered in numerous camps around the region. The involvement of the Chadian government and tribal rebel groups from the region in the Darfur war resulted in numerous casualties among the local people between 2003 and 2005, and culminated in a raid by joint Sudanese-Chadian rebel groups that overran Abéché on the way to the capital N'Djamena in 2008. Throughout the conflict, the region around Abéché served as a retreat area for rebel groups from both sides of the border, exposing local people to alternate rebel attacks and brutal counter strikes by the Chadian army. To de-escalate the conflict, the UN deployed the peacekeeping operation MINURCAT from September 2007 to December 2010, supported by the EUFOR military mission of the EU between March 2008 and March 2009. The French army maintains an airbase with fighter jets in Abéché to the present day.

As political circumstances developed towards a resolution of the Darfur crisis in 2010 and peacekeeping forces withdrew from Abéché, MSF decided to start a project in 2013 because a renewed flare-up of war was expected. MSF's mandate was to take care of the difficult trauma cases in the surgical ward of Abéché's general hospital by dividing some of the tasks and responsibilities between MSF and the MoH. Primarily, MSF anticipated treatment of gunshot and other wounds inflicted by war. However, due to the relatively peaceful conditions during the project period, most of the patients had trauma related to domestic accidents.

The population of Abéché consists of five local groups, generally referred to as 'Northerners', and a variety of immigrant people from southern Chad, equally representing different ethnic groups (Lebeuf, 1959). The Northerners are Muslim tribal groups who share similar Arabic dialects and Arabic genealogies to varying degrees and are engaged in different forms of animal husbandry. They breed cattle, camels, goats or a mix, and follow distinctive forms of nomadism and transhumance. Some of these people are sedentary and have their tribal representatives in town, which traditionally served as a crossroads of caravan trade. Even today, commerce and lorry traffic play prominent roles in Abéché, and are largely controlled by these local groups. They include Maba, Arabs, Sara, Guran and Zaghawa. The latter two belong to the Teda-Deza language group, but can also communicate in Arabic. Their territory is divided by the border of Chad and Sudan. It is rebel groups of the Zaghawa (the ethnic group of President Idriss Déby) that have been involved in the outbreak and continuation of the Darfur crisis (Giroux et al., 2009). Many of these groups are politically marginalised and have high rates of illiteracy due to limited access to education, which is related to their semi-nomadic lifestyle or their rejection of state structures (Arditi, 2003). This is reflected in their absence from white-collar positions in Abéché, and leads to the situation of predominantly Northern patients being treated by Southern medical staff in the hospital. A small number of patients were Southerners who lived in Abéché, but the majority were local Northerners originating from the wider environs.

The general hospital of Abéché was built with German support in the 1970s. At the time of the study, the lack of resources was visible, with a lot of the hospital furniture such as patients' beds dating back to the time of its opening. The open zones around the hospital served as grazing areas for animals, children were playing around uncleared waste, the canteen kitchen for patients was run outside on an open fire and lacked supplies, canalisation pipes were broken, and there was no incineration facility. Inside, it was loud and smelly due to deteriorated sanitation and improper toilet use. Hygiene conditions in the operating theatres were a bit better, but still not at the desired standards. The hospital was roofed by an elevated construction of metal sunshades that guaranteed a certain circulation of air, but produced quite unfavourable acoustics contributing to steady noise from overcrowded corridors. It was an unpleasant place at first sight and – as the study would reveal – was not popular with the community at all.

Consequently, the MSF Holland project's plans included the rehabilitation of the hospital's water and sanitation facilities, the improvement of waste management and the installation of a blood bank, as well as the development of one of the three operating theatres and several patient rooms in the surgical ward. The objective was to deliver emergency surgical aid and to serve as a surgical referral hospital for Caesarean sections and severe trauma cases from the two other MSF projects in Chad; Am Timan and Tissi, close to the border with the Central African Republic. Due to the relief of the Darfur crisis, the project – still in its starting phase – focussed on creating a functional operating theatre providing surgical care for referral patients from Tissi and Am Timan, as well as for the people of Abéché and the Ouaddai region. Instead of treating war victims as initially intended, local cases of trauma that required surgical treatment mainly concerned complicated, open fractures and wounds from a high number of traffic accidents, and burns related to unsafe fireplaces, mostly involving children. There were also a considerable number of stabbings and some gunshot wounds which occurred in the context of local tribal violence.[1]

After the first few months of the project, a worrying tendency became evident – a considerable number of patients refused treatment or left care against medical advice because they were afraid of adverse effects from plaster casts. Local rumours suggested the casts might lead to the unnecessary amputation of limbs. At the same time, traditional bone healers were said to interfere with the activities of the trauma ward and to 'do a lot of harm' to the patients and the community.

Calling for an anthropological perspective

As a result, the project team requested an anthropological assessment in order to understand the presumed "cultural reasons for non-adherence". The study was to "analyse cultural beliefs and perceptions around violence/non-violence related trauma and consequent surgery" (Grohma, 2014), and deliver a concise and comprehensive report. This was expected to help the MSF project team improve the surgical programme and to enhance patient adherence to treatment.

The subsequent anthropological research consisted of an analysis of hospital records, semi-structured interviews and informal conversations with patients, community members and representatives, as well as hospital staff and traditional healers, during a five-week stay in October and November 2014. It did indeed reveal manifold aspects concerning the patients' reluctant acceptance of surgical treatment in the hospital. During the fieldwork, the analysis shifted from the 'culture' of the patients as the focus which had to be understood and adapted to in order to enable project improvement, to the 'culture' of the hospital with its internal dynamics. It became obvious that its malfunctioning and its bad reputation in the community were the core of the problem. A better understanding of interpersonal and ethnic friction inside the hospital, as well as of patients' perception of accessibility, affordability and quality of treatment, became central aims of the investigation. Accordingly, a considerable part of the research was conducted inside the surgical ward observing interactions between patients and staff, as well as between MSF and MoH, and collecting patients' impressions and accounts. Interviews with local nongovernmental organisations and civil society representatives completed the view on local perceptions of the hospital. The main findings of the study included 1) socioeconomic aspects, 2) the hospital as a dysfunctional institution and 3) traditional/alternative healers as a compromise and interface.

Socio-economic aspects

Generally, admission fees and a relatively lengthy admission procedure contributed to a negative image of the hospital within the community. Although MSF was reimbursing fees for the patients, the impression of a costly, corrupt and money-making institution was deeply rooted in the patients' perception. In interviews, the financial aspect – that the hospital was seen to take a lot of money and not use it in an appropriate way – was always named first. This overshadowed MSF's efforts to provide easily accessible and free of charge quality care, since people did not believe it. The fear of being tricked into something very costly was a constant underlying fear of those who had to use the hospital.

Moreover, as in many settings in the region, patients are accompanied by a carer (*garde-malade*), who spends day and night beside the patient, sleeps in the hospital and takes care of the patient's bodily hygiene and nutrition. For that reason, this person is not available for work or household tasks in the family, which is usually a big burden, especially if a mother has to take care of a sick child in the hospital. Consequently, a senior family member, who might bear the financial weight of hospitalisation, had significant power over a patient's admission and duration of stay. This economic aspect was subsequently improved by providing money for food for poor patients and thereby alleviating the economic burden of hospitalisation.

The hospital as a dysfunctional institution

The biggest part of the analysis suggested that cultural reasons played a subordinate role with regard to patients' acceptance of treatment and retention in care. During interviews with patients and community members, it became evident that the hospital itself scared patients away. In the recent past – in particular, during the peak of the conflict – a number of understandable shortcomings had led to the hospital's bad reputation. These were still in place and continued when MSF took over and started running the surgical ward. Actual structural problems concerning the technical and social functioning of the hospital added to the hospital's bad reputation.

The first level of structural problems was identified in the cooperation between MSF and the MoH, which resulted in unequal employment conditions contributing to demotivation and a tense atmosphere in the ward. The hospital was functioning on the basis of long-established hierarchies, working conditions and coping mechanisms, which helped to maintain services despite the lack of basic infrastructure and financial means. In general, the hospital had established a tacit policy of providing minimal information, leaving the patient with little information about the exact nature of their injury, treatment and length of stay. For instance, Ahmed Abu Jumaaya,[2] a young man interviewed at his bedside while he was in traction and struggling with the weights explained that he had not received any information concerning the nature of his fracture, the method of surgery, the duration of his hospitalisation or the possible costs that could arise. He said that he wanted to leave as soon as they removed the weights, which seemed understandable under such circumstances.

On a second level, the antagonism between Southern medical staff and predominantly Northern patients (Lemarchand, 1986) caused frustration and rude behaviour among the former and mistrust among the latter. These levels of conflict could indeed be analysed in a meaningful anthropological way by looking at power relations and cultural differences, as well as negative perceptions and communication barriers between the stakeholders involved. It became evident that 'culture' did have implications for the perception of the hospital, but not, as had been assumed, for the perception of healing and disease per se, which had been believed to be the obstacle to the success of the MSF project. Like a microcosm, the hospital reflected the ethnic composition and the political tensions of the country as a whole. Educated medical doctors and nurses originating from the Christian south of the country were serving in the Muslim town of Abéché, which they perceived as a foreign and hostile environment. There they took care of Muslim Northerner patients, who were largely illiterate and who spoke languages that were understood by only a few local nurses who were not always available. A substantial number of patients were pastoralists or nomads coming from rural places maybe hundreds of kilometres from Abéché with a completely different lifestyle compared to the relatively well-off urban people. Some of the medical staff perceived and treated those patients as dirty and ignorant. Hence, open expressions of disdain, disrespect or neglect towards patients had become common practice (see Yaffré and de Sardan [2003] for similar examples).

As shown with the example of Ahmed Abu Jumaaya, the man in traction, failure to explain symptoms and treatment was the rule rather than the exception. This was reinforced by a language barrier, but even more by an attitude to treatment whereby patients – especially those with a Northern background – were not supposed to ask about their condition. And, given the social gap between patients and staff, most patients adhered to this silent rule. Similarly, the daily ward rounds of physicians (including the MSF surgeon) had the character of a working discussion among medical staff rather than of a dialogue with the patients. An observation from the anaesthetic recovery room additionally demonstrated the lack of respect towards patients. In order to check patients' state of consciousness, the staff fiercely slapped their forehead – when they showed a reaction, they were ready to be transferred to the ward.

Understandably, this unfriendly behaviour contributed to the factors that kept patients away from the hospital or prompted carers to take their relatives away. The fact that the international MSF staff were even less capable than the national staff of speaking the local Arabic dialect only made the situation worse.

The third level of structural problems concerned the quality of treatment delivered by the cooperation between MSF and MoH. Some patients left on the day of admission, others after a few days or perhaps months, but in many cases before their treatment was completed. Those who left after months were cases with difficult healing histories of open fractures or large wounds due to burns that would not close. They left because of unsatisfactory treatment outcomes and went to search for 'better' treatment with traditional healers. Cases were reported where patients' itineraries showed attempts to get the best out of both systems and to avoid pain and adversity where possible. One patient was admitted to the ward, but after he had received an x-ray image, he refused further treatment and turned to the bone healer who could improve his treatment using the x-ray taken at the hospital. These are coping mechanisms resulting from a weak public health system, not culture-specific perceptions of trauma and healing. They show that the health care sectors cannot be neatly divided into traditional, folk and professional, as once proposed by Kleinman (1980). The boundaries are increasingly blurred and, as became evident with the example of bone healers in the urban setting of Abéché, many traditionalists nowadays do have some kind of formal training in biomedicine which they blend with traditional therapies.

Questioning the quality of medical care was epitomised in the rumour of plaster casts leading to amputation. This rumour came under suspicion of being an expression of cultural perceptions of trauma, but in fact turned out to be part of an oral history reflecting true stories from the hospital's recent past. It was not a mere 'culturally bound imagination'. During the Chadian civil war, which lasted from 2005–2010, medical supplies were very limited and the MoH had hired unqualified personnel. Lack of material and medical skills resulted in the treatment of each and every injury – including open fractures – with plaster casts. The inappropriate treatment subsequently led to infection and gangrene, followed by amputations in large numbers. This story originated from the most affected Sixth Battalion, which was based in N'Djamena, but allegedly it happened in all public hospitals in Chad's war zones, including the one in Abéché.

Thus, even aspects that would definitely fall into the sphere of 'culturally determined' health-seeking behaviour – for example, patients preferring treatment carried out by traditional bone healers – could clearly and directly be associated with the deficits of the hospital and the treatment offered by MSF and MoH. Also during MSF's involvement in the hospital, the implementation of modern surgical techniques, such as internal fixation, were not feasible. Although internal fixation is normally contraindicated only in patients who are already infected, in the case of Abéché, this technique was not applied because poor hygiene conditions in the operating theatre carried a high risk of postoperative infections. Complicated fractures were thus treated with external fixations. Depending on the case, fixations were sometimes accompanied by the use of weights to stabilise fractures, a technique which requires hospitalisation for 8–12 weeks, during which the patient is more or less immobile. Along with plaster casts, patients frequently rejected those fixations – especially in combination with weights – as they perceived them not only as inconvenient and painful, but also the sheer sight of them gave rise to many fears and concerns. This was made worse when patients who found themselves with these kinds of fixations after waking up from anaesthesia did not receive any clarification on their post-operative condition.

The study revealed that the lack of information on their condition and the surrounding environment – unfriendly nurses, uncomfortable beds, noise, bad smell, etc. – was not reassuring enough for patients to extend their stay. If a patient had to choose between two treatments, both with uncertain outcomes, they would probably choose the one involving less inconvenience at first sight and being eventually cheaper. It is a fact that – due to financial, structural and hygiene constraints – some of the methods offered by MSF did not correspond with latest standards of biomedicine and were thus prone to competition with traditional healers, who communicated their methods in a friendly and understandable way and promised less painful and more efficient healing prospects.

Traditional/alternative healers as compromise and interface

An array of traditional healers formed some sort of alternative medical sector next to the hospital offering exactly what the facility could not deliver: cheap, quick and often also successful treatment in a personal and friendly environment (El Hag & El Hag, 2010).[3] These alternative healers dedicated more time to the patients and offered easier-to-understand explanations of their fractures than the hospital staff could provide. Of course, at the same time, charlatans and quacks – unskilled people who claim to have medical knowledge – took advantage of people's trust in traditional bone setting and made a living from exploiting trauma patients, often resulting in tragic outcomes (Mathieu et al., 2014).

The anthropological analysis showed that the majority of traditional bone healers were embedded in a local culture of traditional medicine, with a substantial number also being trained in biomedicine or physiotherapy and working in small public health posts. Most had undergone apprenticeships of several years, learnt from family elders who drew their bone healing knowledge from the regionally significant pastoralist culture (it is important to know how to heal animal bones in a semi-nomadic society), or visited teaching facilities for traditional medicine, which exist in southwestern Chad. Therefore, they enjoyed the confidence of many community members – a phenomenon, which is known from other medically pluralistic settings, where patients have a choice between different offers from the traditional, folk and biomedical sectors (Kleinman, 1980). Understanding diseases or fractures and having them explained in culturally appropriate ways was an important element in the choice of treatment.

Nevertheless, the quality of traditional bone healers' work was seen as controversial and had opponents, as well as supporters, within the community members of Abéché. But, like the traditional healers' actions, hospital care and treatment also did not guarantee a successful outcome. In the eyes of the patients, the hospital was an uncertain choice, where they could hope for treatment from a university-trained surgeon, but had to put up with admission fees, bad hygiene, often unfriendly and dismissive behaviour by the hospital staff, and uncomfortable accommodation in a repugnant environment. Traditional healers, on the other hand, were of a different and sometimes dubious quality, but offered less costly services and enabled patients to stay at home for treatment. Basically, patients had a choice between those two suboptimal options – traditional healer or hospital – both with the risk of a bad outcome.

'Translation' of findings into health promotion

The anthropological analysis of the Abéché surgical project has proved again that the strength of anthropology lies in the 'thick description' of Clifford Geertz (Krumeich et al., 2001), linking not only local explanatory models but also social stratification, power and access to a specific situation. While anthropological analysis always takes the broader social, economic and political dimensions into account, at the same time, it zooms into the micropolitics of a specific place, such as the surgical ward of Abéché's hospital. This kind of analysis is a solid ground on which health promotion activities can be built. In the Abéché project, health promotion activities started in March 2015, about six months after the anthropological study was carried out.

Health promotion in this sense is not understood just as a one-way communication in terms of educating patients and carers; more than that, it considers how services can be adapted to the needs of the patients. Eventually, the anthropological assessment led to basic recommendations focussing on how to make a stay in the hospital a more pleasant experience by improving the environment generally and by enhancing staff-patient communication in particular. The suggestion was

Revealing causes beyond culture **187**

to achieve this by involving a representative of local ethnic groups as a facilitator between local patient groups and (mostly international) medical staff. This representative should be fully dedicated to communication, explanation and confidence building. Ideally, they should have considerable knowledge and understanding of both biomedicine (surgery) and traditional medicine, and be qualified to explain to patients the pros and cons of traditional versus biomedical treatment. Additionally, it was recommended to carry out a service promotion campaign focussing on the hospital and the communities of Abéché in order to address people's concerns with the hospital, to explain the role of MSF within the hospital and to detach MSF services from the local perception of the hospital.

As a first step, emphasis lay on improving the overall conditions in the hospital. This included both the organisation of the surgical ward in terms of clearer rules for washing laundry, food preparation and improved hygiene, as well as communication between health care professionals, patients and carers. A skilled and experienced health promoter was recruited to be in charge of these activities. The choice fell on a woman who had worked with MSF for many years in different auxiliary positions and in several projects. The main criteria for her selection was that she had been born and raised in the region, spoke local Arabic – and Masalit as an additional local language – and at the same time had a good command of French, which was necessary for communication with the international MSF staff. She was not only experienced in looking after patients and taking time to listen, but also had a lot of experience in giving very clear and hands-on information. Moreover, her loyalty to MSF and its core values, as well as her dedication to the patients, turned out to be an important input for the medical team.

Due to a lack of human resources, the health promotion strategy focussed on the internal dynamics of the hospital rather than on service promotion, as the surgical ward run by MSF in fact faced an increasing number of emergency patients, and the limits of capacity were reached. Many issues had to be addressed to achieve better hygiene standards in the surgical ward and in the hospital as a whole. MSF international staff jokingly referred to the hospital as a 'hotel and zoo' because numerous carers and animals occupied the free spaces both in the inner and surrounding yards of the hospital. As the hospital did not provide food for its patients, the carers used the yards for cooking and washing their clothes, and this produced huge amounts of waste and sewage. It was a priority to take care of the place and keep it tidy in order to make it less smelly and more pleasant. The use of the (often full) latrines was a particular issue for people, who came from the countryside and had never used a latrine; open defecation is still very common in rural Chad. Some elder community members would blatantly refuse to sit over a 'hole'. Cleaners, on the other hand, were fed up with removing faeces from all round the latrine.

A clear *lack of communication* between patients, carers and health care professionals had been identified as one of the major drawbacks of the project. This was tackled by integrating the health promoter well into the medical team, and especially by including her on the daily ward round. By doing this, she could not only get to know every single patient and understand their medical problem, but could also commit herself to explain to the patients in their own language, and in easy-to-understand non-medical words, what the diagnosis was and what kind of treatment they could expect. This was important because of language barriers in the national and international MSF team, and also because many of the patients and their carers were illiterate people from the countryside, most of whom had never been in contact with biomedical or surgical treatment before. In the presence of the health promoter, patients slowly started coming up with questions which might have been obvious to the medical staff, but not for someone who is hospitalised for the first time. Moreover, the health promoter took time to introduce new patients and their carers into the routine of the surgical ward, such as the use of latrines and the use of spaces designed for cooking, for laundry and for praying. She was in charge of surveying social problems such as lack of money and food. At a later stage, when the economic reasons for leaving the hospital before completing treatment, were analysed, a 'social' system for patients was introduced. MSF supported them financially, covering the cost of food, so it was possible to convince carers to retain patients for continued treatment in the hospital.

Based on the frequent requests of patients, the health promotion team developed specific materials in order to address different topics: general hygiene (including taking care of the patient's hygiene during their hospitalisation), as well as information on plaster casts and external fixations. The fear of plaster casts remained strong, shown by questions such as "Does the surgeon align the bones first, before he puts the plaster?" This illustrates the gap between patients' perception and medical science, as well as the bridge that health promotion can build in such a situation. The focus lay on the message that a plaster cast is basically not all that different from traditional bone setting. The fractured bones are set in the correct position and then supported in order to hold them and let them grow together. Another message targeted the 'plaster cast rumour' by explaining that a well-made plaster can cause no harm. Patients were reminded that in certain cases, a plaster cast should be exchanged: when they felt too much pressure or – in severe stages – if they lost feeling in the affected limb. This proved to be a very important point, as patients were not at ease with their plasters because they could not look inside and monitor the healing process. Wearing a plaster cast in the temperatures of the semi-arid Sahel zone is not a pleasant feeling. In traditional bone setting, on the other hand, the splints and bandages are removed every few days, and the bonesetters check the advancement of the healing process. This, of course, involves much more communication and interaction than the treatment offered by the nurses in the Abéché hospital.

In a second step, the health promotion material focussed on burn victims, as skin grafting turned out to generate a lot of fear among carers. The emphasis here lay on addressing the fear of making yet another wound by explaining that only upper layers of skin are removed to be transplanted onto the burnt skin. The surgical team also identified bad curing rates for burns patients if they were malnourished. Therefore, health promotion sessions tackled the question of how to enhance the patients' diet with more protein-rich food, while taking into account the often-limited financial resources of their families.

Further sessions not only targeted patients and carers, but also personnel, including the cleaning personnel, who got more attention and were more motivated to do their work emptying full latrines and clearing waste in the whole area. Yet another session took place with nurses in order to collectively reflect on their role and duties as health care providers in a playful way. As a result, they all identified empathy, taking care and listening to patients as important duties and responsibilities of their job. Overall, the presence of a person who was familiar with local languages and culture and who was available to discuss patients' social needs tremendously improved the situation in the hospital ward within a few weeks. The health promoter turned into a kind of social worker who was an all-round information point for patients, and with every week of her stay, the trust of patients and carers evolved more and more.

Additionally, new international staff members in the team – especially surgeons and anaesthetists – who often stayed in the project for only a short time, were grateful to receive a comprehensive overview of the cultural and ethnic specificities of the region in general, as well as the internal dynamics of the hospital in particular. The ethnic conflict between Southern staff and Northern patients was taken into consideration when recruiting new staff. Emphasis was placed on identifying more skilled people from the region instead of 'importing' others from distant places and reaffirming existing power relationships. This impact on human resources decisions was also replicated in the Am Timan project.

Seeking contact with traditional bonesetters

Nevertheless, one of the central issues in the Abéché project remained the lack of confidence in the institution of the hospital and its biomedical treatment, which had been built up by the people of Abéché due to bad experiences over the years. Therefore, at a later stage of the health promotion activities, contact with a traditional healers' association was additionally established in order to include them in a chain of communication and to motivate them to refer critical cases to the hospital. This was triggered by the tragic case of Risala, a 10-year-old nomad girl who had lost one lower leg due to the unsuccessful treatment of a simple fracture. Her relatives had sought traditional treatment from a bonesetter and later, when the broken bone had perforated the skin, a wound appeared. So they sought advice from 'Dr Shoukous', a name for drug peddlers who sell all kinds of pharmaceuticals at weekly markets held in rural areas – a common phenomenon in less developed countries (see Bledsoe and Goubaud [1988] for Sierra Leone). The open fracture had become infected and the girl developed gangrene that finally – after weeks of suffering – led to the 'natural' separation of the gangrened leg. When the girl arrived at the MSF hospital, the staff could do no more than amputate the dead part and care for the wound.

This tragic example served as a starting point for addressing the rumours of 'unnecessary amputations' which the hospital was known for. A workshop was organised at the traditional healers' association in Abéché with the aim of bringing together traditional healers and the surgical team of the hospital. To accomplish that, the health promoter had to build bridges between the two opposing parties to allow for a mutual understanding of each other's perspectives. The first and foremost objective, though, was to improve the acceptance of the surgical project and to promote referral of complicated cases to the hospital.

The challenge of such an encounter is to address the sensitive topic of failed treatments without pointing fingers or widening the gap between traditional approaches and biomedical treatment. Therefore, it was necessary to promote an 'integrated approach' (Nwachukwu et al., 2011). During the discussion, it was stressed that traditional bone setting is a good choice for simple fractures, and at the same time, it was emphasised that MSF neither intended to question the traditional bonesetters' skills nor planned to take away their clients. It was important to pay the healers all due respect. Accordingly, it was explained that open fractures absolutely need to be treated in a hospital setting, as the danger of infection is very serious. It was made clear that healers should henceforward refer such cases to the hospital. The healers, on the other side, explained their techniques but also presented their view that hospital staff did not make enough efforts to save affected limbs and tended to amputate early, unnecessarily. At this point, pictures of Risala, the girl who had lost her leg, and another severe case were shown in order to underline what was at stake. The surgical team could explain why the amputation was inevitable, and at this point, the healers agreed. This approach shows how important it is to engage in face-to-face communication in order to develop respect and mutual understanding.

Conclusion

As the analysis of the Abéché project and the implementation of the health promotion programme have shown, a thorough understanding of structural factors – such as the social and political circumstances – is necessary to cope with the daily routines and shortcomings of a surgical ward. The key problem of the Abéché surgical project was *not* a cultural one in terms of patients' perception of disease and acceptance of biomedical treatment, even though it appeared to be at first glance. The underlying causes of the difficulties were definitely structural ones, and patients used their cultural capacities to react to the challenges of the hospital experience. It is not the Abéchians' perception of plaster casts or other forms of treatment that leads to patients leaving the hospital against medical advice, but rather the lived experience of the quality of treatment offered. Moreover, patients do not feel understood when the majority of health care providers originate from different ethnic groups or nationalities. If most patients are illiterate, they suffer if medical staff are unable or unwilling to help them understand the kind of treatment that is performed on them. Furthermore, the final outcome of treatment offered for difficult cases of burns and trauma victims is often not foreseeable, which adds to patients' scepticism about such treatment.

The Abéché project demonstrated that the external perspective provided by an anthropologist in a humanitarian setting can serve as both translation and critique

(Beshar & Stellmach, 2017). It can help to gain new insights and to identify problems that would otherwise have remained concealed by daily routines and a purely medical focus. In some cases, a blind spot can block MSF's perception of its own work and lead to overlooking structural deficits and falsely correlating a problem with cultural causes. In such cases, it is the purpose of a "humanitarian anthropologist" (Leach, 2015) to elucidate that a given problem is precisely *not* a cultural one – even though it might have appeared to be – and to reveal other causes beyond culture.

Notes

1 The anthropological study revealed details about traditions and some reasons underlying local violence that caused on average one to two cases of stabbings or severe beatings per day being referred to the trauma ward. It involved concepts of adolescence among tribal young men in the Ouaddai region for whom the receipt of a dagger and its consequent use – traditionally to protect female clan members or to free an injured animal from its sufferings – constitutes part of a rite of passage. In the context of a post-conflict urban setting with high rates of youth unemployment and drug abuse, this tradition often turned into violent fights between individuals of rival ethnic groups embedded in a system of clan feuds and tribal conflict resolution.
2 Name changed.
3 El Hag and El Hag (2010) point out in their overview of complications caused by treatment by traditional bonesetters that orthodox medical treatment is more effective; however, traditional bonesetters do have success with simple, closed fractures.

References

Abramowitz, S., Marten, M. and Panter-Brick, C., (2014). Medical humanitarianism: anthropologists speak out on policy and practice. *Medical Anthropology Quarterly.* **29**(1), 1–23.

Abu-Lughod, L., (1991). Writing against culture. In: R. G. Fox., ed., *Recapturing anthropology. Working in the present.* Santa Fe: School of American Research Press. 137–162.

Arditi, C., (2003). Les conséquences du refus de l'école, chez les populations musulmanes du Tchad au XXème siècle. *Journal des Africanistes.* **73**(1), 7–22.

Beshar, I. and Stellmach, D., (2017). Anthropological approaches to medical humanitarianism. *Medicine Anthropology Theory.* **4**(5), 1–22. doi:10.17157/mat.4.5.477

Bledsoe, C. and Goubaud, M., (1988). The reinterpretation and distribution of western pharmaceuticals: an example from the Mende of Sierra Leone. In: S. van der Geest and S. Reynolds Whyte, eds., *The context of medicines in developing countries.* Netherlands: Springer. 253–276. doi:10.1007/978-94-009-2713-1_13

Daniel, E.V., (1996). Crushed glass: a counterpoint to culture, or, Is there a counterpoint to culture? In: E. Valentine Daniel and J.M. Peck, eds., *Culture/contexture: explorations in anthropology and literature studies.* Berkeley: University of California Press. 357–376.

de Oliveira Nunes, M., (2014). From application to implication in medical anthropology: political, historical and narrative interpretations of the world of sickness and health. *História, Ciências, Saúde – Manguinhos.* **21**(2), 403–420. Available from: www.scielo.br/hcsm

El Hag, M.I.A. and El Hag, O.B.M., (2010). Complications in fractures treated by traditional bonesetters in Khartoum, Sudan. *Khartoum Medical Journal.* **3**(1), 401–405. [online]. [viewed 17 October 2016]. Available from: http://onlinejournals.uofk.edu/index.php/kmj/article/view/440

Eriksen, T.H., (1993). *Ethnicity and nationalism: anthropological perspectives.* London: Pluto Press.

Foster, G.M., (1976). Medical anthropology and international health planning. *Medical Anthropology Newsletter.* **7**(3), 12–18.

Fox, R.G. and King, B.J., eds., (2002). *Anthropology beyond culture.* New York: Berg.

Giroux, J., Lanz, D. and Sguaitamatti, D., (2009). *The tormented triangle: the regionalisation of conflict in Sudan, Chad, and the Central African Republic.* Crisis States Research Centre Working Papers **2**(47). Crisis States Research Centre, London School of Economics and Political Science, London.

Grohma, P., (2014). *Abéché, its hospital and its environs: an anthropological abstract.* Unpublished MSF report.

Kleinman, A., (1980). *Patients and healers in the context of culture: an exploration of the borderland between anthropology, medicine, and psychiatry.* Berkeley: University of California Press.

Krumeich, A., Weijts, W., Reddy, P. and Meijer-Weitz, A., (2001). The benefits of anthropological approaches for health promotion research and practice. *Health Education Research.* **16**(2), 121–130.

Leach, A., (2015). Exporting trauma: can the talking cure do more harm than good? *The Guardian.* [online]. [viewed 5 February 2015]. Available from: www.theguardian.com/global-development-professionals-network/2015/feb/05/mental-health-aid-western-talking-cure-harm-good-humanitarian-anthropologist

Lebeuf, A.M.D., (1959). *Les populations du Tchad: (nord du 10e parallèle).* Paris: Presses Universitaires de France.

Lemarchand, R., (1986). Chad: the misadventures of the North-South dialectic. *African Studies Review.* **29**(3), 27–41. doi:10.2307/524081

Mathieu, L., Bertani, A., Chaudier, P., Charpail, C., Rongiéras, F. and Chauvin, F., (2014). Management of the complications of traditional bone setting for upper extremity fractures: he experiences of a French Forward Surgical Team in Chad. *Chirurgie de la Main.* **33**(2), 137–143. doi:10.1016/j.main.2014.01.005

Nwachukwu, B.U. et al., (2011). Traditional bonesetters and contemporary orthopaedic fracture care in a developing nation: historical aspects, contemporary status and future directions. *The Open Orthopaedics Journal.* **5**, 20–26. PMC. (Web. 1 December 2016.)

Randeria, S. and Karagiannis, E., (2015). Zwischen Begeisterung & Unbehagen – Ein anthropologischer Blick auf den Begriff der Kultur. In: S. de la Rosa, S. Schubert and H. Zapf, eds., *Transkulturelle Politische Theorie – Eine Einführung.* Wiesbaden: Springer Verlag. 63–83.

van Dijk, R., (1998). Culture as excuse: the failure of health care for migrants in the Netherlands. In: S. van der Geest and A. Rienks, eds., *The art of medical anthropology.* Amsterdam: Het Spinhuis. 243–250.

Wagner, U., (2015). Der Stellenwert der Anthropologie in der humanitären Hilfe am Beispiel von Ärzte ohne Grenzen. *Ethnoscripts.* **17**(2), 156–165. Available from: http://journals.sub.uni-hamburg.de/ethnoscripts/article/view/906/871

Witeska-Mlynarczyk, A., (2015). Critical medical anthropology: a voice for just and equitable healthcare. *Annals of Agricultural and Environmental Medicine.* **22**(2), 385–389. doi:10.5604/12321966.1152099

Yaffré, Y. and de Sardan, J.-P.O., eds., (2003). *Une médecine inhospitalière: les difficiles relations entre soignants et soignés dans cinq capitales d'Afrique de l'Ouest.* Paris: Editions Karthala.

10

"YAYA HANKURI DA MUTANI?" (HOW IS YOUR PATIENCE WITH THE PEOPLE?)

A medical anthropological inquiry into treatment challenges in the Anka Local Government Area, Zamfara Heavy Metal Treatment Project, Nigeria

Annemieke Bont, Marit van Lenthe and Karla Bil

Introduction

This chapter provides one example of how questions of cultural miscommunication have been explored by anthropologists. The investigation demonstrates how perceived treatment failures were in fact the result of Médecins Sans Frontières' interaction with local people. We discuss elements of ethnography from a medical anthropological study of an MSF project caring for children with acute lead poisoning in Zamfara state, Nigeria. The catastrophic event that prompted MSF intervention took place simultaneously in eight villages. Most patients who enrolled in the subsequent treatment programme in 2010 responded initially. However, in one village, MSF faced major challenges. The level of lead in the blood remained high in about 50% of the initial patients. The health promotion team struggled to keep patients in the treatment programme and to motivate mothers to bring their children to clinic appointments. It was at this point that an anthropologist was called in to establish if there was any relation between these problems and what the medical team considered specific cultural issues. The description that follows focuses on this one location where the health of the community remained at risk, from October–December 2014.

The initial outbreak

In March 2010, an MSF team on routine outbreak surveillance responded to a reported increase of child mortality in children under the age of 5 in the regions of Anka and Bukkuyum Local Government Areas (LGAs) in Zamfara state, northern

Nigeria. The investigations that followed drew on support from MSF, the US Centers for Disease Control and Prevention (CDC), the World Health Organisation (WHO) and the Zamfara State Ministry of Health (ZMoH). The investigation found what is to date, history's largest confirmed epidemic of acute lead poisoning.

The outbreak rose indirectly from a spike in the international price of gold. This had led to an increase in the region's long-established artisanal gold mining activities, specifically in deep rock ore mining and processing, as opposed to traditional alluvial mining, which does not cause lead poisoning. Due to the particular geology of certain areas of Nigeria, the ore being processed contained high levels of gold – and also very high concentrations of lead.

For an unknown length of time, village populations had been processing the gold ore inside their villages. While the ore was mined at some distance from the village, it was processed closer to home, where it was pulverised then sifted for gold particles. Increasingly, people used agricultural grinding machines intended to mill grain into flour for this purpose. One factor in the outbreak may have been the widespread adoption of this technique, which raised large, drifting clouds of lead dust (Lo et al., 2012). The gold ore was largely ground in public areas throughout the villages. Other processing activities, such as crushing, washing and gold recovery, took place inside the residential compounds (von Lindern et al., 2011). These activities heavily polluted the living environment with lead dust and residual waste. Whereas over 10,000 people were estimated to be affected by the exposure to lead, children under the age of 5 were most at risk of death or serious acute and long-term irreversible health effects. This was due to the pathological effects of lead on their still-developing physiology, their increased proximity to soil, hand-to-mouth activity and a much higher percentage of absorption of ingested lead than adults. Lead exposure in children can lead to a host of clinical symptoms, such as abdominal pain, arthralgia, clumsiness, staggering, headache, convulsions, behavioural changes and encephalopathy. Of the many organs adversely affected by lead exposure, the central nervous system is the most important. Lead distorts enzymes and structural proteins in the body, and high blood lead levels can cause coma and death (Needleman, 2004).

The response

MSF decided to respond to this emergency even though lead poisoning is usually not an MSF focus. For MSF, this outbreak fell into a category of acute unmet medical needs with high mortality, which justified a response. Over 400 children younger than 5 were estimated to have died of lead poisoning before the June 2010 start of the MSF response in Anka and Bukkuyum LGAs. The medical programme focussed on eight villages that were originally identified as severely affected.

It is well known that artisanal mining is hazardous to health, both directly – by handling toxicants used in extraction – and indirectly – by pollution of the living environment (Dooyema et al., 2011). Whereas the health-related impacts of mercury exposure have been widely documented for more than 40 years (Hilson et al.,

2007), little was known about the type of mining-related lead poisoning found in Zamfara. Lo et al. (2012) report that while there is documentation on environmental lead contamination in small-scale gold ore-processing communities, the literature is limited (Appleton et al., 2001; Betancourt et al., 2005; Odumo et al., 2010; Ogala et al., 2002), and none of the reports explore the correlation between gold ore processing and childhood lead poisoning.

Also, in dealing with lead treatment of this scale and level, MSF found itself on new terrain and convened a group of international experts on lead poisoning to develop a protocol, with input from field teams. As a result, a chelation therapy[1] was provided in hospitals in Bukkuyum and Anka LGAs for acute cases of lead poisoning, and an oral chelation therapy protocol was developed for children with high blood lead levels (BLL), up to the age of 5, as outpatients at MSF clinics at village level.

MSF's inpatient care was effective in addressing the most acute presentations of lead poisoning. However, discharge of patients back into the community presented a problem. Outpatient chelation therapy has limited efficacy if children remain exposed to high lead levels in their homes and villages. Therefore, medical treatment alone would not suffice. Additionally, the chelation treatment protocol prioritised children up to the age of 5. It did not address the medical needs of older children or adults, including women of reproductive age. Thus, the primary method of improving the health of all affected groups was to reduce their exposure to lead. Four main exposure routes for children and adults were identified in these villages (von Lindern et al., 2011, pp. 12–13): incidental ingestion of contaminated soils and dusts (especially a risk for infants and toddlers, given their increased hand to mouth behaviour), consumption of food contaminated by soil and dust sources, ingestion of contaminated water and inhalation of contaminated dusts.

Reducing exposure required deep cleaning the living environment of the village population. This problem was tackled with the help of an engineering firm specialising in environmental clean-up – TerraGraphics Environmental Engineering, Inc (TG). Before beginning treatment of patients at village level, remedial work was undertaken in the affected villages. In all eight villages, as well as other remediation, surface soil from family compounds and contaminated public spaces was removed and replaced with clean soil. The contaminated soil was disposed of in secure landfills.[2]

As part of the response, MSF set up a health promotion to explain the cause of the disease to the community and explain the pathways of exposure to lead, as well as to promote safe ore-processing activities away from the villages to prevent recontamination of the environment. The promotion yielded good results. With the combination of remediation, treatment and prevention activities, the number of patients enrolled in the programme had progressively decreased by early 2014 to approximately 20% of those ever enrolled. As a result, one clinic had by then been closed entirely, with all patients discharged. In two other villages, the MSF had decided to start phasing out the project, based on the remaining number of patients and their anticipated treatment progression.

196 Annemieke Bont et al.

But the programme did not show positive outcomes in all clinic locations. One clinic showed very different results in 2014. Here more than 50% of the original number of patients remained under care with persistently high BLL, while the team was also struggling to stop patients from dropping out of the treatment programme before the BLL fell enough. On top of that, instead of their mothers, or at least an adult carer, some young patients were accompanied by their only slightly older siblings. This was a problem for the medical team, as, from a medico-ethical perspective, children cannot give consent for children, or receive prescriptions on behalf of other children. The team could not effectively pass on dosage information to these siblings, and were uncomfortable trusting pharmaceuticals to such young children.

Efforts from the medical team to address these issues did not lead to structural improvements. It was at that point, at the end of 2013, that the decision was made to request anthropological input in order to understand the social reasons behind a slow uptake of preventive measures by the affected communities. In their words, team members wanted to know if there were: "specific cultural reasons for the . . . challenges [in the village], and if yes, [how] can we address them in the coming year, in order to achieve better results [discharge from programme as per protocol] for the children in the programme?" (MSF, 2014).

Health, illness and the 'cultural context'

Everybody's perceptions of health, illness and health-seeking behaviour are strongly linked to their way of life (Trotter, 1990). Such perceptions are the focus of medical anthropological research, and this case would be no exception. However, as has been highlighted in other chapters in this book,[3] 'culture' or 'lack of education' – while often suggested as possible causes for the challenges encountered – rarely prove to be the real problem. The cultural aspects of the local context can play a part in the response to a medical programme (see Hill-Jackson, 2005) but the main issue often lies on the interactional level; that is, in the dynamics between the care provider and the people they serve (Wilce, 2009).

Therefore, in order to understand the problems outlined, the anthropologist needs to consider the perspectives, beliefs and assumptions of all the parties involved. A familiarisation with the village and its inhabitants was an essential part of this research. This included the socio-political, cultural and economic aspects such as village history, structure and organisation, as well as a study of the community's health understanding and health-seeking behaviour. However, equally important was the analysis of the medical set-up (clinic organisation), the treatment protocol and medical procedures, as well as the clinic-based interactions between medical staff and patients/carers on all these issues.

As the anthropologist had experience of MSF, but not of the setting or the pathology of lead poisoning, the assignment began with 40 hours of preparatory research of the literature on those two elements. Between mid-October and mid-December 2014, six weeks were spent on field research in the project locations.

As the project at this time was achieving good medical outcomes and minimal resistance in most of the project locations, it made sense to spend some time in one of these settings. The anthropologist spent five days in one of the more remote villages where the programme was successful enough to be phased out, and the final patients were about to be discharged from the programme. The remaining time on the project was spent in the main research location, where the programme faced challenges. This allowed the anthropologist to discover different perceptions of the medical programme, and to learn about local differences in village structure and social dynamics.

Data was collected through multiple ethnographic strategies. A total of 85 semi-structured interviews were conducted with 121 respondents, and seven in-depth interviews were held with key Nigerian and international MSF staff. Extensive and repeated observations were conducted in a total of 13 compounds, as well as at the clinic site and in the village's public spaces, and was supported by evidence from informal conversations.

Additionally, the anthropologist made use of the extensive epidemiological data available in surveillance sheets, in combination with a village map drawn up during the remedial phase of the project. Apart from showing village infrastructure and compound locations, this map also included information on lead contamination levels of village public space, household compounds and water sources prior to the remediation. The wealth of information in the surveillance sheets and the village map allowed the anthropologist,[4] in the first phase of their enquiry, to place patients in their household context, as well as to link them to the village mining history and pre-remedial lead contamination levels in the village.

When living is bad for your health

The research location is a larger village a 15-minute drive from Anka, the main town of the Anka LGA in Zamfare State, Nigeria. During the 2012 village count,[5] the total village population was 1,287 people, divided into 211 households. The patients, according to the MSF treatment criteria – children up to 5 years old – were estimated to be around 500. The majority of the village are Muslim Hausa, like the other villages where the MSF programme was established.

In Zamfara's villages, farming traditionally supplies the households with its main food source. The men take primary responsibility for farming the family plot and bringing the harvest home, while the women work inside the compounds to dry and prepare the crops for the household's use. In the farming off-season, men generate income through occupational specialities. Part of the money they earn is used to 'solve family problems', and a part is for them to spend as they like. Most women will also have income-generating activities, performed throughout the year, and sometimes their contribution can be of great importance to the household's subsistence level (Coles & Mack, 1991). With their income, they can financially support female neighbours and relatives in ceremonies and celebrations, and it helps them pay for their daughters' marriages or provide things for the household, their

198 Annemieke Bont et al.

children or themselves. These activities can be performed largely inside the compounds, which is important due to the widespread practice of *Kulle*, wife seclusion, through which the husbands control the movement of women outside the household compound.

Children perform a range of tasks to support the household. They assist with cooking, cleaning and childcare, and they engage in farming with their father or the compound's older women, for whom *Kulle* is less strict. Also, as their mothers are largely bound to the household compounds, children will run errands for them and collect water and firewood. They also contribute to their mothers' income-generating activities by selling the foods and snacks their mothers have prepared (Coles & Mack, 1991). In the research location, the children sell these in the village public space, from compound to compound, or even in the nearby market in Anka.

Life in the main research village is different in the sense that a large number of the village men had been involved in artisanal mining and mining-related activities long before the spike in international gold prices caused the surge in mining in the region. For some households, these activities had been their main occupational speciality, and they spoke with pride about how their village's mining history was the most extensive in the area. This was understandable, as in periods when gold prices were high, their mining had been a source of relative prosperity for their families. Indications of the village's long-term mining history can indeed be found in the village social structure. Village men involved in mining were part of a hierarchical structure, represented by a 'head of miners'. The village also had its own well-respected local 'middle-man', who was connected to the region's gold trade networks.

The location of the MSF programme – Anka and Bukkuyum LGAs – is a low income, rural region, richly endowed with gold deposits, a combination that facilitates artisanal mining. Artisanal mining in general is performed by people living in the poorest and most remote rural areas with few employment alternatives, and as such, the sector represents an important source of income (Kyeremateng-Amoah & Clarke, 2015). As a low-tech, labour-intensive industry with few barriers to entry, artisanal mining has become an alluring alternative livelihood for many (Long et al., 2015).

Indeed, the research location is rural, with high dependency on agriculture and limited alternative employment options. Even when most of the men active in artisanal mining also engaged in farming during the season, they relied heavily on money from mining to support their families; for example, to buy extra food from the market in the nearby town. This reliance made these families vulnerable to changes in gold prices and in mining opportunities, and the lead emergency had a huge impact on their livelihoods.

Once child mortality was found to be related to processing lead–contaminated ore inside the compounds and in the village public spaces, several measures were taken to address the problem. MSF's focus was on treating acutely sick children and on preventive measures such as the remediation of contaminated compounds and the removal of residual waste lead. Other measures taken locally were directed at mining-related activities. The Emirate of Anka's first reaction in March and April 2010 was to impose a general mining ban, quickly followed by a ban on all processing in residential areas, and a safety radius of half a kilometre from the villages. Subsequent actions – a combined effort of MSF, local and state officials and the Anka Emirate – included the closing and dismantling of nearby industrial mining areas and the launch of education on safe mining practices.

For those families with a high dependency on mining, much was at stake. For the men, the general ban on mining meant a direct loss of income-generating activities. As this had been their main occupational speciality for generations, they did not have many alternatives. Those who chose to continue mining either had to do so in more distant locations, travelling to sites in other states for longer periods, or continue mining at nearer illegal sites, disobeying their Emir. However, as there was a large drop in gold prices at the time, even with these options, families still faced hardship. Much of this hardship landed on the shoulders of the women.

In rural Hausa settings, women already carry a heavy burden from the combination of income-earning occupational activities, reproduction and domestic labour (Coles & Mack, 1991), but the study showed clearly that in many of these mining-related compounds, women had taken on responsibilities that were not traditionally theirs. When men were absent for longer periods, mining in distant locations, older men in the household compound or male relatives who might be living in other compounds were officially responsible for the households, but in effect, women were in charge of household issues. Also, whereas women normally used their own money to contribute to occasional ceremonies and celebrations, and to provide items for themselves and the children, a significant number of the women interviewed said that they were now using the money to 'help their husbands'; to support them by providing basic household items, often even food, normally the main responsibility of the men: "We use it to help the husbands with money when they do not have it. We buy the things like soap. Now it is more difficult to find the money to support the household" (Interview 60). "You know we are in the village, sometimes we may wake up and we don't have any food in the house. I can use my money to buy food for my children to eat" (Interview 57). "Although the money [I get] is not that much. . . . At times even, when my husband don't have money to buy food for us, out of what am getting I use it to buy food, and we eat myself and my children" (Interview 24).

With women's income increasingly important for the family, they also dedicated more time to income-generating activities, putting them under constant time pressure. These women clearly struggled to control their daily workload. Sometimes this was stated in a direct answer: "Honestly speaking, work is too much here for us in the village" (Interview 49). At other times, this was revealed indirectly. While spending half an hour in a compound for the study, the following conversation occurred between a respondent and a neighbour, who had asked her to pound some sorghum that morning in return for money, who comes up and starts speaking to the respondent:

Neighbour:	"Up till now these people are still here?"
Respondent:	"That is why I could not do anything today. What an evil thing is that. If my husband comes back, what am I going to give him? What will I tell him?"
Other women:	"So you cannot pound today, right?"
Respondent:	"I don't know when these people will free me."

(Interview 53)

Time pressure on these women trying to manage extra tasks and responsibilities was a real problem. As we will see later, this also played a role in the regular clinic visits needed for their children´s treatment.

It was by comparing outcomes from the research location with the comparison village that the anthropologist was first alerted to local differences in the women's tasks and responsibilities (see Box 10.1). Later on in the research, it became evident that these differences could also be found within the main research location, when comparing mining and non-mining households.

Initially, the anthropologist suspected that these issues were all directly related to the more recent loss of mining income for these families, and that the women had responded by increasing their own income generation. However, closer analyses of the data[6] made clear that the different role divisions and the additional hardship these women spoke of were actually more structural and pre-dated the 'lead emergency'. Also, their household's financial vulnerability was comparable to that of mining communities at large (Hentschel et al., 2003; Kyeremateng-Amoah & Clarke, 2015).

Apart from the direct economic impact and the added burden for the women, these families also felt a threat to their social status. For some, their social standing in the village depended largely on their function in the local mining structure, a standing they now feared losing due to the bad image lead poisoning gave mining activities. Not all residents in this village had been involved in mining, and mining families risked being held responsible, not just for the health of their own children, but also of those children from non-mining families.

The frustration and anger that built up around these issues readily turned against MSF because it was present at village level promoting health issues and safe mining activities. Referring to this period, a male respondent, previously very involved in mining, explained to the anthropologist: "However, if you didn't forget . . . when you people came here, we are just like enemies here. It was later on that we came to understand each other right" (Interview 66).

MSF's activities were regarded with suspicion, and the main issue raised by this group was that mining had been going on for generations and lead poisoning had never been a problem before. What was being questioned was not so much the need for a programme, but more importantly, whether mining was the cause of the emergency. Challenging the causal relation between lead poisoning and mining seemed to be a strategy to fend off responsibility for the emergency and limit any damage to their position in the village.

Possibly this response can be understood as a defence mechanism, a way to cope with a situation in which the main work to support the family is at the same time harming it, and there are no real alternatives available. Other research has shown that knowledge and awareness of the adverse health impacts of artisanal mining does not necessarily affect how miners act or their decisions on avoidance, control and protection against exposure. Indeed, generating a livelihood outweighs the potential negative health outcomes (Charles et al., 2013). A study by Grätz (2009) in northern Benin goes well beyond this. It suggests the emergence of a distinct socio-professional identity among miners, whereby various risks are culturally reconceived as challenges, often affirming that they – as opposed to others – are proud to deliberately choose and master these hazards. These risk-sharing attitudes were observed to lead to a considerable degree of internal cohesion, even despite the various internal disputes. Miners often use this as a means of self-assertion or expression of self-awareness to counter a strong stigmatising discourse (or bad reputation) from outside communities and state agencies (Grätz, 2009). It seems quite possible that a similar dynamic took place among the mining families in response to MSF's programme. The messages MSF was promoting about the miners' main income source bonded them as a group – and as a group, they turned against the programme.

MSF's continual efforts in their health promotions to portray mining as a cause of lead poisoning seemed to have a contrary effect on these families' attitudes towards the project. Instead of welcoming it, they felt compelled to openly question the treatment's effectiveness and largely reject MSF's programme. Indeed, a woman whose children were successfully treated and discharged from the MSF programme early on remembered being scolded and ridiculed for their trust in the programme by other women: "some people used to mock us, telling us that we don't know what we are doing for taking these drugs so seriously" (Interview 55).

When looking at the comparison village, the anthropologist did not find doubt or rejection within the village on the cause of lead poisoning in either of the MSF interventions (see Box 10.2). Also, speaking to the villagers about their mining activities and the lead emergency that followed was unproblematic, whereas, within the research location, this topic was often met with silence, reluctance and sometimes even hostility.

The population of the comparison village easily accepted the MSF's intervention because to them the cause and consequence with regards to the lead emergency was evident, and they still had alternative income generating activities to return to. The high treatment adherence in this location explains the good treatment outcomes, allowing MSF to phase out the programme in this location by early 2014.

But for those families involved in mining for a long time, non-adherence to the treatment, as a way of preserving their standing and their dignity, seems a likely cause for the lack of treatment progress up to the time of the research. This was despite the fact that their children, according to MSF medical data, were actually most in need of treatment. Comparing the MSF surveillance sheets with the compounds' pre-remediation contamination levels marked on the village map, it was clear that those families most involved in mining-related activities also suffered most from the lead emergency. Pre-remediation contamination levels in these families' compounds had been extremely high, and they suffered correspondingly high numbers of deaths among their children. They were also confronted with high levels of lead in their children's blood long after the initial emergency phase. In fact, at the time of the research, it was in these compounds where MSF was seeing most of the children with problematic high levels of lead who were not responding well to the treatment.

If their rejection of the MSF programme was indeed linked to self-assertion, these families would not be won over either by focussing on the cause of lead poisoning or by repeated explanations about how to administer the drugs. So, MSF's approach at the time of the research was not going to produce positive outcomes. A new approach was needed for these families.

BOX 10.1 VIGNETTE: A DESCRIPTION OF A VILLAGE WHERE THE INTERVENTION SHOWED A SUCCESSFUL OUTCOME

Differences in work and household responsibilities as compared to the research location

Tungar Daji is a relatively isolated village of roughly the same size as the main research village. Agriculture is the primary activity for men. In the farming off-season, the men earn money from a large range of occupational specialities. The women are responsible for the household activities and childcare, and most have some income-generating activities throughout the year.

Questions on household responsibilities and use of income were answered light-heartedly and with humour. Asked about their daily activities, women in Tungar Daji explained that they usually busied themselves in the morning with the main household activities – pounding maize or sorghum, cooking and washing. However, by late morning, women had usually finished their main daily activities and only had the evening meal to prepare later in the afternoon. They usually had time to sit down and talk to the anthropologist and made ample time to do so, the atmosphere of the interviews being friendly and quite carefree. When discussing income-generating activities, young women with very small children said they were not usually engaged in anything, instead relying on their husbands to provide for all the family's needs. Some would have minor activities like braiding other women's hair. Some women would pound maize or sorghum for others, sell cooking ingredients from their

"Yaya hankuri da mutani?" **203**

compounds or prepare food which their children would sell in the village. Some of the older women would engage in farming, some offering their work to others, while others would farm their own plots. When asked what women would use their money for, the most frequent answer was to contribute to ceremonies and to buy themselves small private things and treats for themselves and the children. The men's money would be partly used to solve 'family problems', and the rest would be for the men's private use.

Role division between a man and his wife (or wives) was very clear, with the men responsible for providing the family with food, and the women for looking after the household and the children. Two co-wives were joking that "The only thing we are helping him [the husband] with, is with eating what he brings!" [women laugh] (Interview 35). One older woman, honourably nicknamed 'queen of farming' by the members of her compound, joked about the different use of her husband's money compared to the money she made from selling rice from her own farm:

Question: "The money your husband earns, what is it used for?"
Answer: "He uses it for feeding the family! [woman laughs] Or he gives us fura [a millet drink mixed with milk and sugar]. My own, I use it in taking care of the children and celebration."

(Interview 14)

BOX 10.2 ACKNOWLEDGEMENT OF THE ROLE OF MINING IN THE LEAD EMERGENCY AND READY ACCEPTANCE OF THE MSF INTERVENTION

Mining and related activities had not been important for the population in Tungar Daji previously, and only appeared for a relatively short period around the spike in gold prices around 2009. The inhabitants of Tungar Daji explained how in a short time everybody became engaged in pounding activities, "men and women, old and young". Women from a compound would pool their money and pay young men to deliver sacks of ore and have 'pounding competitions' to see who could pound the most. Their eyes would light up when they spoke of these competitions, and they remembered which women did well. Inside the compounds, women would pound using household items, such as mortars and pestles, leaving not only the compounds contaminated with lead dust, but also directly contaminating their main staple foods, sorghum and maize. Men would pound in the village public spaces often using agricultural grinding machines. The ground ore would be 'washed' (panned) in village ponds and nearby streams, further contaminating the village environment.

When asked about the impact of lead poisoning, women pointed out the compounds of families affected. They knew how many children died in these compounds from lead poisoning, which children were in hospital and which children were still in the MSF treatment programme. They would also take the anthropologist to other compounds to show her children who had survived an acute lead poisoning episode but now suffered heavy neurological damage. They would ask her what could be done for these children, and where the parents should take them to be cured. They would describe the burden on these mothers, having to care for such heavily disabled children.

Looking back on the cause of the acute lead poisoning epidemic, the people of Tungar Daji easily recognised a link between the beginning of the mining-related activities and the onset of symptoms. They explained that even though the extra money was a welcome addition to the family income, once they understood this was causing the high child mortality rate, people quickly switched back to their previous activities. The MSF treatment was gratefully accepted and led to a quick drop in the patients' BLL, with subsequent discharge of the patients according to protocol and, by early 2014, a phasing out of the interventions.

When is a child sick? Science versus experience

While part of the village had been critical of the lead treatment from the start, others only developed doubts about it when, after multiple treatment courses, their children were still said to be in need of additional treatment. The two main questions they asked were 1) how could the children still 'have lead' when they actually looked healthy?, and 2) how could lead still be a problem when mining activities in the village had ceased and the village had been cleaned?

It became clear to the anthropologist that MSF's activities were actually valued, but more in relation to other health issues being treated in the clinic than their continued effort to treat the lead poisoning:

> Some people will never believe [that the lead is a problem], especially some of them whose children have never convulsed.[7] For me, I see the importance, because apart from lead, if children are sick, we go to the clinic they will give us drugs for free. If it is for us to buy the drugs with our money, I know the drugs are very expensive. For that we are so thankful for MSF.
>
> *(Interview 54)*

Additionally, it was not well understood why lead would still be a problem now that mining activities had been banned from the village and general involvement in mining had been so drastically reduced. The continued emphasis on the need for treatment and preventive measures by the health promotion team was seen as irrelevant. As one woman said, "When the gold was much in the community, people do talk about it, that it [doing the mining in the village] is wrong, but now that the gold is not much, people don't pay attention to the issue like they do before" (Interview 62).

It seems that a different perception of the children's health and of the long-term remaining impact of lead on health had become a barrier to the community's understanding of, and the motivation for, the lead treatment programme.

'Having lead', or 'being sick'

At the time of the study, while observing interactions between women and MSF staff (both at the clinic and within the compounds), there was visible irritation on both sides. MSF had managed to significantly reduce the number of cases of acute lead poisoning, but results from the blood tests showed that many children still had high BLL. The improvements were much slower in this location than in other project villages. The staff were frustrated by the lack of improvement and blamed the mothers, suspecting that they were not following the treatment protocol.

From the point of view of the community, however, it was not well understood why MSF continued to urge them to bring their children to the clinic for regular visits and was still treating their children for 'lead'. As far as they could see, the children were showing no signs of sickness. Most children by this point were indeed asymptomatic, but suffering from a significant subclinical impact of lead poisoning.

One of the first things that became apparent is that MSF and the village people judged the health of the children in different ways, by using different means. When asked how they knew if a child was sick, mothers would list symptoms they regarded as signs of ill health. The most frequent was 'when the child's body is hot' (fever); other symptoms were vomiting, 'passing stool' (diarrhoea), convulsion, headache, stomach pain, 'when a child does not want to play or eat' and coughing. For the mothers, children who do not show any kind of symptoms and do not complain of feeling unwell are considered to be healthy.

When asked about lead poisoning, called 'lead' by the community, it became clear that this condition proved difficult to grasp for most people, both men and women. Asked what the symptoms of lead poisoning were, the answer was unanimous – convulsion. Other symptoms mentioned (by women) in order of frequency were stomach pain, 'child refuses to eat' (lack of appetite), 'very hot body' (high fever – perceived to be higher than fever from malaria), 'not passing stool' (constipation) and 'child being very thin'.

However, the mothers only associated these symptoms with lead poisoning when these combined, or were quickly followed with, convulsions, so in direct relation to an episode of *acute* lead poisoning. When assessing the children's current condition, these symptoms were rarely understood as a sign of lead poisoning.

Since the beginning of the MSF response, the number of children suffering lead-related convulsions had decreased enormously. Respondents explained that the situation had evolved from a time when they would see a child having convulsions and possibly dying every day, to a time when they witnessed this maybe once every three months. For the majority of respondents, the low frequency of convulsions meant lead poisoning was no longer a problem. However, MSF continued to tell them otherwise.

Most of the women who were asked about the current health of their children – children still being treated by MSF – said they were healthy[8] or 'did not have lead'. The absence of convulsion is crucial in the women's judgement of their children's health in connection to lead. Sickness, and the absence of convulsions, vomiting, diarrhoea, or any kind of symptom the children might regularly have, means malaria to them: "We have spent 13 days in Anka with her, they have been giving her lead drugs, but since then she has never convulsed again, now she only gets sick" (Interview 55). When asked about the children's current health, most people actually believed that their children were healthier than before; they were 'stronger', 'plumper' and had 'good appetite', all signs that were thought to be marks of good health.

This made it difficult to motivate people to give their children the lead treatment. Why would you give medication to a child who is perceived to be healthy? And how motivated will mothers be to administer this medication when they do not see any difference between the child's pre- and post-treatment condition? Especially because the treatment regimen is demanding; the main medication is given together with a number of supplements (zinc, vitamin C, iron and calcium), needs to be administered three times daily, and the length of the treatment varies depending on the outcome of the most recent blood test. In a study on lead poisoning in a Mexican immigrant community, Vallejos et al. (2006) used the 'the health belief model' to explain what was needed for the programme to be effective. First, in order to increase their likelihood of preventing or decreasing their children's exposure to lead, parents must understand the health effects of lead exposure, and they must believe that these effects are severe and their children are susceptible to exposure. Second, parents must believe that the benefits of taking action outweigh any perceived barriers. In the research location, most parents were aware and willing to act during the emergency period of the response, but it seemed to become more problematic once remediation was finished and children became asymptomatic. With no perceived treatment effect, and a demanding treatment regimen, mothers seemed to have other priorities.

MSF did try to make administering the medication easier, offering it already pre-sorted in pill boxes. However, from the mothers' perspective, the lead treatment could easily be perceived as unnecessary, a hassle and possibly ineffective. The same reasoning could be applied to the many clinic visits for lead treatment. Mothers confirmed they would come to the clinic if the child was sick, but when the child was happily playing about, they would have other priorities.

Indeed, the mothers' perceptions of their children's health also affected their decision whether to accompany their children to the clinic. Without exception, mothers explained that when a child is sick, it is a mother's obligation to bring them to the clinic. However, they also agreed that when a child is healthy, they can be taken to the clinic by a sibling. As it is common practice in the village to give young children substantial responsibilities at an early age, taking a sibling to the clinic had, over time, been added to the tasks they were allowed to perform; and, as the clinic was next to the village school just outside the main village entrance, getting there was not considered problematic or dangerous. The accompanying siblings were accustomed to venturing much further outside the village to collect fodder for the compound animals or collect firewood.

MSF's concern about children consenting for their siblings did not appear to be an issue for the mothers, either. A member of the health promotion team, seen as representing MSF at the compound level, would attend the family home the day before a clinic visit to inform the mother why it was necessary, so women did not feel additional consent at clinic level was required. The mothers were by now aware of the different aspects of the treatment, and did not feel the need for additional explanation in the clinic.

The treatment holiday

After the reduction in mining activities and the removal of contaminated soil from the village, people could not understand why 'lead' was still a problem for their children. In fact, the biggest puzzle for them was why MSF was still treating children for their initial contamination with lead, despite the efforts of the medical staff and the health promotion team to explain this. The anthropologist found that a misunderstanding had developed around the part of the treatment protocol which the MSF medical team called the 'treatment holiday'. This is, in fact, a pause in treatment during which the medication can bind to the lead particles, allowing the body to dispose of the lead. After this pause, a blood test is taken to find out how effective the treatment has been. The outcome then defines the length of the next treatment course. Mothers would explain to the anthropologist that the patient got this 'treatment holiday' when "the lead has gone down" or "the lead is down". When the treatment was resumed, responders would describe this as "the lead has gone up again" or "the lead has come back". After looking into this in more detail, it appeared that, over time, the community had come to see lead poisoning as a disease similar to malaria; a child will suffer repeated separate disease episodes, and each time be diagnosed and treated, and each time the disease leaves the body. What does not make it easier is that symptoms for 'lead' and for malaria appear to be the same: "Sometimes their body will be hot and they are sick from malaria, while sometimes they said it is lead, and they give them drugs for lead" (Interview 88).

This kind of confusion around the interpretation of symptoms also emerged in a study in Ghana on mining-related mercury poisoning. Poisoning symptoms were readily interpreted as signs of malaria, and miners would self-medicate using quinine and paracetamol (Hilson et al., 2007). Charles et al. found that this kind of confusion has implications for awareness and subsequent prevention and treatment (Charles et al., 2013).

208 Annemieke Bont et al.

In the case of lead poisoning in the research location, there was confusion not only about the interpretation of the symptoms, but also around the 'way the disease worked' and the 'way the medication worked'. Consecutive treatment courses were no longer understood as part of one long trajectory dealing with the same issue, but as separate treatment courses for single lead 'episodes' in the same way malaria is treated. Many women actually believed that between treatment courses, the lead had gone from the body and that the child was truly healthy, matching their perception of the child as healthy due to the absence of symptoms.

Another problem of understanding had developed regarding those children whose BLL was low enough for a new treatment course to be unnecessary (according to the treatment protocol), but not low enough to be discharged from the programme. These children were asked to come to the clinic for a follow-up blood draw every two months. It was difficult for the mothers to understand that the children still 'had lead', when they no longer received any treatment and, again, were asymptomatic and perceived to be healthy. The MSF health promotion team had a lot of difficulty motivating the mothers in this patient group to bring their children to the clinic for these blood tests. Because many blood tests did not result in any kind of follow-up treatment, mothers no longer saw these tests as relevant.

The other health perception: defining health by clinical facts

Clearly, the mothers' perceptions of health and illness ran contrary to the findings of the MSF medical team. MSF measured the children's health by way of blood levels. The surveillance list showed the full record of laboratory tests for each child indicating their BLL. The MSF medical team judged the child's health and based subsequent treatment needs on these outcomes. These levels indicated the children were 'not cured of lead', and thus were either in need of further treatment or follow-up blood tests to monitor their BLL.[9] But, although these outcomes were evidence to the MSF medical team of a child's need for further treatment, the mothers did not interpret them in the same way. The focus on clinical facts made it difficult at that point for the medical team to hear and respond to the mothers' message that 'our children are healthy'.

It is not so strange that MSF faced these difficulties, as the focus on clinical outcomes and statistics had been vital in the inception and the development of the project. These MSF medical statistics are fundamental to their work; as a medical humanitarian agency, MSF uses this kind of medical data not only to make decisions on gaps and success in public health emergencies, but also to provide evidence for advocacy and policy change (Stellmach, 2016). MSF was able to use the statistics in this way in this project, potentially laying a base for long-term health improvements on a much larger scale.

However, in order to develop a new approach, MSF had to move away from clinical facts and add a different perspective to the programme. This is where the anthropologist was able to step in. By taking a broader and more social view of health perception and health behaviour, and by looking at MSF epidemiological data through a social lens, they could reveal the stories behind the numbers. This proved useful for two reasons: it challenged the limitations of a standardised outcomes approach, and it shifted the emphasis from following the numbers to listening to what the patient's mothers were telling them: "our children are healthy". This would produce a better response and shift the project towards positive treatment outcomes.

In the perception of the village population, the cause for lead poisoning had been addressed with the ban on processing lead-contaminated ore inside the compounds and in the village public spaces, and with the subsequent remediation of the village's contaminated areas. Additionally, at the time of the research the children were perceived as healthy (in fact, healthier than before). Combined with an alternative understanding of lead poisoning and an additional misunderstandings around parts of the treatment protocol, this resulted in a situation whereby the motivation was fairly low to take the lead treatment – a complicated and demanding treatment regime – or to follow up on other protocol-related check-ups. A general apathy towards the programme seemed to have taken over the women. Questions along the lines of "How long will you keep treating our children [for lead]?" came up repeatedly during the research period.

"How long will you keep treating our children for lead?"

While villagers were happy that the MSF clinic supplied medication for their children's primary illness, many of them were no longer persuaded by the lead treatment. The question "How long will you keep treating our children [for lead]?" was an expression of this. To change this attitude the anthropologist made the following suggestions: 1) deal with issues of communication and interaction; 2) concentrate on routes of exposure and recontamination of compounds by lead, and offer support to address this; and 3) improve awareness of compound dynamics and support.

Interaction with families involved in artisanal mining

Clearly, some of the things that worked well in many other projects did not in this one. This was partly connected to the village's mining history; the other locations did not have extensive previous mining activity, and MSF seems to have misjudged the importance of artisanal mining to some of the community. MSF's communication on the health risks of artisanal mining and on preventive measures and treatment was well received at other locations (and by 50% of the initial patients in the research location), but it was not well received by those with (previous) high involvement in mining.

MSF was aware of ongoing mining activities, but responded with a repetition of information on preventive measure and health risks. At the clinic, mothers were reminded how these activities were jeopardising their children's health. It was true that mining activities continued, even though diminished, and it was quite likely that artisanal mining would remain an income-generating activity for many of

210 Annemieke Bont et al.

these families as few other option were open to them, "because up till now, many people don't have any business if not mining activities" (Interview 55).

Particularly for young unmarried men, mining was a way to get a head start in life, something they would not easily step away from:

> They [the young adults] are the majority of the people who go for the mining work, because they only solve their own personal problems, and assist their parents. That is what they will be doing up till the time they get married. I myself I bought a motorcycle with the mining money, a very new one.
> *(Interview 82)*

In some families, the adult men resorted to travelling to more distant locations, where they would stay, mining for longer periods, and this did not cause much concern about recontamination at compound level. In other compounds however, activities continued much closer to home, and some teenagers could be observed during the day carrying panning equipment.[10] In fact, the lull in activities seemed more a result of less opportunity due to low gold prices, and the dismantling of nearby mining locations, than one of higher awareness of the health risks. The anthropologist found that many were simply waiting for new opportunities:

> There is not much gold in the ground now. That is why many people look for other jobs that they are doing. But if we heard that there is gold, we will all prepare to go back to the mining activities. These young boys now, that you are seeing, if there is mining activities, you cannot see them hanging around like the way they do now. [Turning to the boys] Am I lying? [The boys reply:] "No, that is the truth".
> *(Interview 47)*

Conversations around this topic were difficult, and were avoided as much as possible. In the clinic setting, these issues were mostly perceived as accusations because they addressed the harm done to the children. MSF had not found a way to have a constructive discussion on this issue, and it probably would have benefited the project to change how they communicated this topic. MSF needed to accept and respect that, for some people, artisanal mining was going to remain their way of earning a living. Instead of issuing the standard instructions on prevention and treatment, a common ground was needed with much more precise and compound-tailored information and support; for example, by helping to identify the main routes of contamination for each specific compound where children still had high BLL. Most importantly, this needed to involve both men and women, as at the time of the research many of the fathers of patients were unaware that their children were still enrolled in the programme and receiving lead treatment.[11] These fathers – of whom many were still seasonal miners – needed to become aware of the continuous impact of their mining activities on their children's health situation, and MSF could help them to find ways to take on the responsibility for this. Such an approach would also take much of the treatment burden away from the mothers and make the children's health a shared responsibility.

Communication on lead-related health and treatment issues

MSF staff members were very uncomfortable with patients being brought to the clinic by siblings, and put enormous efforts into motivating mothers to accompany their children. As mentioned earlier, this was for reasons of consent; they believed that they could not effectively convey dosage information to these siblings, and they were uncomfortable with giving out pharmaceuticals to such young children. As for dosage information, observations at the clinic site showed that, by now, mothers actually knew this by heart.[12] Among those mothers who doubted or denied the effectiveness of the medication, there was not much worry about the children bringing medication home, but other mothers clearly believed that it should not be given out to children and would pick it up themselves.

The main problem seemed to be that overall, the mothers did not believe that they were given any new information about their children's health on clinic visits, and so there was no compelling argument to attend. This was clearly something MSF had to address. In order to motivate mothers to come to the clinic, MSF needed to make the visit worthwhile and (re-) establish relationships with the mothers. This would allow the treatment and cure of their children to become a concern shared by the mothers and MSF, in which communication was based on dialogue more than on instruction.

MSF could still regain momentum, and enhance treatment motivation, by giving the mothers more insight into the treatment process, treatment effectiveness and the ultimate treatment aim of discharging the patient from the programme. This had not been needed in other locations where treatment progress had been good for all patients, and mothers were motivated to continue the treatment by seeing other children successfully treated and discharged. Because, in the research location, treatment effectiveness could no longer be measured by the successful discharge of others (there were hardly any discharges according to protocol at the time of the research) or judged by the children's physical appearance (at least in the perception of the mothers), MSF needed other ways to give the mothers insight into the treatment outcomes. Despite having no health promotion background, the anthropologist designed a visualisation[13] to illuminate how subsequent treatment courses were still dealing with the initial lead poisoning, countering the current understanding of lead being a recurrent illness like malaria. It also showed what the treatment aim was and where progress was needed to achieve that aim. Individual test outcomes could be inserted to show a patient's pathway towards discharge. The first experiment with the visualisation produced a positive response from the mothers, and the device was later implemented by the health promotion team as a tool in their communication with the mothers.

Another concern about communication was the level of privacy at the clinic. The anthropologist suggested moving some of the interactions, when possible, to the compound level, as the clinic offered little by way of privacy. Often, several mothers who did not belong to the same extended family were waiting inside the doctor's office for outcomes of the blood tests. During the research, it became clear that women did not easily share bad laboratory results, such as an increase of their children's BLL, with others. It exposed them in the village, raising questions about how this could have happened, marking them as a family possibly involved in mining, which, as explained previously, was not discussed openly.

One mother appeared very ashamed and was almost in tears when she shared her experience with the anthropologist. She had been spoken to at the clinic about the condition of her youngest child, with others able to hear:

> Even this child, I took him to the clinic first time, they said he has much lead, so everybody was surprised. How come the child of [name] was affected by lead, I now said it is God that makes him to be affected by lead, as for now that I am giving him drugs, the lead in his blood is coming down now.
>
> *(Interview 42)*

Allowing negative treatment outcomes to become public could have a further negative effect on the trust between the patient's families and MSF. If confidentiality could not be provided at the clinic, it was better to discuss such information in a private space; for example, inside the compound walls. It would also be important to establish the cause of exposure so it could be remedied. This was the case for all patients, but especially when babies were brought to the clinic for a first-time baseline test; mothers appeared to be quite bewildered if the test result showed a considerable level of lead. They had not expected it, and often did not know how it had come about.

A medical issue left unaddressed: assessing recontamination

In this location, there were many signs that children were still being exposed to lead, even after the remedial work. The main indication was the large fluctuations in blood lead levels, but also the treatment programme was still admitting new patients.[14] This concerned the medical team, and in the clinic it was mainly thought to be because of continued mining activities by family members, so it was addressed chiefly by repeating information on safe mining practices and prevention. Keeping an eye on renewed exposure was particularly necessary, however, as the research location was the only one where remediation had not been completed. This was due to a pending government water project which planned to flood the village and its surrounding area in the near future (von Lindern et al., 2011). During the remedial work, it was decided to delay clearing the contaminated ponds around the village until there was more clarity on the project. The villagers had been warned to stay clear of these ponds and not to use mud from them for the maintenance and construction of houses,[15] as this could easily re-introduce lead into the cleared compounds.

If recontamination was indeed happening in this way, it could jeopardise the treatment outcomes; from the start of the project, it had been clear that the treatment would only be effective when children were no longer exposed to lead in their homes or village environment. Ignoring this would also make it very difficult to judge the impact of other factors on treatment failure, and if re-exposure was a problem, it could well play a role in the perception of the medication as ineffective.

After analysing the updated village map and the surveillance sheets, the anthropologist found that many new patients lived in newly built or recently extended compounds, which were possibly constructed with lead-contaminated mud. Their lead positive blood tests could, at least partly, be a result of contamination inside the compound. From observations made around the village, it was clear that mud from untreated ponds was being used, both for construction and for maintenance work after the rainy season – not just on houses, but also on the big mud containers used to store food after the harvest. On one occasion, when the anthropologist accompanied patients and their mothers to their shared compound after a clinic visit, she observed the girls of the group pick up mud bricks from such a pond and carry them into the compound. When asked what they were using them for, it turned out they were building a new room for one of the son's brides, who would soon come to live with them. MSF needed to find out urgently if this indeed was a problem. And if so, it had to be addressed.

Taking into account social dynamics at the compound level

The main reason why health promotion staff visited compounds was to inform mothers about a scheduled clinic visit for their children, or to ask them why they had not shown up and try to convince them of the need to do so. There did not seem to be much awareness of compound dynamics, or of specific issues at play in the compound that could affect the treatment. The principal focus was, as explained previously, on the health of the children as defined by the blood tests, and on trying to keep the children to follow the complicated treatment programme and have them attend to the many clinic visits.

But in this setting, compound dynamics define much of daily life, especially for women of reproductive age. As such, compound dynamics should be taken into account as a factor affecting health behaviour and disease experience. In an attempt to find a good example of this for the MSF team, the anthropologist met one young mother whose 6-month-old baby was recently admitted to the treatment programme. She lived in a compound where all the other children had previously been treated and successfully discharged. She had only just married her husband, one of the younger adults of this compound. After some initial hesitation, she explained that she suspected her child was sick because her husband's business was

214 Annemieke Bont et al.

transporting gold ore with his camel. Being a young wife, she could not address this directly with her husband. Instead, she had raised the issue with her mother-in-law, who had promised to discuss it with the young man's father. However, the mother-in-law had to wait for the right occasion to do so. It is in such cases that there could be a role for the MSF team, first to find or confirm the route of exposure, and then to function as mediator in finding a solution — all in the privacy of a compound.

By engaging at the level of the compound in such a way, it could be possible to remove the barriers individual mothers and patients face but are unable to overcome themselves. However, it is necessary to explore this approach very carefully. In this context, where a great effort is made to keep compound matters private and to adhere to hierarchy, such involvement with compound affairs could also backfire. Nevertheless, awareness of compound dynamics, and of the roles and positions of individual patients and mothers in their respective compounds, would already be a major step forward to building trust in the treatment relationship.

Conclusion

This investigation has demonstrated how perceived treatment failures were a product of interactional dynamics between MSF and the local people. When MSF requested the support of an anthropologist, maybe it hoped to find 'specific cultural reasons' for the lack of treatment success in the remaining patients, and that the programme could be unlocked with a single key. Instead, the anthropologist found that there was no such single key, and that a multitude of issues were at play, largely related to interactional dynamics between MSF and local people.

Initially, MSF saw the health of a child as a clear-cut issue defined by blood tests, and the question of what to do next was essentially defined by the treatment protocol. But this was quite different for one of the villages. Unaware of the many sources of doubt or even rejection of the programme throughout the community, MSF continued to repeat the same messages and information to all patients, their mothers and their families, resulting eventually in refusal and obstruction. It was evident that an alternative definition of health and illness existed, based on different explanations or perceptions of health, ill health and health needs. MSF's approach grew problematic for a community that was particularly influenced by the political economy of mining and its effects on their familial and communal resources.

The anthropological perspective produced a greater knowledge of socio-political aspects and plugged a gap in understanding acknowledged by MSF at a critical stage. In an attempt to make a difference and help the project progress, the medical anthropologist offered a broader social view on health, as well as a sensitivity to the impact of social dynamics on health behaviour. Looking at the available epidemiological information and data through a social lens uncovered issues that might otherwise have been missed.

While MSF was still a few degrees away from understanding how to alleviate lead poisoning, one important outcome of the anthropological assessment was the evidence that a single solution or a unilateral approach to treatment and care was unsuitable on this occasion. The information gathered also revealed how reduced mining activities affected family or household-specific issues, adding extra responsibilities to women's daily workloads.

MSF decided to respond to this emergency, even though its programmes do not usually focus on man-made disasters. Having met all the challenges, the Nigerian example shows what a huge positive impact on people's health such a response can have, not just at treatment level, but also at the level of awareness and prevention. With important collaborations, MSF achieved a crucial and commendable outcome: an admirable response with remediation, an extensive health promotion component, hospital-based emergency treatment and village-based clinics for chelation therapy in eight locations. These elements proved to be fully effective in several locations.

Attention to needs-based projects like this has brought MSF to a point where discussion on the response to environmental health disasters has become part of their strategic planning.

Afterword: where are we now?

MSF has been active in Zamfara state since 2010, and in Niger state since 2015. Since then, MSF has navigated all complexities responding to the life-threatening consequences of acute lead poisoning on children and their families. Areas from treatment to training environmental officers on remediation, residential health promotion, safer mining and occupational health practices are all new for MSF, but we know environmental health risks are here to stay. This requires new approaches, new commitments and the acknowledgement that social circumstances for people whose lives are affected need to be better understood. In Nigeria, we learnt that one village in particular had specific 'resistances' that required considerably more thought.

The visit in 2015 has helped us forward. The lessons learnt and anthropological recommendations from Zamfara were implemented in the Niger state programme from the start, and staff was included with important experience from the former project (including a geologist project coordinator and a sociologist, translator of the anthropological assessment). The commitment remains resolute, and a better understanding of the local social realities and 'politics' has helped shape the health and preventive activities and response. With two international conferences paying attention to the topic, we are moving toward a better social and structural response of a sound (environmental) health policy and a coordinated approach with state and federal ministries (such as the Ministry of Mines and Steel Development, Ministry of Health and Nigeria Centre for Disease Control). Niger state now has the first ever Lead Center, set up by state and federal ministries as result of the second International Lead Conference. This Center focusses mainly on the preventive side of lead poisoning, and will receive the support of MSF on request. In Zamfara state, the increased presence of ministries is advocated for and in progress, which hopefully will result in increased prevention of exposure. This increased focus will also be beneficial for the adolescent miners, which will very likely require a different approach. The next step for MSF is to coordinate joint efforts to write comprehensive guidelines including topics such as outbreak investigation, diagnostics, surveillance, anthropology, epidemiology, toxicology/pathology, treatment, residential and occupational health, environmental health and safer mining. These guidelines will be developed in close collaboration with stakeholders from state and federal ministries of Nigeria, international partners and MSF.

Addendum: changes made to the project since 2015

Since 2015, there has been progress for people living and working with exposure to industrial pollutants as a result of the involvement of non-profit organisation called Occupational Knowledge International (OKI). This organisation is dedicated to improving public health through advances in working with communities, industry and governments to improve conditions. Those advances include health promotion linked to re-exposure; for example, putting in place hand washing stations, changing areas and separate eating areas for workers, and identifying high-risk children and putting a special focus on adolescents to address recontamination for mining related activities in this age group. Use of data tools and an important counselling approach have also contributed. Whilst out of the scope of MSF, there is a considered progress on the de-criminalisation of artisanal mining alongside public health measures.

Main developments

In 2015, for treatment adherence, direct observation of treatment has been introduced through community workers per ten children.

From 2016, the MSF treatment criteria and protocol includes children younger than 4 years old; younger people (14–18 years old) are also defined as such until their status changes through marriage.

In 2018, a second international conference on lead poisoning was held in Nigeria, with a high involvement of the national authorities at local, state and federal levels.

In 2019, a pilot project for health promotion and public health measures was launched to introduce safer mining practices.

Notes

1 Chelation therapy is a medical procedure. Chelation agents are administered to the body and can bind to heavy metals, and the body can then excrete these heavy metals.
2 Detailed information on the remediation process can be found in the report by von Lindern et al. (2011).
3 See Chapter 4 by Doris Burtscher.
4 With help from the anthropologist, the main research location village map was updated in October 2014, and newly built compounds were added and numbered. At the request

of the anthropologist, this information was also used subsequently to update the surveillance list, as for numerous children the compound number was missing. This made it difficult to get a precise impression of the impact of lead poisoning on the compound.

5 Done by MSF.

6 The difference in role division and women's description of their hardship first became apparent by comparing data from the main research location with the 'comparison village'. However, later in the analyses, the anthropologist found that the same differences were also found in the main research village when comparing mining households with non-mining households. Comparing descriptions of use of income, workloads and household responsibilities of older and younger women from mining related compounds, the more structural nature of the specific social context and economic situation of these households became apparent.

7 Convulsion was still being perceived as the main indication of lead poisoning.

8 Children who at that moment had other health problems, such as malaria or diarrhoea, were considered to be sick, but not to be sick from the lead.

9 When children had a BLL between 30 and 45 μg/dL, a child was not eligible for treatment but could not be discharged, according to the treatment protocol. These children needed to remain in the programme for blood tests in order to monitor the development of BLL over time. If the level moved above 45μg/dL, they would receive further treatment.

10 Used to wash gravel in a pan to separate out gold.

11 Attention to compound dynamics was important, as this was likely to be a result of the specific socio-cultural dynamics between men and women at compound level. Men and women had clearly defined tasks and child health was not a topic to be shared, except when a child was sick and needed (paid) treatment which required the father's consent and support.

12 They were able to name each drug and supplement and explain how and when to administer the tablets.

13 The visualisation was effected by making a comparison to a river, with rising water levels standing for rising BLL and rising risk, whereas a dry riverbed or very low water stood for the BLL level (below 30μg/dL) that allowed discharge. The child's initial BLL was indicated in this picture as a starting point, and with each test result, the new blood value added to the visualisation.

14 Blood samples were taken from neonates, and the majority of babies had some level of lead in their blood when first tested, but the rates would start to rise rapidly from about 8 months old, an age when they had started oral exploration of their environment. As incidental ingestion of contaminated soil and dust through hand-to-mouth activity was found to be one of the main causes of exposure (von Lindern et al., 2011, p. 12), it seemed likely that exposure to lead in their homes was the main cause.

15 The whole village consists of traditional buildings made of earth or mud, materials that need frequent maintenance due to erosion throughout the year. Lead-contaminated ponds were the main source for bricks and mud used for such maintenance (von Lindern et al., 2011, p. 28). Use of mud from the contaminated ponds was observed when remediation activities resumed after the rainy season.

References

Appleton, J.D., Williams, T.M., Orbea, H. and Carrasco, M., (2001). Fluvial contamination associated with artisanal gold mining in the Ponce Enriquez, Portovelo-Zaruma and Nambija areas, Ecuador. *Water Air Soil Pollution*. **131**(1), 19–39. doi:10.1023/A:1011965430757

Betancourt, O., Narváez, A. and Roulet, M., (2005). Small-scale gold mining in the Puyango river basin, Southern Ecuador: a study of environmental impacts and human exposures. *EcoHealth*. **2**(4), 323–332. doi:10.1007/s10393-005-8462-4

Charles, E., Thomas, D.S.K., Dewey, D., Davey, M., Ngallaba, S.E. and Konje, E., (2013). A cross-sectional survey on knowledge and perceptions of health risks associated with arsenic and mercury contamination from artisanal gold mining in Tanzania. *BMC Public Health.* **13**(1), 74. doi:10.1186/1471-2458-13-74

Coles, C. and Mack, B.B., (1991). Women in twentieth-century Hausa society. In: C. Coles and B.B. Mack, eds., *Hausa women in the twentieth century.* Madison: University of Wisconsin Press. 3–26.

Dooyema, C.A., Neri, A., Lo, Y.-C., Durant, J. et al., (2011). Outbreak of fatal childhood lead poisoning related to artisanal gold mining in North-western Nigeria, 2010. *Environmental Health Perspectives.* **120**(4), 601–607. doi:10.1289/ehp.1103965

Grätz, T., (2009). Moralities, risk and rules in West African artisanal gold mining communities: a case study of Northern Benin. *Resources Policy.* **34**(1–2), 12–17. doi:10.1016/j.resourpol.2008.11.002

Hentschel, T., Hruschka, F. and Priester, M., (2003). *Artisanal and small-scale mining: challenges and opportunities.* MMSD, iied/Earthprint, 94. [online]. [viewed 16 January 2019]. Available from: http://pubs.iied.org/pdfs/9268IIED.pdf

Hill-Jackson, V., (2005). Culture matters in high risk, lead poisoned communities. *Practicing Anthropology.* **27**(3), 9–14. doi:10.17730/praa.27.3.pn2081618h74u717

Hilson, G., Hilson, C.J. and Pardie, S., (2007). Improving awareness of mercury pollution in small-scale gold mining communities: challenges and ways forward in rural Ghana. *Environmental Research.* **103**(2), 275–287. doi:10.1016/j.envres.2006.09.010

Kyeremateng-Amoah, E. and Clarke, E.E., (2015). Injuries among artisanal and small-scale gold miners in Ghana. *International Journal of Environmental Research and Public Health.* **12**(9), 10886–10896. [online]. [viewed 25 February 2016]. doi:10.3390/ijerph120910886

Lo, Y.-C., Dooyema, C.A., Neri, A., Durant, J. et al., (2012). Childhood lead poisoning associated with gold ore processing: a village-level investigation – Zamfara State, Nigeria, October-November 2010. *Environmental Health Perspectives.* **120**(10), 1450–1455. doi:10.1289/ehp.1104793

Long, R.N., Renne, E.P. and Basu, N., (2015). Understanding the social context of the ASGM sector in Ghana: a qualitative description of the demographic, health, and nutritional characteristics of a small-scale gold mining community in Ghana. *International Journal of Environmental Research and Public Health.* **12**(10), 12679–12696. doi:10.3390/ijerph121012679

MSF, (2014). *Terms of reference for medical anthropologist Zamfara Heavy Metal Poisoning.* MSF archives, Operational Centre Amsterdam.

Needleman, H., (2004). Lead poisoning. *Annual Review of Medicine.* **55**, 209–222. doi:10.1146/annurev.med.55.091902.103653

Odumo, O.B., Mustapha, A.O., Patel, J.P. and Angeyo, H.K., (2010). Multielemental analysis of Migori (Southwest Kenya) artisanal gold mine ores and sediments by EDX-ray fluorescence technique: implications of occupational exposure and environmental impact. *Bulletin of Environmental Contamination Toxicology.* **86**(5), 484–489. doi:10.1007/s00128-011-0242-y

Ogala, J.S., Mitullah, W.V. and Omulo, M.A., (2002). Impact of gold mining on the environment and human health: a case study in the Migori gold belt, Kenya. *Environmental Geochemistry and Health.* **24**(2), 141–157. doi:10.1023/A:1014207832471

Stellmach, D., (2016). *Coordination in crisis: the practice of medical humanitarian emergency.* Ph.D. thesis, University of Oxford. [online]. [viewed 16 January 2019]. Available from: https://ora.ox.ac.uk/objects/uuid:c81d8b4a-4e73-4bbb-b66f-7c84885ab9b8/download_file?file_format=pdf&safe_filename=2016%2BStellmach-Thesis%2BMaster%2BCopy%2Bfor%2BDissemination%2528updated%2529.pdf&type_of_work=Thesis

Trotter, R.T. II, (1990). The cultural parameters of lead poisoning: a medical anthropologist's view of intervention in environmental lead exposure. *Environmental Health Perspectives*. **89**, 79–84. doi:10.1289/ehp.908979

Vallejos, Q., Strack, R.W. and Aronson, R.E., (2006). Identifying culturally appropriate strategies for educating a Mexican immigrant community about lead poisoning prevention. *Family and Community Health*. **29**(2), 143–152. Available from: www.ncbi.nlm.nih.gov/pubmed/16552291

von Lindern, I.H., von Braun, M.C., Tirima, S. and Bartrem, C., (2011). *Zamfara, Nigeria lead poisoning epidemic emergency environmental response*. Moscow: UNICEF Programme Cooperation Agreement and TerraGraphics Environmental Engineering Inc. [online]. [viewed 1 January 2019]. Available from: http://docplayer.net/43486164-Zamfara-nigeria-lead-poisoning-epidemic-emergency-environmental-response-final-report.html

Wilce, J., (2009). Medical discourse. *Annual Review of Anthropology*. **38**, 199–215. doi:10.1146/annurev-anthro-091908-164450

11

DEALING WITH THE BODY SOCIAL

An ethnography of dialogue in a health clinic, South Tehran, Iran

Mitra Asfari; Introduction by Mathilde Berthelot

Introduction

Médecins Sans Frontières has been present in Iran since 1991. For more than 20 years, their projects have mostly addressed the needs of Afghan refugees in various provinces or supported local facilities during emergency responses to natural disasters. In 2012, a project targeting other groups of vulnerable people was launched in Tehran. This new project offered a comprehensive package of medical, psychological and social services to drug users and the homeless, categories at high risk of contracting communicable diseases such as viral hepatitis, tuberculosis and HIV. High stigmatisation of these categories is a factor in patients' exclusion from care and their self-neglect when sick. There was an operational decision also to include in our target group the Iranian gypsies – Gorbat – because they are exposed to various risks but cannot easily find or access health care when needed. All this is a new field for MSF. It requires a new approach from MSF staff, as the patients are quite different from what MSF staff are used to in the context of primary health care for refugees. Tensions erupted and questions were raised on the scope of our intervention. We wanted to take time to know more about these people – especially the Gorbat – in order to understand better how to approach them and tackle their needs, as well as integrating them better into our activities. It was a chance to work with Mitra Asfari, an anthropologist who has unique expertise with these largely unknown people. This collaboration had the aim of improving our knowledge about the people in order to have a better approach – not only to their medical needs, but also to the consideration of the people in their environment – to establish a relationship that would benefit both the patient and the care provider.

This chapter describes the situation in an MSF clinic in South Tehran. The clinic is in a poor urban quarter, where the cost of renting a property is one of the cheapest in the Iranian capital. This quarter, Darvāzeh Gār, is adjacent to the Grand

Bazaar of Tehran, and commercial storage occupies most of its area. Migrants, such as young single men and families, seeking to work in the Bazaar and to rent rooms in this quarter constitute the majority of the inhabitants of Darvāzeh Ġār. Among them there are Afghan families; however, their arrival in this neighbourhood is relatively recent. There are also Iranian rural migrants: Ispahani, Azeri, Kurd and Lor. All these migrants have their own ethnic networks and live in shared houses. Most of the time, each nuclear family occupies one room. All households share a yard which has a bathroom and a water tap. Another group has arrived in this neighbourhood in the last ten years. The habitants of Darvāzeh Ġār call this group 'Ġorbati', which means exiled/strange/strangers. This name is one that neighbouring groups have always given to these people, but now they have appropriated it and refer to themselves as Ġorbat.[1]

Most of the inhabitants of Darvāzeh Ġār work on the borders of the Bazaar as peddlers or drug sellers. Ġorbat women and children beg or are street vendors at crossroads, while Ġorbat men sell drugs or gamble. This quarter gains its reputation not only because of its migrant inhabitants, but also because of an expanded market for drugs. As the name of the quarter (Darvāzeh Ġār) implies, it was one of the ports of ancient Tehran. Darvāzeh means port and Ġār was the name of one of the villages of Ray in Greater Tehran. Migrants used to arrive at the city of Tehran from Ray and other southern parts of Iran through this port. Historians and urban observers have written about the use and abuse of drugs, prostitution and violent gangsters in this part of the town since 1871, from the moment Tehran became the capital (Shahri, 2002).

Today, Tehran municipality considers this neighbourhood to be problematic (mo'zal) and pathologic (āsibxiz) because of its residents and their activities. Migrants (especially single men), drug users, homeless people (kārtonxāb) and Ġorbat are all elements that the municipality wants 'to remove' (bezodāyad) from this quarter. The municipality considers that it is not ideal to have these elements situated next to the Grand Bazaar, so it plans to develop this quarter and turn it over to commercial use by constructing several malls and entertainment centres. This will not be possible without 'cleaning up or purging' (pāksāzi) the quarter of its 'pathologies' (āsib-hā).

Thus, the MSF project focussed on people who are subject to different forms of rejection from health care. Female homeless drug users, excluded from public health care because of stigmatisation, constitute the first and main target group of this project. The clinic also accepts male drug users now that a mobile clinic has started to operate. The extreme social stigma that drug users experience in the Iranian context has been observed by MSF staff members, who accompany drug users to public hospitals. This stigma is also noted by researchers (Ghiabi, 2016), and by citizens who watch the negative messages spread by the media of the Islamic Republic (television, movies, advertisement billboards) against people who are mo'tād (addicts). In fact, the government creates this stigma, and the repercussions can be seen on urban Iranians' behaviour towards drug users.[2] The other stigmatised group that the MSF clinic accepts consists of Ġorbat women and children. However, the acceptance of this group as a target faces challenges.

222   Mitra Asfari

One month after the clinic opened, a 'Gypsy population'[3] (as MSF local staff call Gorbati) started to arrive. That is how I, as a 'Gypsy-expert anthropologist',[4] started to work with MSF. At first, MSF wanted to include them in the target group, but soon Gorbat patients overwhelmed the clinic. Going to the clinic in groups consisting of several women and children, taking over the space of the clinic, making noise and sometimes fighting together were the first problems that Gorbati made for the clinic as soon as they discovered MSF and its services. Once they started to visit the clinic regularly, the staff faced the problem of making them respect the clinics' rules and discipline. In order to do this, they hired a peer worker from the community, a young man who had the experience of working with other local NGOs. They also contacted me to obtain some ethnographic information about the Gorbat.

My first intervention in the clinic was a presentation to the staff in order to give them an anthropological insight into the Gorbat.[5] At this time, the 'Gypsy population', as they used to call them in the clinic, was not part of the target group. The decision whether to include them or not was going to be made after my presentation. However, this presentation brought up an interesting point of view from the local staff regarding 'Gypsies'. During this presentation, I communicated some important points about 1) the sociocultural organisation (community structure, family structure and household economy, gender relations, nutrition, relation to space and habitat), 2) health and hygiene in daily life (how the body is perceived and used, maternal perceptions of child health and illness, regular diseases, high risk environment, drug use, decision-making) and 3) access to health care.

Surprisingly, this brought up very different reactions among the clinic staff. On one hand, the project coordinator and social worker concluded from the presentation that the clinic should include the Gorbat, especially women and children, because they live in a high-risk environment and experience rejection from public health care in the same way that the target groups do. In other words, they are subject to stigma because of their behaviour and their 'habitus'. On the other hand, most of the local staff (nurses and doctors) refused to acknowledge that the Gorbat need MSF services. They argued that these people are able to obtain insurance and take advantage of public health care. They also argued that the Gorbat are not financially in distress and are able to afford medical expenses. Others were doubtful about their professional relationship with them and kept asking if "there is any hope that they change one day" (*omidi hast ke ina ye rooz taġir konan?*), or "how would we be able to change them?" (*mā mitūnim taġirešūn bedim?*). Thus, a contentious situation regarding the Gorbat emerged in the clinic. It could be argued that some 'localised institutional' values collided with those of international staff and the social team in MSF; perceptions of discipline and politeness in a health care structure clashed with MSF principles of inclusion and access to health care without discrimination. The MSF principles convinced international staff to include the Gorbat, while national doctors and nurses remained doubtful.

In the end, the decision made by MSF was to accept 'Gypsies' as a target group. However, the problems mentioned by the locally hired medical staff continued. They remained confused in triage about who to accept and who to refuse. They

Dealing with the body social **223**

kept in mind that MSF should accept: "poor Gypsies, not those who come with stylish and nice clothes or dyed hair . . . for it costs a lot to dye hair like this".[6] This confusion was resolved with a social worker and myself, assuring nurses and certain doctors that every individual who belongs to this group lives in an unstable economic system, and when they come to the clinic, they make an effort to wear their best clean clothes. Nurses and some doctors kept complaining about their 'Gypsy' patients, saying, "Gypsies do not need MSF services, they do not respect basic discipline in the clinic and they come for superficial problems like headache or simple cold, although we have more serious problems to take care about". Social workers and Medical Reference (which is an international unit overseeing medical team activities) rejected these complaints and believed every single problem was worth addressing. Medical Reference planned a brainstorming session for the staff in order to clear their mind of prejudice and ethnocentrism.[7] During the discussion, the representative from Medical Reference said, "we, as a humanitarian organisation, need to adapt ourselves to different populations, as I have to wear a scarf in your country. There is no question about populations adapting to our organisation". During the session, staff brought up questions about dirtiness, bare feet, lack of discipline, loudness, insistence and too many children.[8] I tried to give the staff some examples of the effort the Ġorbat make in order to 'adapt' themselves (for example, wearing their nice clothes). The conclusion of one of the staff at the end of this brainstorming session was: "They will never change!" (*hič vaqt avaz nemišan!*).

Here we face the problem of rejection by local MSF staff that we will try to explain by going back to the historical socio-cultural conflicts between the Iranian majority and various minorities, particularly of itinerant groups such as the Ġorbat. This problem includes several actors: the majority of the Iranian urban population, the Ġorbat (as an Iranian minority of semi-urban semi-rural people), public authorities and public health centres. Another task within the field of medical anthropology was to evaluate the level of mutual comprehension between patients and the medical staff. A patient-centred communication includes four domains: "the patient perspective, the psychosocial context, shared understanding, sharing power and responsibility" (Epstein et al., 2005). Through my own research with Ġorbat patients, I realised that the doctors and nurses were often not understood by the patients. Patients started accusing MSF doctors of being 'good for nothing', so as a result, they did not follow the treatment. The problem of irregular consumption of medicine and discontinuous treatment constitute habits that I have previously observed during my fieldwork among the Ġorbat while working with MSF. Thus, I proposed the research project within the MSF clinic that is presented in this chapter.

In fact, it was during my PhD fieldwork that I gathered fundamental and ethnographic data about the Ġorbat. Based on participant observation, recordings and semi-structured interviews, I gathered all my field data during five years of an intense relationship with this group. They live in Tehran, but they are unknown to the majority of Tehrani citizens. Furthermore, scientific literature – or any documentation – about them is almost non-existent. Thus, a field study was the best way of becoming better acquainted.

In the first section of this chapter, I will present the Ġorbat by describing their sociocultural organisation and daily habits concerning health and hygiene. The second section will develop the question about the historical socio-cultural conflicts between Ġorbat and neighbouring groups, and it will consider the attitude of the latter toward the former in order to understand the rejection of the Ġorbat in the context of the MSF clinic. The third section will present health matters as they are perceived among the Ġorbat in the context of modern medical thought. It will also present some key points of interactions between Ġorbat patients and medical staff, in order to understand gaps between actual and ideal treatment.

The methodology of this project consisted of focussing on medical staff and 'Gypsy patient' communication to highlight areas of misunderstanding and conflict. In order to do this, with the consent of medical staff and patients, I recorded medical consultations of 'Gypsy patients' over ten weeks.[9] I tried to ask patients about their feelings and their perception of the medical visit and to undertake semi-directive interviews in order to understand their idea of illness. I also made observations in the households of patients and followed them during their treatment in order to complete this data gathering.

The Ġorbati people

Community structure

Historically, the Ġorbat were itinerants, *doregard* in their own language. They did not own any land or herds of animals. They used to live in tents, travelling from one village to another. They always had one or two specified itineraries between two camps. The people we will talk about in the present paper are partly settled in the north of Iran, in Bābol, a city in the province of Māzandarān. They started semi-sedentary life there in the reign of Mohamad-Reza Shah who made land reforms and encouraged itinerant groups and nomads[10] to settle on the land he offered them. The Ġorbat continue to move between Tehran and Bābol several times a year. There are other Ġorbat groups in other cities of Māzandarān and other provinces of Iran. There are also groups of Ġorbat in Afghanistan who claim to be originally from the east of Iran (Rao, 1982).

Rao (1985) considers the Ġorbat to be a peripatetic group. According to her, the term 'peripatetic' corresponds to groups who move towards other groups in search of clients and for other economic reasons. A peripatetic group does not practice any kind of food production; thus, its members make small tools to sell to other groups or provides them with services (music, circumcision, etc.). The occupation of every single member depends on belonging to a clan. Historically, each clan had a specific occupation and was endogamous.[11] Furthermore, Rao points out that because of their despised professional activities, they always experienced rejection from neighbouring populations. This could also have provoked their endogamy.

Each Gorbat settlement is composed of several clans, and therefore several extended families. In Māzandarān, important Gorbat clans live in Sāri, Bābol and Qaem Shahr. In Sāri, they have several neighbourhoods, while in Bābol, they have only one. However, these neighbourhoods are strictly homogenous, and nobody without a kinship connection to the Gorbat inhabitants lives among them. Each neighbourhood contains several lineages which intermarry. It may happen that a lineage comes to have the reputation of being the most important, or some individuals obtain a high-ranking status because of their wealth. However, this status only lasts for a short period. As the financial situation is never stable, there is no permanent hierarchy and the status of the lineages fluctuates.

Before their settlement and urban life, Gorbat men were mostly blacksmiths or carpenters and used to create small kitchen and agricultural tools, and the women sold these artefacts in villages or among nomad tribes. Nowadays, because of the decrease in agricultural activity among villagers and the urbanisation of nomad tribes and the Gorbat themselves, men stopped working but women continued selling small objects at the crossroads of cities. Women also beg, accompanied by children of their lineage or the lineage of their husband.

Gorbati are Muslim Shia; however, they never receive a religious education, and as a result, they do not have a daily practice. The only rituals that categorise them as Shia are their annual pilgrimage during *Muharam*[12] and their pilgrimage and devotion to Imam Reza.[13] Gorbat speak both Gorbat, their own dialect derived from Iranian Persian, and the official Persian. Most of them also know the dialect of Māzandarān (māzani). They claim to belong to a wider ethnic group sharing the same language. That is the reason we can consider them to be a 'language community'.

Family structure

The status of family members varies according to gender and age. In general, the woman is responsible for earning money (by street vending or begging) and organising the household. She takes care of infants and manages the labour force of older children living at her house, ensuring that they care for younger ones and gain money. She is responsible for the nutrition of babies and showing children over about 5 years old how to work at crossroads by begging or street vending.

Older children are carers responsible for their siblings, nieces and nephews. Depending on the woman of the household (who can be their mother, aunt, elder sibling or cousin), the child must go to work at the crossroads. They have a very high mobility inside their lineage and circulate through several households. It is indeed very rare to see a child staying in one household. They learn from the age of 3 to go about by themselves in the neighbourhood, to go to the grocery store and even to beg within the neighbourhood. They even eat as they wish.

Because of this unstable lifestyle, hygiene measures are neglected. Almost no soap is used in Gorbat houses. They buy a new shampoo for each shower. In general, objects do not have a long life in a Gorbat home. Things such as documents,[14]

226 Mitra Asfari

clothes, money and medicines often get lost. Hardly any objects are subject to care and protection.

The man is responsible for the management of the household's income. Depending on their family, lineage or clan, men work or are unemployed. Those who are not officially active sell drugs (mostly heroin and methamphetamine) on a small scale. Those who are officially active work on and off as street vendors. The whole income, as well as that gained by women and children, is supposed to belong to the man. Then he decides how to spend the money and how to distribute it among household members – and, eventually, among community members. All lineage and clan members go several times a year to celebrate *arūsi*. These famous celebrations have a financial solidarity function for the whole community. There, considerable amounts of money are transferred from one family to another, from one lineage to another. Each amount that is given should eventually be paid back to the donor with interest. These celebrations thus constitute one of the very important pillars of the ethnic group.

Historical context and cultural conflicts

Relation to space

Because of the itinerant lifestyle of these people and the high mobility of children between different households, it is interesting to analyse the relation of the Gorbat to space. This aspect is indeed crucial for understanding how they seem in public spaces. They have historically never owned fields. They used always to camp on a field and the appropriation of the surrounding area used to happen collectively and spontaneously. Everywhere they camp, even if it is only for a brief period, they must pretend to own the land. This spontaneous relation to space also defines the collective identity of the Gorbati in contrast to non-Gorbat. In fact, it is the gathering of the clan members in the same place, which helps them appropriate each new field, even temporarily. Furthermore, surrounded by other members of the group, each individual feels safe. Thus, the relation to space directly depends on the presence of other Gorbat, so an individual who stays alone will feel lost and unsafe. This is also the reason why they rarely move individually through the city and generally try to have company. The discriminating attitude of the wider society, which reminds them that they are not in the right place, i.e. at home,[15] plays a determinant role in the feeling of insecurity. Each time they move as a group, they feel at 'at home' (in-group), and impose themselves on other people already present there who have to move aside or put up with hostile behaviour. Thus, the Gorbati often appear violent and imposing.

Their concentration in particular neighbourhoods probably occurs for the same reasons. They are merely trying to confirm their presence and their group identity. Meanwhile, the high circulation of adults and children between different households, and a high number of people living in one room, create an unstable form of habitat. In Darvāzeh Gar, because of its history and its special form of real estate, renting is for short periods, between one month and a year. Not every Gorbat household has a rental contract. Sometimes, they sublet from relatives. Permanent housing is non-existent, so the Gorbat are highly mobile and live in unstable groups.

Reasons for rejection

According to historical accounts and my analysis of individual subjectivity in a situation when Gorbat and non-Gorbat meet, the reasons for their rejection may originate in the sphere of religion and beliefs. The majority of Iranians consider the Gorbat to be 'bad Muslims' (Rao, 1982), even though the Gorbat embody a despised status that the Islamic value system seems to justify and accept because the status of the mendicant is believed to personify the space between God and Muslims.

Furthermore, they have been subjected to other forms of rejection to do with matrimonial rules and commensality. For the non-Gorbat people of Iran (nomad and sedentary, rural and urban), it is forbidden to marry Gorbat and to eat with them. Members of some groups that have special ethnic costumes do not allow Gorbat to wear their costume. This restriction limits Gorbat options for places to settle. As mentioned previously, the Gorbat don't have an Islamic education because of their semi-sedentary lifestyle and failure to attend school. The lack of an Islamic education might have provoked this rejection of them. One of my observations of non-Gorbat versus Gorbat interaction revealed that non-Gorbat people often fear 'dirtiness' and 'debauchery'[16] in contact with Gorbat. In a Tehran subway, I heard a non-Gorbat woman tell a Gorbat child, "Don't touch me! You are going to make me dirty!"

After an analysis of the underlying beliefs of this statement, I suggest that the dirtiness refers to substances of the body that Islam considers impure. In fact, Muslims consider urine impure and believe it renders the whole body impure while urinating. The only way to purify the body, at least for women, is to rinse the urinary area with clear water. The dirty face, hands, feet and clothes of the Gorbat make the non-Gorbat believe that they, particularly the children, have not been in contact with water for a long time; thus, they suspect that the Gorbat are impure. Although the dirtiness of the body is a physical and concrete fact, the 'impurity' of the Gorbat derives from symbolic concepts that the cultural and religious value system of non-Gorbat Iranians imposes. Thus, there are both physical and symbolic factors to take into account. Khosrokhavar (1997) also considers this symbolic perception of impurity important. In his study of an eastern suburb of Tehran (Taleghani), Khosrokhavar observes conflicts between non-Gorbat migrants and labourers and one of the Gorbat clans. He believes that the dirtiness that migrants and labourers assign to the Gorbat is of a symbolic order. He concludes that this attitude towards the Gorbat serves a unifying function for the other groups in the inner city. He suggests also that the Gorbat use their physical dirtiness as a way to maintain their borders with the other groups. Thus, Khosrokhavar defines the symbolic order through the concept of *paki* (cleanliness), which, in the belief system of

228 Mitra Asfari

the non-Ġorbat residents, represents both the cleanliness of the body and the purity of the soul. This concept is invoked to distinguish Muslims from non-Muslims.

> In Persian, 'paki' semantically means both physical and moral purity. Physical dirtiness of Ghorbatis seems to be a challenge in order to incarnate the moral impurity. The language operates here symbolically to transpose the semantic meaning into the semiotic one. For the majority of Taleghani inner city's residents, with heterogeneous cultural features and a lack of unity, the dirtiness of Ghorbatis becomes an excellent factor of differentiation and recognition as outsiders.
>
> *(Khosrokhavar, 1997, p. 325; translation mine)*

Regarding these symbolic differences between Ġorbat and non-Ġorbat, the former has limited spheres of interaction with the latter. According to Barth (1969), who also wrote about Ġorbat in the south of Iran (Barth, 1961):

> these are groups actively rejected by the host population because of the behaviour or characteristics positively condemned, though often useful in some specific way. . . . Their identity imposed a definition on social situations which gave very little scope for interaction with persons in the majority population, and simultaneously as an imperative status represented an inescapable disability that prevented them from assuming the normal statuses involved in other definitions of the situation of interaction.
>
> *(Barth, 1969, p. 31)*

In his theory concerning 'ethnic boundaries', Barth argues that in ethnic encounters, the situation of interaction is socially prescribed. Both groups may agree on this prescription, but their agreement will not go beyond the prescribed situation.

> Stable inter-ethnic relations presuppose such a structuring of interaction: a set of prescriptions governing situations of contact, and allowing for articulation in some sectors or domains of activity, and a set of proscriptions [prohibitions] on social situations preventing inter-ethnic interaction in other sectors, and thus insulating parts of the cultures from confrontation and modification.
>
> *(Barth, 1969, p. 16)*

It seems that medical practice belongs to a proscribed sphere of interaction in non-Ġorbat versus Ġorbat encounter. As Barth points out, these spheres are 'breakers of taboos'. The question of the purity and impurity of the body touches one of these taboos. We can observe that the medical sphere confronts Ġorbat and non-Ġorbat cultures on the subject of the body and all the taboos it concerns. As predicted by Barth, in proscribed spheres, there is confrontation, but there is also modification.

In fact, Ġorbat use of medical facilities seems to be a recent habit. They used to go to hospitals only in emergencies, for children with convulsions or in cases

Dealing with the body social **229**

of severe accidents. The medical consultation is a new habit. Since the opening of the MSF clinic, which receives Gorbat patients free of charge, their health-seeking behaviour has considerably changed. As MSF started by accepting only women and children, we can only observe this change in feminine habits. It is important to investigate the reasons that encourage – or force – Gorbat to consult a doctor or seek medical care, and so to face non-Gorbat beyond the agreed spheres of interaction.

After this brief explanation of the historical rejection of Gorbat in the Iranian context, the difficulties that Iranian MSF staff face could be explained as a new proscribed sphere of interaction with Gorbat patients, although this rejection, concerning the body and unconscious religious taboos involved in this sphere, happens more in public health facilities. I observed that MSF staff also face other difficulties in their interaction with Gorbat patients that will be discussed in the next section. These symbolic aspects of the body unconsciously determine all physical interaction, which is why they are so important for ethnographic studies.

Health care structures: a new sphere of interaction

In Darvāzeh Gār, because of the age of the houses and the high mobility of its migrant inhabitants, there is little maintenance of buildings. Also, infrastructure, such as gas and electricity networks, is mostly unofficial and unsafe. In their domestic space, whether in Tehran or Bābol, the Gorbat do not observe safety measures. Unsheathed wires and extensions of gas hoses pass through rooms and living spaces, and no security measures are taken into account for young children. Therefore, scalding, burns and electrocution happen frequently. Apart from car and motorbike accidents, burns are one of the most frequent emergency cases that bring Gorbat to hospitals.

Physically violent interactions among Gorbat individuals also cause numerous injuries. Nevertheless, not all serious injuries bring Gorbat to a doctor. The importance of the injury is socially determined; an injury is worth medical care according to how much it prevents someone from doing their daily duties. I will develop different aspects of pain from the Gorbat point of view in the next section.

The majority of Gorbat children do not have identification documents or health insurance. However, this does not seem to prevent them getting a medical consultation. In an emergency, close relatives will help by lending money and ID cards.

How are they received in medical centres?

According to my observations and interviews with social assistants, the reception of Gorbat people in public hospitals, where they usually go, is subject to discrimination based on three different categories:

1   Hospitals, which have received Gorbat people for several years, might be hostile to them because their bad reputation for not respecting hospital rules and escaping without paying has been confirmed by experience.

230 Mitra Asfari

2 Hospitals have difficulties receiving Ġorbat because most of them do not have official documents.
3 The third category of discrimination is based on some socio-ethnic considerations as developed in this chapter. Preconceived ideas like dirtiness, impurity or being a non-Muslim inhibit medical staff from providing normal health care.

Ġorbat experience this discrimination as a hostile attitude. Often, the medical staff blame them because of: "their carelessness regarding children" (*be bače hāšūn ahamiat nemidan*), "being bad mothers" (*mādarhāye badi hastan*) or "not respecting hygiene measures and discipline" (*asan behšdāt o nazm e bimārestān o rāyat nemikonan*).

Observation of Ġorbat mothers indicates that they 'fear' (*mitarsam*) going to the hospital. Which really means they are 'afraid' of being called 'a bad mother' (*migan če mādar-e badi hasti to*). For mothers who use drugs, it is obviously more frightening to go to hospital – and other official institutions – because of the stigma concerning drug users and the risk of being arrested.

> These women with coloured hair, black skin, long skirts, who talk loud, are so insolent and think they have all rights, they have very low IQ. They don't understand anything, don't know how to take care of their children, don't want to collaborate with the medical staff. When we ask them to do this or that, for example to close the bed rails for the safety of their child, they become violent, start to yell and don't even understand what it is for!
>
> (*A nurse in Shahid Fahmideh hospital,*[17] *2015*)

During child hospitalisations, I witnessed an important lack of mutual understanding between the medical staff and Ġorbat parents. The medical staff do not explain the causes of the sickness or the treatment to parents. They communicate only through medications, but parents – especially young parents – do not understand the variations of medicinal use. The fact is that older parents do not bother to accompany their own children to hospital. Young parents, older siblings or cousins are the principal attendants. They are unfortunately inexperienced and very little informed about medical practices. Thus, the causes of the disease are never made clear for young carers, and the lack of care continues. According to these observations and the results of the research I carried out on the interactions between Ġorbat patients and medical staff at the MSF clinic, on one hand, the Ġorbat patient is not familiar with modern medicine's epistemology and, on the other hand, medical staff are not familiar with Ġorbat reasoning about health problems. Most of the time, a Ġorbat patient does not recognise any relationship between their health problem and the questions medical staff ask. This communication gap between Ġorbat and modern medicine in their approach to body and illness makes a barrier to Ġorbat access to health care. I will discuss this issue later in this chapter.

Each time a sudden death happens in the Ġorbat community, long and lively discussions take place among clan members. Everyone tries to understand and, at the same time, to explain the reasons for the death. Electrocution and appendicitis are examples of complete incomprehension. Why and how electricity can bring about death is not clear. A simple 'stomach ache' which kills is just as weird, because it leads to strange interpretations. After the explanations from the doctor about the death of a child from appendicitis, close relatives of the child understood the statement as follows: the child is dead because he consumed a banana and a *Sandis* (a brand of fruit juice). It seems that the medical explanation about an organ that resembles a banana, called the appendix, leads to a reformulation concerning a banana and *Sandis*. The result is total incomprehension.

Thus, Gorbat patients might refuse important medical intervention because of problems with communication – they misunderstand. In some cases, they might refuse because of financial difficulties. But let me emphasise that financial problems are not a consistent barrier in Gorbat social life. Lack of cash is immediately critical without being a continuous problem. Getting and spending money are always subject to considerable fluctuations. One household can be rich and poor at different moments of the year. Everyone passes through moments of wealth and poverty. Being wealthy is not an established status for most of the Gorbat; wealthy households are quite rare. Another factor that we should take into consideration is the cash flow tradition among clan members and financial solidarity among close relatives. Note that in moments of crisis, such as a sudden hospitalisation, close relatives help the patient overcome the expense. This solidarity is nonetheless subject to some variations. If the person in need is in debt or their relatives are away, the payment is likely to cause problems. Therefore, I would like to stress that financial difficulties among the Gorbat is not a constant problem, and assessment of its importance in an evaluation of the family context is needed.

However, perceived wealth was one of the main problems that MSF local staff had with Gorbat patients. They argued that these patients appeared wealthy enough to go to the public hospitals. Here, we touch on another feature of the local value system regarding humanitarian actions. In the Iranian context, largely because of Islamic influence, humanitarian action is perceived as an act of charity. Charity is defined within Islamic codes and is seen to be the distribution of money or free services among the poor. The stigmatised or despised do not come under the definition of people in need. Therefore, the Iranian MSF staff had difficulties understanding the difference between poverty and stigma. While the main preoccupation of MSF was to provide medical services for stigmatised people, the local staff kept thinking that they had to accept only people with financial difficulties.

Role of other NGOs in modifying Gorbat health-seeking behaviour

Local NGOs in Darvāzeh Gār offer a basic education about personal health and hygiene for children. They also provide practical help such as bathrooms, clean clothes and slippers. Their social services consist of accompanying children and mothers to hospital when needed. They do understand the stigmatisation to which the Gorbat are subjected in hospitals, and believe that accompanying them has helped the Gorbat to consult doctors more easily and to gain self-confidence.

Local NGOs' intervention on behalf of children with the common cold happened to become very significant for Gorbat mothers. Paying attention to children with a cold is now considered to be a sign of being a 'good and considerate parent'. Making soup for sick children is, for instance, one way to express their motherhood in a social way, because the practice of cooking for children is rare in Gorbat culture.[18] More and more mothers are trying to change their habits in order to be able to despise other mothers for 'not caring' or for being 'bad mothers'. They use exactly the same terms used against them in hospitals. It seems that NGOs in Darvāzeh Gār have had obvious effects on Gorbat habits of health-seeking behaviour. They have opened a new sphere of interaction, yet the social prescriptions are not totally agreed on by both sides. In Gorbat social life, this change is a sociocultural modification rather than a medical habit. For instance, NGOs focussed on a special issue (the common cold) that is generally ignored by the Gorbat but became a feature of self-presentation and representation in the group, which is very important in their culture. Bringing the child to the doctor because of a simple cold is a cultural representation rather than a medical comprehension of the child's health. This observation brings us to the representation of the body and its social functions among the Gorbat.

Conflicts on treating the body social

Body as a tool

In Gorbat interactions, the body serves as a medium for symbolic and identity representation. From birth, the informal education they get leads children to develop two important ideas about their bodies: 1) to gain consciousness about their gender and 2) to raise the tolerance threshold when facing pain, humidity and fatigue.[19]

Physical exchanges between young members of the lineage with infants are always firm and forceful. From a young age, the Gorbat are encouraged 'to impose their cruelty' (*zālemgiri*) and 'not to show any sign of weakness' (*bi orzegi*). This means being strong physically, dominant in confrontations and resistant to pain. Every Gorbat child learns these basic values from their first physical interactions with peers and other relatives. Gorbat children learn that numerous pains and injuries are irrelevant because of a lack of concern from adults. They are supposed to tolerate these pains without complaining; otherwise, they will be severely blamed and/or punished. As Gorbat children grow up, these physical exchanges and the perceived irrelevance of some sorts of pain make their bodies highly tolerant of pain.

An 8-year-old girl, Baran, came to the MSF clinic accompanying her older sister and their niece. Their referral to the clinic was for the niece, who had serious otitis. It was by pure chance that the doctor realised that Baran had an injury on her foot. The doctor asked the older sister to open a case file for her in the clinic so that she would be able to visit and have her foot treated. The doctor, nurses and

Dealing with the body social **233**

I sensed the pain Baran was feeling only by seeing her injuries. She never expressed any feeling of pain. Even though an inappropriate shoe caused her injuries, she was still wearing the other hurting shoe. These injuries over three days did not seem to bother Baran nor stop her from walking around. She obtained ointment and a dressing on her injuries, but pulled them off as soon as she got home. This anecdote illuminates the different perception of pain in two different value systems.[20] As Le Breton (2009, p. 325) notes, medical discourse takes into account the physical aspect of pain, while the individual feels pain according to an interpretation grid, a world of meanings and values specific to their socio-cultural being.

During adulthood, the social dimension dominates the way the body is perceived. It becomes a site of social representation. Marital status for women, for instance, is reflected in the colour of their hair, and their body should be plump and fertile. Men represent authority, strength and attractiveness. They spend considerable time and money on their appearance (haircuts, clothes, etc.). As social bodily practices, tattoos and cosmetic surgery should also be mentioned. These practices are common among men and women, and communicate social codes and values. An astonishing number of cosmetic nose surgeries among Gorbat men and women reveals the importance of the social and representative function of the body.[21] Each surgery represents the spontaneous wealth of the individual. The fear of medical structures seems to disappear when social reputation is at stake.

Thus, the social body is much more concentrated on representative aspects than on health matters. Being fat for married women and having children young are not a consideration of the health of the woman, but about her social duties. Men keep up their appearance to look handsome and to please women, especially when they are polygamous. Children must be strong and independent. They are constantly encouraged to defend themselves against their peers and to dominate them physically. At the same time, their daily activity is begging, which necessitates its own physical techniques.

These forms of the socialisation of the body reappear in the relationship that Gorbat adults maintain with their body. In fact, the Gorbat learn to ignore many sensations from their bodies in order to keep only a social utility for this part of their being. All the practices concerning the body are intended to be a message. In other words, the body is a more powerful medium of communication than language.

The relationship the Gorbat have with their bodies could be considered to be 'utilitarian'. The description of women and children's practice of mendicancy can reveal this relationship. With a thorough observation before, during and after begging sessions at various crossroads in Tehran, we can analyse this practice with reference to the performance theories of Turner (1988). We have to emphasise that begging in the daily life of the Gorbat corresponds to the definition by Turner of a ritual act. Each sequence of this ritual is a scene of what Turner calls a "metatheatre" or a "social drama". Referring to Goffman, for whom the world of social interactions is a stage full of ritual acts, Turner suggests that:

> the dramaturgical phase begins when crises arise in the daily flow of social interaction. Thus, if daily living is a kind of theatre, social drama is a kind of

metatheatre, that is a dramaturgical language about the language of ordinary role-playing and status-maintenance which constitutes communication in the quotidian social process.

(Turner, 1988, pp. 75–76)

This daily process, with its dramaturgical language, scene settings and crises made in the public space, is what we can observe in the practice of mendicancy at the crossroads. Here, the body plays a crucial role in the whole process of interactions with passersby.

In other words, the main tool of this performance remains the body. All gestures, body language, rhythm of the body and facial mimics serve to enter the scene of mendicancy. Outside the scene, the Ġorbat woman walks straight, keeps her head up and her shoulders back. During the mendicancy, she has fallen shoulders, head bent to one side and she drags her feet on the floor. Thus, entering the space-time of mendicancy means to act bodily in order to represent a legitimate image of a person in need. In the Iranian context and in the Islamic belief, widows and orphans have the most legitimate profile for begging. The whole Muslim community is responsible for their protection. Therefore, Ġorbat mendicants act according to these rules for legitimation using their body and language as crucial tools to project the correct image. Marcel Mauss showed the anthropological importance of studying the body. He mentioned the importance of the body as a tool for work and for the other cultural themes it might represent: "The body is the first and the most natural instrument of Man.. . . his first and most natural technical object and also his technical means" (Mauss, 2004, p. 372; translation mine).

Thus, the body is a tool that the Ġorbat use to survive both socially and economically. The body must follow the individual and obey their social intentions. This understanding of the body is in contradiction with medical understanding, which focusses on the body as an object that requires special care in order to be treated and healed.[22] Sometimes, a medical treatment requires patients to adjust their work and daily habits. This is problematic for the Ġorbat, who consider that the body is merely required to do whatever is needed. For instance, in order to treat some bodily conditions, one of the measures to take is to adapt nutrition to the body's requirements. For the Ġorbat, nutrition rarely has a direct relationship with the body. It is often a social matter.[23] Asking Ġorbat to change their habits in order to respect their bodily needs is inconceivable – unless, of course, their body itself is unable to do the necessary daily tasks.

What does illness signify?

Consulting a doctor does not happen unless a serious physical problem threatens the individual. To the question "What do you define as a state of illness?" Ġorbat patients replied, "When the person passes out" (*vaqti ğaš kone*). Illness signifies an overwhelming handicap preventing the individual from doing their daily activities. The same is true for pain. As long as it does not stop daily activity, Ġorbat do not consider pain to be an illness. Therefore, they define health as the condition of the body that allows the individual to do their social duties. Gorbat social life encourages each individual to tolerate pain and other discomforts. Thus, unless Gorbat men have severe injuries or bone fractures, they do not consult a doctor. Children and women are changing their habits, even though their definition of illness has not changed. Sometimes they come to the MSF clinic, not because they feel ill, but because they need medical advice (for example, in cases of genital infection).

In general, as the clinic staff can assert, the most common illness that Gorbat parents recognise regarding their children is, as they say, "simple fever and chills" (*ye tab o larz e sāde*). Before MSF came to the neighbourhood, they used to wait until a child was convulsing before consulting a doctor. But being in contact with local NGOs has raised parents' awareness of flu. In fact, contracting flu is very common among the children, probably because of their working conditions and their hygiene. They work in cold weather with bare feet and inadequate clothes, and they do not have enough food and rest. However, the concern that Gorbat mothers have about flu is not to prevent the child worsening, but to maintain the social representation of being a good mother. They still do not define flu as an illness.

Besides flu, diseases that parents recognise as important are impetigo (*zarde zaxm*), diarrhoea (*eshāl*), broken bones (*šekastegi*) or serious burns (*sūxtegi*).[24]

Impetigo mainly affects young children and is significant to parents because of its contagiousness. As many children live in the same house, and as physical interaction and the sharing of possessions is common among them, skin infections spread rapidly. It seems that impetigo has been a problem for a long time because the Gorbat have some traditional rituals to prevent contagion. They burn a thick tissue on the roof and throw the burning tissue in the air. They also try to keep children apart during the outbreak. However, they do not treat skin infections caused by the minor injuries that are extremely common among children. In fact, no superficial injury deserves parental attention. Furthermore, they only care about diarrhoea, bone fractures and severe burns while children are too young to be able to look after themselves.

All other common diseases (such as parasites, infections, skin diseases and anaemia) noticed by the clinic staff or other NGOs are not considered to be important for Gorbat parents because they do not stop the children from going about their daily activities. Some young parents are well aware of anaemia among children and easily obtain iron supplements. However, they do not use medication properly. They mostly feed children with milk and do not consider changing their feeding habits because they do not consider anaemia an important problem for children.

Vaccination, for another example, does not seem to be accepted as a normal health matter for maternal care. A Gorbat mother was concerned about the vaccination of her child which had been delayed by several years. She said that if the child was not vaccinated he would not be accepted at school. I kept asking her, "Why was the vaccination important?" She kept replying, "Not to get sick, not to have fevers and chills, and to be accepted in school". The specificity of each vaccination was not clear for the mother. The interesting point is the mother's concern for school.

236 Mitra Asfari

She does not believe that the vaccination itself is very important. However, she does not want to be rejected or blamed by officials or administrators in front of other mothers. The rejection of being called a 'bad mother' was much more her concern than protecting her child from diseases that she did not even know about.

The absence of causal reasoning in understanding the causes of illness

This great gap between the Gorbat on one side and modern medicine on the other, over their ideas about the body and illness, brought my attention to consultations in the clinic and moments of misunderstanding between patients and medical staff. With the Gorbat's construction of body and illness, medical discourse seems very strange, because it has completely different paradigms. The surprise and astonishment of both patient and medical staff is evident during their conversation.

This explains why most of Gorbat referrals to the clinic are for gynaecological problems (genital infections) or the common cold. In order to adapt their consultations to Gorbat patients, midwives undertake more comprehensive sessions explaining all the habits that may cause infections. They encourage patients to change their clothing and improve personal hygiene. This advice does not seem to convince the Gorbat women, who rarely argue by cause and effect when it comes to treatment. Following their utilitarian view of the body, they do not accept any changes to social or daily behaviour. Thus, we face two levels of misunderstanding: 1) the causal relation between physical facts, such as the connection between the hygiene of underwear and genital infections and 2) the medical idea of the body, which does not seem to make sense in Gorbat logic and, conversely, the utilitarian idea of the body that the medical staff equally do not accept.

Medical understanding of the body demands some modification in daily activities for treatment (taking medication at the right time, changing daily habits like clothing, food, physical exercise, etc.). These demands are unacceptable in the Gorbat way of life. For the Gorbat, the life of an individual depends on the collective life. For example, if the group moves, the individual must move. Thus, the body follows the individual, and the individual follows the collective. This social structure stops the Gorbat from changing their view of the body, which does not match medical evidence.

While medical discourse is solely based on scientific evidence and seeks causes in order to deliver a diagnosis, the Gorbat do not employ a cause-and-effect logic to understand or to explain their health problems. During medical consultations in the MSF clinic, the doctor or midwife asks questions in order to detect relevant symptoms. However, for the Gorbat patient, these questions are irrelevant; she does not connect the questions with her problem, and so she is likely not to answer in a useful way. Because the Gorbat do not accept a causal approach towards health matters, women often face difficulties following medical reasoning about their bodies. For instance, it is not always clear to these patients that dirty bathrooms or not wearing underwear may cause uterine infections.

Ġorbat regularly claim that there is no reason for their illness and it happened without any known reason: "The sickness just happened among us"[25] (*Marizi-e dige oftade*). Nowadays, they mostly believe that the devil's eye may threaten a child's life, as well as a love relationship. Diseases are not believed to be a consequence of malicious prayer or thought.

We can also note some traditional ways of treating certain diseases in Ġorbat tradition. However, the young generation – as well as some older people – are increasingly losing faith in these traditional methods, saying that "they are useless" (*fāyde nadāre*). They believe modern medicine is much more useful than traditional remedies, but there are good and bad doctors. Accordingly, they prefer doctors who they can relate to; doctors who try to make them understand the reasoning. Good doctors are also seen to be those who are likely to give a good quantity of medicine. Nevertheless, by consulting medical staff, some physical conditions are gradually becoming accepted as the causes of disease.

There is, in fact, a communication gap. Semantically and technically, the Ġorbat patient faces an unknown world when coming to a health centre. The medical staff encounters the same communication problem as the patients. Staff members do not have access to their usual ideas about the body, health and illness. This situation seems to impose a form of symbolic violence on the Ġorbat people, and sometimes results in a violent response towards the medical staff. The whole verbal and non-verbal communication with medical staff concerns the body and brings up all the conflicts underlying both symbolic systems.

An ethnographic example of the symbolic violence that Ġorbat patients face in health care situations is the blame directed at Ġorbat mothers for not knowing how to treat their children. In the clinic, I observed several times Ġorbat patients being blamed for coming to the doctor because of a common cold:

> *Faghat vase ye sarmāxordegi ūmadi? Ādam vase ye sarmāxordegi mir-e doctor? Key šomā mixāin in čizā ro yād begirin? Āxe man as dast-e šomā čikār konam?*

> You came only for your common cold? You should not come to the doctor for a common cold! When are you going to learn all these things? What am I supposed to do with you?

The Ġorbat try to impose themselves and to make the medical staff believe that their problem – even a common cold – is worth being treated. In this way, they introduce an element of violence into the medical situation.

Conclusion

In this humanitarian situation, there is a large problem of access to health care which is neither merely political nor economic. In this MSF programme, which aims to provide medical services to stigmatised people, there is even stigma and rejection within the MSF clinic. One of the target groups is the Ġorbat, who do

238 Mitra Asfari

have access to public insurance and health care. However, they do not have proper access to health care. This rejection happens initially because the Ġorbat do not look after their documents properly and lose them very often. On top of this, their rejection happens at the interactional level; it happens when reception and medical staff mistreat them or refuse to provide them with proper treatment, saying that they are aggressive and troublesome.

In order to understand this conflict, we must look at a deeper level of interaction between Ġorbat people and the wider Iranian society. In fact, both sides are interacting in a situation which is not socially prescribed, since the Ġorbat have a limited site of interaction with the wider society (which takes place mostly at the roadside). Historically, Ġorbat people only interact with neighbouring societies in restricted spheres, mainly to do with mendicancy and peddling. The wider society, the municipality and all health structures have troubled relations with Ġorbat, especially when their interaction goes beyond 'prescribed spheres'.

For this reason, the intervention of the MSF as an external agent might reduce conflict. However, the Iranian MSF staff fought against the idea of including Ġorbat women and children in MSF's target groups. Their arguments about the financial and political situation of Ġorbat people did not correspond to reality. Theoretically, the Ġorbat have access to health care, but in practice, they experience rejection. Some of the local staff continue to claim that "there is no hope of changing this population" (*hič omidi be taġir-e ina nist*) and "they are only making trouble" (*faqat moškel ijād mikonan*), even though "they do need MSF's services" (*niāzi be xadamāt-e M.S.F. nadāran*). Others tried to learn more about Ġorbat ways of thinking, their daily habits and beliefs, and to adapt their communication methods to patients.

Reasons for rejection were found in historical and symbolic explanations. On one hand, the local staff of MSF belong to the wider Iranian society, and it takes some time for them to overcome the symbolic barriers (for example, the question of purity) that separate them from this minority/pariah group. On the other hand, in the actual Iranian urban context, humanitarian work depends on the definition of Islamic charity and how it is understood as a way to help the poor. For Muslims, charity is specifically about providing help to those who are suffering financially. Nevertheless, all the negative messages that the municipality of Tehran spreads about the Ġorbat have a great influence on every citizen. The negative messages suggest that people practising mendicancy are rich and connected to mafia networks. Therefore, any small signs of temporary wealth made Ġorbat patients seem to the local staff to be 'rich'. It was found that cash circulates rapidly in the Ġorbat community, and a temporary acquisition of an expensive object does not mean that that person is wealthy. However, MSF's purpose was to provide health services to people suffering from stigma, not poverty. When the excuse of perceived wealth was rejected, local staff continued insisting that the Ġorbat must change their behaviour in order to be accepted in the public health system.

As Barth (1969) pointed out, in cultural encounters we need socially prescribed spheres of interaction. For the Ġorbat, there is a need for a prescription designating a new sphere of interaction with new components. All the crucial elements – such

Dealing with the body social **239**

as the body, illness, markers of time and space, individual and collective considerations, and the Islamic definition of purity and impurity – must be taken into account.

Addressing the resistance of the local staff was one part of my mission in the MSF project. The other part that I, personally, wanted to work on was the misunderstanding between medical staff and Gorbat patients. This part revealed important points about their different views of the body and illness. In the context of Gorbat health-seeking behaviour, the body turned out to have many social functions, as well as serving as a tool. This is a social construction that alienates the body from a medical approach.

This ethnographic study leads us to the work of Augé (1986) about the anthropology of illness. He believes that illness is embedded in social, religious and cultural life, and constitutes an anthropological object. According to this theory, the study of representations of illness is a crucial way of pinpointing the system of thought that gives rise to individual behaviour. In other words, the social dimension of illness will bring to light symbolic dimensions of culture (such as the relation to the body, religious feeling, and an individual's interactions with the social). In this study, we found confirmation of Augé's theory in Gorbat social and symbolic systems. Through observation of therapeutic behaviours and beliefs, we can, in fact, reach the social dimension of illness. That is to say, the Gorbat intellectual framework helps us to think about illness. In the same way, through observation of treatment and the attitudes of medical staff toward Gorbat patients, we observed the interrelation between the dominant culture and this minority group. In other words, studying the body in the context of illness and treatment sheds light on the sociohistorical and cultural dimensions of Gorbat and non-Gorbat coexistence.

Furthermore, knowledge about the social organisation and cultural values of both sides (Gorbat patient and MSF medical staff) helps us understand their respective representations of body and illness. This is what can be extracted from Augé's work for the purpose of investigating medical humanitarian situations. Illness and the cultural system are interrelated, and understanding one requires an understanding of the other. This gives us a new insight about ethnography in humanitarian situations that is not merely about studying the 'target population', but also about adopting a vision and widening observations to include the socio–political contexts in which all actors live. Using an interdisciplinary approach to the study of all the actors involved will help to improve the understanding of such a multi-actor scene. A humanitarian organisation – with its sociocultural system and preconceptions, local actors and their understanding of the humanitarian subject (involving illness and poverty), and, last but not least, the historical and cultural relationships between these local actors – are all ethnographic objects. As Fainzang (2000) recalls, modern medicine is also an anthropological object. In ethnographical situations, we must give equal weight to discourse, concepts and values. Modern medical practices imply sociocultural subjectivities. In other words, as an anthropologist in a humanitarian situation, all the different symbolic systems at stake must be grasped. These systems may represent an administrative institution, modern medicine, a minority group, a majority group or an association. These systems might be in symbiosis, in conflict or merely overlapping. Thus, in order to establish how they interact, whether they collaborate or oppose each other, the study of the underlying logic of each symbolic system is essential for the anthropologist.

Notes

1 Within the Gorbat, each clan has a name according to its former occupation or the name of its ancestor. These names remain unknown to non-Gorbat people.
2 Unfortunately, I am not going to discuss these main targets of the clinic here. However, this definitely requires a thorough ethnographic study.
3 *Kowli* in Persian.
4 The title of my position in MSF.
5 Later, I collaborated with the social team on several health promotion programmes among the Gorbat.
6 *Kasāee ke moškele māli dāran qabūl konim, na ūnāee ke bā mūye rang karde o lebāsāye ānčenāni miān. Midūni rang kardan-e mū be in šekl čeqadre hazine dāre.*
7 An attitude which consists of rejecting moralities, religion, social forms and aesthetic standards of other people while prioritising one's own values.
8 These qualifications correspond to how urban and rural Iranians describe Gypsy (*kowli*) people.
9 This happened only on Saturday, because Saturday is a holiday for the Gorbat, and this is when they usually came to the clinic.
10 Nomads own herds and their chiefs (within their hierarchic society) own lands, while itinerant groups possess neither herds nor lands and they do not recognise any individual as a chief. There is no hierarchy among them.
11 A matrimonial custom whereby individuals marry members of their own lineage, clan or ethnic group.
12 An important month in Shia calendar. They celebrate the anniversary of the martyrdom of the third Shia Imam (Hussein) and his family. Gorbat have a special pilgrimage for this occasion in Māzandarān. They walk from their neighbourhood to a sanctuary which might vary from one year to the next.
13 The eighth Shia Imam whose sanctuary is in Iran (at Mashhad, in the province of Khorasān).
14 According to Iranian law, Gorbat are Iranian and can obtain identification documents. However, they often lose documents and birth certificates. This carelessness makes it difficult for them to have identification cards, and is the main reason why most of them are undocumented. The same problem occurs with their health insurance documents.
15 Because their name means 'exiled' or 'stranger'.
16 This was how people used to warn me of the 'dangers' of discussing and socialising (in a general sense) with Gorbat during my fieldwork.
17 A hospital for sick children, close to Darvāzeh Gār, where Gorbat go following their installation in the neighbourhood.
18 Cooking is a Gorbat wife's favour for her husband in case of rivalry with co-wives. It also can be the young husband's favour to his wife when she comes home after work.
19 In this chapter, we are going to develop only the second educational point on the body social.
20 MSF clinic South Tehran Project. January 2017.
21 This practice is also very common among non-Gorbat Iranians.
22 I extracted this from the consultation sessions in the MSF clinic from conversations with the medical staff. This view of the body does not pretend to be the most objective definition in medical discourse, and takes into account the subjectivity of medical actors.

23 While the wider society condemns commensality with Gorbat, a Gorbat rule forces each individual to share their food with people who are present at the time. Only in very rare cases, such as pregnancy, breastfeeding and old age, might they keep food to themselves.
24 Almost 99% of Gorbat children experience burns.
25 They even claim this with contagious diseases.

References

Augé, M., (1986). L'anthropologie de la maladie. *L'Homme*. **26**(1–2), 81–90.

Barth, F., (1961). *Nomads of South Persia: the Basseri tribe of the Khamseh Confederacy*. Oslo: Oslo University Press.

Barth, F., (1969). *Ethnic groups and boundaries: the social organization of culture difference*. Bergen and Oslo: Universitetsforlaget.

Epstein, R.M., Franks, P., Fiscella, K., Shields, C.G., Meldrum, S.C., Kravitz, R.L. and Duberstein, P.R., (2005). Measuring patient-centered communication in patient-physician consultations: theoretical and practical issues. *Social Science and Medicine*. **61**(7), 1516–1528. doi:10.1016/j.socscimed.2005.02.001

Fainzang, S., (2000). La maladie, un objet pour l'anthropologie sociale. *Ethnologie comparée. Revue électronique semestrielle* (1).

Ghiabi, M., (2016). *The medical republic of Iran and the art of managing disorder*. Communication in the 11th biennial of *Iranian Studies*, Vienna.

Khosrokhavar, F., (1997). Nouvelle banlieue et marginalité: la Cité Taleghani à Khak-e Sefid. In: C. Adle and B. Hourcade, eds., *Téhéran, Capitale bicentenaire*. Téhéran: Institut Français de recherche en Iran et Tehran. 307–344.

Le Breton, D., (2009). Entre douleur et souffrance: approche anthropologique. *L'information Psychiatrique*. **4**(85), 323–328.

Mauss, M., (2004). Les techniques du corps. *Sociologie et anthropologie*. 365–388. Paris: PUF.

Rao, A., (1982). *Les Gorbat d'Afghanistan: aspects économiques d'un groupe itinérant* Jat. Paris: Institut d'Iranologie de Téhéran Ed.

Rao, A., (1985). Des nomades méconnus: pour une typologie des communautés péripatétiques. *L'Homme*. **95**, 97–120.

Shahri, J., (2002). *Tehran-e qadim* (Ancient Tehran). Tehran: Moein Editions.

Turner, V., (1988). *The anthropology of performance*. New York: PAJ Publications.

12

EPILOGUE

The new missionaries – an anthropological reflection on humanitarian action in critical situations

Frédéric Vandenberghe and Jean-François Véran

The humanitarian agent in critical situations

The justification of humanitarian work is post-secular: it is at once humanist, professional, medical and legal. The mission of Médecins Sans Frontières, as stated in its charter, is founded on universal medical ethics and the right to humanitarian assistance. It is an attempt to operationalise the Hippocratic oath in catastrophic situations of emergency or, less extremely, in troubled situations where the usual conditions of medical practice do not apply.

Following Dewey, French pragmatists call those situations "critical moments" (Boltanski & Thévenot, 1999, p. 359; see also Boltanski & Thévenot, 1991, p. 220). They are characterised, both at patient and context levels, by radical ruptures of standard medical routines that need to be accommodated by innovative redefinitions of the situation of action. The protocols of aid work define and specify prescribed modes of actions for critical situations (e.g. earthquakes, epidemics), gaps in local medical response (the absence of a protocol for sexual violence, for instance) and enclaves (i.e. specific territories with access barriers, such as hyperviolent urban settings). Protocols can therefore be considered to be an attempt to establish routines of a second order in critical moments.

Today's missionaries are humanitarian agents. Usually, they are professionals at the highest levels of accomplishment, trained and skilled in cutting-edge theoretical knowledge, technologies of intervention, practical lines of treatment, surgical procedures and other areas of expertise. They do not follow the classical model of academic knowledge production (blue sky research with independent peer review). Their knowledge is interdisciplinary, contextual, practical and applied. Unlike academic knowledge, applied knowledge is not autonomous, but heteronomous. Geared to the solution of practical problems, its ends and means are defined by third parties who set the agenda and define the parameters of evaluation and success (Gibbons et al., 1994).

Typically, the humanitarian worker is, before their humanitarian engagement, a highly qualified, well-paid, successful doctor or nurse, logistician, administrator or project coordinator with a university degree. Whether they come from the Northern or the Southern hemisphere, humanitarian workers are often individuals with a moral sensibility and a sense of compassion. Following Archer's (2003) typology of the modes of reflexivity as exhibited in internal conversations, we can say that they are 'meta-reflexive' individuals; i.e. critical idealists with values and a mission in life. In search of both useful and meaningful action, they want to have a positive impact on the relief of human suffering. They are 'paradoxical individuals' in the sense that, against all expectations, they leave their zone of comfort within the mainstream of their profession to make a mark on the world. Whatever their personal reasons may be, they decide to dedicate a part of their lives to alleviate the suffering of distant others, even if it is limited in time and, eventually, career considerations need to be taken into account. An MSF assignment is an excellent credential indeed.

Once the decision is taken, the professional becomes a humanitarian worker who, following the attendance of a practical crash course by MSF (named PPD: *préparation au premier départ*, preparation for first departure), is flown into a critical setting to start their assignment. The crash course is neither theoretical nor technical; it is operational and formed in two parts. One is general and consists of an induction into the structure and general proceedings of the organisation. The other is specific and consists of learning the guidelines and protocols that are specific to MSF within each area of competence. Through a series of case studies and group simulations, it aims to instil new guidelines of action for emergency settings where standard practices do not apply (or only apply conditionally, partially). The knowledge that is dispensed is of a practical nature. It has nothing to do with the explicit inculcation of humanitarian morals or philosophical worldviews. Rather, it aims to form the habitus of the practitioner and to prepare them for the field (Bourdieu, 1977).

The operational character of the training explains why explicit knowledge ('know that') is less important than practical knowledge ('know how'), and why the normative content is limited to the basic MSF charter and its implication for everyday professional behaviour. Knowledge has to become effective in 'operational chains' of action that allow the humanitarian worker to assist with confidence and competence in situations of high unpredictability. In practice, it corresponds to a systematic presentation of a working environment that is not highly technological, well resourced, predictable or rational. The habitus is systematically disarticulated and reassembled, reconfigured and retrained to react automatically to critical moments, in accordance with the protocols and security guidelines. During this induction course, the initial humanitarian imagination of the worker is rapidly brought down to earth. The missionary has lost zeal, but gained efficacy.

All the same, when the professional arrives on the scene, they still encounter a world they could not have foreseen. The definitions of the situation break down and they are forcefully brought back to realities that defy the expectations acquired during formation at university and in previous professional exercise. By this we do not mean to imply that the humanitarian professional world considers its practice to be mere *bricolage* and just-in-time adaptation. Quite the contrary, the regime of action is not one of continuous convenience and invention but consists of "the plan" (Thévenot, 1995, pp. 411–434). It is an engineer's world. It is designed and believed to be a world ruled by medical protocols, logistical procedures and security guidelines that are engineered to make emergency response rational, orderly, observable, describable, predictable – in short, "accountable" (Quéré, 1987, p. 97; see also Garfinkel, 1987).

Risk mitigation is a top priority. In huge logistic headquarters in Europe, prefabricated hospitals are stored in containers, ready to be shipped by special airplane and recently also by zeppelin. Protocols are in place for up to three lines of treatment to face the complications of any epidemic. Complex supply routes are traced. Detailed contingency plans are designed. The MSF Toyota Land Cruisers are purpose-built, with no on-board electronics, so they can be repaired anywhere in the world. Everything is put in place to make the emergency response professional, with as little space for improvisation as possible.

What the previous chapters show, however, are the limits of this particular sociotechnical 'dispositive' that comes with the regime *en plan* (on paper) of the engineer. A dispositive is an assemblage of heterogeneous factors (Dodier & Barbot, 2016, p. 421). Technological, logistical and operational factors are joined with economic, political and cultural factors. Between the first series and the second series, there is a hiatus, though – something does not work. The human has not been properly factored in. Manifestly, something has escaped strategic planning. 'Human factors' are seen as the culprit. The emergency response to the spectacular 2014–2015 Ebola epidemic in Sierra Leone was alleged to have been slowed down and made complicated by mourning rituals involving inter-human body contact (Fairhead, 2016). In contexts with exceptional HIV prevalence and incidence, improper health-seeking behaviour of people becomes an obstacle to their care and their adherence to medication. In sexual and reproductive health projects, the survivors of sexual violence may come after the 72-hour window of prophylactic efficiency, or they may not come at all. The very presence of a centre for treatment of cholera is threatened by accusations that deaths are caused by witchcraft or international conspiracy. As the preceding chapters have shown, this is when anthropologists are called in to explain the situation and point to a solution. Almost invariably, they arrive at the paradoxical conclusion that humans are the main impediment to proper humanitarian assistance. Those who should be treated do not want to be treated in the ways defined by the humanitarian protocols. The protocols were meant to facilitate humanitarian action, but in fact, they often make it more difficult – and sometimes impossible.

The situation reminds us of the achievements of Science and Technology Studies. Initially, in the philosophy of science of Popper and consorts, and also in the sociology of knowledge of Mannheim, social and cultural factors were only invoked to explain the deviation from the truth. The truth itself was deemed universal, rational, transcendental. It was not seen as the result of social or cultural factors. When the members of the Edinburgh School developed their strong programme in the sociology of knowledge and advocated the "principle of symmetry" (Bloor, 1976, p. 5),

Epilogue **245**

the situation was reversed. Not only deviation from the truth, but the truth itself should be analysed and understood as a social and cultural artefact. Our humanitarian workers, now in place, soon discover that the conditions of veracity of their concepts and the functionality of their protocols are bound to the social context in which they were acquired. Without knowing it, humanitarian workers project their own conditions of professional practice onto the local situation. Their technical competencies make them stop noticing human contingencies. Protocols that were meant to deal with uncertainty and risk did not cover the contingent conditions of their own efficacy. This shows that the distinction between the rational and non-rational does not hold. The rational cannot understand its own irrationality. Despite attempts to understand, it is all too easy to play the blame game and accuse the local people of irrational beliefs and erratic behaviour. The anthropologists' main contribution is not to unveil mysterious local cosmologies, but to help the humanitarian workers acknowledge the blind spots of the organisation's operational knowledge in the first place. Just like Lévi-Strauss' scientist, the engineer is in fact a *bricoleur* (Lévi-Strauss, 1962, p. 11). The main task of humanitarian anthropology is not to denounce and relativise Western knowledge, but to reflect on the practical impediments that have to be understood and overcome for the humanitarian action to be successful.

Technology and the human deficit

Bernard Stiegler is a philosopher of technology. In 1979, he robbed a bank and was condemned to jail (Stiegler, 2003). In captivity, he realised he was denuded and bereft of the usual trappings of modernity: television, cars, sofas, leisure, etc. Through the window, he could see the blue sky, and he began to reflect on the importance of technology in everyday life. He conceived incarceration to be a "technological epoché" (p. 92); that is, a suspension of the exteriorisations of the body that make freedom possible. What was significantly missing was a stable, materialised, taken-for-granted environment that could provide conditions of stability and security. Henceforth, he would only have access to the outside world through memory.

The humanitarian worker on an assignment finds themself in a similar situation. Following a "critical event" (Das, 1996, p. 1), like the chemical accident in the Union Carbide Factory in Bhopal that intoxicated and killed scores of people, the 2010 earthquake in Haiti, the South Sudan conflict or the chronic hyperviolence in Honduras, the humanitarian worker realises in action – albeit negatively – the importance of highly industrialised conditions in their ordinary practice as medical doctor, logistician, water sanitation engineer, etc., in overdeveloped societies. They are well aware that the adequate differential diagnostic of febrile syndromes requires sharp lab tests, which would be standard back home but are not available, and that, consequently, they will have to work with only clinical and probabilistic diagnoses. They learn how to plan and manage a supply chain, but they are faced with the reality that when the medication is blocked at the border, there isn't anything to carry. The water and sanitation expert knows that still waters are perfect breeding sites for *Aedes aegipti*, but it won't be possible to build the drainage system for adequate vector control.

Although MSF training has contemplated all these issues and simulated multiple crisis scenarios, the one worse than the other, they tend to envisage and evaluate local conditions from the point of view of a default position of full access and full control of all the variables in play. As a result, the local situation is always defined negatively as a deficit in terms of what would be required and is, one way or another, continuously missing. They can't help it, but the extreme conditions often provoke harsh judgement of the locals by the international staff: the health structure is constantly collapsed because of poor planning, supply chains are moribund because of endemic corruption, local nepotism makes adequate human resources impossible. Without being fully aware of it, our humanitarian worker relapses and spontaneously reactivates the judgement of their former self, the missionary who not only continuously compares two worlds but also establishes "differential valences" (Héritier, 2005) between the two and orders them in a hierarchy of development. In his book on humanitarian reason, Fassin speaks of an "ontological inequality" (2007, p. 520) between two humanities – on the one hand, those who voluntarily sacrifice their lives to save lives; on the other hand, those whose lives are sacrificed by catastrophes. In theory, heroes and victims belong to the same humanity; in practice, however, the two humanities are unequal. The value of one life is worth much more than the value of the other. What holds for their value also holds for their knowledge.

Confronted with a technological deficit, the representative of science and reason blames the local people for the practical consequences of a project's difficulty reaching its target populations and meeting its operational goals. The technological deficit is thereby transformed into a human deficit. The failure of the humanitarian worker is due to the irrational practices and improper health-seeking behaviour of the locals. To the co-workers, the national professionals on the team, the misjudgement and misattribution of the cause of failure by the international professional is blatant. As they feel co-responsible, they feel they are being judged, as well. In private, they often complain about racial prejudices and colonial stereotypes of the humanitarian workers. As a member of the national community who occupies an intermediary position between the international staff and the locals, the co-worker is 'epistemologically privileged': they can see the mechanisms of domination (colonialism, racism, patriarchy, etc.) that interfere with the smooth execution of the project because as a national; they are subject to the mechanisms and can feel them, as it were, on the skin. While this knowledge may be of use to make the organisation as a whole more reflexive, open and democratic, aligning its lofty principles with organisational practices and thus reducing the difference in status between its personnel (Fassin, 2010), it does not solve the practical issues that are the result of a missing interface between a technological and a socio-cultural assemblage.

Like the internationals, the co-worker is a highly skilled professional. As a national, they not only know the protocols of the international organisation, but they would also know how to adapt them to the local context or, if necessary, when and why to simply bypass them. The co-worker from the national team has contextual knowledge to which the international worker has no access and of which they have no direct experience.

We are not fetishising 'local knowledge' here. What matters in situations of emergency is 'practical knowledge' – not explicit knowledge ('know that'), but implicit knowledge ('know-how'), knowledge in action that allows one to understand and resolve social and political problems. If one does not know how to handle the local context, problems may quickly become intractable. The co-worker is also vulnerable to pressures from the discipline in which they operate. Embedded in local power relations and network constraints, the co-worker can at times put a project at risk. Clientelism, and indeed corruption, are endemic in extreme situations, and constitute a permanent risk factor for international organisations. We are not suggesting here that the so-called local staff are more corruptible than the international staff because they are embedded in the local culture. It is about exposure and vulnerability. The first ones usually live with their families, have regular wages in contexts where formal work is scarce, and live and circulate in these humanitarian situations, while the international staff may have early curfews and very restricted movements imposed by security guidelines. Local staff are also usually identified in their communities as MSF workers. For all these reasons, local staff are more exposed to targeted blackmail, extortion or threats of all kinds than their international counterparts.

The protocols of engagement do mention that information needs to be context related. And they do provide a context-analysis toolkit, but this analysis does not go any deeper than the context itself as understood by the humanitarian workers themselves. Two dimensions are missing: a hermeneutic one (Gadamer, 1960) and an ethnomethodological one (Garfinkel, 1967). The hermeneutic dimension has to do with the symbolic layers of knowledge in the background that pre-structure, pre-interpret and pre-define the situation for all the people involved. The ethnomethodological dimension involves a myriad of inconspicuous context-specific details that can neither be anticipated nor imagined by an outsider. The two dimensions converge in the necessity of an 'emic' understanding (i.e. from the perspective of someone within the culture) of the context that is both symbolic and practical. Even when we are dealing with 'insiders' and 'outsiders', we always need to reconstruct from within the different perspectives people enact when they adhere to the goals of the project. Three factions are at play: the international staff, the national co-workers and the local people. The task of the anthropologist is to reconstruct these three perspectives. By showing different understandings of the same situation, the anthropologist can reveal misunderstandings that impede a fluent coordination between all the people involved in the drama of humanitarian intervention.

Some chapters in this book reveal the mismatch between the perspectives of international staff and their co-workers. The latter often believe that the international staff are so involved with the organisation itself and its protocols that these become ends in themselves. Instead of being a means to intervene in the situation

248 Vandenberghe and Véran

with efficacy, the protocols are followed and implemented 'ritualistically'. Following Merton, the ritualist pays extreme attention to routines and institutional norms at the risk of being counterproductive (Merton, 1968, p. 205). In the end, the stability of the protocols sometimes leads to inaction.

Often, MSF's own organisational culture of protocols and guidelines gets in the way of true operational efficiency. It is not rare that an MSF emergency response is indeed perceived as important, but also relativised by national co-workers and local people within a context whereby basic survival at all levels is at stake. It is not rare that an MSF priority project with a high level of engagement does not match the perspective of local people and their perception of what is a priority. It is important to note that by 'perspective', we do not mean, as shown constantly in this book, some kind of cultural perspectivism that only the anthropologist can see through their analytical lenses (Viveiros de Castro, 2009), but conversely, a more 'practical sense' of what matters when a socio-economic and/or political system is collapsing. In this sense, one of the tasks of the anthropologist is not to add deeper cultural analysis to context analysis, but to facilitate communication and understanding between the local people, the national staff who know the local stakes and the organisation that aims to intervene for the welfare of the people who need help.

The other task of the anthropologist is to help the humanitarian workers to remember that a technological deficit should not be interpreted as a human deficit. The 'assistance gaps' that are invoked as motives for providing assistance cannot be transfigured into human deficits to explain later why the assistance is not working properly. For example, if the reason for the project is the lack of a national protocol for integral assistance to the survivors of sexual violence, the lack of adequate health-seeking behaviour by survivors cannot be held to be the reason for the project's difficulties in reaching its target population. Rather, the anthropologist's task is to reverse the argument to show that while no medical resolution is sought by the survivors and their families, other resolution modes are at play, such as mediation with the perpetrator, mob justice or deliberation by traditional authorities. The issue is therefore not 'atavism', 'cultural acceptance' or 'social anomie'. What people actually do in such situations may not be convergent with the objectives of the organisation, to provide medical and mental health assistance, but that does not mean that they are acquiescing to their distress. To be able to intervene better, one has to know what the options are of the people who need help, and combine them with the objectives of the humanitarian organisation.

As medical technology advances in wealthy over-developed countries, the 'gap' takes another meaning. The absence of high-tech medicine such as computer-assisted surgery, intelligent prosthesis or 3D printing in humanitarian settings haunts the imagination of medical staff. Day by day, they have a feeling of missing vanguard tools and chemicals they know exist elsewhere, and they themselves become part of the gap they were supposed to fill in in the first place. The absence of high-tech medicine becomes more and more difficult, and continuously reminds the staff that humanitarian settings produce a disruptive conception of humanity whereby humanitarian action is precisely supposed to restore and defend the belief in the

MSF charter and principles of engagement. Two humanities encounter each other in the context of an assignment. Re-configurable, modifiable and commodified cybernetic organisms that can be artificially augmented are in confrontation with fragmented and diminished bodies in pain. The post-human is standing face to face with a human reduced to bare life without any qualification (Agamben, 1998). As a modern discipline that is haunted by its post-modern imagery, anthropology is also confronted with its own past and future. Its conceptual apparatus is challenged by the appearance of an improbable otherness. The other is no longer the exotic other; neither is it the post-modern post-human, but a human body between life and death. This, in all its simplicity, is not the "Death of Man" (Foucault, 1966, p. 398), but more simply and without any epistemic layers, the death of a mere human being. This is ultimately what anthropology in humanitarian situations is about: it is about how this encounter with absolute otherness engages the responsibility of a whole discipline not just to reflect on different conceptions of mankind, but to apply its knowledge so that the medical staff can fulfil its mission to 'save lives'. By bringing back all the social, cultural and political complexity, anthropology shows that a suffering body is always more than mere life. Humanitarian situations where anthropologists are useful are the ones where this demonstration is needed.

Worldwide, the economic, technological and political transformations are destabilising the parameters of existence. The coming together of rising inequality ('neo-liberalism'), ecological challenges (the 'Anthropocene') and the insurgence against liberal democracy ('populism') provoke a global sense of insecurity that inevitably trickles down to the humanitarian experience during a project. Terrorism, armed conflict, urban violence, international crime, pseudo-natural catastrophes, climatic migrations, spectacular epidemic outbursts and the increasing pandemic threat: all these dramas are interwoven and create a general atmosphere of danger and risk. Countries with collapsed infrastructures may well offer an advanced observation deck on "the coming anarchy" (Kaplan, 1994, pp. 44). Scarcity, crime, overpopulation, tribalism and disease are rapidly destroying the social fabric of our planet.

We know that in the global society, natural catastrophes are socially manufactured and human tragedies are ever more precipitated by changes in the natural environment. As Latour (2015) has shown, there is now an inversion of the geological times − once extremely slow and now accelerated, and the political times − once accelerated and now bound to inertia. For humanitarian assistance, the intermingling of biomedical and social issues leads to special challenges. The 2014–2015 Ebola outbreak stretched the emergency response to the limit. In a context of spatial mobility and temporal acceleration, the international incapacity to address sudden variations of scale in failing states was evident. The insufficiency of the logistic coordination and of the medical protocols showed that international organisations are challenged by the difficulties of dealing with 'translocal' problems. The spectacular return of malaria in zones where it had been previously eradicated or under control is evidence not only that the global response to 'modern' epidemics is inadequate, but, worse, that it has lost its capacity to deal with infections that were already known about in the Middle Ages. Periodic infections like leishmaniasis, tuberculosis and diphtheria are locally resurging, while arboviruses like zika, chikungunya and dengue spread worldwide in a warming world, along with the globalisation of travel and migration.

After a post-Second World War period of recognition and expansion of the rights of refugees and migrants, we are now witnessing a global rejection of their moral and political status. The story of the *Aquarius* illustrates well this turn of the tide. The MSF-assisted boat that rescued migrants alongside the Libyan coast was repeatedly denied landing in Europe in 2018. Its Panamanian flag was revoked and, despite an international campaign by MSF, it had to cease all activities. For an organisation like MSF that gained a reputation and sense of engagement in 1974 during the Vietnamese boat people crisis, this is quite disconcerting. The same types of activities that built its moral foundation are now openly decried and criticised. The politicisation of humanitarianism denies MSF its core principle of neutrality, and may even lead to the outright criminalisation of its activities. The organisation is being intimidated: the line that separated humanitarianism and warfare was always thin. No wonder that the suspicion of disguised imperialism is reactivated in times of global disorder.

These geopolitical issues not only appear in the public documents and internal discussions of MSF; they also have immediate repercussions at the project level, where they are translated into operational questions. How to address environmental health within the limits of MSF's medical activities? How to impact on the medical and mental health consequences of urban violence? How to develop an adequate epidemic response in post-colonial times where accusations and suspicions are rife? How to assist migrants while not exposing them to police harassment and gang extortion? These are some of the practical questions that arise alongside – and during – humanitarian aid. They are raised among project teams during the routine of meetings, health promotion sessions, situation reports and informal discussions at night. The anthropologist, when called, is just one more figure at the table.

References

Agamben, G., (1998). *Homo Sacer: sovereign power and bare life.* Stanford, CA: Stanford University Press.

Archer, M., (2003). *Structure, agency and the internal conversation.* Cambridge: Cambridge University Press.

Bloor, D., (1976). *Knowledge and social imagery.* Chicago: Chicago University Press.

Boltanski, L. and Thévenot, L., (1991). *De la justification: les économies de la grandeur.* Paris: Gallimard.

Boltanski, L. and Thévenot, L., (1999). The sociology of critical capacity. *European Journal of Social Theory.* **2**(3), 359–377.

Bourdieu, P., (1977). *Outline of a theory of practice.* Cambridge: Cambridge University Press.

Das, V., (1996). *Critical events: an anthropological perspective on contemporary India.* Delhi: Oxford University Press.

Dodier, N. and Barbot, J., (2016). La force des dispositifs. *Annales. Histoire, sciences sociales.* **71**(2), 421–450.

Fairhead, J., (2016). Understanding social resistance to the Ebola response in the Forest Region of the Republic of Guinea: an anthropological perspective. *African Studies Review.* **59**(3), 7–31.

Fassin, D., (2007). Humanitarianism as a politics of life. *Public Culture.* **19**(3), 499–520.

Fassin, D., (2010). *La raison humanitaire: une histoire morale du temps présent.* Paris: Seuil.

Foucault, M., (1966). *Les mots et les choses: une archéologie des sciences humaines.* Paris: Gallimard.

Gadamer, H.-G., (1960). *Wahrheit und Methode: Grundzüge einer philosophischen Hermeneutik.* Tübingen: Mohr.

Garfinkel, H., (1967). *Studies in ethnomethodology.* Englewood Cliffs: Prentice Hall.

Gibbons, M., Limoges, C., Nowotny, H., Schwartzman, S., Scott, P. and Trow, M., (1994). *The new production of knowledge: the dynamics of science and research in contemporary societies.* London: Sage.

Héritier, F., (2005). La valence différentielle des sexes. In: M. Maruani, ed., *Femmes, genre et sociétés: l'état des savoirs.* Paris: La Découverte.

Kaplan, R., (1994). The coming anarchy: how scarcity, crime, overpopulation, tribalism, and disease are rapidly destroying the social fabric of our planet. *The Atlantic.* (February), 44–76.

Latour, B., (2015). *Face à Gaïa: huit conférences sur le nouveau régime climatique.* Paris: Editions La Découverte.

Lévi-Strauss, C., (1962). *La pensée sauvage.* Paris: Plon.

Merton, R.K., (1968). *Social theory and social structure.* New York: Free Press.

Quéré, L., (1987). L'argument sociologique de Garfinkel. *Réseaux.* **27**, 97–136.

Stiegler, B., (2003). *Passer à l'acte.* Paris: Galilée.

Thévenot, L., (1995). L'action en plan. *Sociologie du Travail.* **37**(3), 411–434.

Viveiros de Castro, E., (2009). *Métaphysiques cannibales: lignes d'anthropologie post-structurale.* Paris: PUF.

INDEX

Note: Page numbers in *italics* indicate a figure and page numbers in **bold** indicate a table or box on the corresponding page.

4H 166–168

access; and assumed supremacy of formal health care 130–131; and the context of HIV/AIDS in Homa Bay, Kenya 114–115; and culture 129–130; and fieldwork in Homa Bay 117–121; and the impact of anthropological research 131–133; interaction of multiple barriers 126–127; late arrival of patients to MSF-run Clinic B 117; and the Luo ethnic group 115–116; and MSF involvement in the control of the HIV/AIDS epidemic in Homa Bay 116–117; patients' fear of defaulting from medical recommendations 125–126; patients' health-seeking pathways 121–122; poor diagnostic capacity of the formal health sector 122–125; working with beneficiaries 127–129
'Access for more' 46–50
acculturation 10–11
adapted services 109–110
Afghanistan *see* Khost province (Afghanistan)
Agamben, Giorgio 140, 149–151
agency 144–145; *see also* humanitarian agent; political agents
AIDS *see* HIV/AIDS
alternative healers 185–186

Anka Local Government Area (Nigeria) 193, 197–202, 214–216; assessing recontamination in 212–213; communication on lead-related health and treatment issues in 211–212; families involved in artisanal mining in 209–211; health, illness and the 'cultural context' in 196–197; initial outbreak in 193–194; response to outbreak in 194–196; role of mining in lead emergency 203–204; science versus experience in 204–209; social dynamics at the compound level in 213–214; successful outcome in 202–203
anthropology: added value of 12–15; affirming the basis for 27–29; anthropologists 19–20; calling for an anthropological perspective 181–186; and changes in humanitarian politics and practice 34–36; and changing humanitarian contexts 29–34; and the conflict in Khost province 95–96; and cultural translation 9–12; and 'danger signs' related to delivery 101–103; and delivery at home or hospital 103–105; and ethics in social science 61–63; and ethnography of women seeking safe birth 97–98; and future humanitarianisms 36–37; and good ethical relations between people 63–66; and health promotion and adapted services

109–110; and HIV/AIDS 117; and the humanitarian agent in critical situations 242–245; in humanitarian situations 1–9; impact of research 131–133; integrating social sciences with Operations 57–59; and the issue of 'shame' 98–99; mapping of **16–17**; and marriage 99; of modern epidemics in Haiti 162–171; at MSF 15–20, **16–17**; how MSF frames ethical review 66–72; MSF Khost maternity clinic 96–97; in MSF medical operations 41–42, **57**; in MSF medical operations (1996–early 2000s) 42–46; in MSF medical operations (2009) 46–50; in MSF medical operations (2012) 50–56; and MSF surgical project 178–179, 190–191; and the need for social science in developing humanitarian health operations 39–41; and the notion of 'culture' 179; and the paradox of safe birth 93–95; and Pashtun society in the context of war and insecurity 98; and pregnancy 99–101; project setting 180–181; and the referral system 105–107; seeking contact with traditional bonesetters 189–190; studies in Homa Bay project **57**; and technology and the human deficit 245–250; in the time of outbreak 137–139; 'translation' of findings into health promotion 186–189; a way forward 72–74; *see also* medical anthropology

Archer, Margaret 243
armed conflict, changing 30–32
Aron, R. 7
artisanal mining 209–211
ART treatment initiation 45–47, 50–51
Asfari, Mitra 220
assessment 212–213
associations 144–145
assumptions **87–89**; supremacy of formal health care 130–131

barriers 126–127, *128*
Barth, F. 10, 228, 238
Beaussan, outreach at **170**
beneficiaries 127–129
benefits 65–66
biomedical perspective 156–162
birth 93–95; and the conflict in Khost province 95–96; and 'danger signs' for delivery 101–103; delivery at home or at a hospital 103–105; ethnography 97–98; and health promotion and adapted

services 109–110; and the interaction of medical anthropology and humanitarian work 107–109; and the issue of 'shame' 98–99; and marriage 99; and the MSF Khost maternity clinic 96–97; and Pashtun society in the context of war and insecurity 98; and pregnancy 99–101; and the referral system 105–107
blame 119–127
blog **139**
blood lead levels (BLL) 195–196, 204, 208, 210, 212, 217n9, 217n13
body, as a tool 232–234; *see also* body social
body social 220–224, 237–240; community structure 224–225; conflicts on treating 232–237; family structure 225–226; and health care structures 229; reasons for rejection 227–229; and reception in medical centres 229–231; relation to space 226–227; and the role of NGOs in modifying health-seeking behaviour 231–232
bonesetters 189–190
Brazilian Medical Unit (BRAMU) 156, 175n3
Burtscher, Doris 15

causal reasoning 236–237
causes 178–179, 190–191, 236–237; and anthropological perspective 181–186; and the notion of 'culture' 179; and project setting 180–181; and seeking contact with traditional bonesetters 189–190; and 'translation' of findings into health promotion 186–189
Centers for Disease Control and Prevention (CDC) 154, 158–159, 162, 167–168, 172, 174, 194
Chad 180–181, 184–187
cheering 99–101
chikungunya 169–171
children 204–209; and treatment 209
cholera 168–169
clinical facts 208–209
Clinic B 116–121
communication 211–212
Community Health Advisory Boards (CHAB) 52–53
Community Mobile approach (COMMOB) 52–55
community structure 224–225
compassion 4–5
comprehensive health centres (CHC) 96–97, 102–105, 165–166

254 Index

compromise 185–186
conflict, on treating the body social 232–237; *see also* cultural conflicts; Khost province (Afghanistan); war
contact, with traditional bonesetters 189–190
contamination 10–11
context: affirming the basis for anthropology in humanitarian contexts 27–29; and changes in humanitarian politics and practice 34–36; changing humanitarian contexts 29–34; and future humanitarianisms 36–37; historical 226–232
critical situations 242–245; humanitarian agent in 242–245
critique 4–9; limits of 8–9
Cuba 157, 159–160, 167
cultural conflicts 226–232
cultural context 196–197
cultural translators 9–12
culture 129–130, 178–179, 190–191; and anthropological perspective 181–186; and assumed supremacy of formal health care 130–131; challenging the notion of 179; and the context of HIV/AIDS in Homa Bay, Kenya 114–115; and fieldwork in Homa Bay 117–121; and the impact of anthropological research 131–133; and interaction of multiple barriers 126–127; and late arrival of patients to MSF-run Clinic B 117; and the Luo ethnic group 115–116; and MSF involvement in the control of the HIV/AIDS epidemic in Homa Bay 116–117; and patients' fear of defaulting from medical recommendations 125–126; and patients' health-seeking pathways 121–122; and poor diagnostic capacity of the formal health sector 122–125; and project setting 180–181; questioning 129–130; re-location of 11–12; and seeking contact with traditional bonesetters 189–190; and 'translation' of findings into health promotion 186–189; uses and abuses of 9–10; and working with beneficiaries 127–129

danger signs 101–103
death 140–142
debate 7–8
defaulting 125–126
deficit *see* human deficit
dengue fever 154–156, 171–175; and an anthropology of modern epidemics

in Haiti 162–171; dengue resistance 156–162; fieldwork narratives from Léogâne **164–165**; and outreach at Beaussan **170**; taxonomic trap of 160–162
denial *see* institutions, institutional denial
design *see* study design and preparation
diagnosis *128*; diagnostic capacity 122–123; differential diagnostic 156–157; missed diagnosis 123–125
dialogue 220–224, 237–240; and community structure 224–225; and conflicts on treating the body social 232–237; and family structure 225–226; and health care structures 229; and reasons for rejection 227–229; and reception in medical centres 229–231; and relation to space 226–227; and the role of NGOs in modifying health-seeking behaviour 231–232
differential diagnostic 156–157
direct obstetric complications (DOCs) 94–97, 99, 101, 103, 108–109
diseases, traditional Luo 124; *see also maladiblan* (white's disease); sent diseases
distrust **143–144**
Dominican Republic 159, 171, 174
dysfunction, hospital as 183–185

Ebola, and harsh messaging *141*; *see also* Ebola survivors
Ebola Management Center (EMC) 136, 138–140, 142, 145–148, 150
Ebola survivors 136–137, 149–150; and anthropology in the time of outbreak 137–139; building the survivor's identity 142–144; and distrust **143–144**; ongoing support for 148–149, *149*; and relativism **146**; and revival of associations and agency 144–145; and the rite of passage from death to life 140–142; stigmatisation of 145–148; surviving in the time of outbreak 140
editors 15–18
emergency 77–80, 91; ethnographic vignette 85–91; and research management in the field 81–85; statements, knowledge and assumptions **87–89**; and study design 80–81; *see also* humanitarian emergency; lead emergency
engagement 7–8
epidemics 154–156, 171–175; anthropology of 162–171; dengue resistance 156–162; fieldwork narratives from Léogâne **164–165**; and outreach at Beaussan **170**

Index **255**

Eswatini 16

ethical considerations: gaining ethical approval **69–71**; good ethical relations between people 63–66; how ethics in social science are framed 61–63; how MSF frames ethical review 66–72; a way forward 72–74

ethical review, how MSF frames 66–68

ethics: ethical issues within MSF 68–72; good ethical relations between people 63–66; in social science 61–63; why ethics are different for social science 65–66

ethnography 77–80, 91, 220–224, 237–240; and community structure 224–225; and conflicts on treating the body social 232–237; and family structure 225–226; and health care structures 229; and the practice of humanitarian emergency 85–91; and reasons for rejection 227–229; and reception in medical centres 229–231; and relation to space 226–227; research management in the field 81–85; and the role of NGOs in modifying health-seeking behaviour 231–232; statements, knowledge and assumptions **87–89**; and study design 80–81; of women seeking safe birth 97–98

evidence, laboratory 'evidences' 157–159

experience, science versus 204–209

facts *see* clinical facts

families: family structure 225–226; interaction with 209–211; *see also* birth; children

fear 125–126

field, research management in 81–85

field setting 117–118

fieldwork: experiences and challenges 119–121; in Homa Bay 117–121

fieldwork narratives **164–165**

focus 80–81

focus group discussions (FGDs) 137–139

formal health care *see* health care, formal, assured supremacy of

formal health sector *see* health sector, formal

Foucauldian perspective 3, 8–9

Foucault, Michel 6, 13, 25, 150; *see also* Foucauldian perspective

Gorbati people 19–20, 220–224, 237–240; and the body as a tool 232–234; causal reasoning 236–237; community structure 224–225; family structure 225–226; and health care structures 229; modifying health-seeking behaviour of 231–232; reasons for rejection 227–229; reception by medical centres 229–231; relation to space 226–227; what illness signifies 234–236

Gypsies 220, 222–224; *see also* Gorbati people

Haiti, anthropology of modern epidemics in 162–171; *see also* Léogâne (Haiti)

happiness 99–101

healers *see* alternative healers; traditional healers

health: and 'cultural context' 196–197; defining 208–209; when living is bad for your health 197–202

health care, formal, assumed supremacy of 130–131

health care structures 229

health clinics 220–224, 237–240; and community structure 224–225; and conflicts on treating the body social 232–237; and family structure 225–226; and health care structures 229; and reasons for rejection 227–229; and reception in medical centres 229–231; and relation to space 226–227; and the role of NGOs in modifying health-seeking behaviour 231–232

health needs, changing 33–34

health operations *see* humanitarian health operations

health perception 208–209

health promotion *149*, 178–179, 190–191; and adapted services 109–110; and anthropological perspective 181–186; and challenging the notion of 'culture' 179; and project setting 180–181; and seeking contact with traditional bonesetters 189–190; 'translation' of findings into 186–189

health sector, formal *128*; failing patients 119–127; poor diagnostic capacity of 122–123

health-seeking behaviour 93–95, *120*, 121–122; and the conflict in Khost province 95–96; and 'danger signs' for delivery 101–103; and delivery at home or at a hospital 103–105; ethnography 97–98; and health promotion and adapted services 109–110; and the interaction of medical anthropology and humanitarian work 107–109; and the

256 Index

issue of 'shame' 98–99; and marriage 99; modifying 231–232; and the MSF Khost maternity clinic 96–97; and Pashtun society in the context of war and insecurity 98; and pregnancy 99–101; and the referral system 105–107

HIV/AIDS 166–168; context of 114–115; MSF involvement in the control of 116–117; *see also* HIV/AIDS treatment; HIV project in Kenya

HIV/AIDS treatment: and assumed supremacy of formal health care 130–131; barriers to *128*; context of HIV/AIDS in Homa Bay, Kenya 114–115; and culture 129–130; and fieldwork in Homa Bay 117–121; and the impact of anthropological research 131–133; and interaction of multiple barriers 126–127; and late arrival of patients to MSF-run Clinic B 117; and the Luo ethnic group 115–116; and MSF involvement in the control of the HIV/AIDS epidemic in Homa Bay 116–117; and patients' fear of defaulting from medical recommendations 125–126; and patients' health-seeking pathways 121–122; and poor diagnostic capacity of the formal health sector 122–125; and working with beneficiaries 127–129

HIV project in Kenya 41–42, **57**; 1996–early 2000s 42–46; 2009 46–50; 2012 50–56

Homa Bay (Kenya) **57**; and assumed supremacy of formal health care 130–131; conducting fieldwork in 117–121; and the context of HIV/AIDS in 114–115; and culture 129–130; impact of anthropological research in 131–133; interaction of multiple barriers 126–127; late arrival of patients to MSF-run Clinic B 117; and the Luo ethnic group 115–116; and MSF involvement in the control of the HIV/AIDS epidemic in 116–117; patients' fear of defaulting from medical recommendations 125–126; patients' health-seeking pathways 121–122; poor diagnostic capacity of the formal health sector 122–125; working with beneficiaries 127–129

home delivery 103–105

hospital: delivery at 103–105; as dysfunctional institution 183–185

human deficit 245–250

humanitarianism: affirming the basis for anthropology in humanitarian contexts

27–29; and changes in humanitarian politics and practice 34–36; changing humanitarian contexts 29–34; future 36–37; 'Western' 34–36; *see also* medical humanitarianism

humanitarian action: and the humanitarian agent in critical situations 242–245; and technology and the human deficit 245–250

humanitarian agent, in critical situations 242–245

humanitarian architecture, changing 30

humanitarian contexts: affirming the basis for anthropology in 27–29; changing 29–34

humanitarian discourse 36

humanitarian emergency 85–91

humanitarian health operations 39–41; integration with social sciences 57–59

humanitarian order, reform of 12–15

humanitarian politics and practice, changes in 34–36

humanitarian settings, impact of anthropological research in 131–133

humanitarian situations 1–3; and the added value of anthropology 12–15; anthropology in 3–4; and anthropology at MSF 15–20, **16–17**; and critique 4–9; and cultural translation 9–12

humanitarian work, and medical anthropology 107–109

identity, and survivors 142–144

illness: in children 204–209; and 'cultural context' 196–197; and signification 234–236; understanding causes of 236–237

insecurity, Pashtun society in 98

institutions: hospital as dysfunctional 183–185; institutional denial 122–123

interaction 229

interface 185–186

intervention: acceptance of **203–204**; successful outcome **202–203**; *see also* medical intervention

interview techniques 83–85

Iran *see* South Tehran (Iran)

Kenya: HIV project in 41–42, **57**; HIV project in (1996–early 2000s) 42–46; HIV project in (2009) 46–50; HIV project in (2012) 50–56; *see also* Homa Bay (Kenya)

Khost province (Afghanistan) 93–95; conflict in 95–96; and 'danger signs' for

Index **257**

delivery 101–103; and delivery at home or at a hospital 103–105; ethnography 97–98; and health promotion and adapted services 109–110; and the interaction of medical anthropology and humanitarian work 107–109; and the issue of 'shame' 98–99; and marriage 99; MSF Khost maternity clinic 96–97; Pashtun society in the context of war and insecurity 98; and pregnancy 99–101; and the referral system 105–107

Khost Provincial Hospital (KPH) 96, 104–109

knowledge 40–43, 54–58, **87–89**, 159–160, 185–187, 214–220, 242–249; and ethical considerations 63–66; and ethnography of malnutrition 85–90

laboratory 'evidences' 157–159

late arrival of patients 117

lead emergency 193, 197–202, 214–216; assessing recontamination 212–213; communication on lead-related health and treatment issues 211–212; health, illness and the 'cultural context' 196–197; initial outbreak 193–194; interaction with families involved in artisanal mining 209–211; response to outbreak 194–196; role of mining in **203–204**; and science versus experience 204–209; and social dynamics at the compound level 213–214; successful outcome **202–203**

Léogâne (Haiti) 154–156, 171–175; and an anthropology of modern epidemics in Haiti 162–171; dengue resistance 156–162; fieldwork narratives from **164–165**; outreach at Beaussan **170**

Liberia 136–137, 149–150; anthropology in the time of outbreak in 137–139; building the survivor's identity in 142–144; and distrust **143–144**; ongoing support for survivors in 148–149, *149*; and relativism **146**; revival of associations and agency in 144–145; the rite of passage from death to life in 140–142; stigmatisation of survivors in 145–148; surviving in the time of outbreak in 140

life 140–142; when living is bad for your health 197–202

Luo ethnic group 53–54, 115–116, 123–124, 129–131; traditional diseases **124**

maladiblan (white's disease) 159–160, 162, 166, 174

malnutrition 77–80, 91; ethnographic vignette 85–91; and research management in the field 81–85; and study design 80–81

mapping **16–17**

marriage 99

maternal child health (MCH) 39

maternity clinic 96–97

medical anthropology 193, 197–202, 214–216; assessing recontamination 212–213; communication on lead-related families involved in artisanal mining 209–211; health and treatment issues 211–212; health, illness and the 'cultural context' 196–197; and humanitarian work 107–109; and initial outbreak 193–194; and response to outbreak 194–196; role of mining in lead emergency 203–204; science versus experience 204–209; social dynamics at the compound level 213–214; and successful outcome 202–203

medical centres, reception by 229–231

medical humanitarianism 93–95; and the conflict in Khost province 95–96; and 'danger signs' for delivery 101–103; and delivery at home or at a hospital 103–105; ethnography 97–98; and health promotion and adapted services 109–110; interaction of medical anthropology and humanitarian work 107–109; and the issue of 'shame' 98–99; and marriage 99; and the MSF Khost maternity clinic 96–97; and Pashtun society in the context of war and insecurity 98; and pregnancy 99–101; and the referral system 105–107

medical intervention 5–6

medical operational perspective: and HIV project in Kenya 41–42, **57**; and HIV project in Kenya (1996–early 2000s) 42–46; and HIV project in Kenya (2009) 46–50; and HIV project in Kenya (2012) 50–56; and integration of social sciences with Operations 57–59; and social science in humanitarian health operations 39–41

medical recommendations 125–126

medical strategy 93–95; and the conflict in Khost province 95–96; and 'danger signs' for delivery 101–103; and delivery at home or at a hospital 103–105; ethnography 97–98; and health promotion and adapted services 109–110; and the interaction of medical

258 Index

anthropology and humanitarian work 107–109; and the issue of 'shame' 98–99; and marriage 99; and the MSF Khost maternity clinic 96–97; and Pashtun society in the context of war and insecurity 98; and pregnancy 99–101; and the referral system 105–107
messages *141*
methods 118–119
mining **203**–**204**; artisanal 209–211; *see also* lead emergency
Ministry of Health (MoH Chad) 178, 180, 182–184
Ministry of Health (MoH Haiti) 157
Ministry of Health (MoH Kenya) 46–47, 50–51, 116
missionaries: and the humanitarian agent in critical situations 242–245; and technology and the human deficit 245–250
Mission des Nations Unies pour la Stabilisation en Haïti (MINUSTAH) 168, 171, 174
mosquitoes 162

narratives *see* fieldwork narratives
neutrality 80–81
NGOs 162–163, 168–174, 231–232, 235
Nigeria *see* Anka Local Government Area (Nigeria)

objectivity 7–8, 80–81
observation techniques 83–85
outbreak 193–194; anthropology in the time of 137–139; surviving in the time of 140
outreach **170**

Pashtun society 93–95; and the conflict in Khost province 95–96; in the context of war and insecurity 98; and 'danger signs' for delivery 101–103; and delivery at home or at a hospital 103–105; ethnography 97–98; and health promotion and adapted services 109–110; and the interaction of medical anthropology and humanitarian work 107–109; and the issue of 'shame' 98–99; and marriage 99; and the MSF Khost maternity clinic 96–97; and pregnancy 99–101; and the referral system 105–107
patients: blaming 119–127; fear of defaulting from medical recommendations 125–126; health-seeking pathways *120*, 121–122; late arrival of 117; *see also* beneficiaries

people: changing 32–33; good ethical relations between 63–66
perception *see* health perception
personal protective equipment (PPE) 142, 148
pluralistic health settings 130–131
political agents 136–137, 149–150; and anthropology in the time of outbreak 137–139; building the survivor's identity 142–144; and distrust **143**–**144**; and ongoing support for survivors 148–149, *149*; and relativism **146**; and revival of associations and agency 144–145; and the rite of passage from death to life 140–142; and stigmatisation of survivors 145–148; and surviving in the time of outbreak 140
politics 154–156, 171–175; and an anthropology of modern epidemics in Haiti 162–171; and dengue resistance 156–162; fieldwork narratives from Léogâne **164**–**165**; and outreach at Beaussan **170**
pregnancy 99–101; *see also* birth
preparation *see* study design and preparation
préparation au premier départ (PPD) 243
project setting 180–181

qualitative research 18–19
quality 105–107

racial argument 159–160
reasoning *see* causal reasoning
recommendations *see* medical recommendations
recontamination 212–213
referral system 105–107
rejection 227–229
relativism 9–11, **146**
research management 81–85; *see also* qualitative research
resistance, dengue 156–162
response 194–196
risks 65–66
rite of passage 140–142

Sartre, Jean-Paul 7
science 204–209
sent diseases 163–166, **164**–**165**; *see also* *maladiblan* (white's disease)
shame 98–99
signification, and illness 234–236
social dynamics 213–214
social science: and ethical issues within MSF 68–72; ethics in 61–63; integration

with Operations 57–59; mapping of **16–17**; need for 39–41; why ethics are different for 65–66
social scientists 40–41
socio-economic aspects 182
South Sudan **69–71**, 77–80, 91; ethnographic vignette 85–91; and research management in the field 81–85; and study design 80–81
South Tehran (Iran) 220–224, 237–240; and community structure 224–225; and conflicts on treating the body social 232–237; and family structure 225–226; and health care structures 229; and reasons for rejection 227–229; and reception in medical centres 229–231; and relation to space 226–227; and the role of NGOs in modifying health-seeking behaviour 231–232
space 226–227
statements **87–89**
stigmatisation, of survivors 145–148
strategy *see* medical strategy
study design and preparation 79–81; observation and interview techniques 83–85; and the practice of humanitarian emergency 85–91; research management in the field 81–83
successful outcomes **202–203**
Sudan *see* South Sudan
surgical project 178–179, 190–191; and anthropological perspective 181–186; and the notion of 'culture' 179; project setting 180–181; and traditional bonesetters 189–190; and 'translation' of findings into health promotion 186–189
Stringer, Beverley 98
survivors *see* Ebola survivors
Swaziland *see* Eswatini
synthesis 14–15

taxonomy, and dengue fever 160–162
TB 42–48
technology 245–250
traditional bonesetters 189–190
traditional healers 185–186
traditional Luo diseases **124**
traditional treatment 123–125

translation 3–4, 132–133, 186–189
treatment 207–209; lead-related 211–212; traditional 123–125; *see also* treatment challenges
treatment challenges 193, 197–202, 214–216; assessing recontamination 212–213; communication on lead-related health and treatment issues 211–212; families involved in artisanal mining 209–211; health, illness and the 'cultural context' 196–197; initial outbreak 193–194; response to outbreak 194–196; role of mining in lead emergency 203–204; science versus experience 204–209; social dynamics at the compound level 213–214; successful outcome 202–203
trust 105–107

Venables, Emilie **139**
Véran, Jean-François 8, 15
voluntary medical male circumcision (VMMC) 52–54

war 30–31, 78–79, 98, 140–141, 180–181, 184–185
Weber, Max 7
wife inheritance 49, **115**, 116, 130
women, ethnography 97–98; *see also* birth
World Bank 30
World Health Organisation (WHO) 46, 94, 133n3, 147, 194

Zamfara Heavy Metal Treatment Project 193, 197–202, 214–216; assessing recontamination 212–213; communication on lead-related health and treatment issues 211–212; families involved in artisanal mining 209–211; health, illness and the 'cultural context' 196–197; initial outbreak 193–194; response to outbreak 194–196; role of mining in lead emergency 203–204; science versus experience 204–209; social dynamics at the compound level 213–214; successful outcome 202–203
Zamfara State Ministry of Health (ZMoH) 194